40 DIGITAL PHO
RETOUCHING TECHNIQUES
with Photoshop Elements 5.0

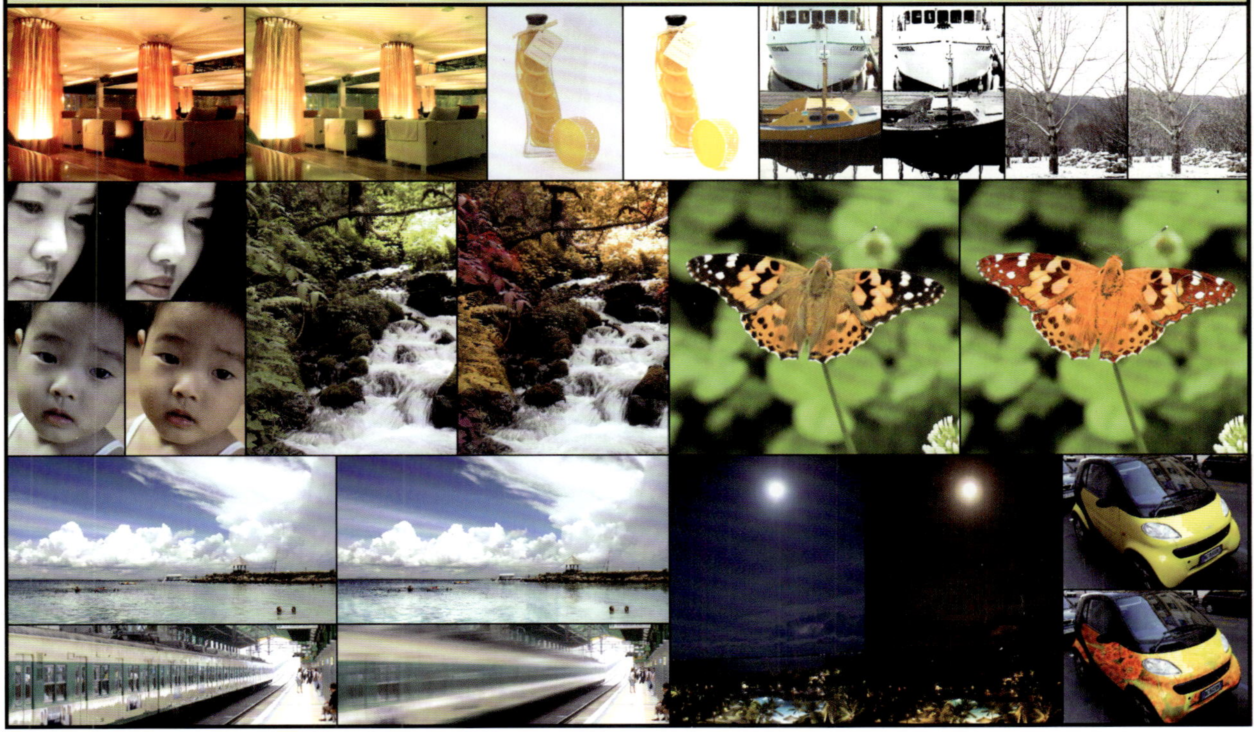

Y.

ISBN: 978-89-314-3370-8

Printed and bound in the Republic of Korea.

How to contact us:

E-mail: support@youngjin.com
feedback@youngjin.com.sg

Address: Youngjin.com
997-10, Daechi-dong, Gangnam-gu
Seoul 135-502, Korea

Credits

Production Manager: Suzie Lee
Developmental Editor: Rachel Lake, Publication Services, Inc.
Project Manager: Lorie Donovan, Publication Services, Inc.
Editorial Services: Publication Services, Inc.
Book Designer: Litmus
Cover Designer: Litmus
Production Control: Jay Won, Misook Kim

A Note from the Author

The aim of this book (and the others in the Go Digital series) is to show you how to use a simple tool to produce professional-quality work that you can be proud of, whether you are a commercial photographer or hobbyist. As a whole, this book provides a comprehensive tutorial on Photoshop Elements 5.0, but each technique is explained step by step, so you can focus on creating the effects you want.

Though this book may be results-oriented, it is not short on good pedagogy. If you have no prior experience with image-editing software, the best approach is to first read the Introduction, which contains background information and basic skills you need to try out the techniques.

If you have some experience with an image-editing program, you can start with any of the 40 techniques to augment your editing skills. All of the examples used in this book are carefully selected for their educational value, industry relevance, and artistic quality. With the release of Photoshop Elements 5.0, the instruction and exercises have been reviewed and updated to ensure that you can explore the full range of what Photoshop Elements can do. The new workspace is fully explained, and you'll be confidently manipulating photos in no time.

Let's get started!

Zack Lee

Contents

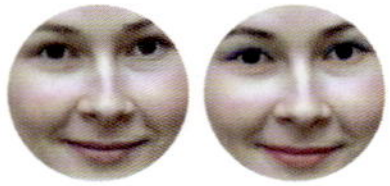

Introduction | Warming Up to Photoshop Elements 5.0 7

Key Features 8
Understanding Pixels and Resolution 10
Understanding Image File Formats 14
Touring the Welcome Screen 17
A Closer Look at the Photoshop Elements 5.0 Editor Window 21
Essential Photoshop Elements Know-How 24
Opening an Image File 24
A Closer Look at the Organizer Window 27
Saving an Image File 29
A Closer Look at the Save As Dialog Box 30
A Closer Look at the Save for Web Dialog Box 31
Changing the View 32

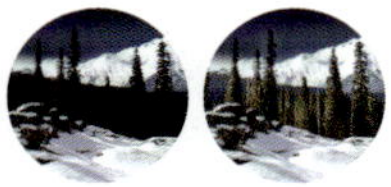

Chapter 1 | Correcting Contrast 35

1 Diagnosing the Problem 36
2 Correcting Blurred Images 38
3 How the Pros Do It 40
A Closer Look at the Levels Dialog Box 42
4 Correcting Backlighting 43
5 Brightening a Specific Spot 46

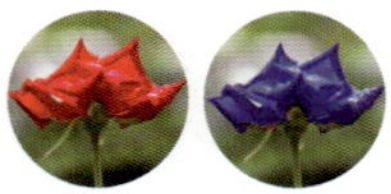

Chapter 2 | Manipulating Colors 49

6 Changing a Color 50
A Closer Look at the Hue/Saturation Dialog Box 52
7 Replacing a Color 53
8 Correcting Improper White Balance Using Color Variation 55
9 Turning Color Photos into Black-and-White Images 59
10 Coloring Black-and-White Photographs 62
11 Creating a Sepia-Toned Picture 65
Blending Colors 67
12 Turning Summer into Fall 68
13 Making Detailed Color Changes 72
A Closer Look at the Color Replacement Tool Options Bar 75

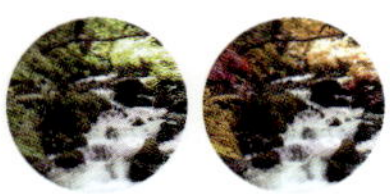

Chapter 3 | Enhancing Portraits 77

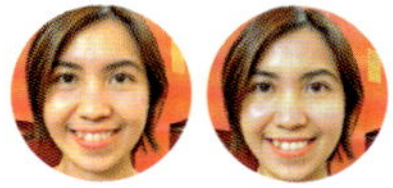

14 Removing Red Eyes 78
15 Removing Facial Blemishes 80
16 Applying Makeup 85
17 Creating Bigger Eyes and a Sharper Chin 91
18 Revising a Portrait Using Adjust Color for Skin Tone 96
19 Opening Closed Eyes 98
20 Selective Focusing 102
21 Creating a Studio Background and Picture Package 106
22 Adding a Picture Frame 116

Chapter 4 | Editing Skills and Special Effects 121

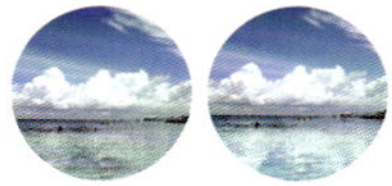

23 Automatically Separating Scanned Images 122
24 Opening and Processing a Camera Raw Image File 123
25 Adjusting Image Size and Shape 126
26 Cleaning Up Backgrounds 135
Using the Shift Key for Straight Lines 138
27 Creating Reflections 139
28 Adding Type Effects 142
29 Altering Perspective 144
30 Combining Images 147
31 Defringe Layer 151

Chapter 5 | Very Special Effects 157

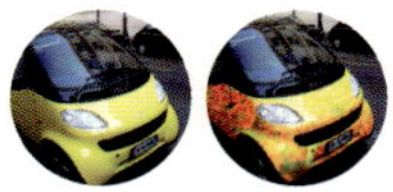

32 Stitching Panoramas 158
33 Adding Motion Blur 161
34 Giving Photos an Antiqued Look 163
35 Maintaining Texture While Repainting an Object 166
36 Let It Snow 171

Chapter 6 | Using and Sharing Images 175

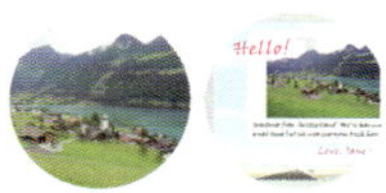

37 Making a Greeting Card 176
38 Maintaining Photographs with Album Pages 179
39 Making a Web Banner 187
40 Making a Web Photo Gallery 192

Contents of the Supplementary CD 196

Index 197

40 Digital Photo Retouching Techniques

with Photoshop Elements 5.0

Introduction

Warming Up to Photoshop Elements 5.0

Photoshop Elements is an easy-to-use image-editing program designed specifically for novice users and amateur photographers. It comes with all the basic features of Photoshop, a popular graphics program used by commercial artists and designers, but at only a fraction of the cost. Compared to Photoshop, Photoshop Elements has a significantly simpler editing process; its novice-friendly interface allows you to quickly and effortlessly correct, enhance, and retouch images.

In this book, you will learn how to edit and work creatively with your images in Photoshop Elements. From Chapter 1 onward, you will explore 40 real-life techniques listed in order of difficulty and grouped thematically. But before you jump into editing mode, read this chapter for an introduction to the key features of Photoshop Elements and for some background knowledge about computer graphics editing.

Key Features

Focus on image retouching

Photoshop Elements may be a cut-down version of Photoshop, but the user experience is completely different. The most obvious difference is that classic Photoshop features and functions have been reorganized or tailor-made to suit photography enthusiasts. The program is great for retouching images, such as sharpening blurred pictures, correcting overexposure, and fixing red eyes. All these can be done with a few clicks of the mouse or by changing a few parameters' values.

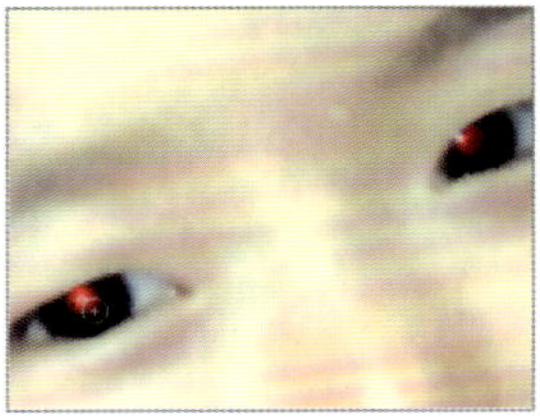

▲ Red eyes caused by using a flash

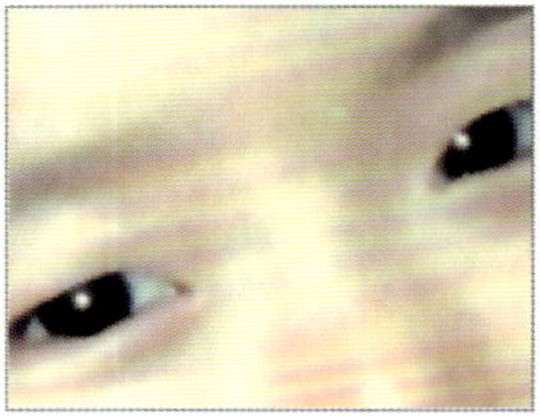

▲ Using the Red Eye Removal Tool to fix red eyes

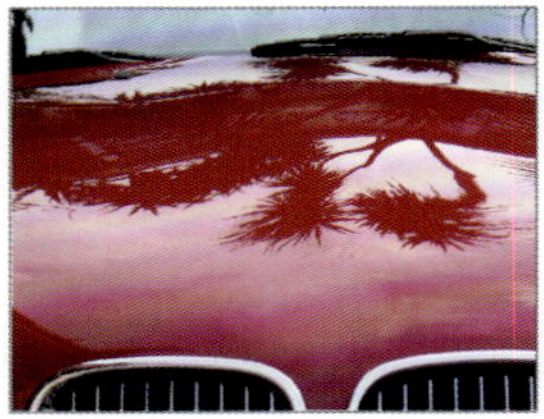

▲ Original image of a car

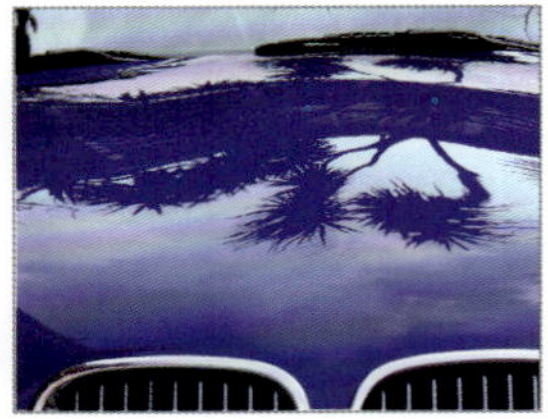

▲ Changing the color of the car

Creative photography

Photoshop Elements enables you to color images or enhance them by adding a picture frame, snow, or a myriad of other special effects. You can also combine several images to create a unique mosaic.

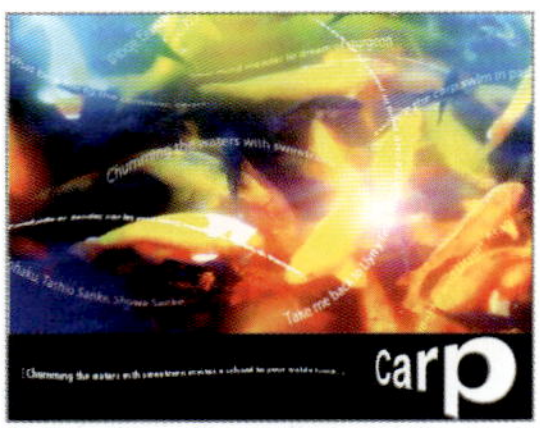

▲ Creative image retouching using the Brush Tool

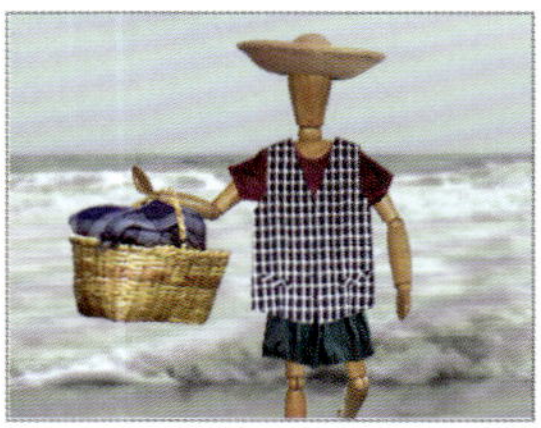

▲ Blending a picture of an artist's mannequin into the beach

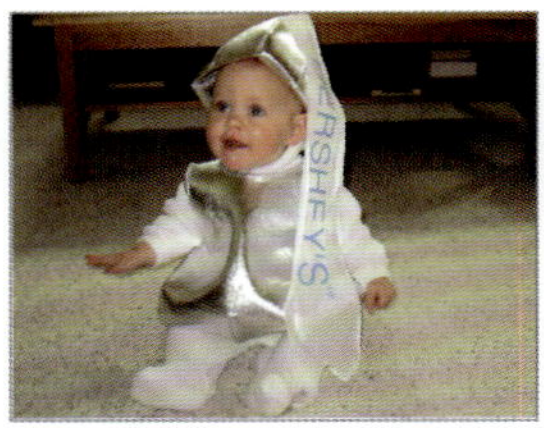

▲ Original picture of a baby

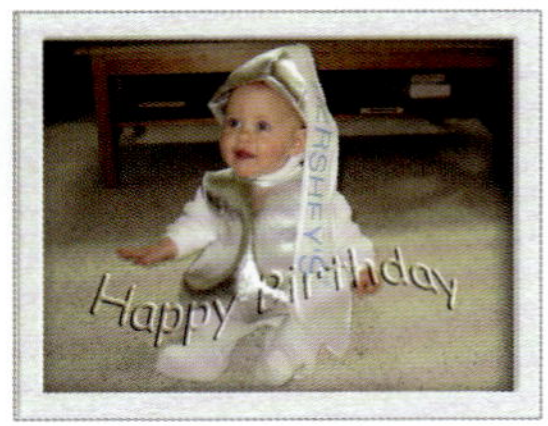

▲ Adding a picture frame and text effects

Usability

If you are an avid photographer, you know that locating an image from the hundreds or thousands of images stored on your computer is a tiresome and time-consuming process. Photoshop Elements 5.0 makes finding and organizing images a less painful process with the easy-to-use Organizer window. The Organizer lets you search for images in many ways and allows you to tag and organize your files. You can also view an image's metadata.

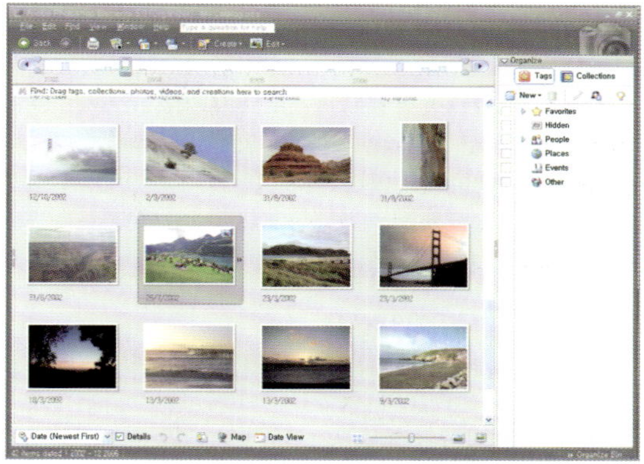

▲ Mac users should note that the Organizer window (above) is not found in the Mac version of Photoshop Elements.

Flexibility

Photoshop Elements is a flexible program that lets you do more than retouch images. The program makes it easy for you to create slide shows, photo albums, postcards, calendars, Web photo galleries, VCDs, and DVDs using your images. A great way to explore these options is through the Welcome Screen, which lets you jump straight to the relevant window or dialog box for your project. Photoshop Elements also has flexible printing options, allowing you to arrange several images on the same page for printing.

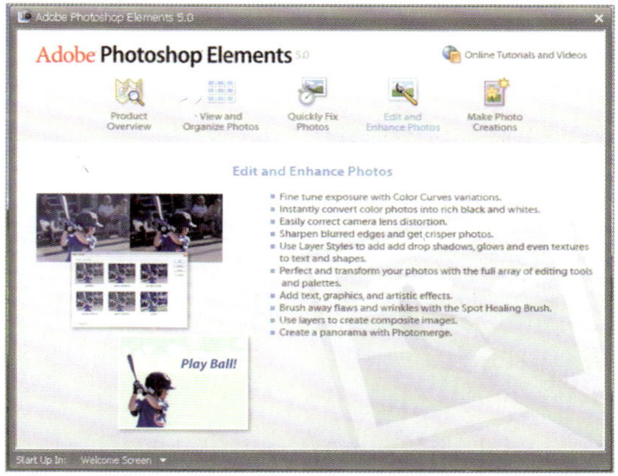

▲ Most of the exercises in this book are performed in the Standard Edit workspace. To open the workspace, select Edit and Enhance Photos in the Welcome Screen.

Understanding Pixels and Resolution

What are pixels?

If you blow up a scanned image or a picture taken using a digital camera, you will see that the image is composed of small squares. These small squares are the smallest unit in an image and they are called pixels (short for picture elements). An image usually contains thousands of such pixels, each with its own color information and packed closely together. Optical illusion causes our eyes to take in the composition of pixels as a complete image. When you modify a certain area of an image, you are actually changing the pixels within that area. How well you modify these pixels will determine the quality of the final picture.

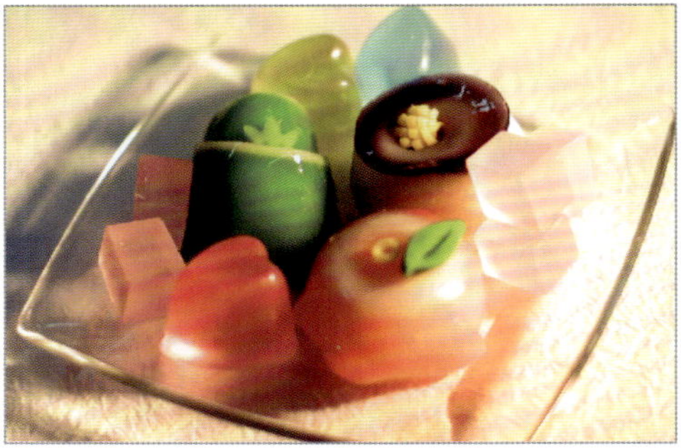

▲ The image at its original size

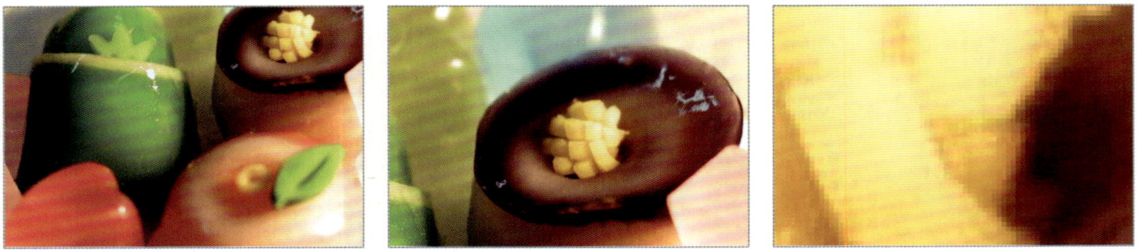

▲ The more you magnify the image, the more apparent the pixels become.

What is image resolution?

Image resolution refers to how compactly pixels are packed in an image. Image resolution is measured in pixels per inch (ppi). A resolution of one pixel per inch (1 ppi) means that there is one pixel in an area measuring one inch by one inch. A resolution of 10 pixels per inch (10 ppi) means that there are 10 pixels along each side of the same one-inch square. Thus, the higher the resolution, the more pixels there are in the image, and the better the quality of the image, because a higher resolution allows for more details.

The relationship between image resolution and file size

The resolution of an image has a direct impact on file size. Although the image quality gets better at higher resolutions, the file size also increases.

- The file size of the image on the right, which has a resolution of 300 ppi, is 1.23 megabytes (MB).

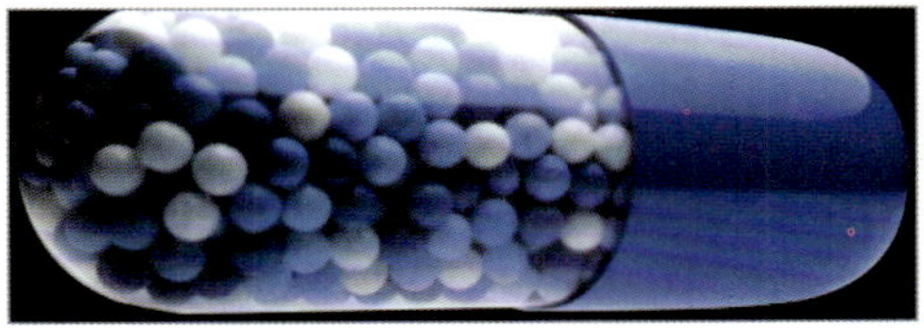

▲ Image size: 1.23MB

- The same image at 72 ppi has a smaller file size of 73 kilobytes (KB), because the image is made up of fewer pixels.

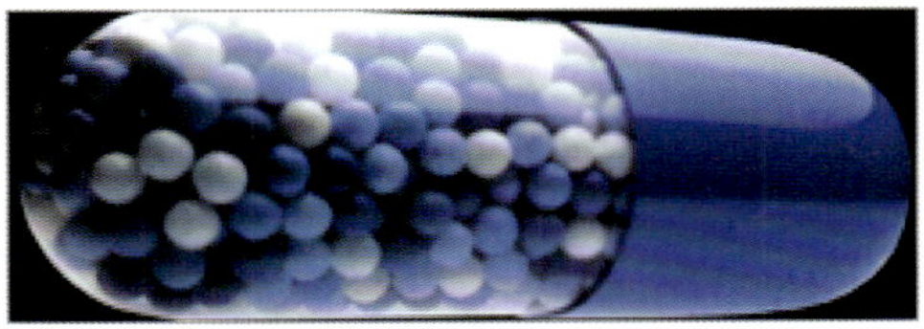

▲ Image size: 73KB

- At 36 ppi, the file size of this image is even smaller, at 18 kilobytes.

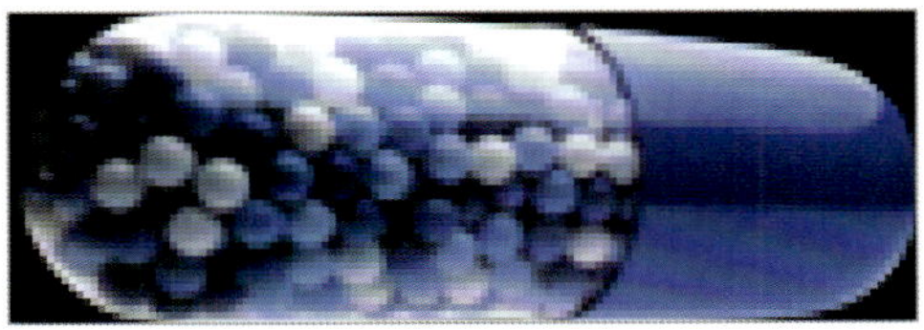

▲ Image size: 18KB

The difference between low- and high-resolution images

The image shown has an area of 3.94 inches by 2.63 inches and a resolution of 180 ppi. This means that there are 709 pixels along the width of the image and 473 pixels along the height. This works out to a total of 709 × 473 (or 335,357) pixels for the entire image.

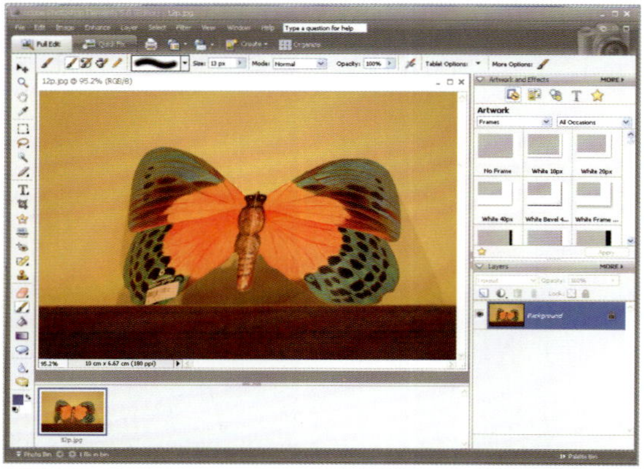

▲ Image resolution: 180 ppi

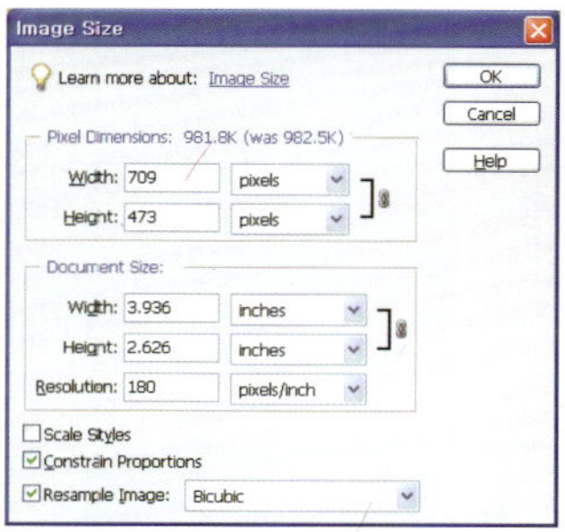

▲ Width: 709 pixels, height: 473 pixels

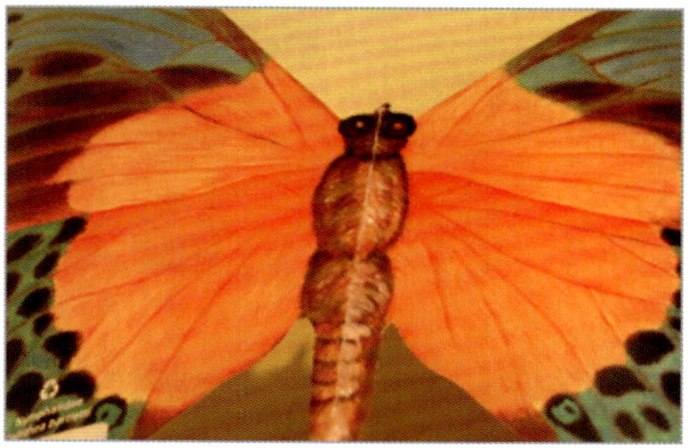

▲ Magnifying the image

Using the preceding example, if you leave the image size alone and reduce the resolution to 72 ppi, there will be 284 pixels along the width and 189 pixels along the height. The image will have a total of 284 × 189 (or 53,487) pixels.

Because you did not change the image size, there is no difference in the size of the printed image. The image, however, will be less sharp because the resolution is lower (72 ppi compared to the original 180 ppi). This image is of lower resolution than the high-resolution image generated at 180 ppi.

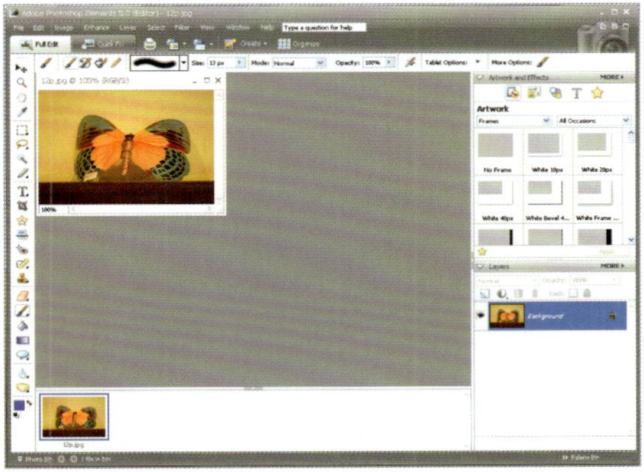

▲ Image resolution: 72 ppi

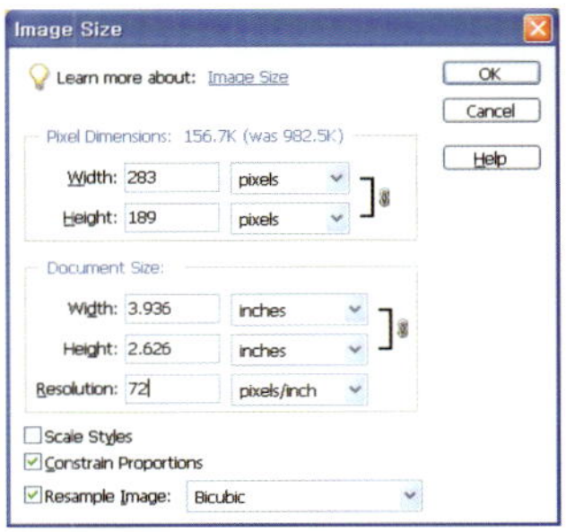

▲ Width: 283 pixels, height: 189 pixels

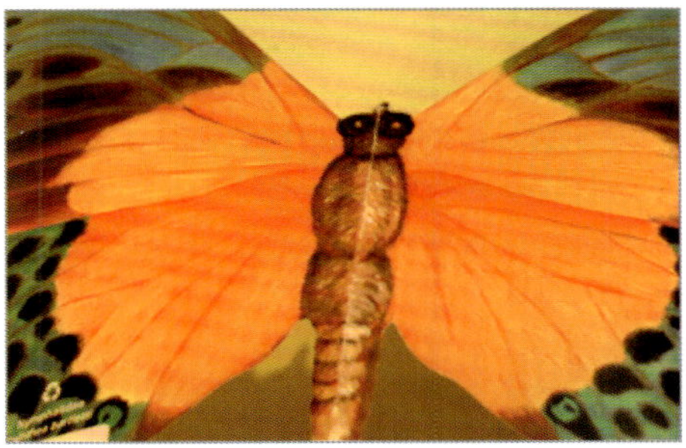

▲ Magnifying the image

Units of Resolution

Resolution may be measured in pixels per inch (ppi) or dots per inch (dpi). Ppi refers to the number of pixels per inch in a digital image. The resolution of a scanned image, for instance, is measured in ppi. Dpi refers to the number of dots that a printer can print per inch. The resolution of a printout is measured in dpi. In Photoshop Elements, you can set the image resolution to pixels per inch or pixels per centimeter.

Understanding Image File Formats

Photoshop Elements allows you to save image files in different formats for different purposes. Factors such as file size and quality have to be considered when choosing a file format. The following file formats are supported by Photoshop Elements:

Adobe file formats

▶▶▶ Photoshop (*.PSD, *.PDD)

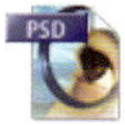

These file formats are exclusive to Photoshop and Photoshop Elements. Files saved in these formats tend to be larger than other image file formats because all layer and channel information is saved. Despite a larger file size, this format is useful because when you open it again, it allows you to work on the file exactly as you left it.

▶▶▶ Photoshop PDF (*.PDF, *.PDP)

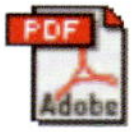

The Portable Document Format is the file format commonly used for sharing documents over the Internet because of its flexibility and widespread compatibility. Photoshop Elements recognizes the generic PDF format and also the Photoshop PDF format.

Generic PDF files, in general, are created using Adobe Acrobat. You can open generic PDFs in Photoshop Elements, but you can only save them in Photoshop PDF format. A file saved in Photoshop PDF format can only contain one page, whereas a generic PDF can contain multiple pages. You should also remember that when a generic PDF file is loaded into Photoshop Elements, hyperlinks and all other Adobe Acrobat attributes will be changed into images.

File formats suitable for the Web

▶▶▶ CompuServe GIF (*.GIF)

GIF, or Graphic Interchange Format, is a file format that saves images in 256 or fewer colors. Because of this, it is not suitable for most continuous-tone images but works well for images with large areas of solid colors and crisp details.

▶▶▶ JPEG (∗.JPG, ∗.JPEG, ∗.JPE)

JPEG, an acronym for Joint Photographic Experts Group, is an image file format that retains all the color information of an image but reduces file size by selectively throwing away data.

JPEG is most useful for saving photographs and other continuous-tone images. Images can be compressed at different levels. A higher level of compression gives a smaller file size but also a lower image quality, whereas a lower level of compression results in a larger file size but a higher quality image.

▶▶▶ PNG (∗.PNG)

PNG, or Portable Network Graphics, is a file format that was developed as an alternative to GIF and is intended for Web usage. Like GIF, PNG-8 supports 8-bit color depth or 256 colors and is suitable for images with few variations in color. PNG-24, on the other hand, supports 24-bit or 16,777,215 colors, which are about all our human eyes can see, so it is recommended for continuous-tone images. In addition, PNG-24 supports many levels of transparency, unlike JPEG.

Print and other file formats

▶▶▶ Photoshop EPS (∗.EPS)

EPS, or Encapsulated PostScript, allows files to be shared by most graphics, illustration, and page-layout programs, such as PageMaker and QuarkXPress. EPS images are best printed on PostScript-enabled printers. Many color separators and printers accept images in this format.

▶▶▶ BMP (∗.BMP)

BMP, a standard image format used on Windows-compatible machines, allows you to set the color depth to control image quality and file size.

▶▶▶ PICT (∗.PCT, ∗.PICT)

PICT, the standard image format for Macintosh environments, allows for 16-bit and 32-bit color depth settings. It is especially suitable for compressing flat-color images.

▶▶▶ PCX (*.PCX)

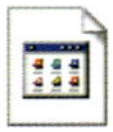

PCX is a bitmap file format widely supported on both Windows-compatible and Macintosh machines.

▶▶▶ TIFF (*.TIF)

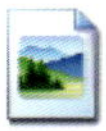

TIFF, or Tagged-Image File Format, is a flexible bitmap file format supported by most graphics, illustration, and page-layout programs. It is often used for cross-platform file exchange.

▶▶▶ PIXAR (*.PXR)

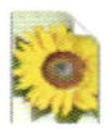

The PIXAR format, developed and named after the Pixar computer technology used in the making of the movie *Toy Story*, is used most frequently on PIXAR computers. It is also supported on the Macintosh.

▶▶▶ TGA (*.TGA, *.VDA, *ICB, *.VST)

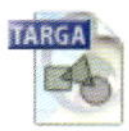

TGA, or Targa, is designed for systems using the Truevision video board. It automatically creates alpha channels that include 256 or fewer shadows, and it can be easily combined with background images in Photoshop Elements or other image-editing programs.

▶▶▶ RAW (*.CRW, *.ORF, *.RAF, *.NEF, *.MRW)

“Raw” refers to a file that has a record of the raw, unprocessed data captured by a camera sensor. A raw file is not a single file format. All digital camera makers use their own technology to record and save a raw format. For instance, Nikon’s raw format has the .NEF file extension, whereas Olympus uses the .ORF extension. Only mid-range and above digital cameras are capable of saving an image in a raw file format because of the large file size. With entry-level cameras, the raw data from a camera sensor is automatically processed and compressed into JPEG files, resulting in a loss of data or quality.

Touring the Welcome Screen

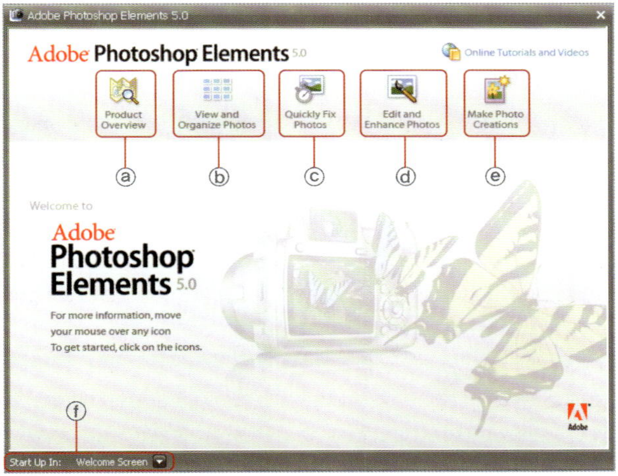

ⓐ Product Overview

Click on this button for an introduction to Photoshop Elements. The product information will display in the Welcome Screen itself. You can select Product Overview or Upgrading from a Previous Version of Photoshop Elements? in the lower-right corner of the Welcome Screen for additional information regarding these topics.

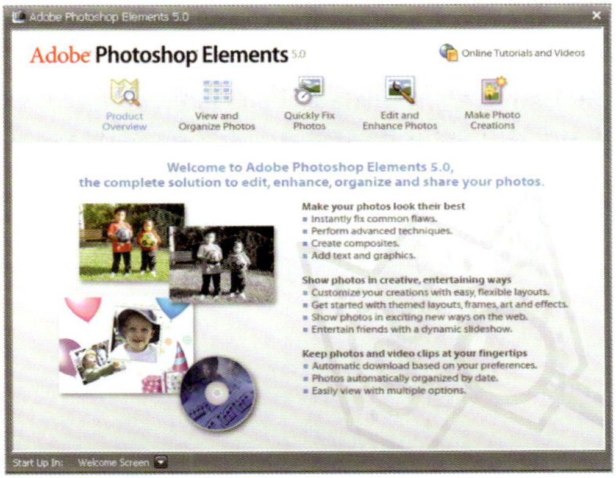

ⓑ View and Organize Photos

Selecting this button launches the Organizer window. The Organizer window makes it easy for you to find and organize your images. This window is not available in the Macintosh version of the program.

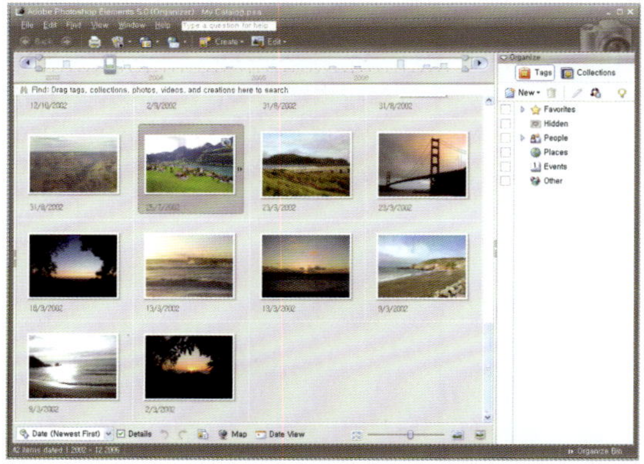

ⓒ Quickly Fix Photos

If you want to perform some simple editing on an image, click on the Quickly Fix Photos button to open the Quick Fix workspace in the Editor window. The title bar indicates that this is the Editor window. In the top-left corner, you can also see that the Quick Fix button is selected. The Quick Fix workspace lets you fix common and easily corrected problems such as those related to color and lighting.

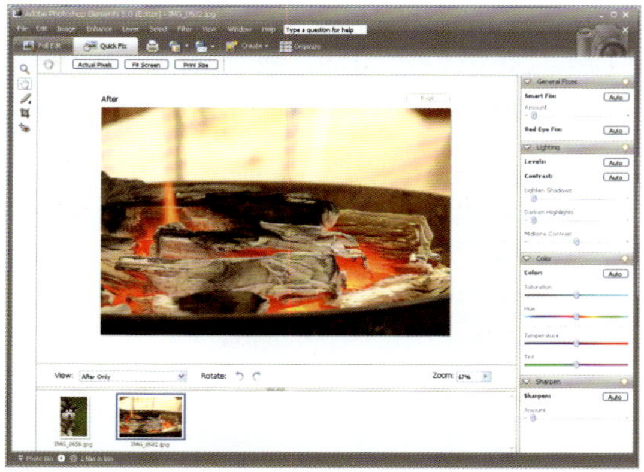

ⓓ Edit and Enhance Photos

Selecting this button launches the Standard Edit workspace in the Editor window. The Standard Edit workspace is where you can access all of Photoshop Elements' editing commands, tools, and palettes. Unless otherwise stated, almost all of the exercises in this book are carried out in this workspace.

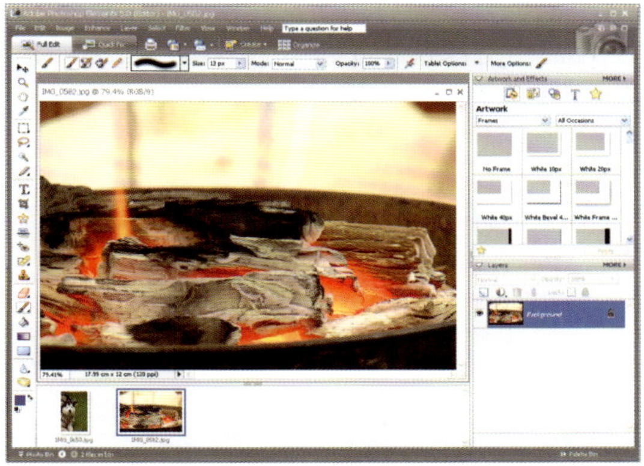

ⓔ Make Photo Creation

The Make Photo Creation button opens the New Photo Layout dialog box, where you can change the size, shape, etc., of the images and frames. After making all the selections, an image can be inserted from the Editor window. Furthermore, you can create slide shows, photo albums, postcards, and more by clicking on the Create button from the Shortcuts bar in the Editor or Organizer window.

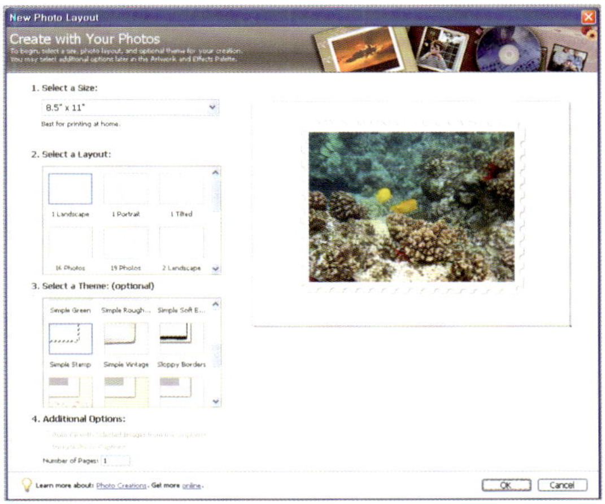

▲ New Photo Layout window

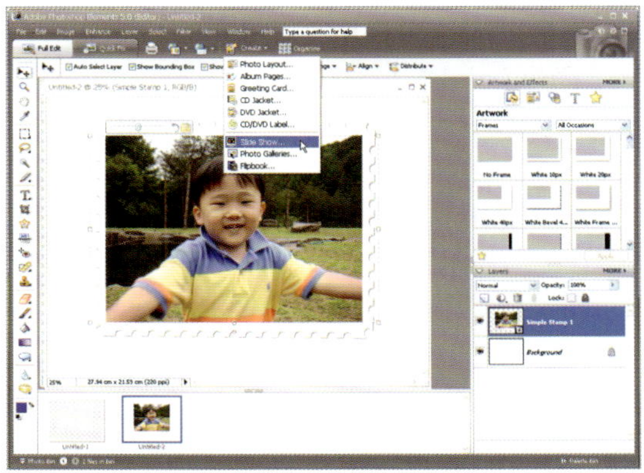

▲ Clicking the Create button

Introduction

ⓕ Start Up In

If you find it a hassle to go through the Welcome Screen every time you launch Photoshop Elements, you can tell the program to launch in the Editor or Organizer window using the Start Up In menu. If you change your mind, simply select Window > Welcome to open the Welcome Screen and make a new Start Up In selection.

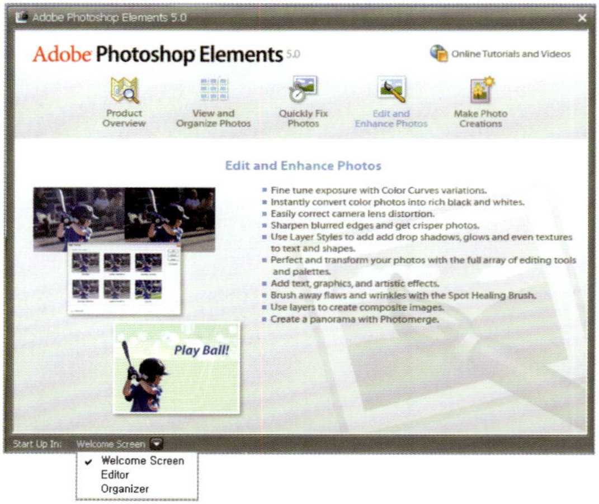

A Closer Look at the Photoshop Elements 5.0 Editor Window

The Editor Window contains two workspaces, the Quick Fix workspace and the Full Edit workspace, and you can toggle between these two workspaces by selecting the Quick Fix or Full Edit buttons. Because the Full Edit workspace contains a more complete editing environment, let's take a look at the Full Edit workspace and its various features in this section. After you become familiar with the Full Edit workspace, you will find it easy to explore the Quick Fix workspace on your own.

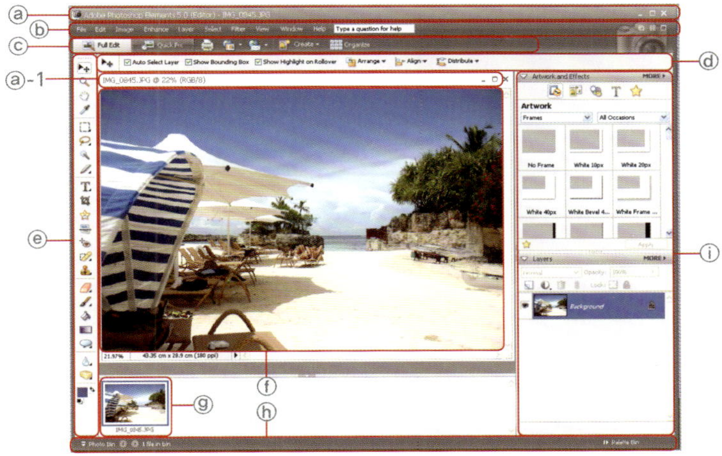

ⓐ, ⓐ-1 Title bar

The title bar displays the name of the image file, the magnification at which the image is being viewed, and the image mode (bitmap, grayscale, indexed color, or RGB).

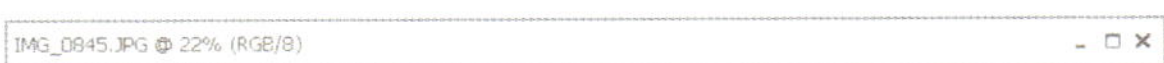

ⓑ Menu bar

The menu bar displays menus for the various commands available in Photoshop Elements. Clicking on a menu item will pull down the associated submenu.

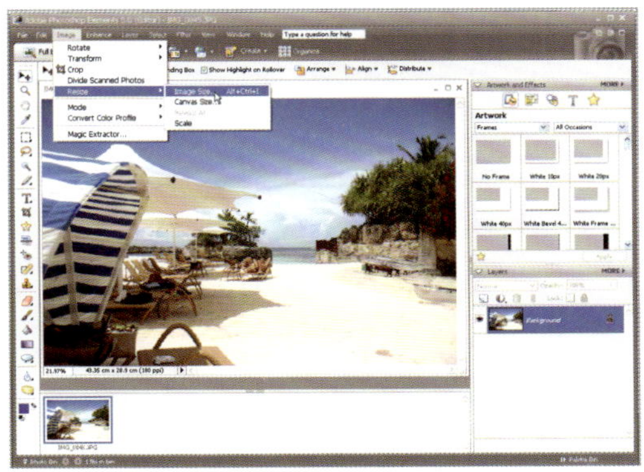

▲ Selecting Image from the menu bar

ⓒ Shortcuts bar

The Shortcuts bar is where you can find icons for commonly used functions such as the Quick Fix button, which allows you to make quick corrections to an image; the Print button, which lets you print online; and the Create button, which lets you create slide shows, photo galleries, and more.

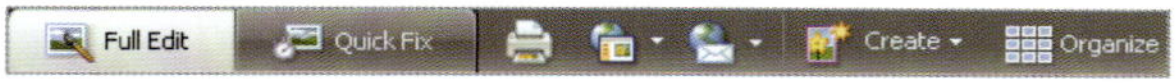

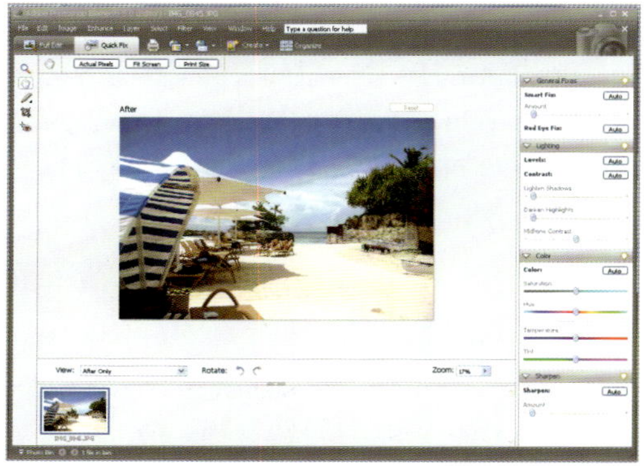

▲ Clicking the Quick Fix button

ⓓ Options bar

The options bar allows you to configure the options for a tool you've selected.

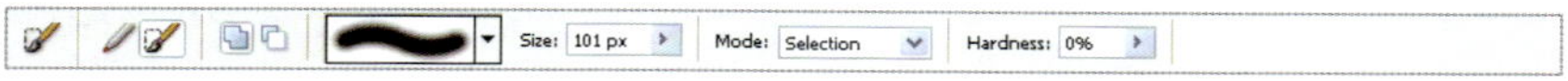

ⓔ Toolbox

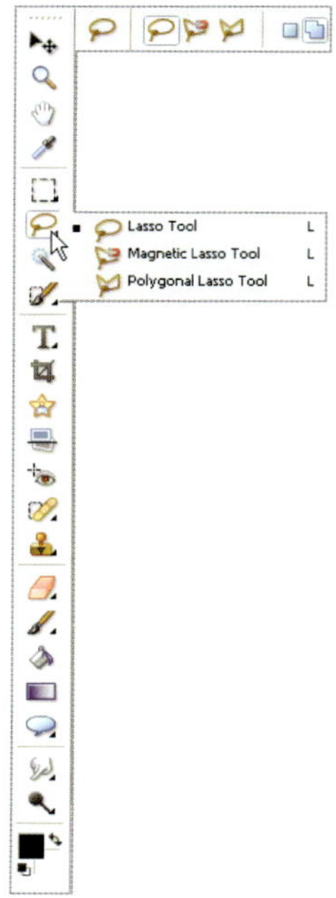

The toolbox contains all the tools you need for working on images, including selection, drawing and painting, correction, and navigation tools. Placing the cursor over a tool will reveal the tool's name and the keyboard shortcut for accessing the tool. This text is called the tool tip. At the bottom of the toolbox are two color swatches that you can use to set the foreground color (i.e., your tool color) and the background color.

A small triangle at the lower-right corner of a tool indicates that the tool has additional tools associated with it. These are called hidden tools. Clicking the right mouse button or holding a left mouse button click on a tool will reveal the hidden tools.

ⓕ Active image area

This is the area where the current active image is displayed.

ⓖ Photo Bin

The Photo Bin shows you a thumbnail of all the images that are currently open in the Standard Edit workspace. You can click on an image's thumbnail to make the image the active file in the workspace.

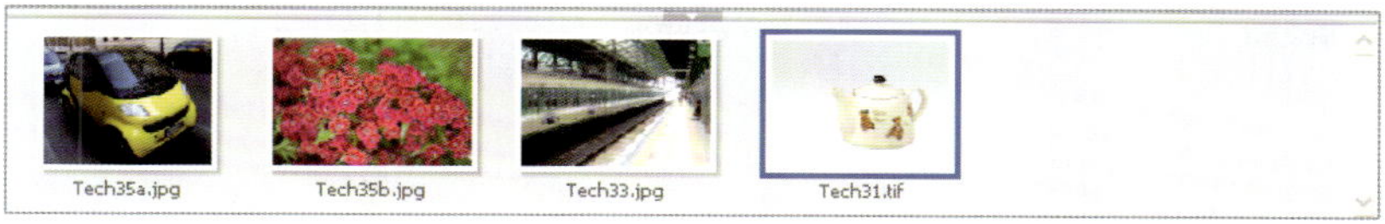

ⓗ Status bar

The status bar displays the status for the current image, namely the zoom ratio, the image dimensions, and information about the active tool.

ⓘ Palette Bin

Photoshop Elements comes with 8 palettes, each with different functions to help you monitor and modify images. The palettes can be accessed from the Window menu. You can keep the palettes in the Palette Bin or leave them in the work area.

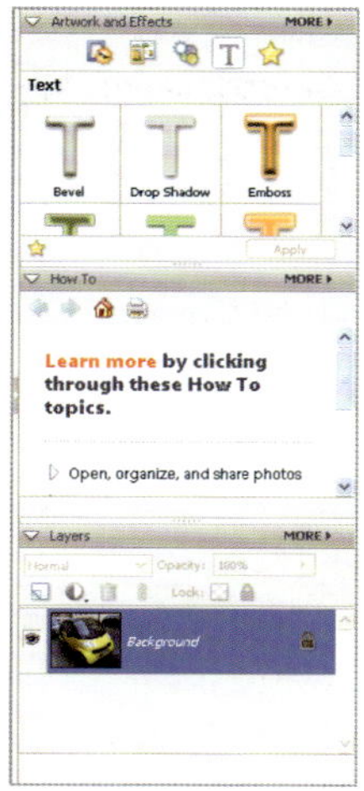

▶ Click on the Filters tab in the Palette Bin to view the Filters palette.

Essential Photoshop Elements Know-How

Now that you have an understanding of the Photoshop Elements interface, we will devote the rest of this introduction to showing how to perform some essential steps in the program. In the following pages, you will learn how to open and save an image file, and change the view of the image window.

Opening an Image File

There are three ways to open an image file in Photoshop Elements:

Using the File > Open command

1. Select File > Open from the menu bar.

The Open dialog box appears.

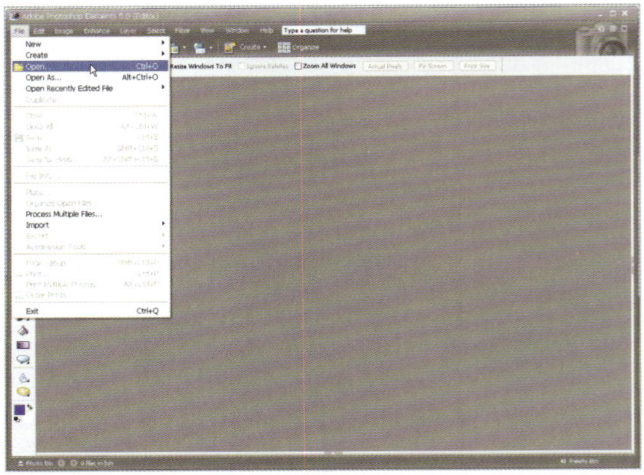

2. Select the image file from its folder. Click Open.

The selected file will appear in the Photoshop Elements image window.

tip You can also open an image file using the keyboard shortcut Ctrl + O. See the note on page 29 for information on Macintosh key commands.

Double-clicking on an empty workspace

1 Double-click on the empty workspace. This is the gray background where the image window will appear when a file is opened.

The Open dialog box appears.

2 Select the image file from its folder. Click Open.

The selected image file will appear in the Photoshop Elements image window.

Using the organizer

1 Click on the Organize icon in the shortcuts bar.

The organizer opens in a new window.

2 Select File > Get Photos and select the location where the photos can be found. For this exercise, let's select From Files and Folders.

After you have selected the photos, you do not need to perform this step again because the photos can be found in the Photo Browser.

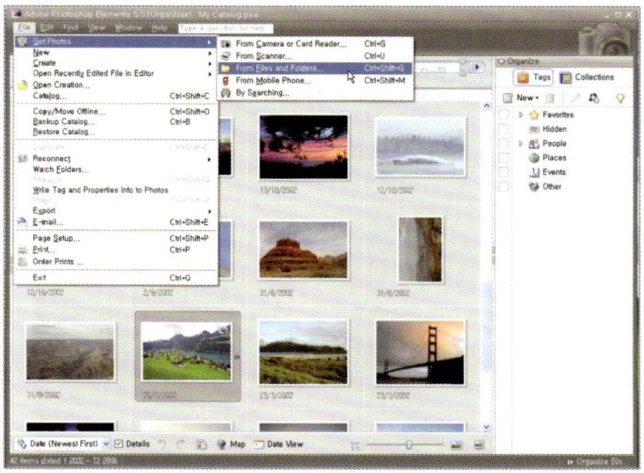

③ When the Get Photos From... dialog box appears, locate the image and click Get Photos or OK.

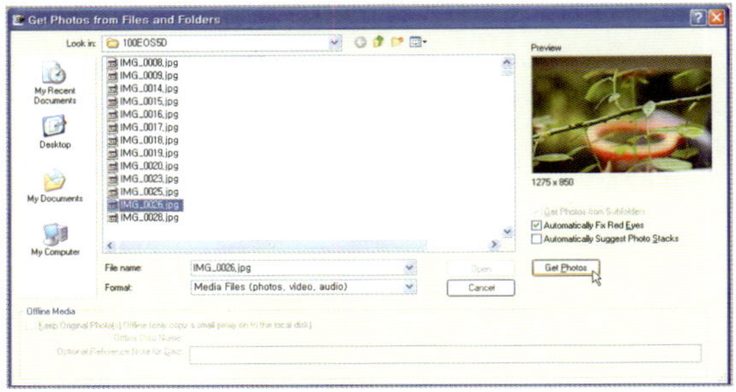

④ In the Photo Browser, you can see the image's thumbnail. Right-click on the image and select the workspace that you want to edit the image in. You can choose Auto Fix Window, Go to Quick Fix, or Go to Full Edit.

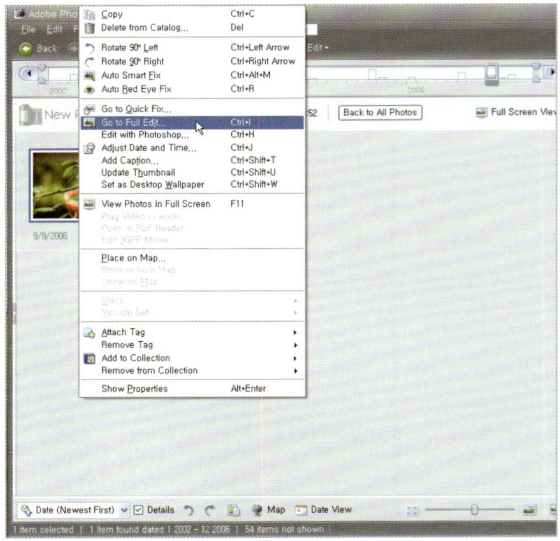

A Closer Look at the Organizer Window

The Organizer window contains the Photo Browser workspace and the Date View workspace. Because the Photo Browser workspace is more commonly used than the Date View workspace, we will only look at the Photo Browser workspace in this section. The Date View workspace looks and works like any computer calendar program so you will probably find it easy to explore the workspace on your own.

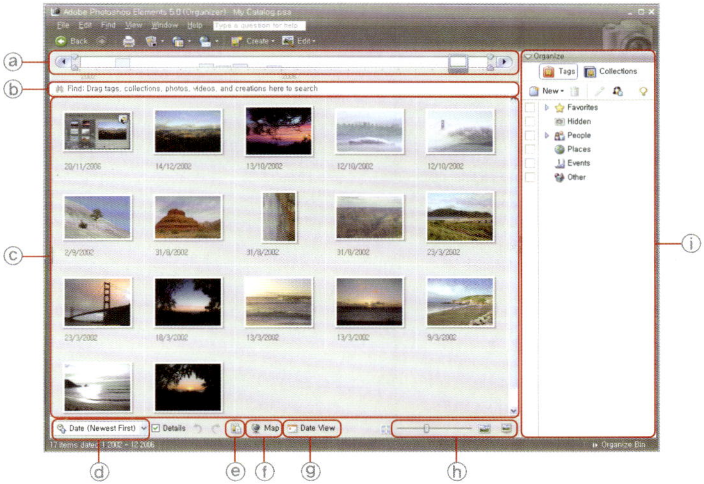

ⓐ Timeline

A bar on the timeline indicates the volume of images taken on that day on the timeline. If you click on a bar, the main window will show you the images taken on that day.

ⓑ Find bar

You can drag a tag from the Tag pane on the right to the Find bar to quickly locate the images that are tagged with the selected tag. You can also drag a photo to the bar to find similar photos, but this feature can be rather tricky to use effectively.

ⓒ Main window

The main window contains the thumbnails of images that you have selected for review.

ⓓ Photo Browser Arrangement

You can change the order of how the photographs are arranged in the Main Window. Date (Newest First) will arrange starting with the latest photography viewed, and Date (Oldest First) will arrange starting with the oldest photography viewed. Import Batch will show the date and time in which the photograph was pulled out from the hard drive. Folder Location will open a folder window on the left side of the main window, allowing you to view the folders in your computer.

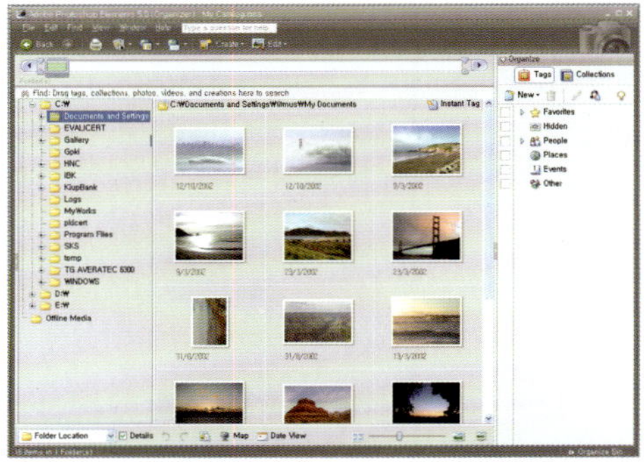

ⓔ Show or Hide Properties

Once clicked, the Properties window will appear and the information–such as file size and folder location–of the selected photograph can be seen. You can also input simple notes and/or captions to the selected photograph.

ⓕ Show or Hide Map

A map will appear when this button is clicked. You can drag the image to the location where you took the photo in the map to keep track of where the photo was taken.

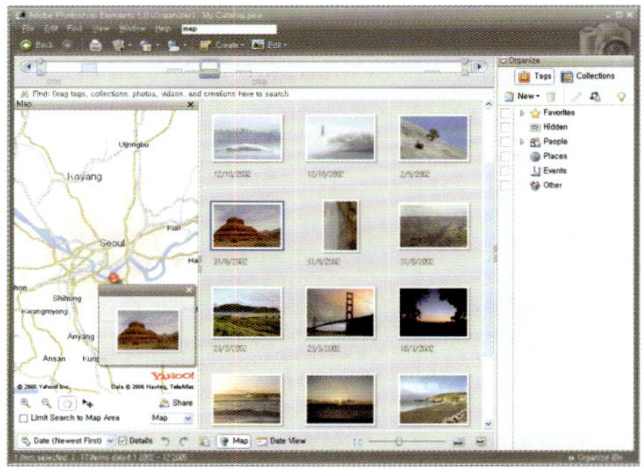

ⓖ Date View

The Date View workspace lets you look for images and files in a calendar format.

ⓗ Thumbnail size slider

Dragging the slider's handle to the left makes the thumbnails smaller whereas dragging to the right makes them larger.

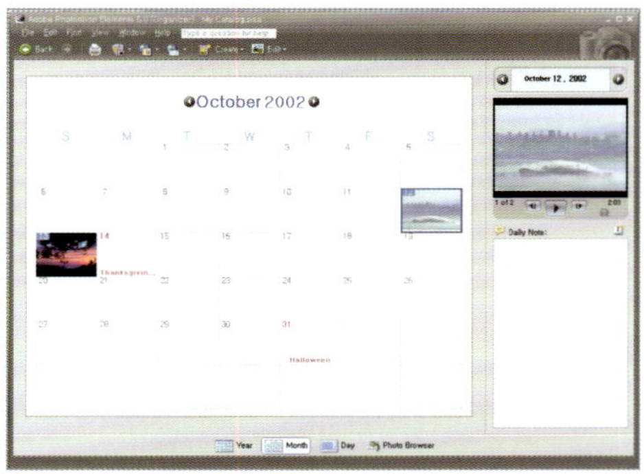

ⓘ Tags and Collections panes

You can tag or add an image to the Tags and Collections panes to organize and quickly access your files.

Saving an Image File

Using the File > Save command

Select File > Save from the menu bar to save the image file using the same name in the current file format. If you save an image using File > Save, the original image will be overwritten by the changes made.

Using the File > Save As command

1. Select File > Save As from the menu bar.

   The Save As dialog box appears.

2. Type in the file name and select the image format.

3. Click Save.

Using the File > Save for Web command

1. Select File > Save for Web from the menu bar.

   The Save for Web dialog box appears.

2. Click OK.

   The Save Optimized As dialog box appears.

3. Type in the file name. Click Save.

Keyboard Shortcuts on the Macintosh

Photoshop Elements runs on both the Windows and Macintosh operating systems. The program functions the same on both platforms, but there are a few keyboard differences. For example, the shortcut to open a file in Photoshop Elements is Ctrl + O in Windows; it's Command + O on the Mac.

Throughout this book, the keyboard shortcuts given are based on the Windows platform. Mac users should have no problem following along if they learn a few keyboard equivalents:

Windows	Macintosh
Shift	Shift
Alt	Option
!	Command (or "apple" key)
right-click	Ctrl +click

A Closer Look at the Save As Dialog Box

The Save As dialog box lets you define how an image file should be saved. Let's look at some of the options.

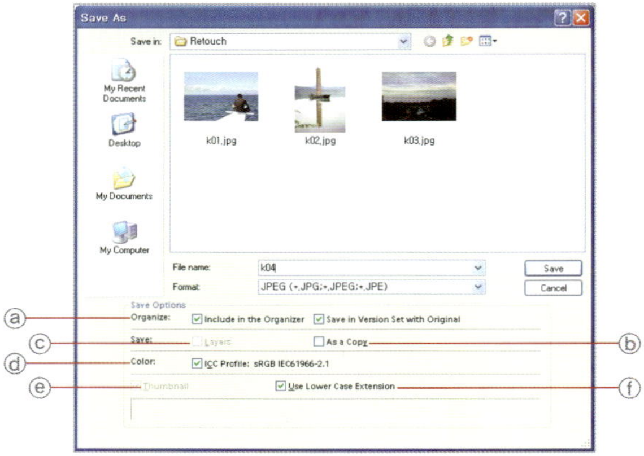

ⓐ **Organize**: Check these options to include your edited image in the organizer, and to save both versions in a Version Set.

ⓑ **As a Copy**: Check this option to save the image file as a copy, leaving the original image intact. The new file has the word "copy" in the file name.

ⓒ **Layers**: This feature will be activated if you have used layers in the image file. Check this option to preserve the layers. If you do not check this option and save the image as an image file (whether JPEG or other file formats), the layers will be merged with the background layer.

ⓓ **Color**: Check this option to save the color information of the image.

ⓔ **Thumbnail**: Check this option to create a thumbnail for the saved image file. This thumbnail will be shown in the Open dialog box when the File > Open command is selected.

ⓕ **Use Lower Case Extension**: Check this option to have the file format extension displayed in lower case. If not selected, the file format extension will be displayed in upper case.

A Closer Look at the Save for Web Dialog Box

The Save for Web dialog box allows you to adjust settings that determine the size and quality of images saved for the Web and to save files as GIF animations. It also lets you preview the effects of the settings you make.

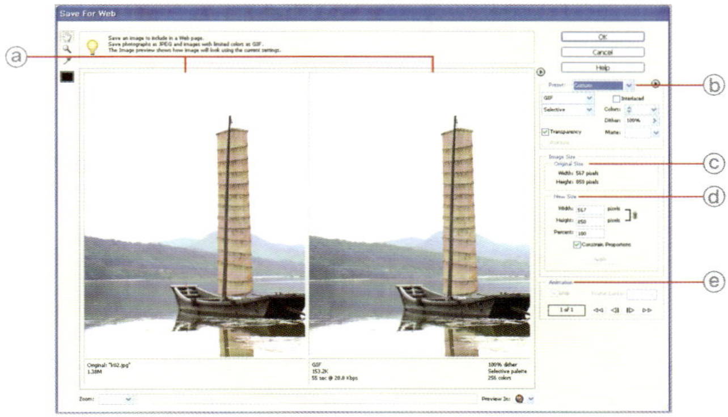

ⓐ **Preview window**: Displays the original image on the left and the optimized image on the right. Also shows the file size and loading time for each image.

ⓑ **Preset**: Displays the compression file formats and color depth options available.

ⓒ **Original Size**: Displays the image size and resolution of the original image.

ⓓ **New Size**: Allows alteration of the image size and resolution.

ⓔ **Animation**: Saves file as an animated GIF file.

Why Optimize?

A large, high-resolution image will take a long time to load on a Web page. To keep downloading speed fast, images need to be saved in one of the compression file formats and settings need to be adjusted in order to preserve the best possible quality at the smallest possible size. This process is known as optimizing an image.

Changing the View

It is often necessary to zoom in on certain parts of an image for more detailed work. This section describes how you can use the Zoom Tool and the Hand Tool to change the view of the image.

Zooming in on a selected area

1. Select the Zoom Tool ( ) from the toolbox.

2. Click and drag over the area you wish to magnify.

The selected area will be magnified and shown in the active image window.

tip The zoom ratio is shown on the title bar at the top of the window.

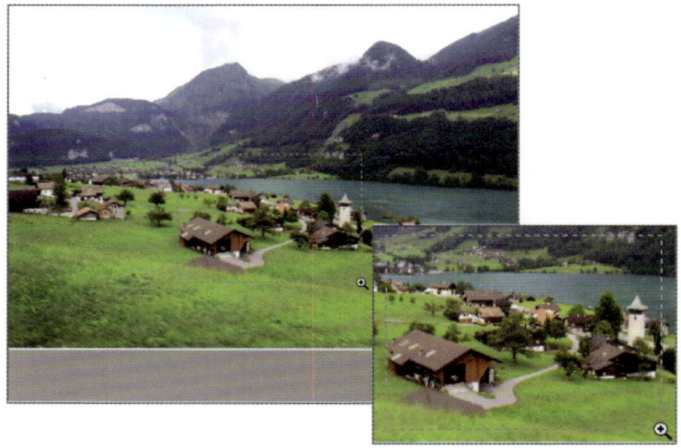

Zooming in on the entire image

1. Select the Zoom Tool ( ) from the toolbox.

2. Click on the image window to magnify the entire image.

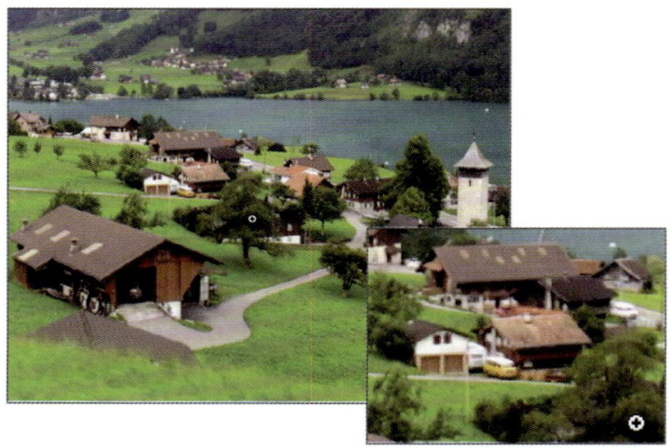

Zooming out from an image

1 Select the Zoom Tool ( ) from the toolbox.

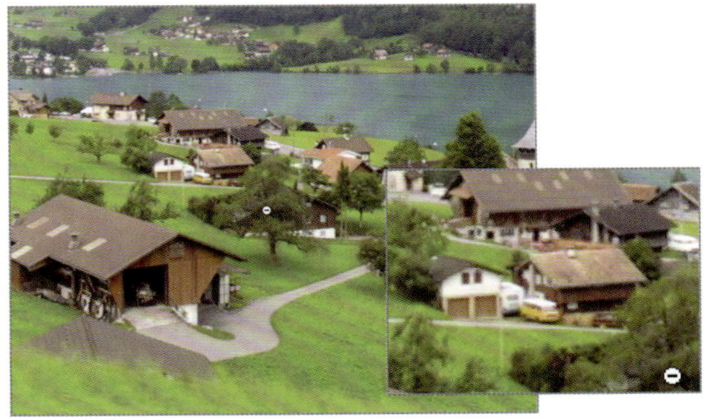

2 Hold down Alt .

The mouse pointer changes to .

3 Click on the image to zoom out.

tip Press Ctrl + Spacebar to change the cursor or selected tool to the Zoom In Tool. Press Alt + Spacebar to convert to the Zoom Out Tool.

Moving the magnified image

After you have zoomed in a few times on an image, you may no longer be able to see the entire image in the image window. In such cases, you must use the Hand Tool to move your view to another part of the image.

1 Select the Hand Tool ( ) from the toolbox.

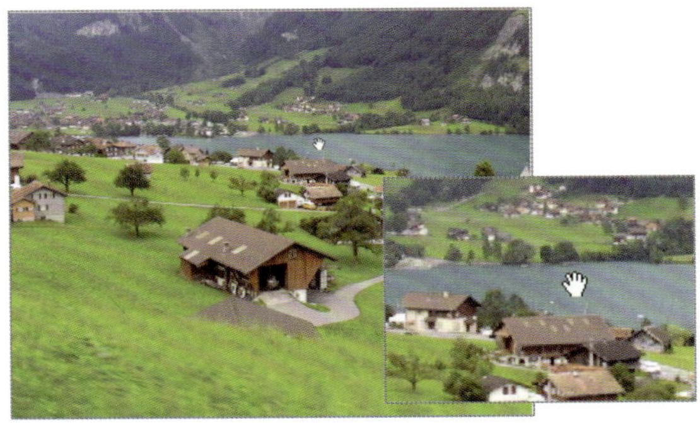

2 Click and drag the tool in the image window to move the image.

tip Press and hold down Spacebar to switch from a selected tool to the Hand Tool.

Using Keyboard Shortcuts

- Ctrl + 0 : Resizes the image to fit the Photoshop Elements window so the entire image is visible.
- Ctrl + Alt + 0 : Displays the image at 100% view.
- Ctrl + + : Magnifying the zoom of the image also increases the size of the image window.
- Ctrl + Alt + + : Magnifying the zoom of the image does not change the size of the image window.
- Ctrl + - : Reducing the zoom of the image also decreases the size of the image window.
- Ctrl + Alt + - : Reducing the zoom of the image does not change the size of the image window.

40 Digital Photo Retouching Techniques

with Photoshop Elements 5.0

Chapter 1

Correcting Contrast

If you are a photography enthusiast, you know that light is the defining factor in photography. You probably also know that getting the perfect lighting conditions for the right exposure is sometimes out of your control. Backlit photos, for instance, are sometimes unavoidable.

In this chapter, you will learn how to evaluate the contrast of an image in Photoshop Elements and correct the problem like a pro. In addition, you will make an out-of-focus picture appear more focused by increasing the contrast of the image.

01 Diagnosing the Problem

Overexposed Image

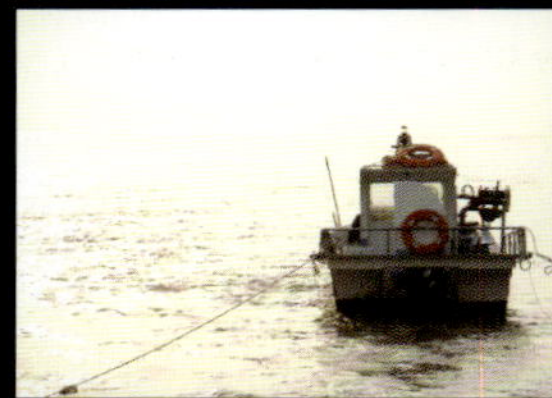

Underexposed Image

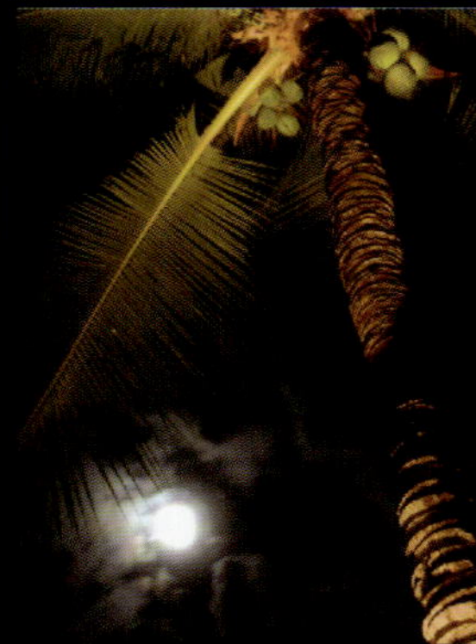

One of the most common problems in taking pictures is getting the right exposure. Although you can tell just by looking whether an image is under- or overexposed, you can make more accurate corrections if you use the Histogram function in Photoshop Elements.

About the histogram

The histogram works by mapping the number of pixels at each tonal value. If the pixels are concentrated in the shadows, this means that the image has more dark areas. An image with pixels more or less evenly spread across the histogram would have a full tonal range. By understanding the information provided in the Histogram dialog box, you will know exactly which part of the histogram needs adjustment when correcting the image tone.

Analyzing an overexposed image

1. Select File > Open from the menu bar.

   The Open dialog box appears.

2. Open the **Sample\Chapter 1\Tech0101.tif** file from the supplementary CD.

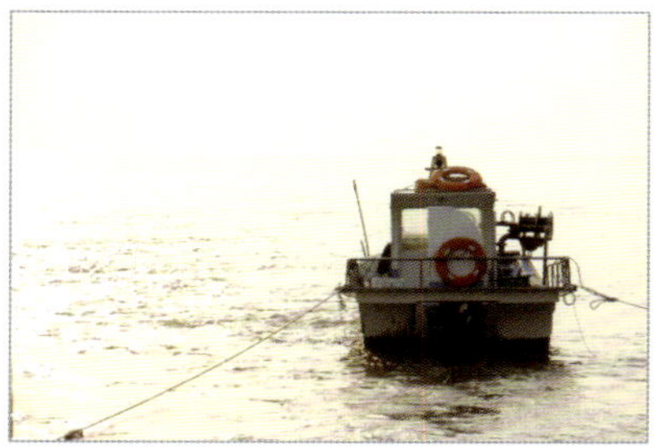

③ Select Window > Histogram from the menu bar. When the Histogram dialog box appears, check that **Luminosity** is selected under the Channel option.

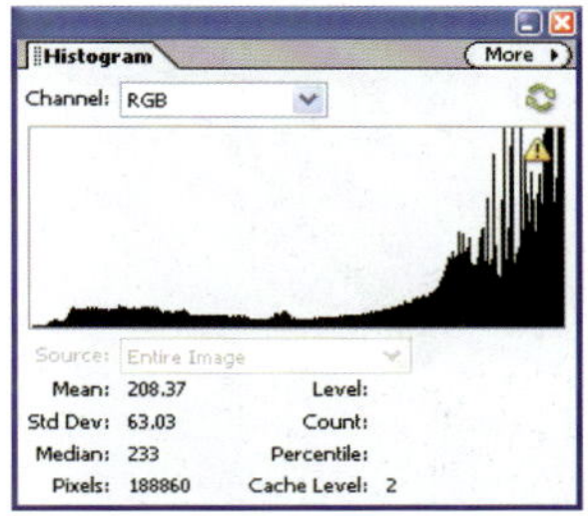

Notice that the right side of the histogram is extremely high. This is an indication that the image is too bright. Such an image is known as a high-key image.

④ Click OK to close the Histogram dialog box.

You can also choose to plot the intensity of the reds, greens, and blues in the image if you are working with an RGB image.

Analyzing an underexposed image

① Select File > Open from the menu bar.

The Open dialog box appears.

② Open the **Sample\Chapter 1\Tech0102.tif** file from the supplementary CD.

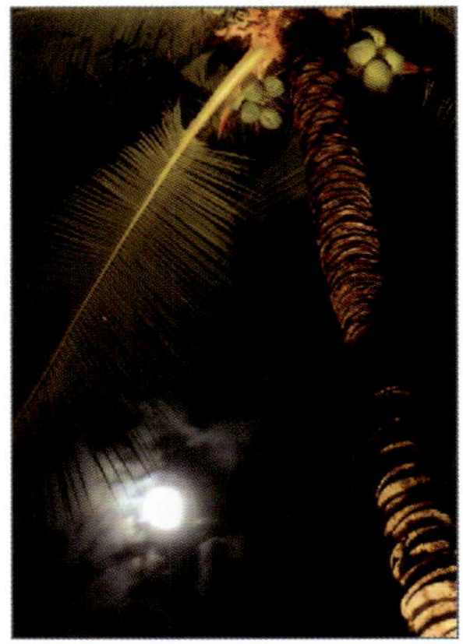

③ Select Window > Histogram from the menu bar.

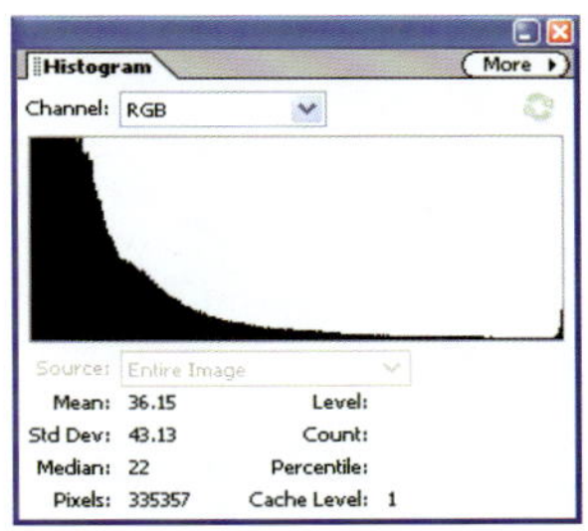

The Histogram dialog box appears. In contrast to the previous histogram, the left side of this histogram is very high. This is an indication that the image is too dark. Such an image is called a low-key image.

In addition to high-key and low-key images, average-key images also need to be fixed. Average-key images are those with a concentration of pixels in the middle portion of the histogram. These images tend to look dull because they are dominated by grays or midtones.

02 Correcting Blurred Images

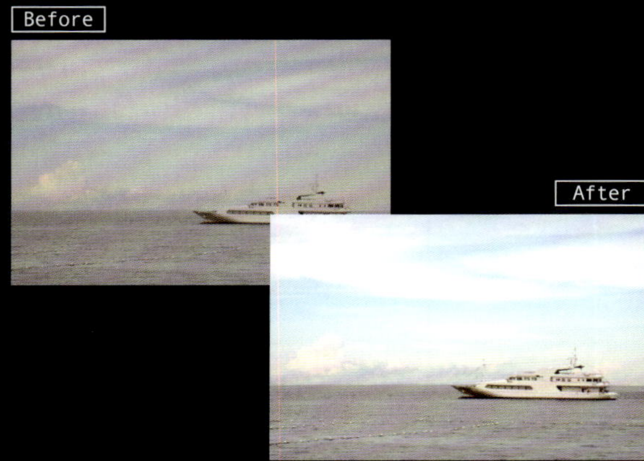

If your image is slightly out of focus, you can increase the brightness and contrast to make it appear sharper. If you have a very blurred image, however, there is no way that you can make it look focused. The best thing to do is to shoot the photo again. Always remember the GIGO (pronounced gee-go) principle. GIGO is short for Garbage-In, Garbage-Out. It is a computer term to describe that the output will only be as good as the input.

(1) Select File > Open from the menu bar.

The Open dialog box appears.

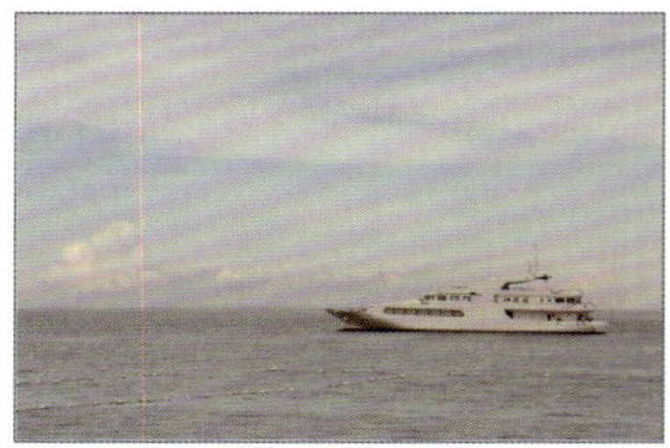

(2) Open the **Sample\Chapter 1\Tech02.tif** file from the supplementary CD.

(3) Select Enhance > Adjust Lighting > Brightness/Contrast from the menu bar.

The Brightness/Contrast dialog box appears.

(4) Set Brightness to **25**. Click on the Preview checkbox to view the effect without closing the dialog box.

Note that the image is now brighter.

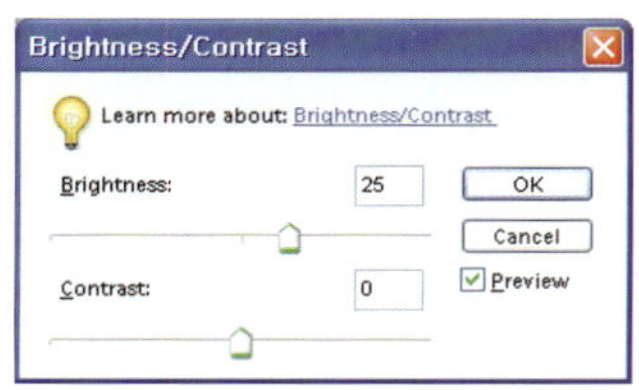

tip Always preview the image when making changes to the contrast. This is to make sure that the colors are not compromised for the sake of sharpness.

5 Set Contrast to **40**.

This makes the image look sharper.

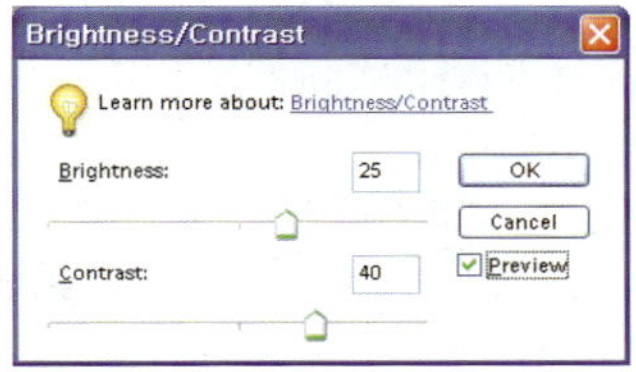

tip In most cases, setting the Contrast to twice the Brightness value you just entered will produce the best results.

6 Click OK.

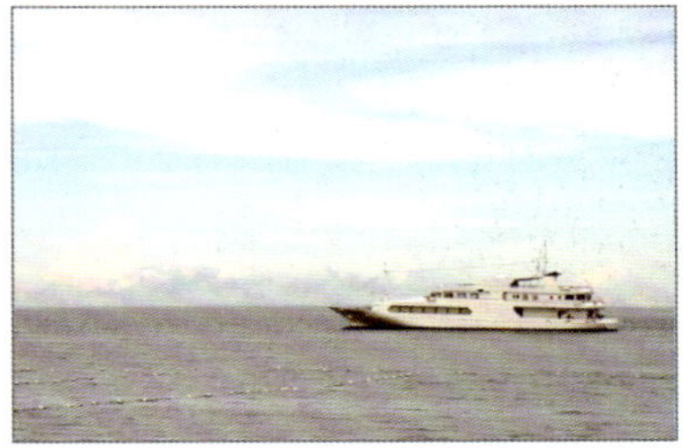

tip You can also change the brightness or contrast by using the slider bars, but typing in a value is quicker and more accurate, especially if you want to apply the same setting to a few images.

tip Press the Alt key to change the Cancel button to the Reset button. You can then reset the Brightness and Contrast values to 0 by clicking the Reset button.

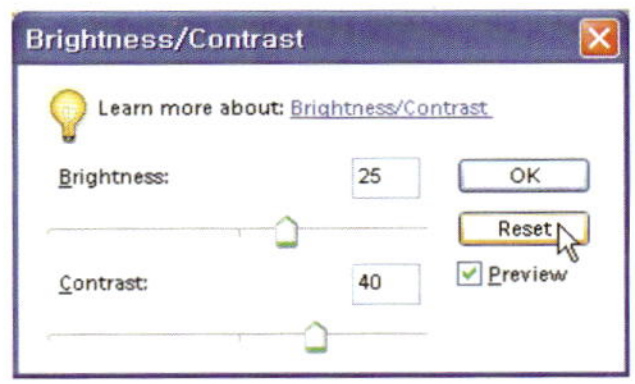

tip Generally speaking, you must adjust the contrast whenever you change an image's brightness. If you brighten up an image without adjusting the contrast, its shadows will look too bright, making the image look like a faded photo.

In the example to the right, the Contrast has been increased to 70. At this high level of contrast, the image is almost turned into a black-and-white picture.

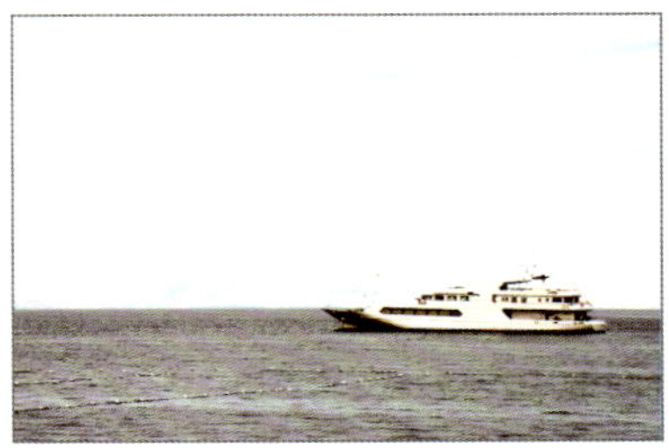

03 How the Pros Do It

Before

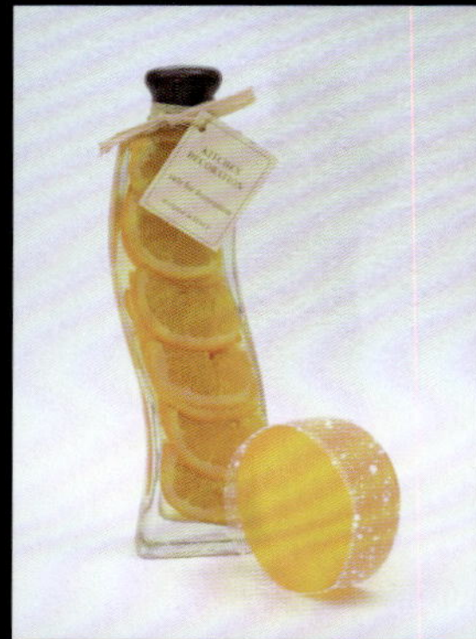

After

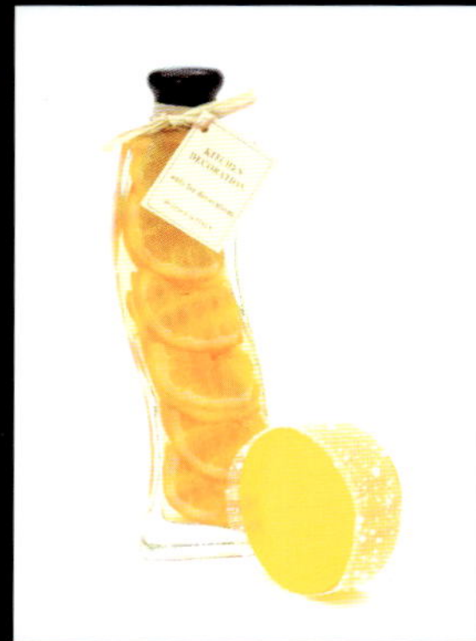

Commercial photography usually requires sophisticated equipment that is beyond the budget of most hobbyists and amateur photographers. Using the Levels command in Photoshop Elements, you can correct and enhance product images taken using digital cameras to achieve professional-looking results.

Brightness/Contrast versus Levels command

While the Brightness/Contrast command can be used to change the brightness and contrast of an image, the Levels function is more sophisticated because you can make specific changes to the shadows, highlights, and midtones of an image.

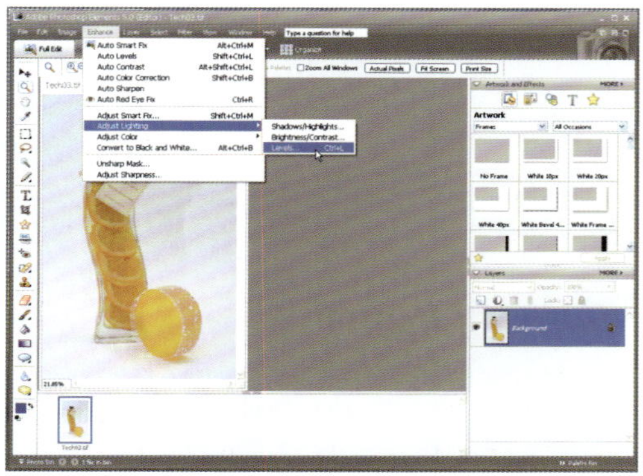

1 Select File > Open from the menu bar.

The Open dialog box appears.

2 Open the **Sample\Chapter 1\Tech03.tif** file from the supplementary CD.

This slightly dull image can be brightened to give the objects a fresh appeal.

3 Select Enhance > Adjust Lighting > Levels from the menu bar.

tip Some users magnify an image to view a particularly problematic or important section when making changes to contrast. Although this is a fast way of correcting glaring weaknesses, it makes it difficult to obtain an optimal overall image setting. Therefore, it is recommended that a contrast that is appropriate for the overall image be applied before the image is magnified.

4 The right side of the histogram in the Levels dialog box is high, indicating that the image is quite bright. Drag the white triangular slider directly below the Input Levels histogram from the right to the left, as shown in the figure.

This brightens the already bright regions of the image and removes the light background tone.

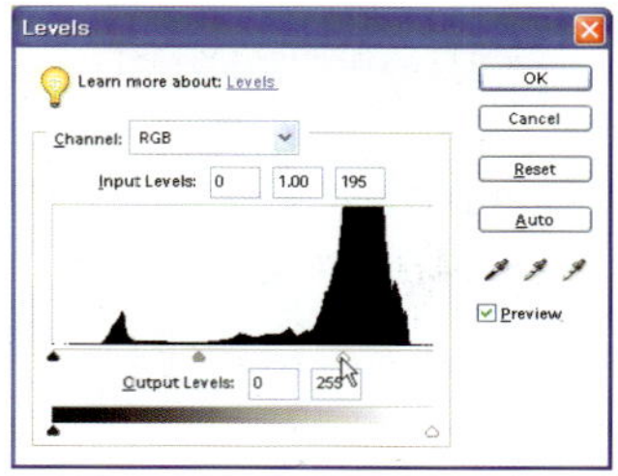

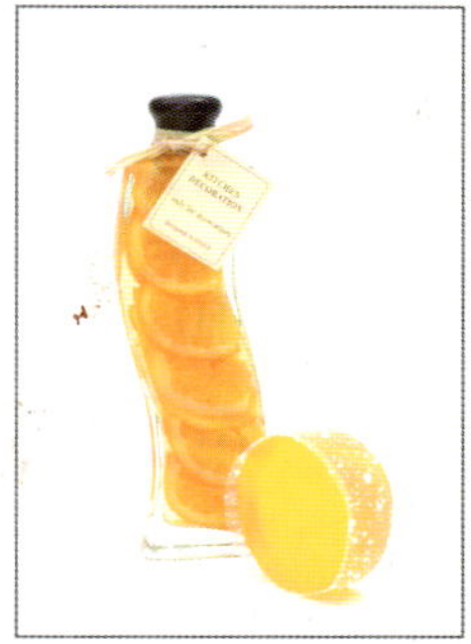

5 Drag the black triangular slider directly below the Input Levels histogram toward the right, as shown in the figure.

This darkens the darker pixels in the image and increases the overall contrast of the picture as a result.

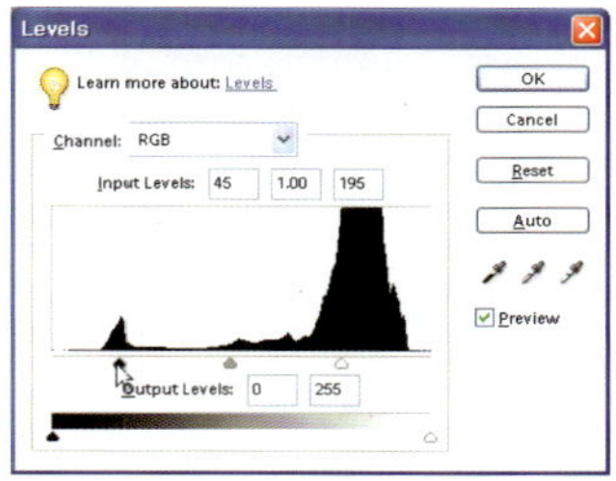

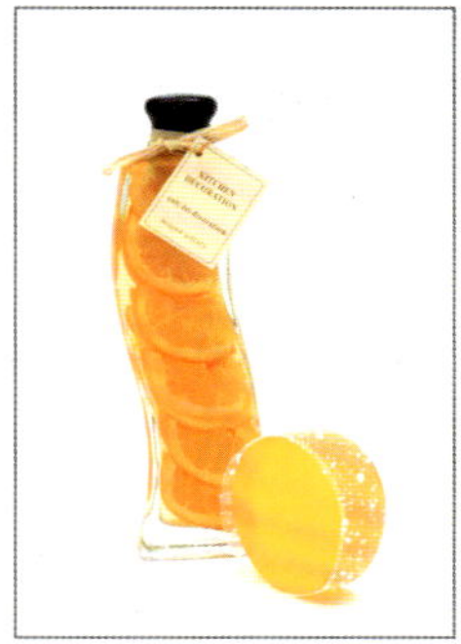

tip As you move a slider, the value in the corresponding Input Levels text field changes to reflect the new input. You can also adjust the histogram by entering the values in the text fields directly instead of moving the sliders. This is especially useful if exact values are needed.

6 Drag the gray triangular slider toward the left to brighten the midtones of the image.

In this example, entering an intensity value of 45 in the first Input Levels field (for the black slider) means that all pixels to the left of 45 will become black. A value of 195 in the third field (for the white slider) means all pixels to the right of 195 will become white. A value of 1.30 in the middle field brightens the midtone regions slightly.

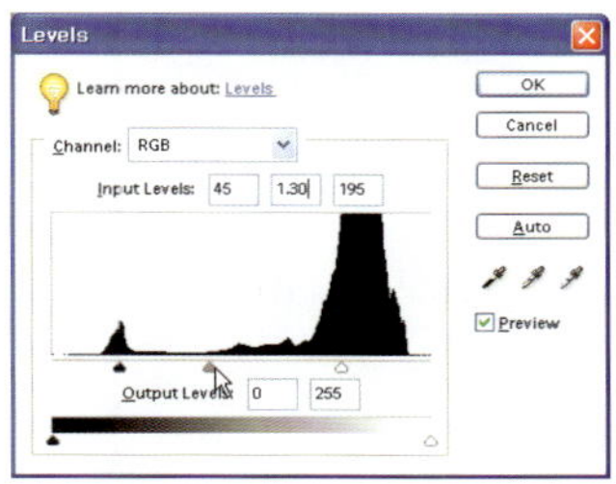

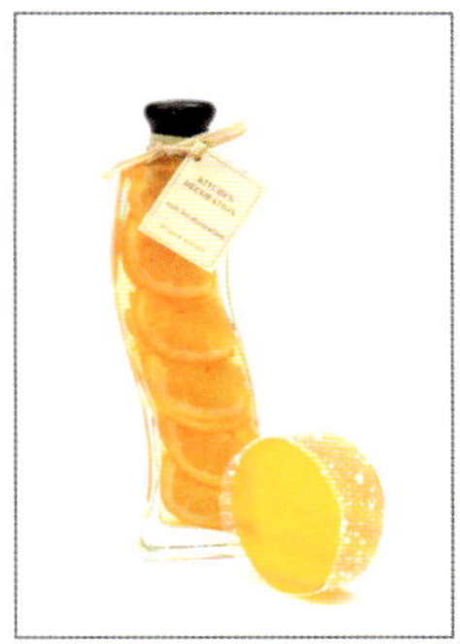

A Closer Look at the Levels Dialog Box

The Levels dialog box consists of a channel menu, a histogram, an input slider bar, and an output slider bar. The input slider bar is used to correct the brightness and contrast of images, while the output slider bar is used to set the tonal range of the image.

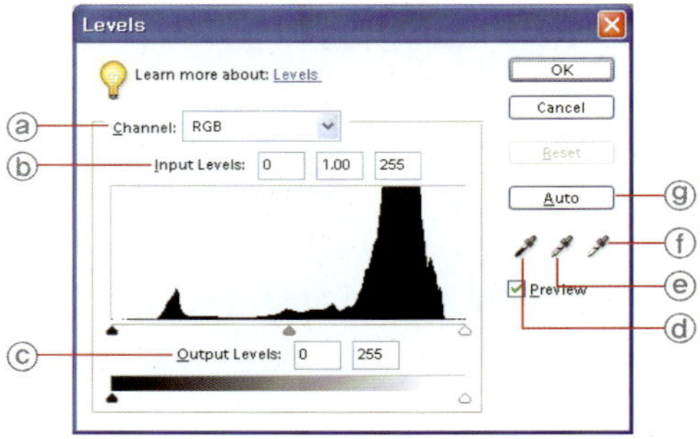

ⓐ **Channel**: You can adjust the intensity of an image's tonal values or its red, green, or blue values by selecting the channel from the drop-down menu.

ⓑ **Input Levels**: You can adjust the shadows, midtones, and highlights of an image by entering the values in the Input Levels text fields or by adjusting the three input sliders below the histogram.

ⓒ **Output Levels**: You can change the overall image's tonal range by moving the two output sliders below the Output Levels text boxes. Dragging the white arrow toward the left darkens the overall image, while dragging the black arrow to the right brightens the overall image.

ⓓ **Set Black Point**: If you click the Set Black Point eyedropper and then click on a pixel on the image, all pixels darker than the selected pixel in the image window will become black. Clicking this eyedropper on areas that are 100% black will have no effect.

ⓔ **Set Gray Point**: This is used to configure the midtones of the image. Clicking the Set Gray Point eyedropper on the image will apply the color contrast of the selected pixels as the midtone for the entire image.

ⓕ **Set White Point**: If you click the Set White Point eyedropper and then click on a pixel on the image, all pixels brighter than the selected pixel in the image window will become white. Clicking this eyedropper on areas that are 100% white will have no effect.

ⓖ **Auto**: You can automatically enhance the contrast of an image by clicking Auto. This option is the same as the Enhance > Auto Levels command in the menu bar.

04 Correcting Backlighting

Before

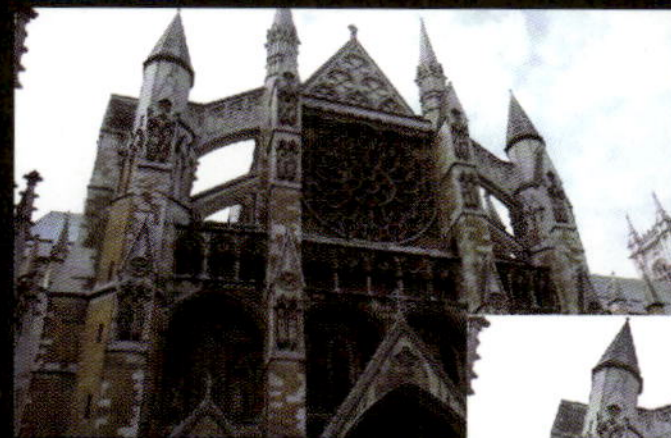

After

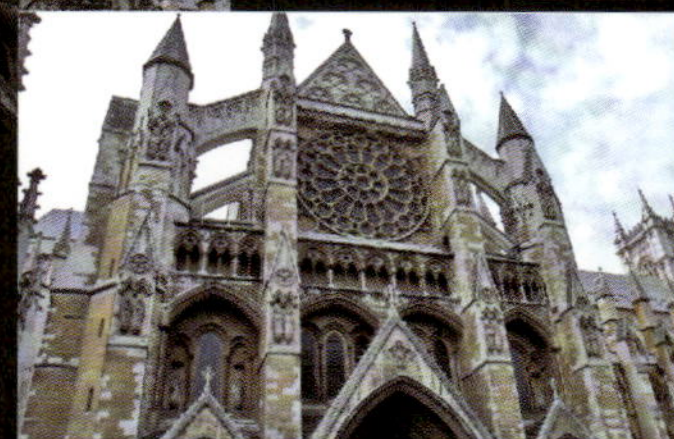

Backlighting often causes exposure problems in pictures. In the Before image on the left, the building is backlit by the bright, sunny sky. As you can see, the sky looks overly bright while the building and other parts of the image appear slightly dark. The Shadows/Highlights feature in Photoshop Elements will help you correct such problems.

1 Choose File > Open from the menu bar.

The Open dialog box opens.

2 Open the **Sample\Chapter 1\Tech04.tif** file from the supplementary CD.

You can see that the sky is too bright while the building is in shadow.

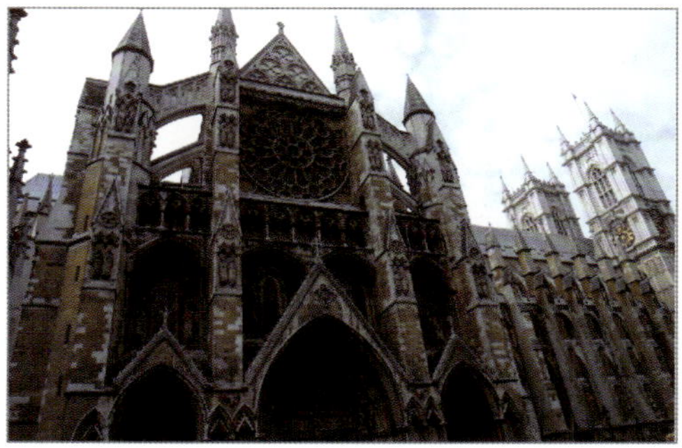

3 Select Enhance > Adjust Lighting > Shadows/Highlights from the menu bar.

The Shadows/Highlights dialog box appears.

(4) To brighten up the building, move the Lighten Shadows slider to a value of **70%**.

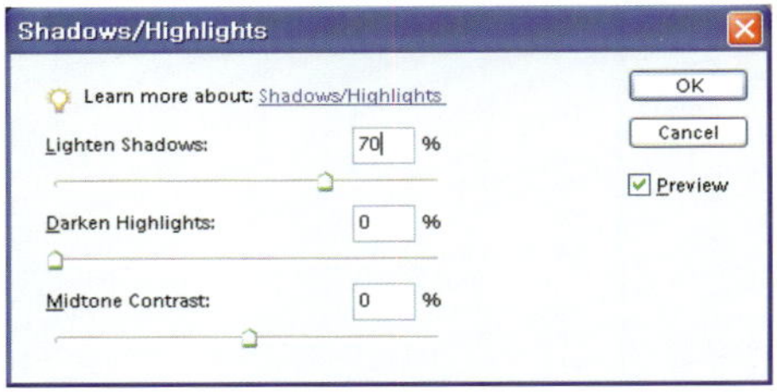

(5) You will see that this only brightens up the building and that the sky's luminosity did not change.

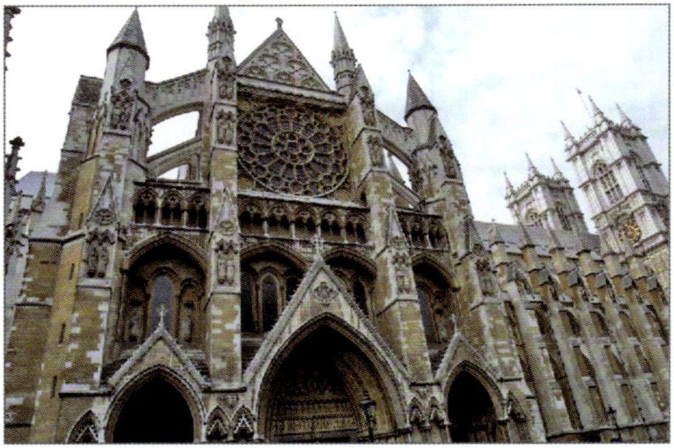

(4) Now, let's darken the sky. In the Shadows/Highlights dialog box, increase the Darken Highlights value to **30%**.

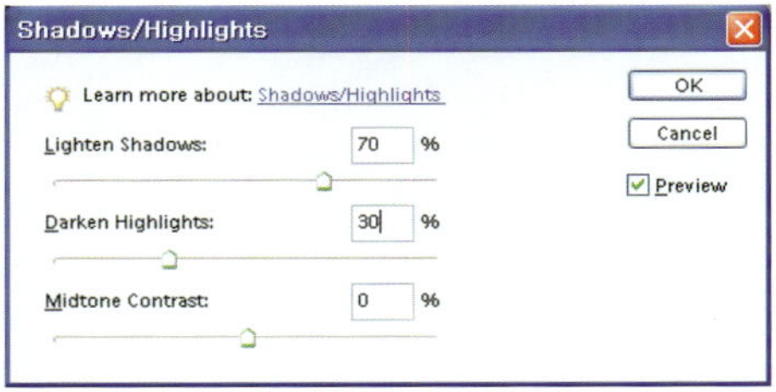

7 By darkening the sky, you can now see the clouds more clearly.

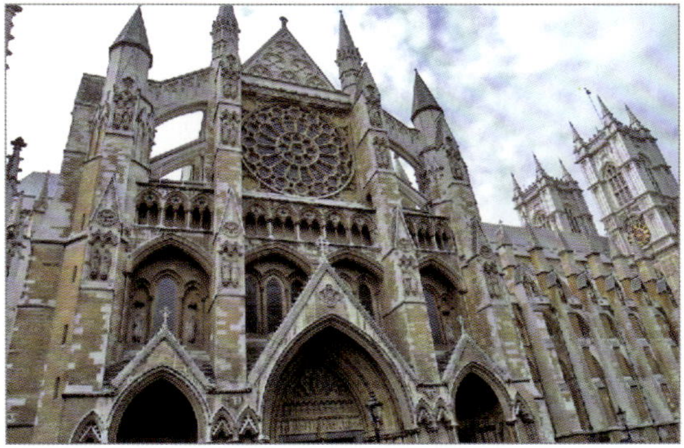

8 Because the building looks slightly washed out, let's increase the midtone contrast to bring out all the details. In the Shadows/Highlights dialog box, increase the Midtone Contrast to **20%**.

Click OK when you are done.

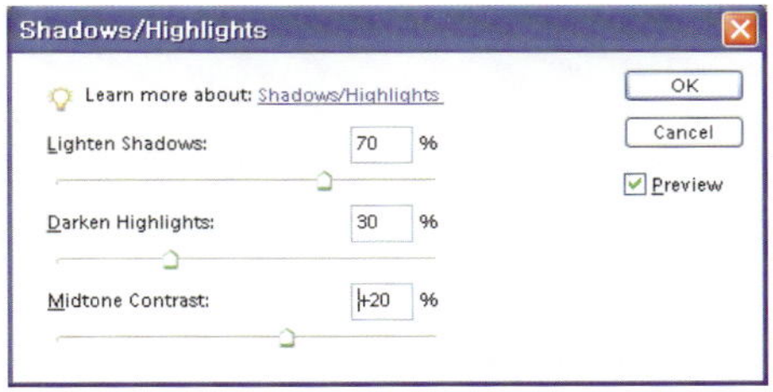

9 As shown in this example, the Lighten Shadows and Darken Highlights sliders are useful for adjusting the brightness of the light and dark areas in a picture, while the Midtone Contrast slider is used to improve the picture's contrast. Combined, these functions make the Shadows/Highlights feature of Photoshop Elements perfect for correcting backlighting problems.

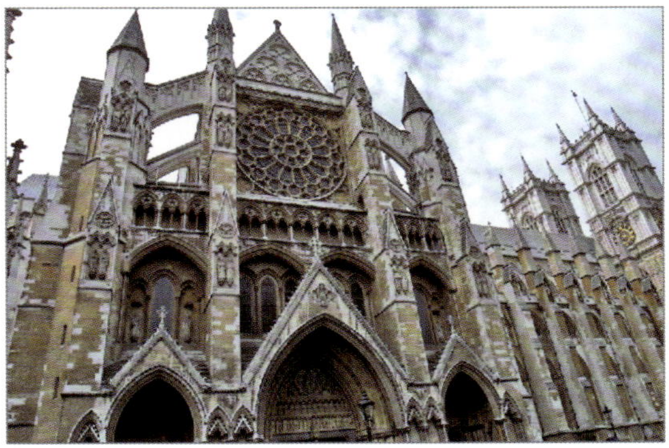

05 Brightening a Specific Spot

Before

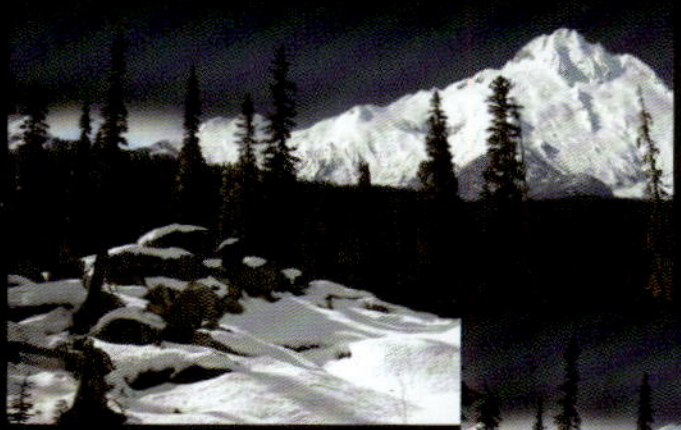

After

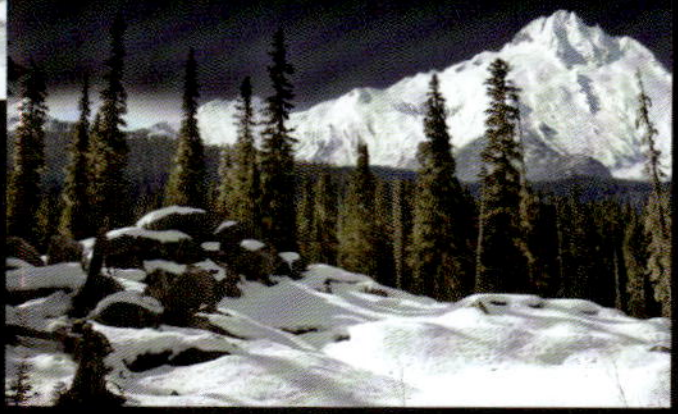

Occasionally, you may need to brighten or darken only specific areas of an image without affecting the other parts. To make such precise adjustments, you need to first select the area you intend to work on. You also have to make sure that the corrected area blends in with the image. All this can be done easily in Photoshop Elements.

1. Select File > Open from the menu bar.

The Open dialog box appears.

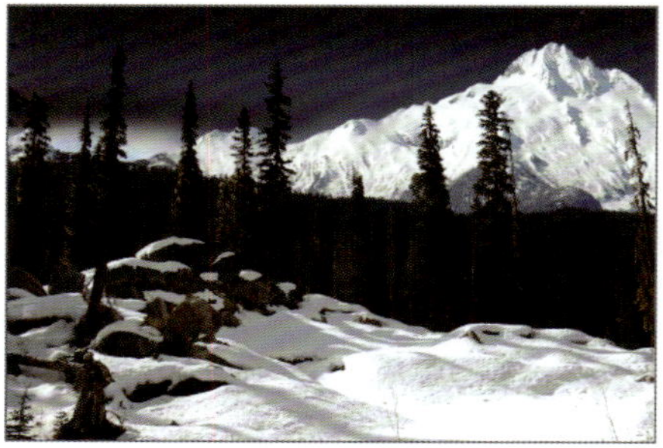

2. Open the **Sample\Chapter 1\Tech05.tif** file from the supplementary CD.

This snow-covered winter picture is too dark except for the areas covered by snow.

3. Select the Lasso Tool ( ) from the toolbox.

4. Use the Lasso Tool to outline the dark areas.

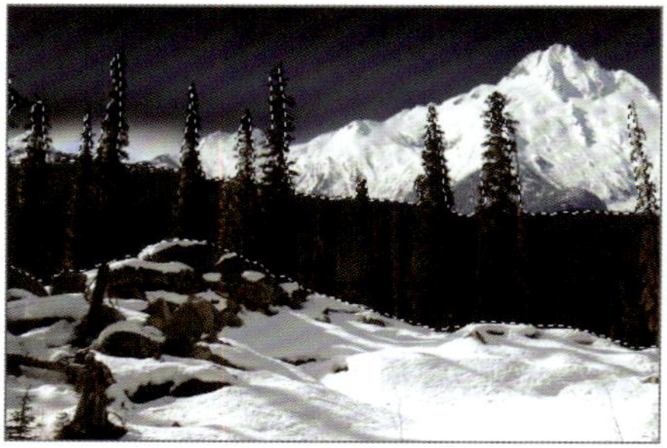

5 Click on Select > Feather from the menu bar.

The Feather Selection dialog box appears.

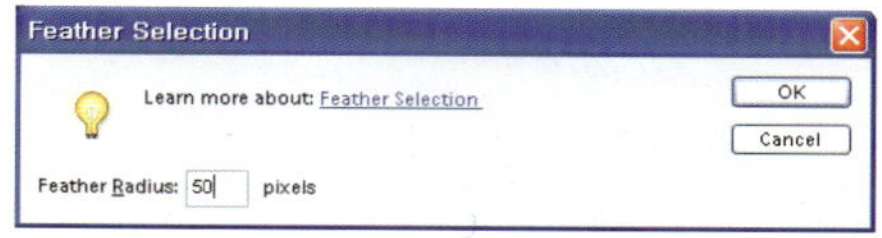

6 Set Feather Radius to **50**.

7 Click OK.

This softens the edges of the selection and blends it in with the rest of the image.

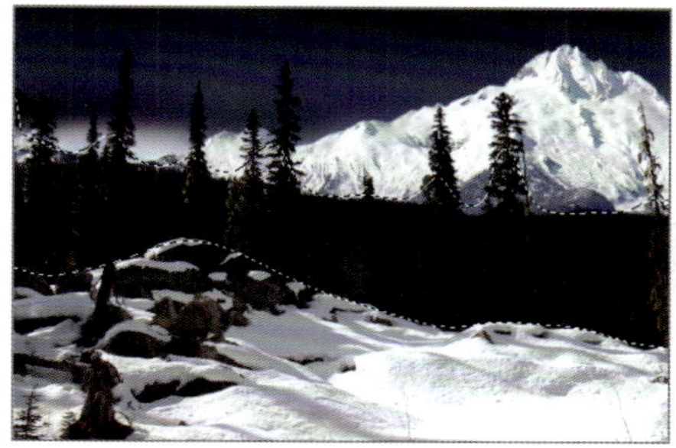

8 Select Enhance > Adjust Lighting > Levels from the menu bar.

The Levels dialog box appears.

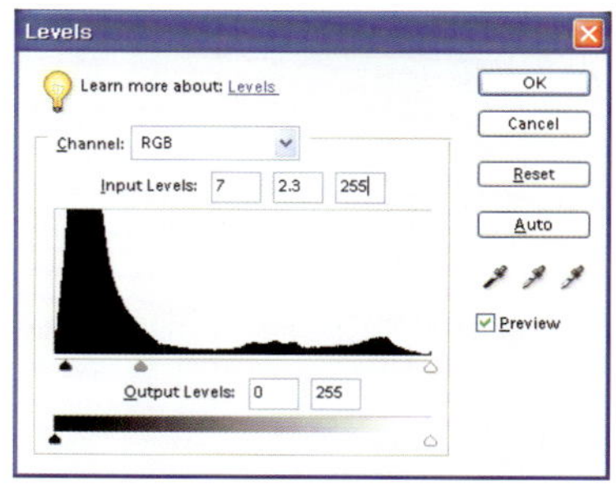

9 Set the Input values to **7**, **2.3**, and **255**.

tip Check the Preview option in the Levels dialog box to preview the changes made in the dialog box on the actual image.

10 Click OK.

The selected areas become brighter.

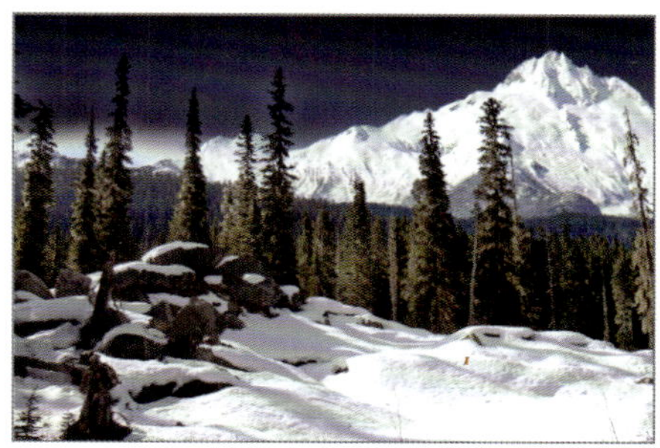

11 Choose Select > Deselect from the menu bar or press Ctrl + D.

This deselects the selection.

40 Digital Photo Retouching Techniques

with Photoshop Elements 5.0

Chapter 2
Manipulating Colors

You can tweak colors in Photoshop Elements as easily as a chameleon changes the color of its skin. In this chapter, you will learn a combination of techniques that will let you correct an image's color or create some interesting visual effects. For instance, you can change a color picture (or just portions of one) into black and white, create a sepia-toned image, and transform a photo of summer into fall. This chapter will show you how to create a multitude of new images from just one picture.

06 Changing a Color

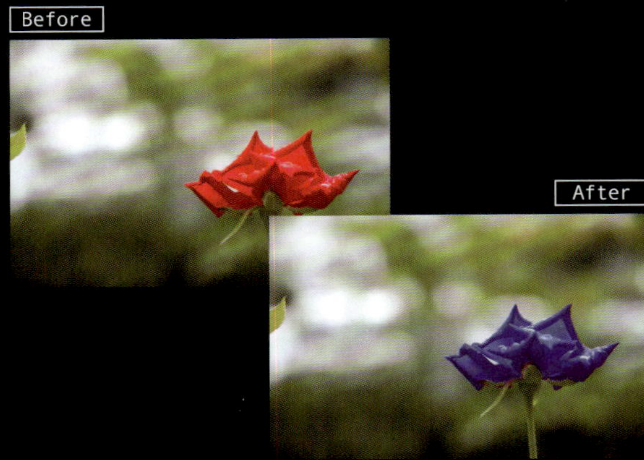

You can easily change the hue, saturation, and brightness of an image in Photoshop Elements with the Hue/Saturation command. This feature for improving overall colors is also useful when you only want to change a specific color. You can, for instance, make all the blues in the image appear darker without affecting the rest of the image. The command also lets you create monotone or duotone images from black-and-white or color images.

1. Select File > Open from the menu bar.

   The Open dialog box appears.

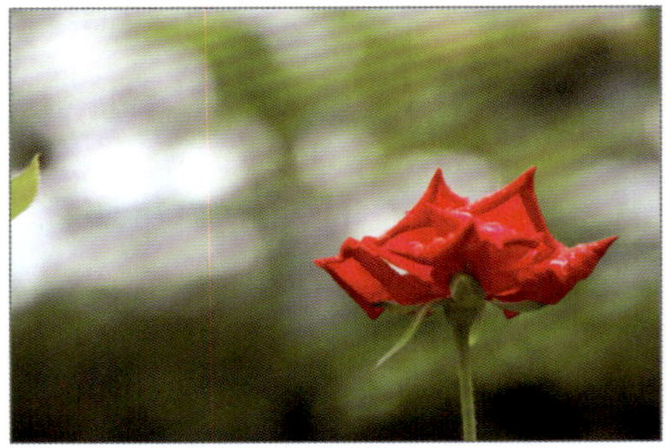

2. Open the **Sample\Chapter 2\Tech06.tif** file from the supplementary CD.

   The following steps will show how to change the color of the rose from red to blue.

3. Select Enhance > Adjust Color > Adjust Hue/Saturation from the menu bar.

   The Hue/Saturation dialog box appears.

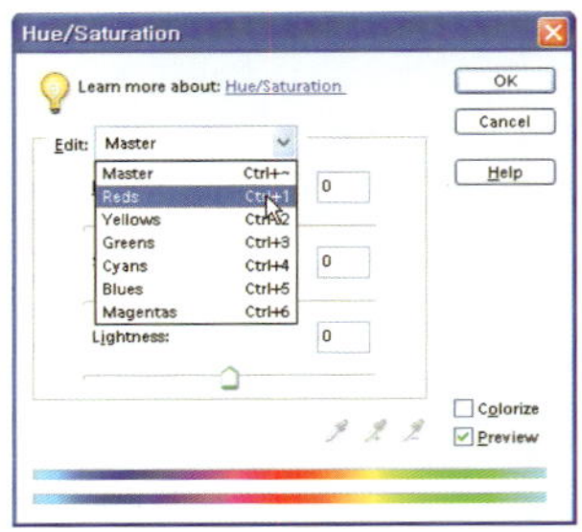

4. Select **Reds** from the Edit menu.

   Now you can only edit the red areas in the image.

5 Move the Hue slider to a value of **–120**.

This changes the color of the flower from red to a purplish blue.

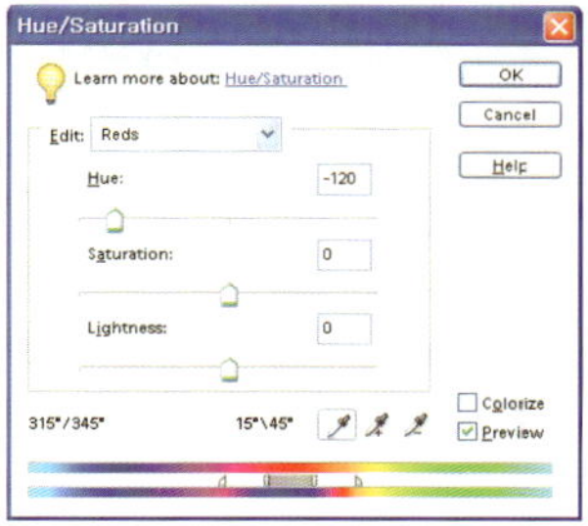

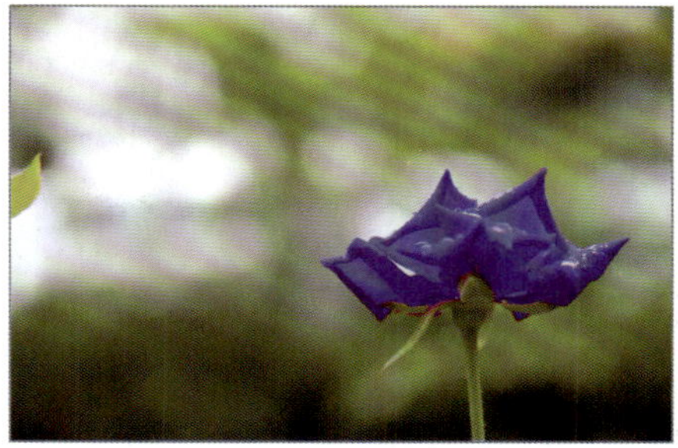

6 Select **Magenta** from the Edit menu.

This limits you to editing the purplish areas in the image.

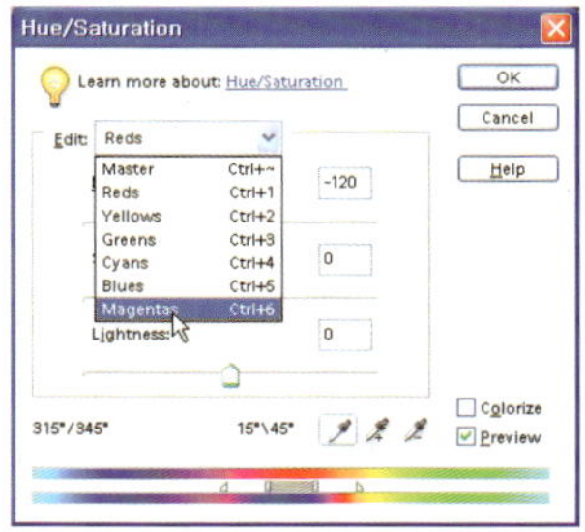

tip If you select Master from the Edit menu, your changes will affect the entire image. You can still change the color of the rose in Master mode, but to do this, you will need to use the Lasso or Magic Wand Tools to select the rose before changing the color values in the Hue/Saturation dialog box.

7 Move the Hue slider to a value of **–100**.

The red-tone water droplet on the rose is changed to a blue-tone water droplet.

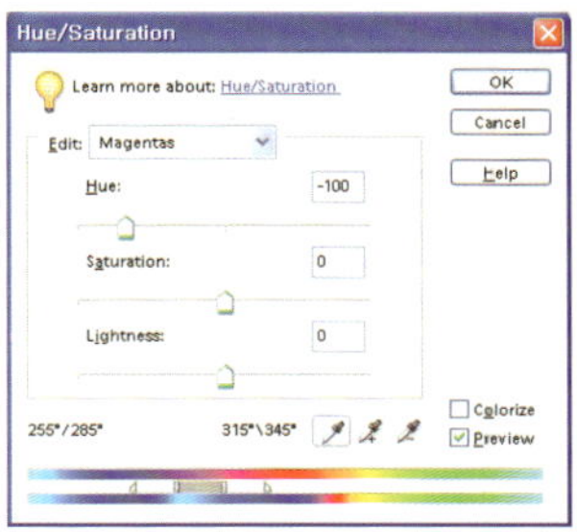

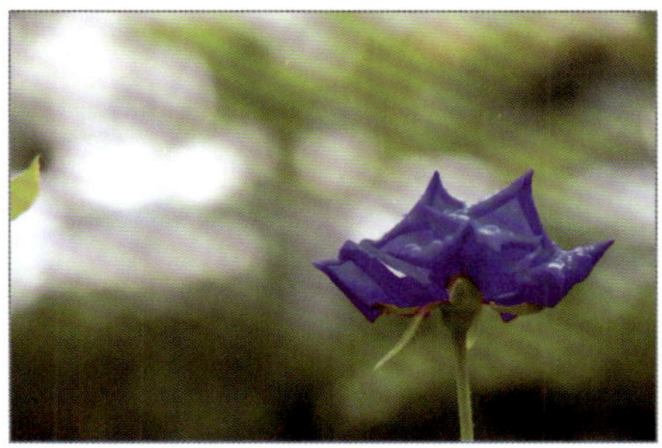

Chapter 02

8 For a more natural looking revision, slightly reduce the saturation of the blue rose. Select Red from the Edit menu and move the Saturate slide to **–40**.

9 Click OK.

The flower is now a brighter blue.

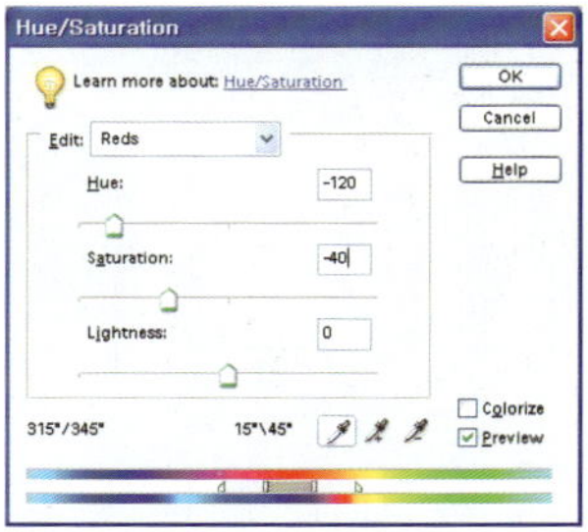

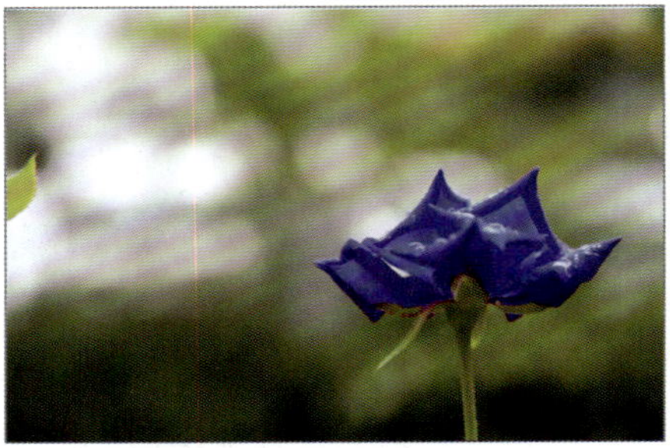

A Closer Look at the Hue/Saturation Dialog Box

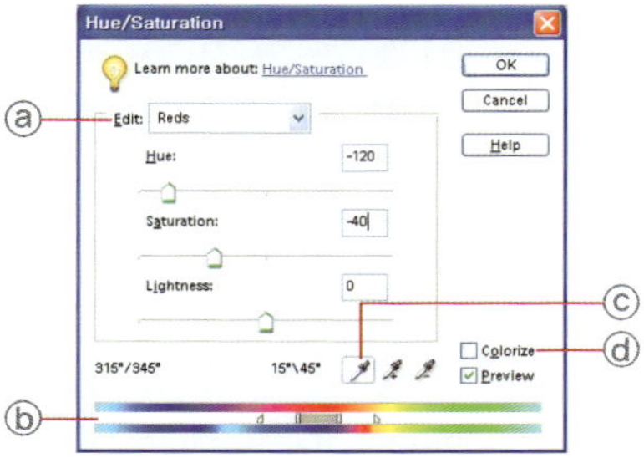

ⓐ **Edit**: You can choose to edit only one color in the image by selecting it from this menu. To edit all the colors in the image, choose Master.

ⓑ **Color bars**: The top color bar shows the color distribution of the original image. The bottom color bar shows the color distribution after making the Hue adjustments.

ⓒ **Eyedropper**: The eyedropper is only available if you selected the Master option from the Edit menu. The eyedropper is useful for making adjustments to different colors in the image using the same values.

ⓓ **Colorize**: You can turn an image into monotone (black and white) or duotone (black, white, and one color) by selecting this option.

07 Replacing a Color

Before

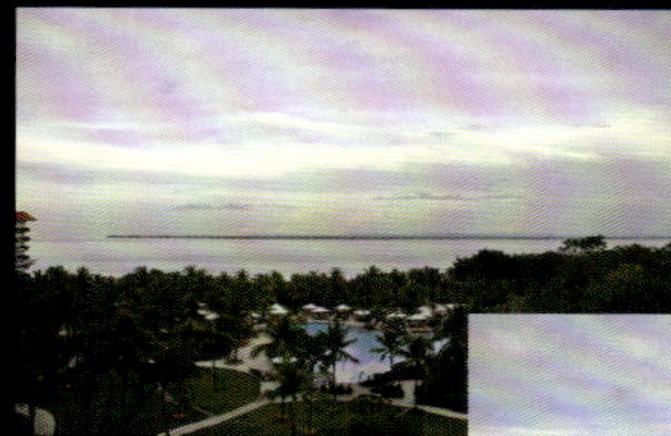

After

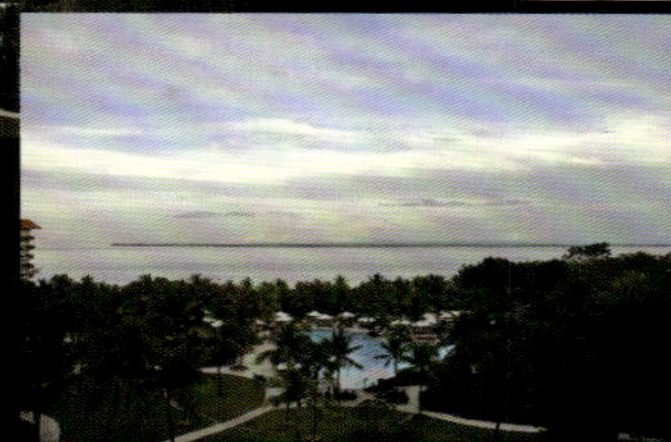

By using the Replace color command, you can change the color, saturation, and the brightness of an area of a picture without selecting a specific area. In this section, you will learn to transform an picture of a sky with reddish tone, due to an improper white balance setting, into a bluish tone sky, which will look like it has been taken with a polarizing filter attached.

1. Select File > Open from the menu bar.

The Open dialog box appears.

2. Open the **Sample\Chapter 2\Tech07.tif** file from the supplementary CD.

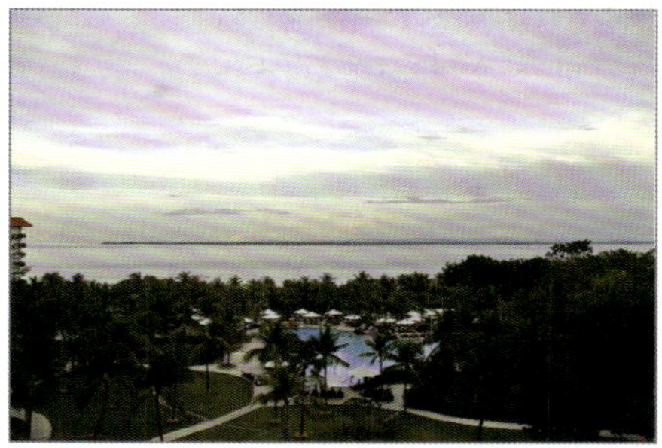

3. Select Enhance > Adjust Color > Replace Color from the menu bar.

The Replace Color dialog box appears.

4. Select the Eyedropper Tool ( ).

5. Click on the purplish tones in the sky to select these areas.

The color selected using the Eyedropper Tool appears in the Sample window of the Replace Color dialog box.

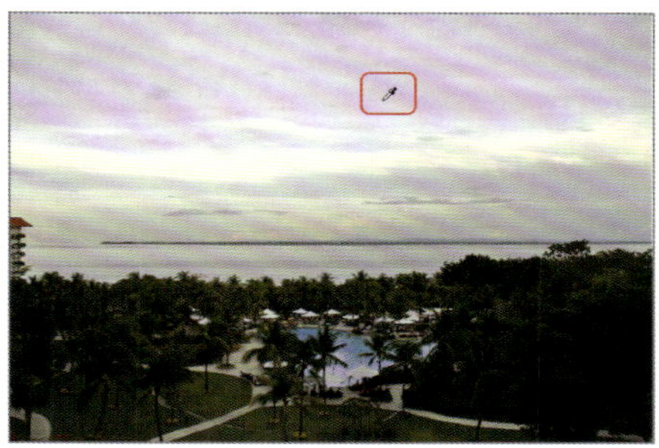

⑥ Move the Fuzziness slider to a value of **110**.

This selects the majority of the purplish areas in the sky so you can correct all the other purplish areas in addition to what you have already selected.

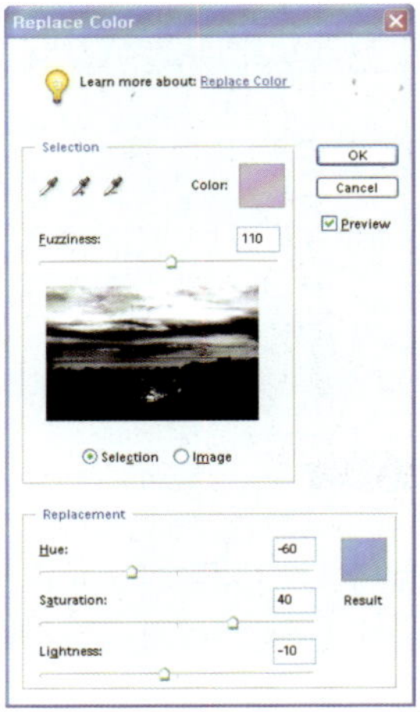

⑦ Change the tone of the sky from red to blue by moving the Hue Slider to **–60** and sharpen the blue tone by changing the Saturation to **40**. Then, darken the picture by changing the Lightness to **–10** to increase the contrast between the blue tone of the sky and the white clouds.

tip In the Replace Color dialog box, check the Selection option in order to view the extent of your selection in the preview box. The white areas represent the areas selected for modification, while the black areas will not be affected by any color corrections.

⑧ Click OK.

The image now has the original bluish tone, instead of a reddish one.

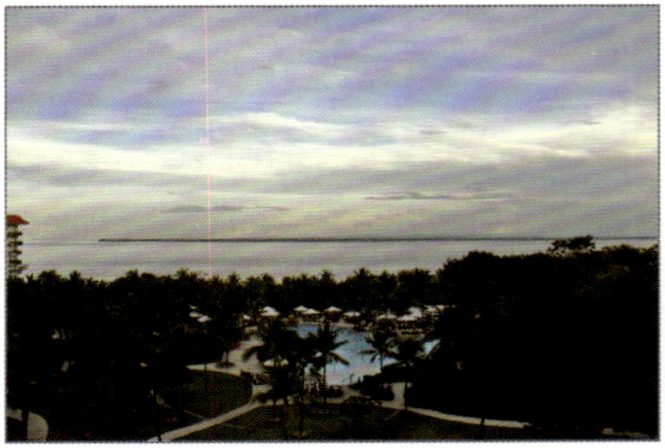

08 Correcting Improper White Balance Using Color Variation

Before

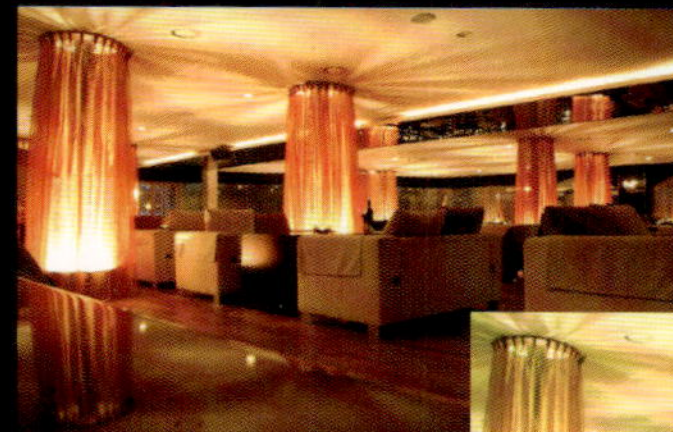

After

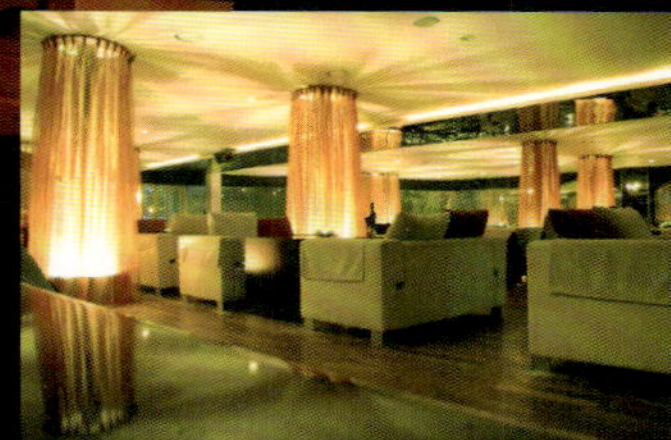

It is not easy to take an ambient picture in a dark or poorly lit indoor setting. Using a flash will only make the photograph lose its unique ambient atmosphere. With the help of the Color Variation in Photoshop Elements, revising the ambiance of a photograph is possible by changing the color and brightness.

1 Click File > Open from the Menu bar.

The Open dialog box appears.

2 Open the **Sample\Chapter 2\Tech08.tif** from the supplementary CD.

A photograph of an indoor setting with red lighting, taken without a flash, will generally have a red tone.

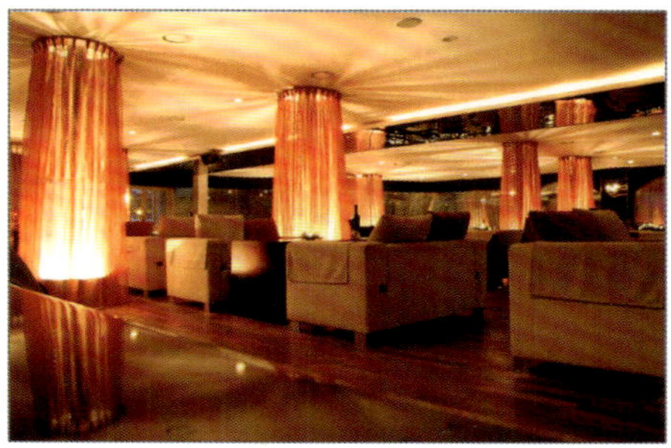

③ To revise the general color and brightness of the photograph, click Enhance > Adjust Colors > Color Variations in the Menu bar.

The Color Variations window will appear.

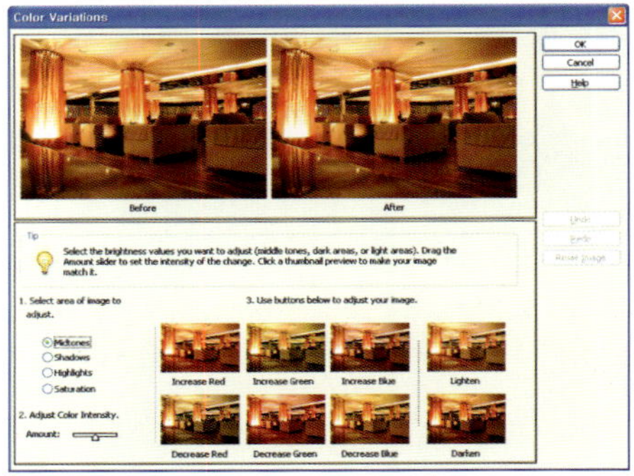

④ To add a blue tone to the generally red-toned photograph, click **Increase Green**.

You can see in the After window that the general tone of the photograph has changed to blue after green has been added.

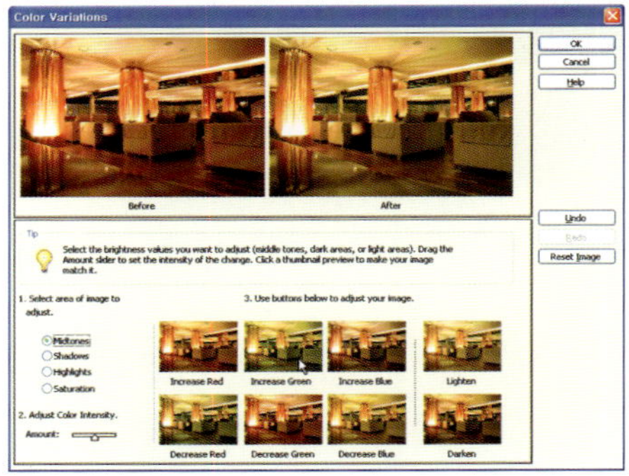

⑤ Now, click **Lighten** to brighten the photograph.

You can see in the After window that the photograph has become brighter.

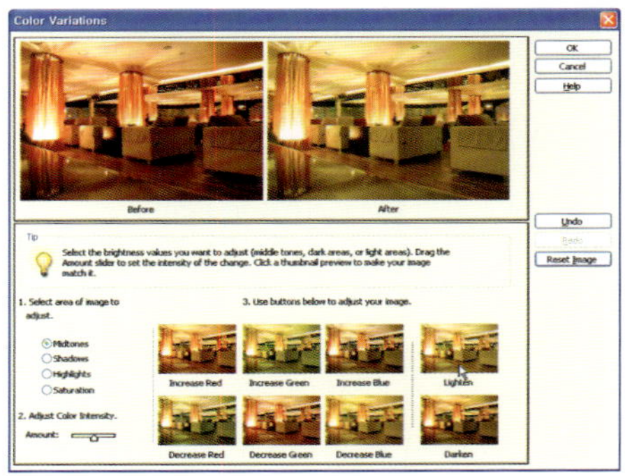

6 To enhance the blue tone, click on **Decrease Red**.

You can see in the After window that the general tone of the photograph has changed to blue after the red has been reduced.

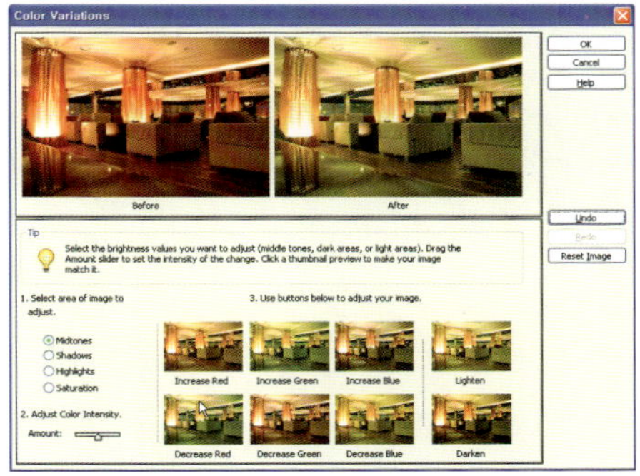

7 To enhance the red in the bright areas of the photograph, select **Highlights** under Select Area of Image to Adjust and click **Increase Red**.

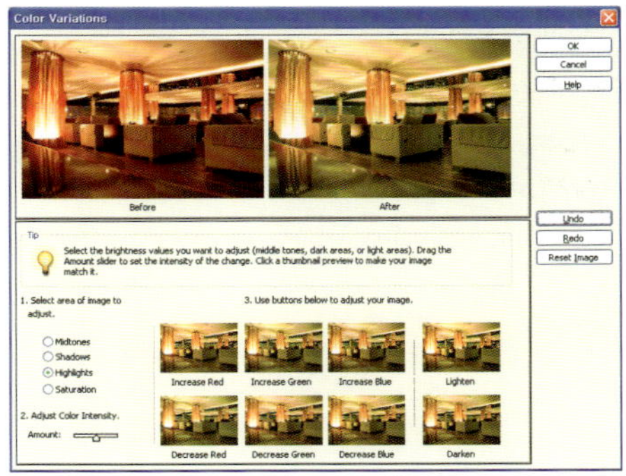

8 To enhance the blue tone in the darker areas, such as the sofas and the tables, select **Shadows** under Select Area of Image to Adjust and click **Increase Green**.

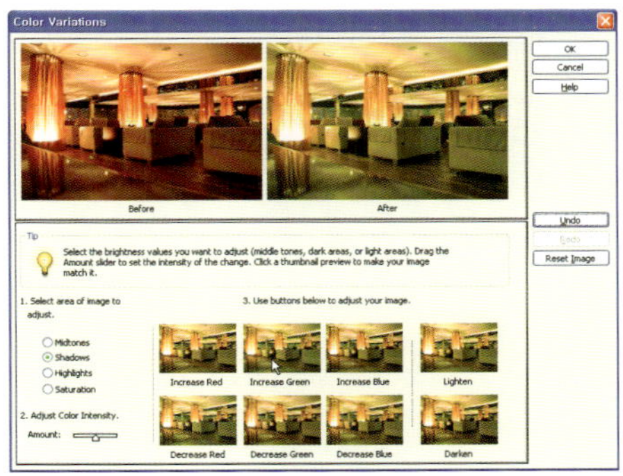

9 You can see the complete revised photograph by clicking the OK button. As you can see from this exercise, a photograph taken with the wrong white balance or a photograph that is generally composed of one color can easily be corrected using Color Variation.

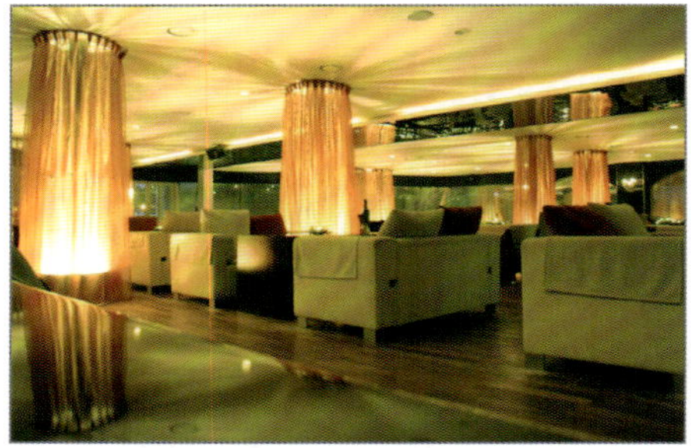

Using the Adjust Color Curves

Newly added to Photoshop Elements 5.0, this function allows you to correct the tone color and brightness of an image without disturbing the general gradient of the original image. Open the Adjust Color Curve window by clicking on Enhance > Adjust Color > Adjust Color Curves from the menu bar. Click on the appropriate thumbnails to correct the Shadows, Midtones, Highlights, and Contrast. Furthermore, in the Advanced Options, you can make fine corrections using the slide bar and the curve line in the graph for each option.

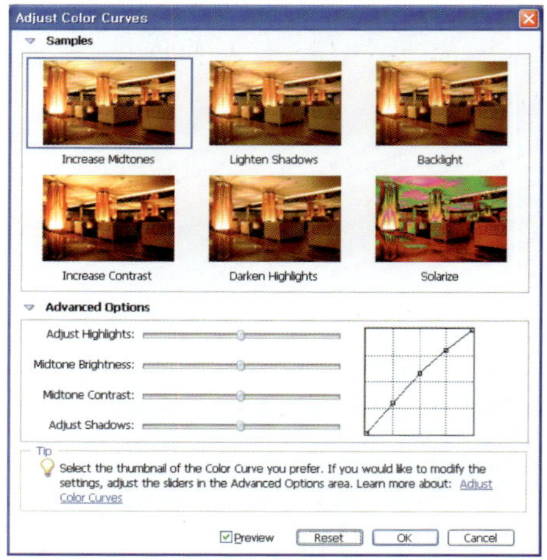

09 Turning Color Photos into Black-and-White Images

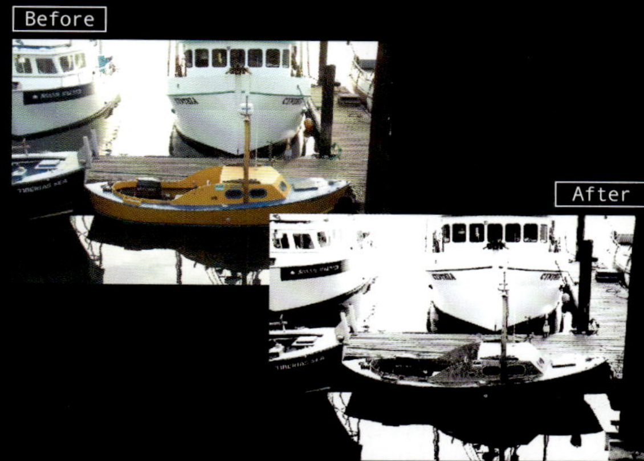

Sometimes, you will discover after a shoot that an image would have looked better in black and white. Black-and-white images are particularly suitable for journalistic-style photography or for evoking a sense of nostalgia. You can turn a color image into a high-contrast black-and-white image to emphasize the lines and shapes in the shot.

1. Select File > Open from the menu bar.

The Open dialog box appears.

2. Open the **Sample\Chapter 2\Tech09.tif** file from the supplementary CD.

3. Select Enhance > Adjust Color > Remove Color from the menu bar.

This removes all the color information so the color image is rendered in shades of gray.

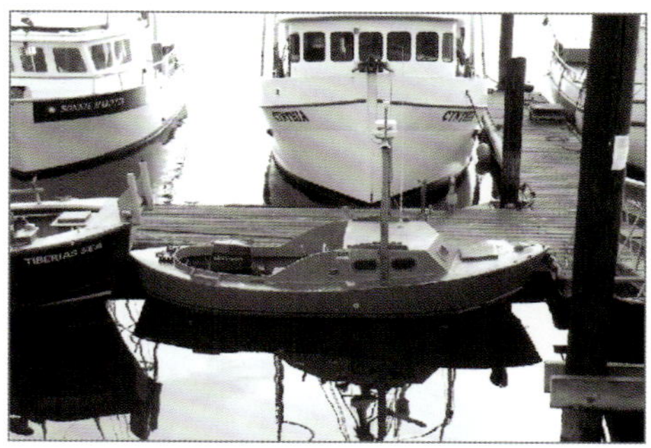

④ Select Enhance > Adjust Lighting > Levels from the menu bar.

The Levels dialog box appears.

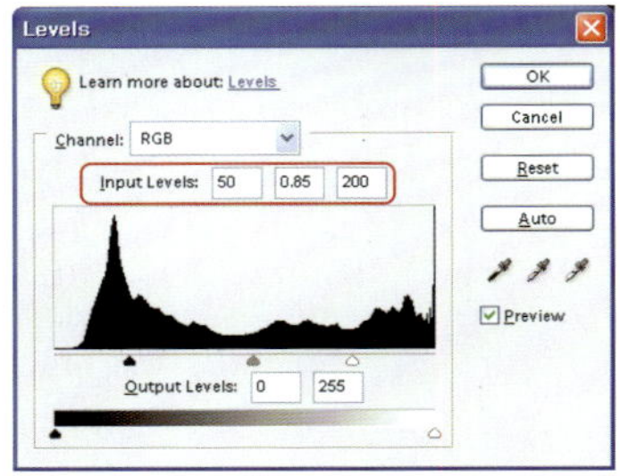

⑤ In the Input Levels text boxes, enter **50**, **0.85**, and **200**, respectively.

⑥ Click OK.

This will increase the highlights and midtones in the image.

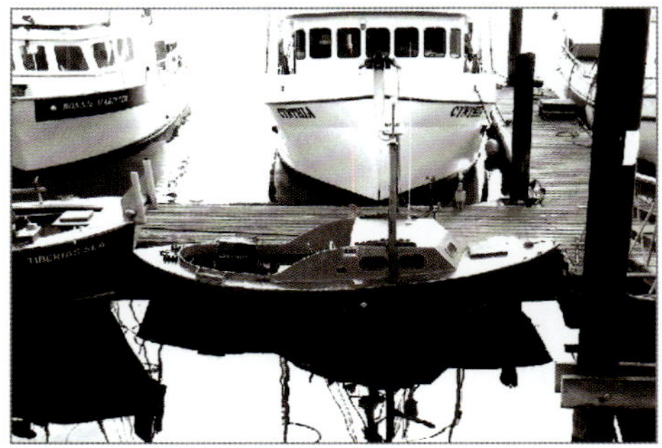

⑦ Click and drag the Background layer in the Layers palette onto the Create a New Layer icon ( ) to make a copy of the layer.

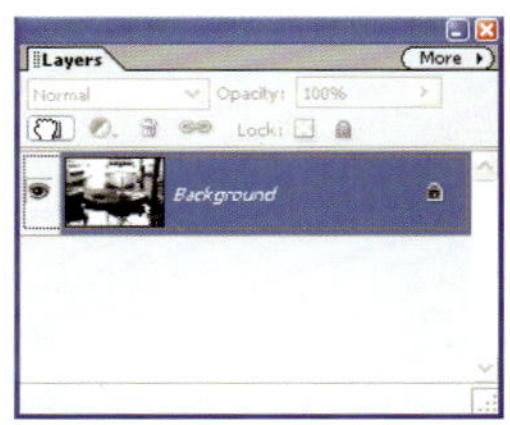

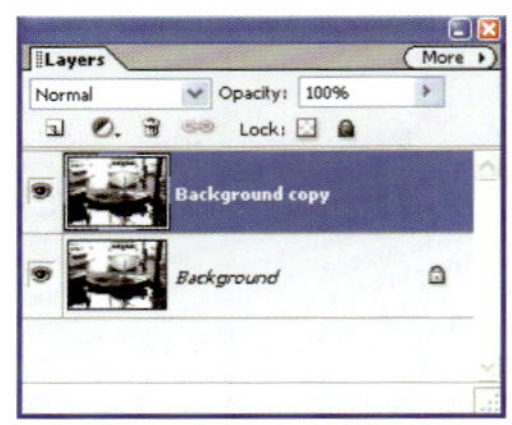

⑧ Select Filter > Adjustments > Threshold from the menu bar.

The Threshold dialog box appears.

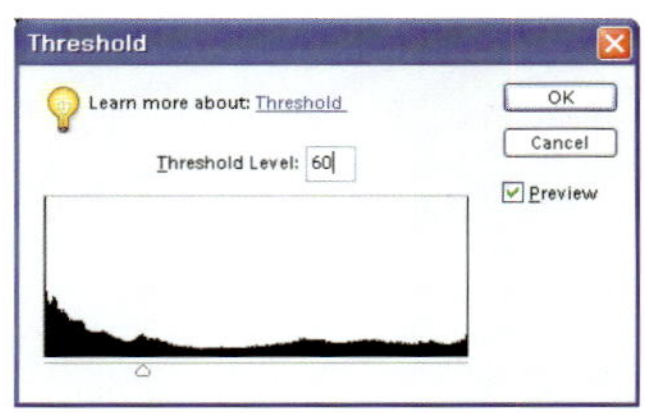

⑨ Move the Threshold Level slider to a value of **60**.

10 Click OK.

The image changes from shades of gray to pure black and white.

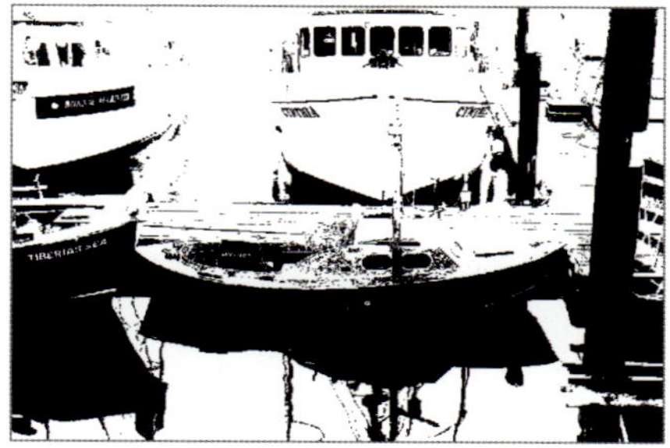

tip The Threshold command transforms color and grayscale images into high-contrast black-and-white images. Pixels lighter than the stated threshold value will be converted to white, while pixels darker than the threshold value will be turned into black. In general, the higher the threshold value, the more black the image will contain.

11 In the Layers palette, change the blending mode to **Overlay** for any layers with altered threshold values.

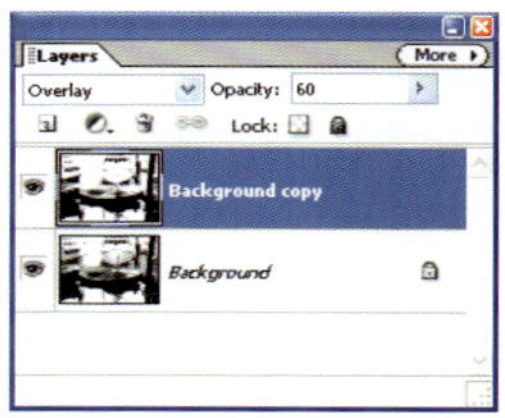

12 In the same palette, change the layer's Opacity to **60%**.

The result is a high-contrast black-and-white image.

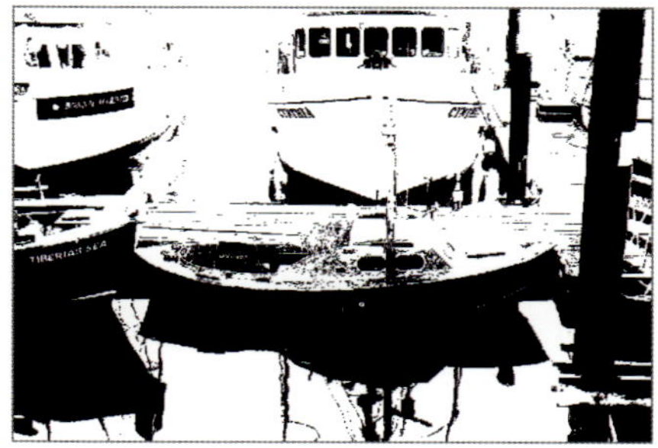

tip A simple way to create a black-and-white photo using the Convert to Black and White function

Newly added to Photoshop Elements 5.0, the Convert to Black and White function provides commonly used styles to create a black-and-white photo. Thus, you can create various types of black-and-white photos with just the click of your mouse. Furthermore, you can change the brightness of your black-and-white photo by clicking on the appropriate thumbnails and also change the intensity by using the Adjustment Intensity.

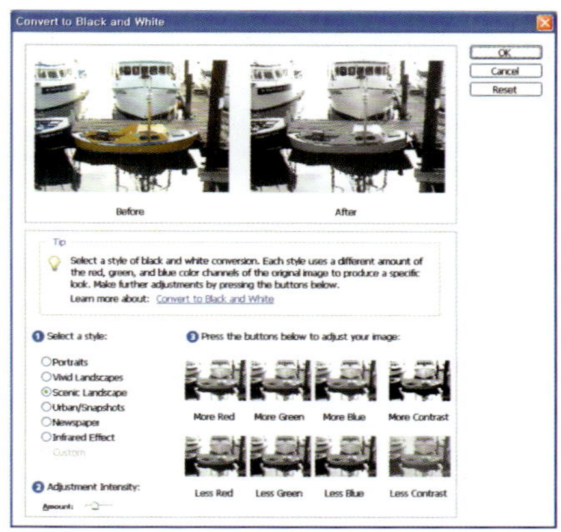

10 Coloring Black-and-White Photographs

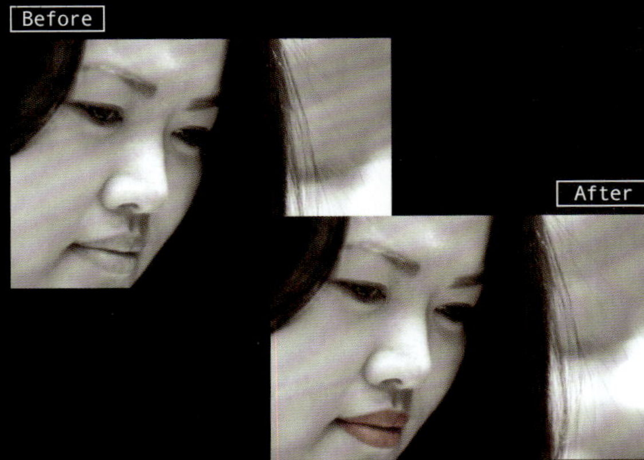

If you have some old black-and-white family photos, try turning them into color images in Photoshop Elements. The colors will inject vibrancy into the images and give them a different kind of look. Selective coloring can also make a simple photo more exciting.

(1) Open the **Sample\Chapter 2\Tech10.tif** file from the supplementary CD.

(2) In order to color a black-and-white photograph, the image mode needs to be changed. To do this, click on Image > Mode > RGB Color from the Menu bar.

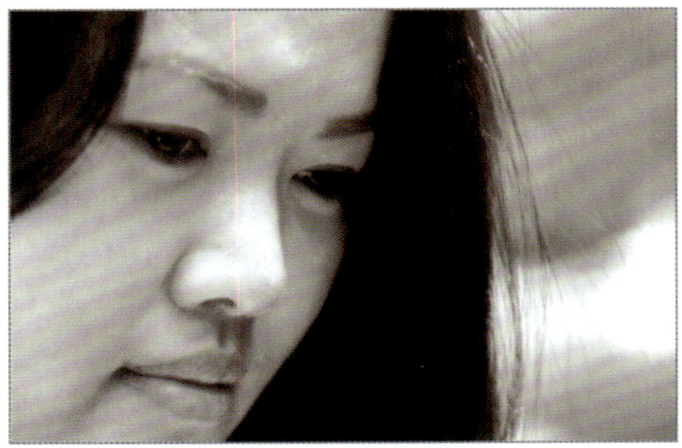

3 Let's add color to the lips. Select the Zoom Tool ( ) from the toolbox, then click and drag over the lip area.

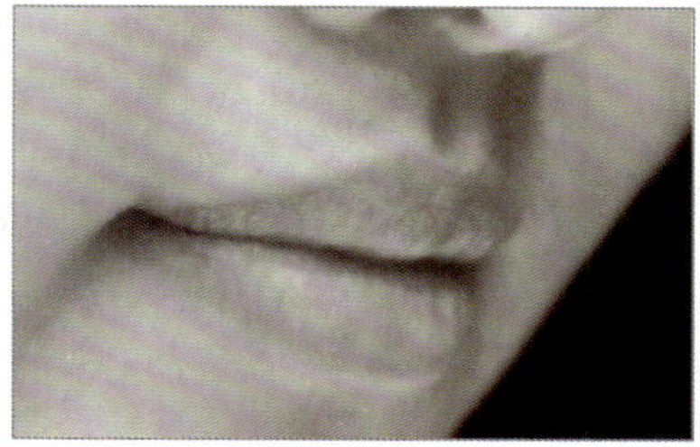

4 Click on the Selection Brush Tool ( ) from the toolbox.

5 Set the brush size to **10px**, the Mode to **Selection**, and the Hardness to **0** in the Option bar.

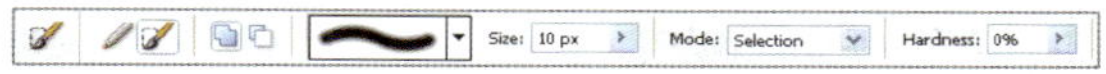

6 Click and drag to select the lip area.

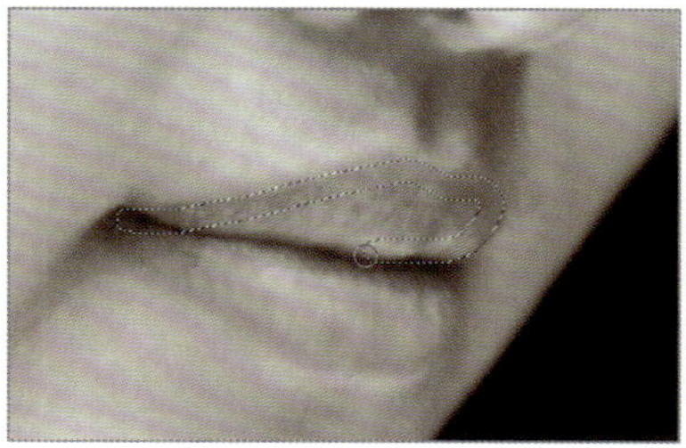

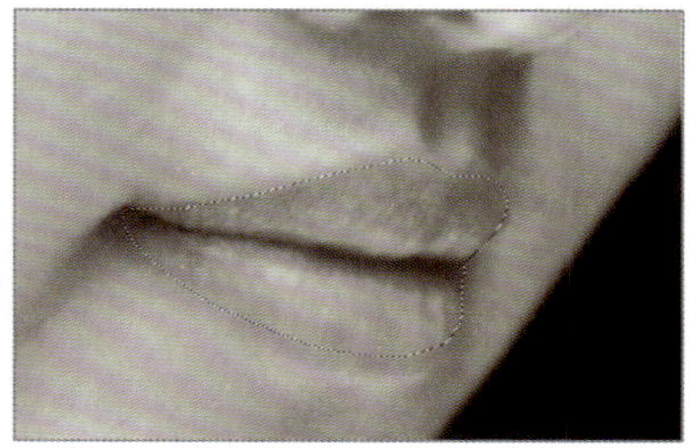

7 Click on Select > Feather from the Menu bar. A Feather Selection dialog box will open. Input **3** for Feather Radius and click OK. The borders of the selected area will become smoother.

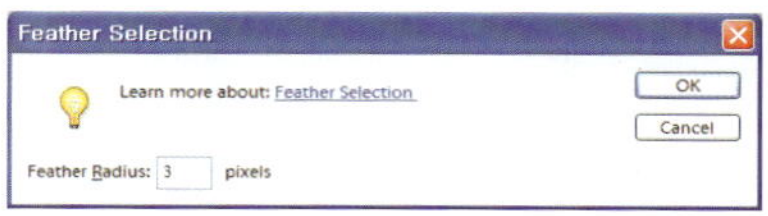

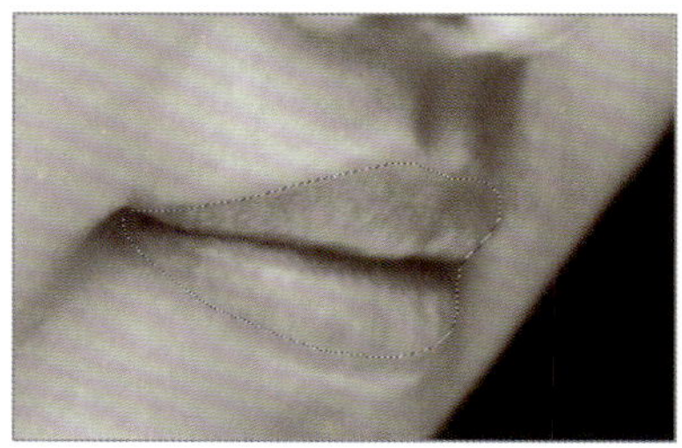

8 Now you must save the selected area. Click on Select > Save Selection from the Menu bar and a Save Selection dialog box will open. Input **New** for Selection, **lip** for Name, and check **New Selection** for Operation. Click the OK button.

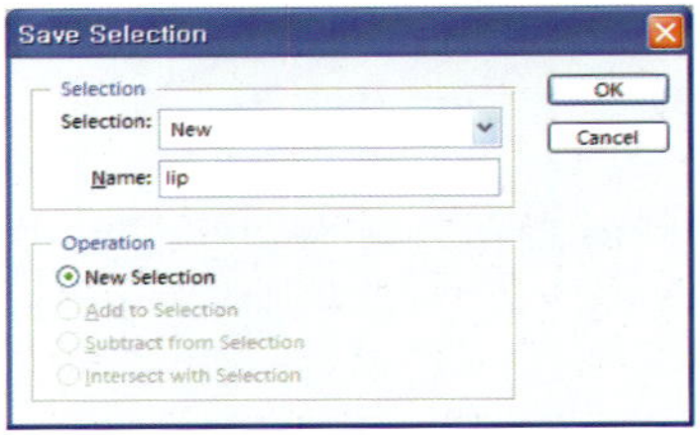

tip If you want to change the color after you have saved the selected area, you can recall the selected area and change the color of the image. You can do this by using the Select > Load Selection menu.

9 Click on Enhance > Adjust Color > Adjust Hue/Saturation from the menu bar and a **Hue/Saturation** dialog box will appear.

10 Check Colorize, then set the Hue at **360**, Saturation at **15**, and Lightness at **–18**. Click the OK button.

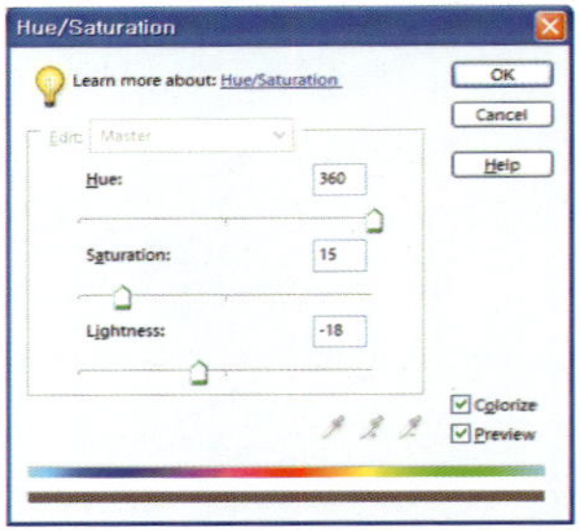

11 Now deselect the colored lip by pressing Ctrl + D.

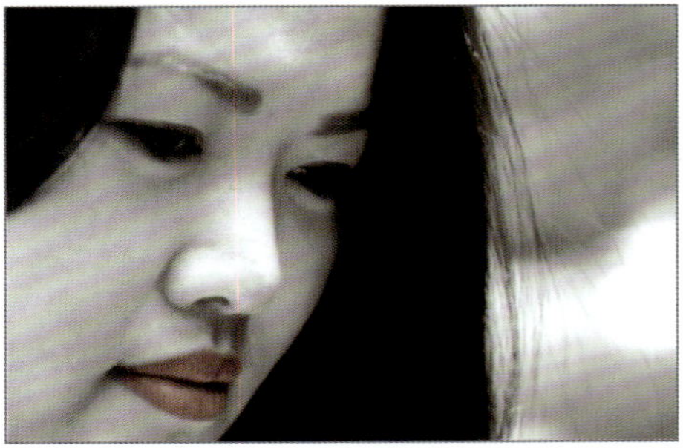

11 Creating a Sepia-Toned Picture

Before

After

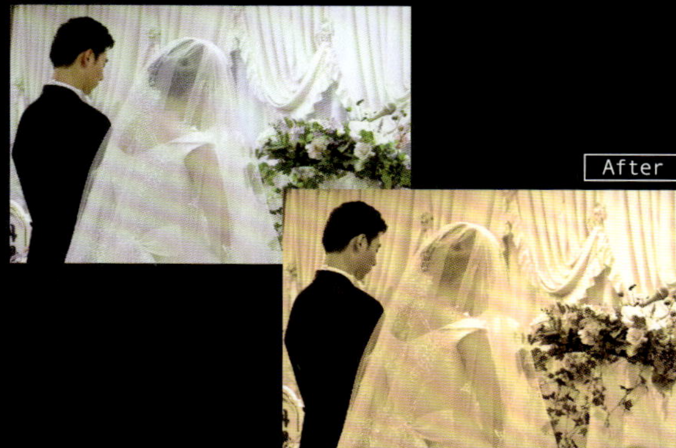

Vintage photographs often come in a single color tone. A common example is the sepia-tone picture, which consists of predominantly brown tones. Sepia-toned images these days usually feature people, although this really depends on the photographer's preference. This section describes the steps needed to change colorful photographs into sepia-toned ones.

1. Select File > Open from the menu bar.

   The Open dialog box appears.

2. Open the **Sample\Chapter 2\Tech11.tif** file from the supplementary CD.

3. Select Enhance > Adjust Color > Remove Color from the menu bar to turn the image into a black-and-white one.

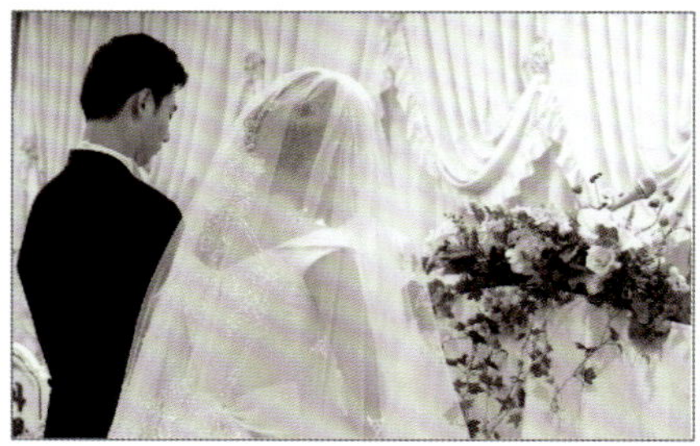

4. Select Enhance > Adjust Smart Fix from the menu bar.

   The Adjust Smart Fix dialog box appears.

5. Drag the Fix Amount slide bar to the right and set it at **120%**. You can see the change as you drag in the image window.

   A sepia-tone photograph is usually made by filling in a black-and-white photograph with one color. Therefore, it is recommended to have a high setting for the contrast of brightness.

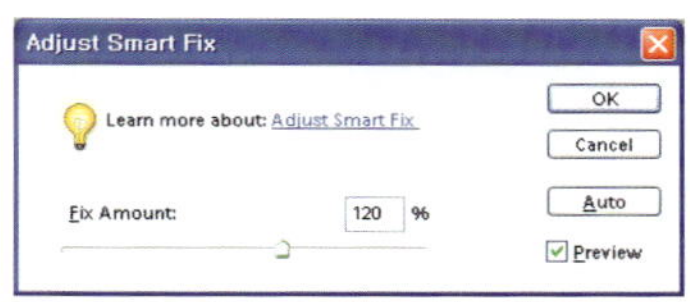

(6) Click OK.

The resulting image has a higher contrast level than the original one.

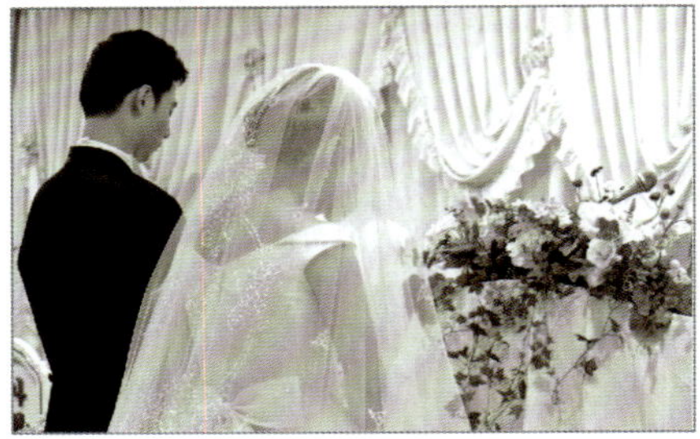

(7) Choose Layer > New Adjustment Layer > Photo Filter from the menu bar. When the New Layer dialog box appears, click OK.

You will see the adjustment layer, Photo Filter 1, added to the Layers palette. The Photo Filter dialog box will also appear.

(8) In the Photo Filter dialog box, check that the Filter option is selected and then select Sepia from the Filter drop-down menu. Set the Density to **100%** and click OK.

The Filter drop-down menu contains a list of commonly used photo filters. You can also set the color of the filter by clicking on the color swatch next to the Color option.

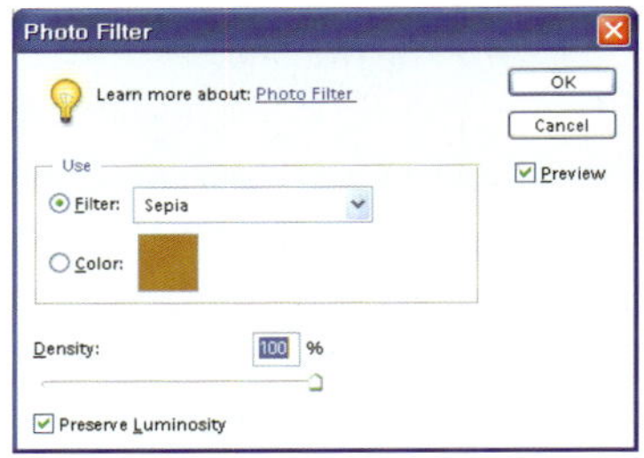

(9) The result is a sepia-toned image.

To undo the changes and restore the original picture, select the adjustment layer and click on the Delete Layer icon ( ) in the Layers palette. You will be asked if you want to delete the layer mask. Click Yes. Click on the Delete Layer icon ( ) again. You will be asked if you want to delete the layer. Click Yes.

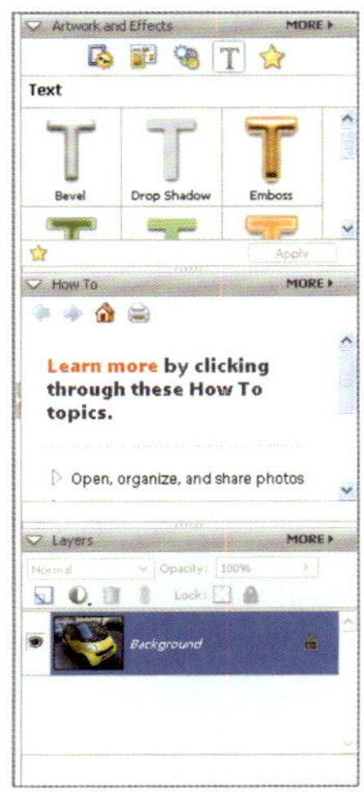

Blending Colors

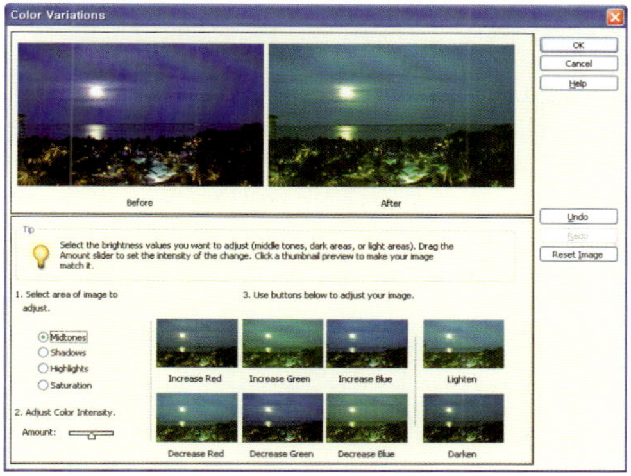

Like the Photo Filter, the Color Variations command, which is accessed by selecting Enhance > Adjust Color > Color Variations from the menu bar, can be used to alter the tone of an image. The key difference between the Photo Filter and the Color Variations command is that the latter lets you selectively tailor your tonal changes. With the Color Variations command, you can choose to selectively alter the highlights, midtones, or shadows. The Photo Filter, on the other hand, will apply the selected tone to the entire image.

◀ The Color Variations dialog box is very user-friendly. Simply follow steps 1 through 3 in the dialog box to alter the tone of an image.

You may be familiar with the artist's color wheel, which shows us how color inks combine to form new colors. The primary colors in an artist's color wheel are cyan, magenta, and yellow. Theoretically, these three colors should combine to form black, but the impurities in the inks produce a deep gray instead. In order to achieve pure black, color printers come with not only cyan (C), magenta (M), and yellow (Y) inks, but also a black (K) ink. So for printing, we use the CMYK color model.

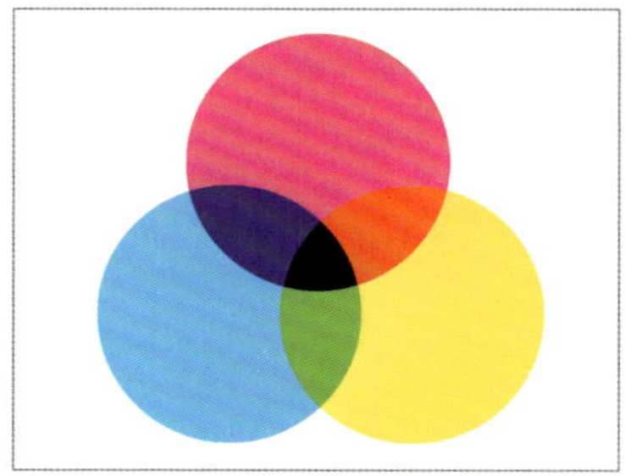

▲ The artist's color wheel

The colors on a computer screen, however, are actually light rays, so they do not have the same properties as color inks. The three primary colors of light are red (R), green (G), and blue (B). When these three colors are combined, we get white instead of black. Take some time to study the RGB color wheel, as shown here, so that you will find it easier to change colors on a computer.

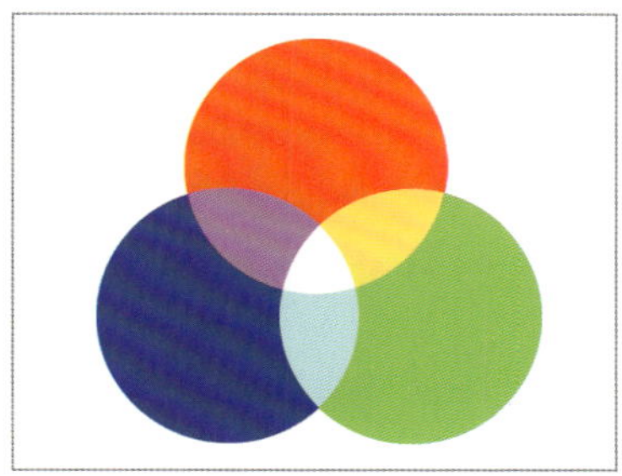

▲ The RGB color wheel

12 Turning Summer into Fall

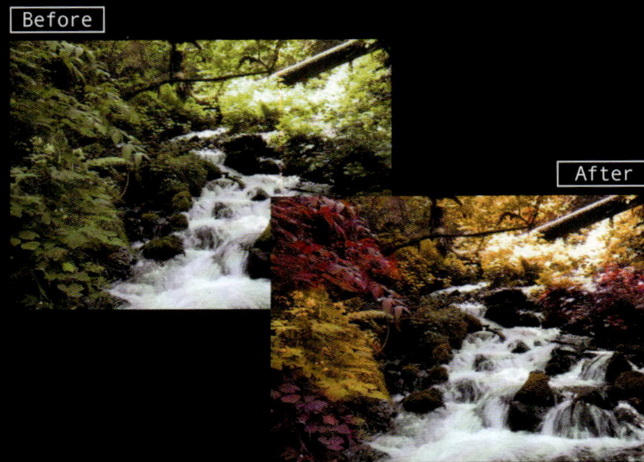

Each season has its representative colors, but fall is particularly bright and colorful. In this section, you will learn how to turn green summer leaves into reddish or yellowish autumn colors.

1. Select File > Open from the menu bar.

The Open dialog box appears.

2. Open the **Sample\Chapter 2\Tech12.tif** file from the supplementary CD.

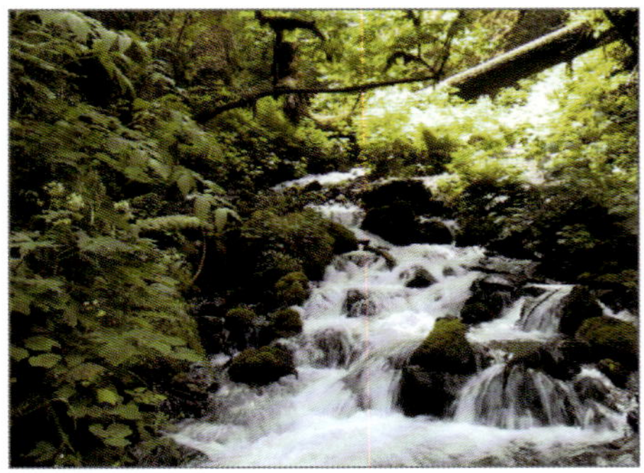

3. Select Enhance > Adjust Color > Adjust Hue/Saturation from the menu bar.

The Hue/Saturation dialog box appears.

4. Change the Hue setting to **–30**.

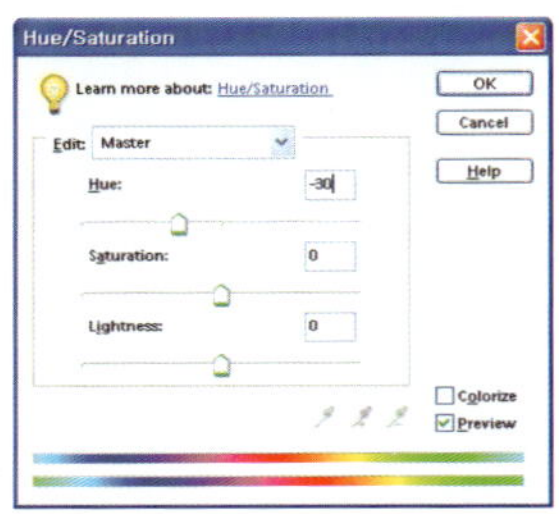

5 Click OK.

The overall image now has a brownish tone.

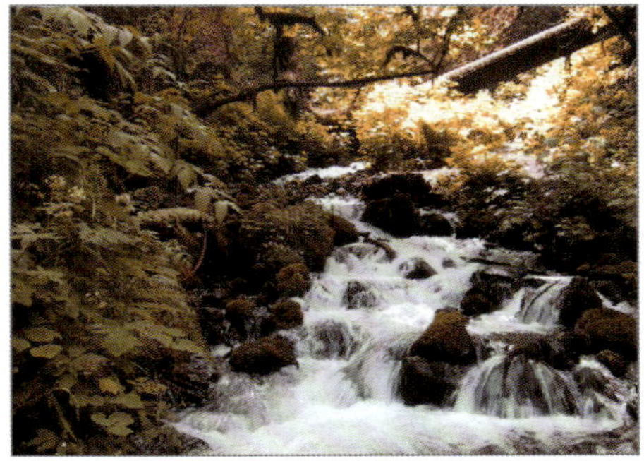

6 Select the Lasso Tool ( ) from the toolbox.

7 In the options bar, set Feather to **20 pixels**.

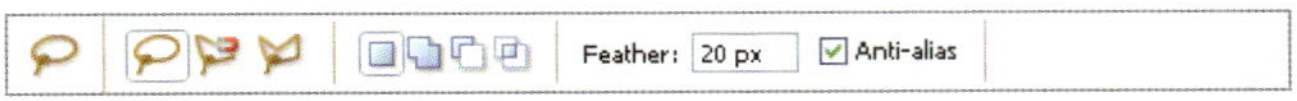

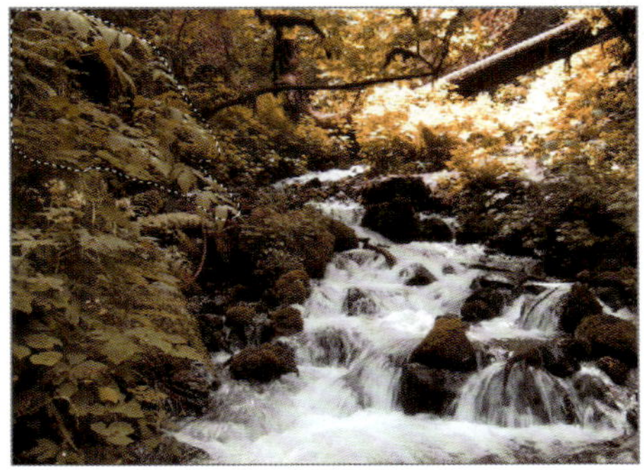

8 Click and drag over a bunch of leaves on the left side of the image to select them.

tip To soften the edges of the selection border, always set a Feather value greater than **0** before changing the color. The greater the Feather value, the fuzzier the edges. A Feather value of **0** will give the selection border an abrupt edge.

9 Click the Add to Selection icon ( ) in the options bar.

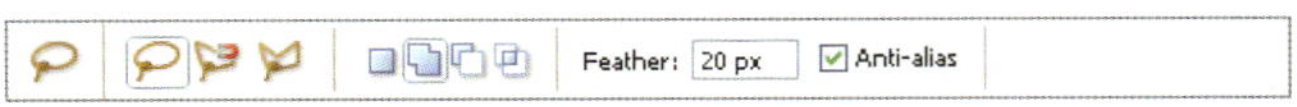

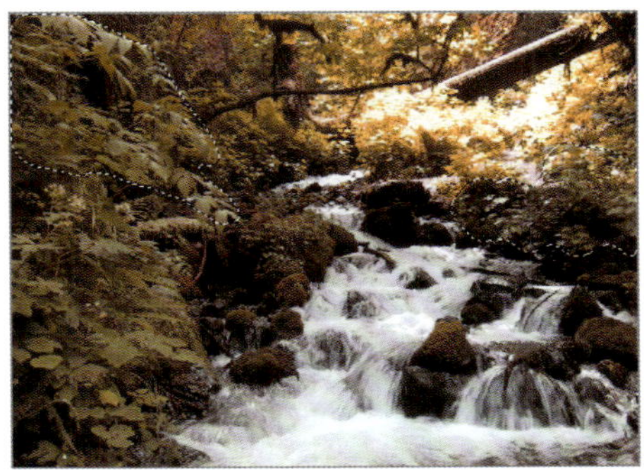

10 Click and drag the tool over the leaves on the right side of the image to add them to the selection.

(11) Press Ctrl + U or select Enhance > Adjust Color > Adjust Hue/Saturation from the menu bar.

The Hue/Saturation dialog box appears.

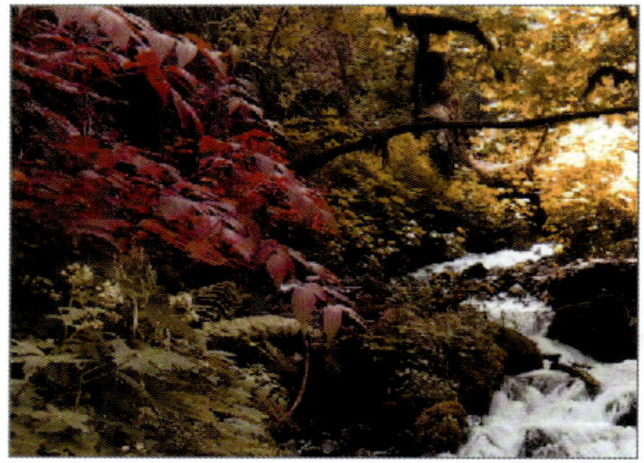

(12) Set Hue to **–55** and Saturation to **+25**.

(13) Click OK.

This changes the colors of the leaves to a warm autumn red.

(14) In the options bar of the Lasso Tool ( ), click on the New Selection icon ( ).

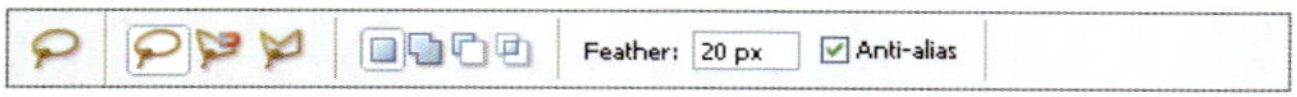

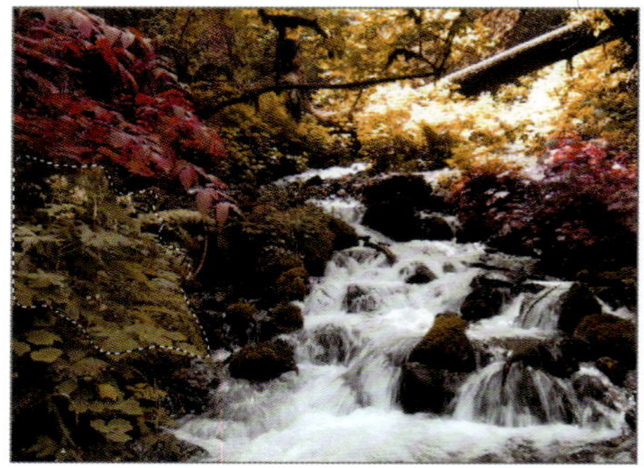

(15) Select the leaves on the left side of the image, as shown.

(16) Click on the Add to Selection icon ( ) in the options bar.

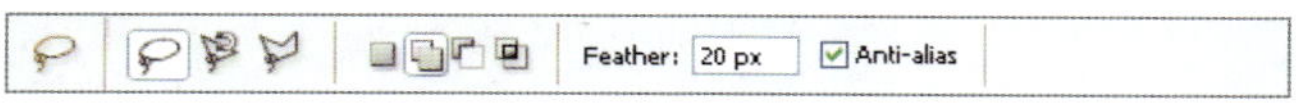

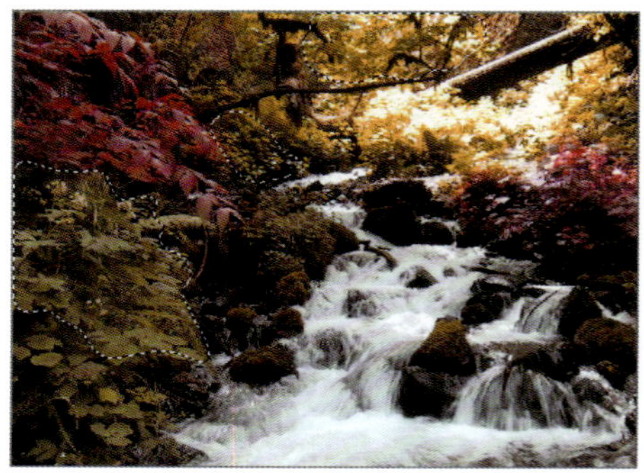

(17) Click and drag the tool over the other two areas, as shown.

(18) Press Ctrl + U or select Enhance > Adjust Color > Adjust Hue/Saturation from the menu bar.

The Hue/Saturation dialog box appears.

(19) Set Saturation to **+65**.

(20) Click OK.

This turns the selected areas yellow.

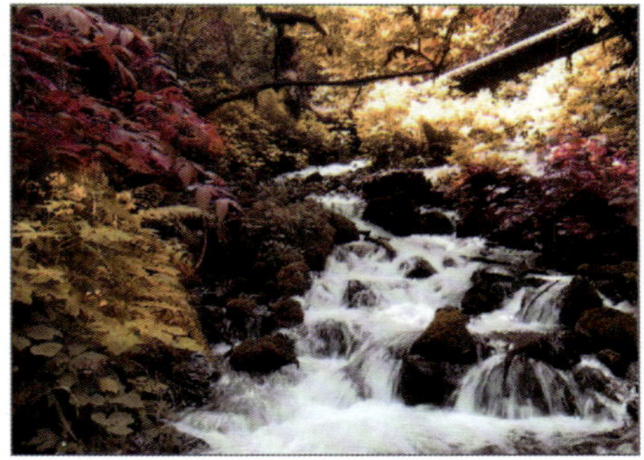

(21) In the options bar of the Lasso Tool ( ), select New Selection ( ).

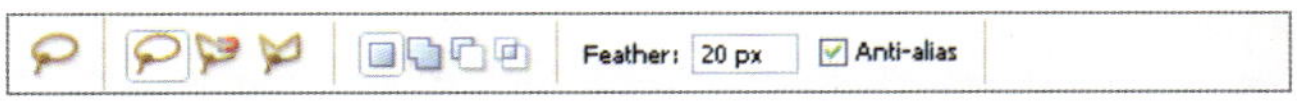

(22) Select the leaves in the lower-left corner.

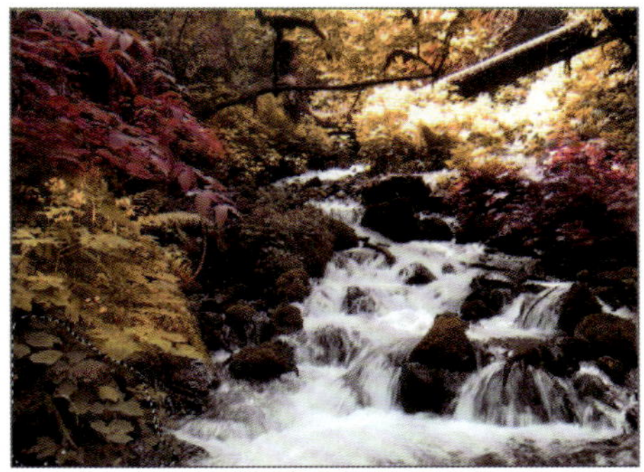

(23) Open the Hue/Saturation dialog box. Set Hue to **–70**.

(24) Click OK. Press Ctrl + D to deselect.

This turns the selected leaves slightly purplish.

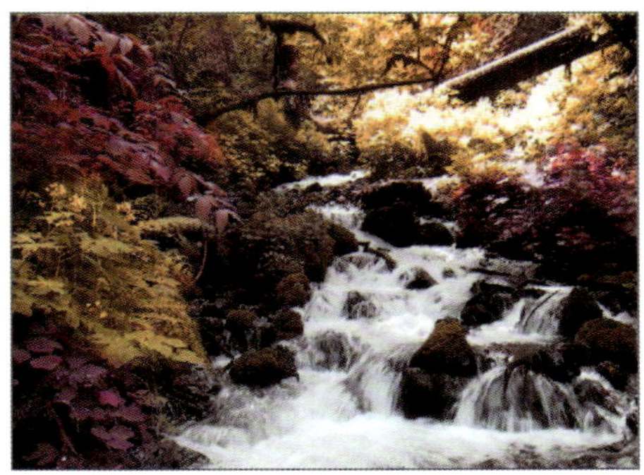

13 Making Detailed Color Changes

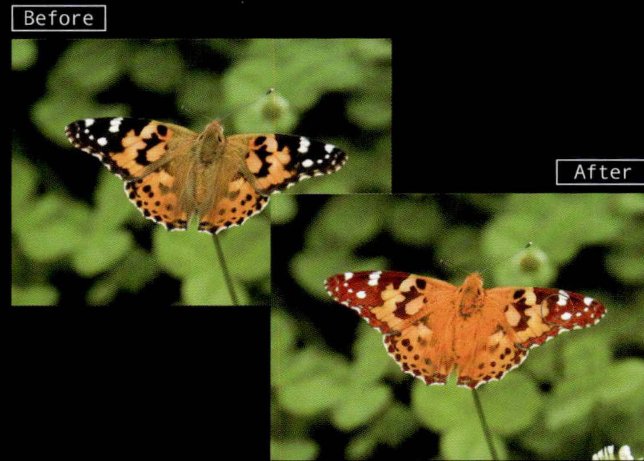

There are many ways to change the color in a specific area of an image, but most of these methods require that you select the area that you wish to change. The problem with making a selection first is that you could end up with a distinct and unnatural-looking border around the altered area. In this chapter, you will learn to use the Color Replacement Tool to change specific colors without making a selection.

1. Choose File > Open from the menu bar.

The Open dialog box appears.

2. Open the **Sample\Chapter 2\Tech13.tif** file from the supplementary CD.

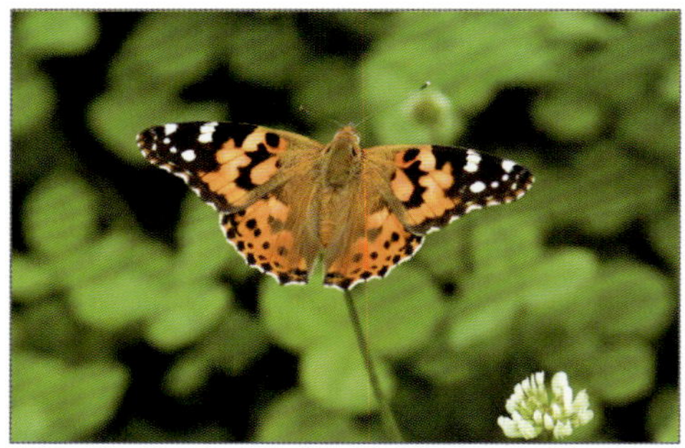

3. Select the Color Replacement Tool ( ) from the toolbox. In the options bar, set the Brush Diameter to **60 pixels**, Sampling to **Once** ( ), and Limits to **Discontiguous**.

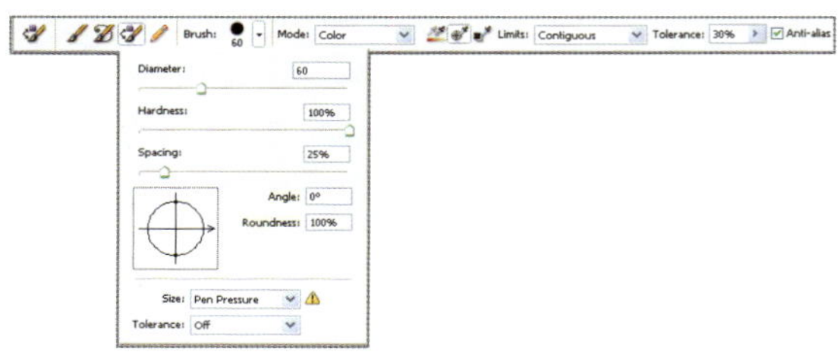

④ Click on the Set Foreground Color icon ( ) in the toolbox and set the RGB values to **245**, **125**, and **5**, respectively. Click OK.

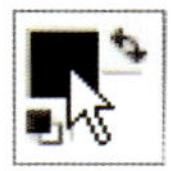

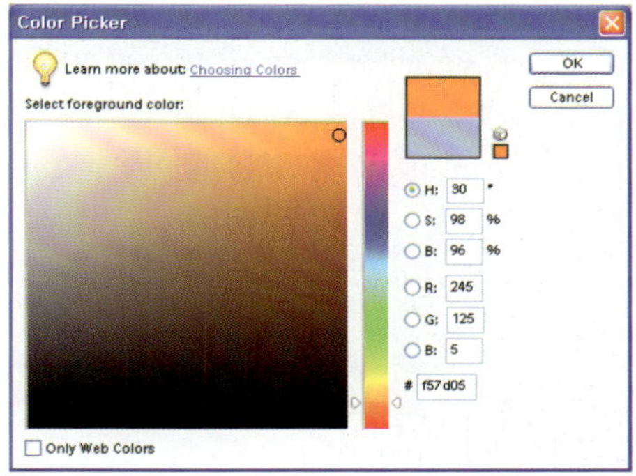

⑤ Click on the center part of the butterfly, as shown here.

You can see that the brownish tint has been replaced by the orange hue that you selected in the previous step.

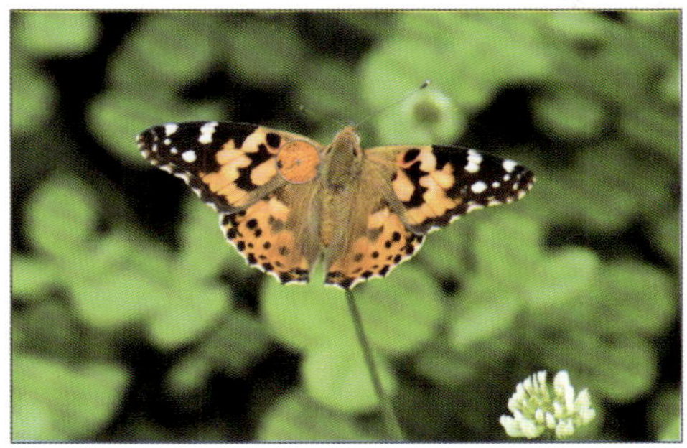

Ⓥ The crosshair in the center of your pointer determines the color that will be replaced. For example, if you click with the crosshair on a black area and then start dragging, only the black areas will be replaced—even if you drag over other colors.

⑥ Click and drag over the center part of the butterfly, as shown.

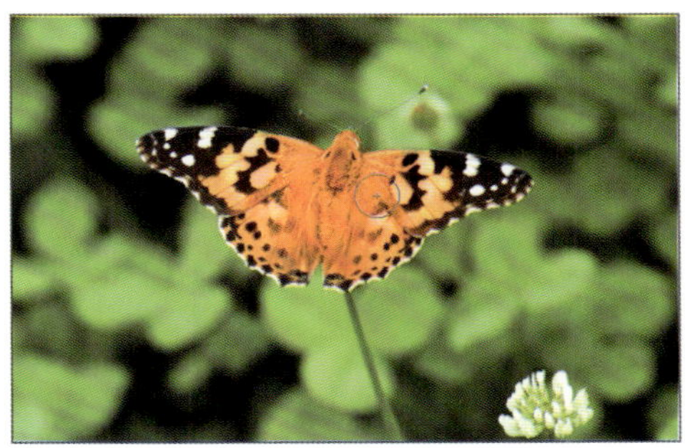

7 Select the Eyedropper Tool ( ) from the toolbox. Hold down the Alt key and click on a black part of the butterfly.

In the toolbox, you can see that the background color has been set to black.

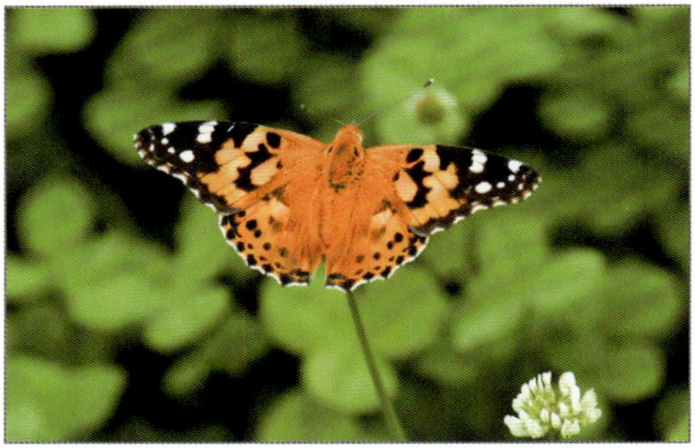

8 Select the Color Replacement Tool ( ) from the toolbox and choose **Background Swatch** ( ) from the Sampling drop-down menu in the options bar.

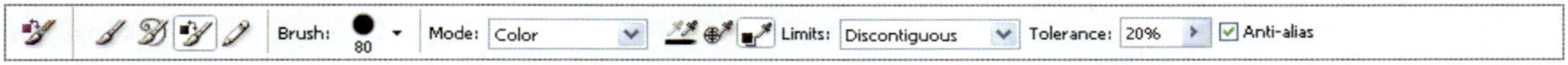

9 Click on the Set Foreground Color icon ( ) in the toolbox and change the RGB values to **245**, **5**, and **5**. Click OK.

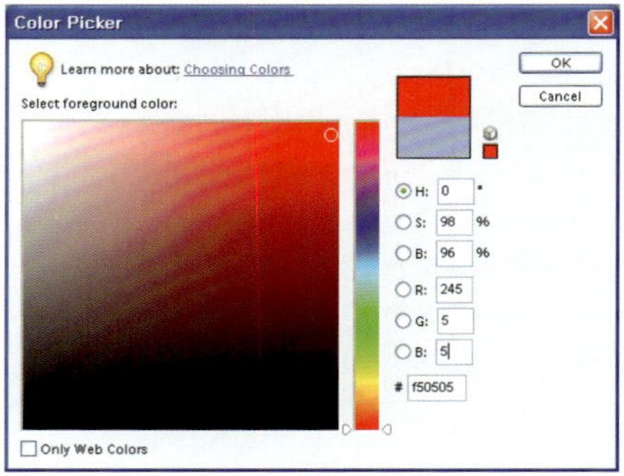

10 Click and drag over the black areas of the butterfly.

11 Because Sampling was set to Background Swatch in step 8, you can see that only areas in the background color (black) are replaced with red.

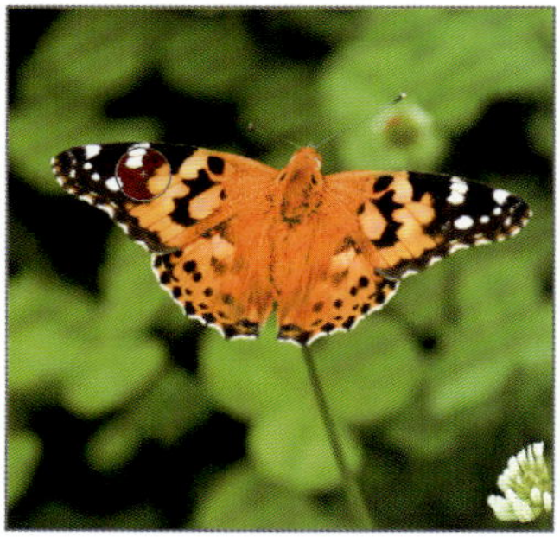

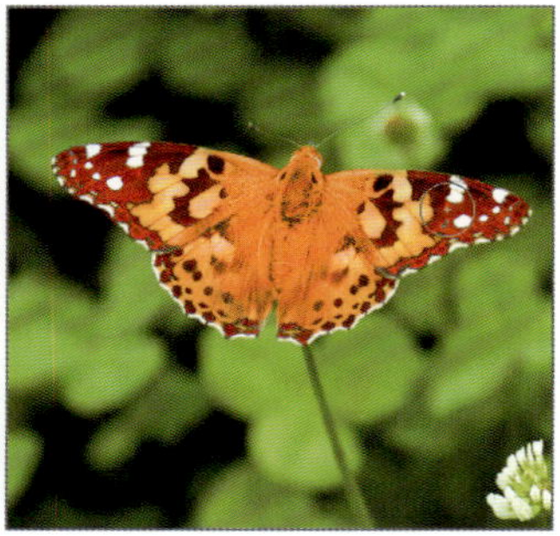

A Closer Look at the Color Replacement Tool Options Bar

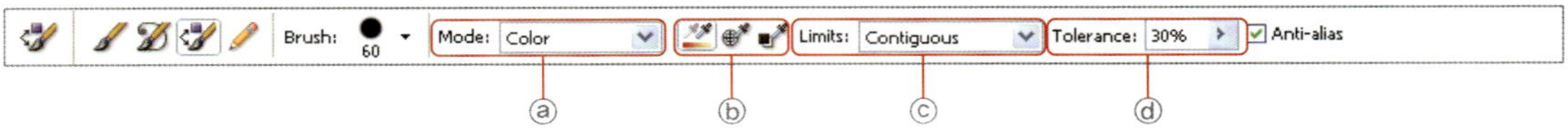

ⓐ **Mode**: Determines the blending mode used. You can choose to replace the Color, Hue, Saturation, or Luminosity in the image.

ⓑ **Sampling**: Choose from three sampling options. The Continuous ( ) option samples the color to be changed continuously, which means the tool will sample as you drag. The Once ( ) option samples the color from the first click of your drag. This option is useful when you want to replace a specific color. The Background Swatch ( ) option samples with the selected background color. This means that the tool will only replace a color in the image if it matches the background color.

ⓒ **Limits**: The Limits option allows you to decide whether the color will be replaced in a contiguous or discontiguous manner. The Contiguous option only replaces the specific "patch" of color (or colors) that you click with the mouse pointer. The Discontiguous option replaces all instances of the selected color in the image, whether they are connected to the location you click or not.

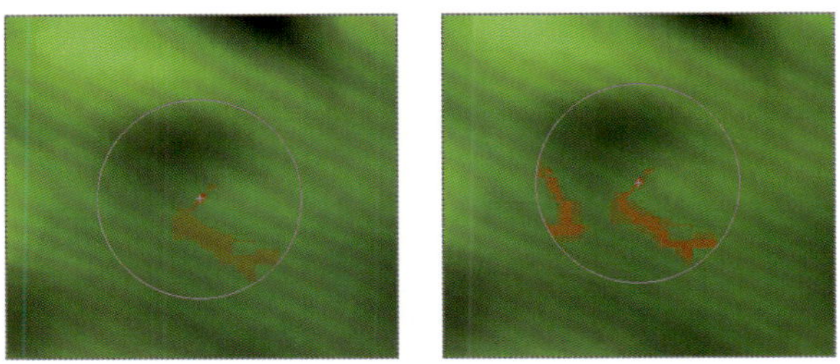

▲ The difference between the Contiguous option (left) and Discontiguous option (right).

ⓓ **Tolerance**: The Tolerance value in the options bar determines the range of colors that will be replaced by the Color Replacement Tool. A low tolerance value only replaces colors that are very similar to the selected color, while a high tolerance value replaces a wider range of colors.

40 Digital Photo Retouching Techniques

with Photoshop Elements 5.0

Chapter 3

Enhancing Portraits

While it is sometimes possible to reshoot a landscape, retaking a bad portrait shot is more difficult. In the worst-case scenario, you may never get the chance again. So instead of a reshoot, try to correct the offending portrait in Photoshop Elements. It will save you time, and the program offers numerous tools to digitally polish your subject.

14 Removing Red Eyes

When you use a flash to take a picture of people or animals in a low-light environment, your subjects can end up with red eyes. In this section, you will learn to use the Red Eye Removal Tool to remove red eyes. The Red Eye Removal Tool, which replaces the Red Eye Brush Tool found in older versions of Photoshop Elements, makes it easier than ever to correct problems with red-eye.

Before

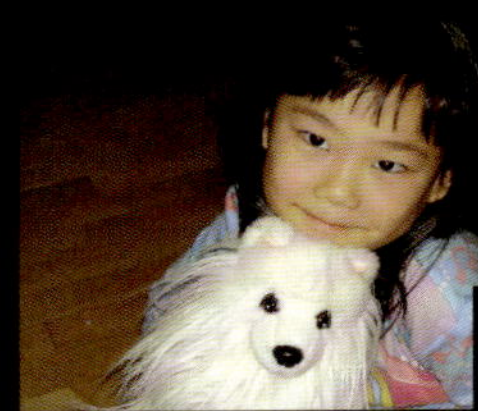

After

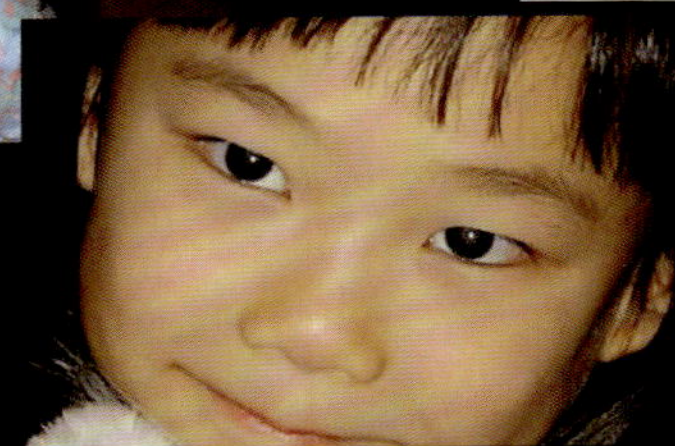

① Select File > Open from the menu bar.

The Open dialog box appears.

② Open the **Sample\Chapter 3\Tech14.jpg** file from the supplementary CD.

Note that the subject has red eyes.

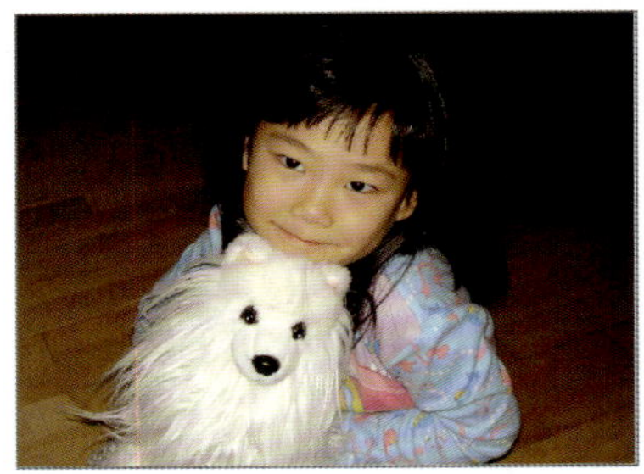

③ Press Ctrl + Spacebar and click on the image window to maximize the window to **200%**.

This step is optional but highly recommended, as you will need a magnified view to work on an area as small as the pupil of the eye.

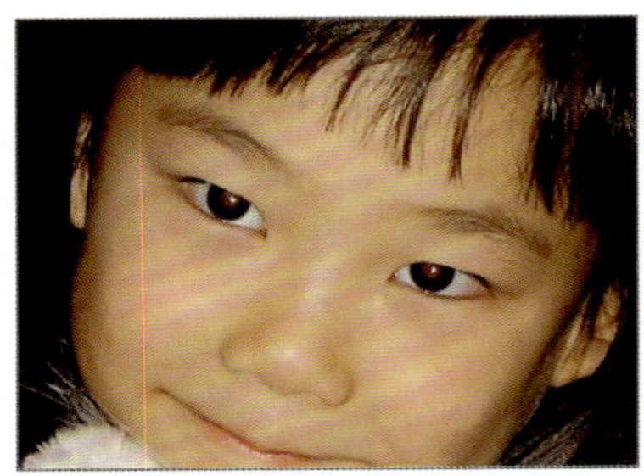

4 From the toolbox, select the Red Eye Removal Tool ( ). In the options bar, check that the Pupil Size is set to **50%** and the Darken Amount to **50%**.

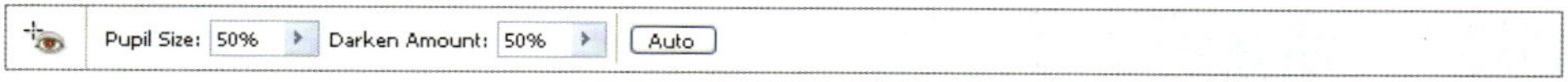

5 Click and drag over an eye to remove the red glow.

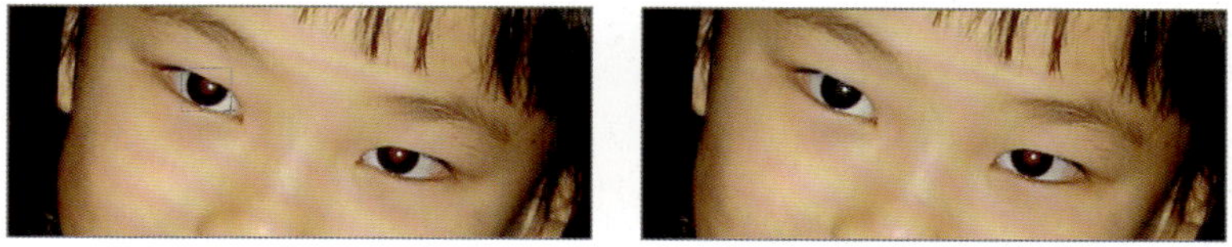

6 Repeat the step on the other eye.

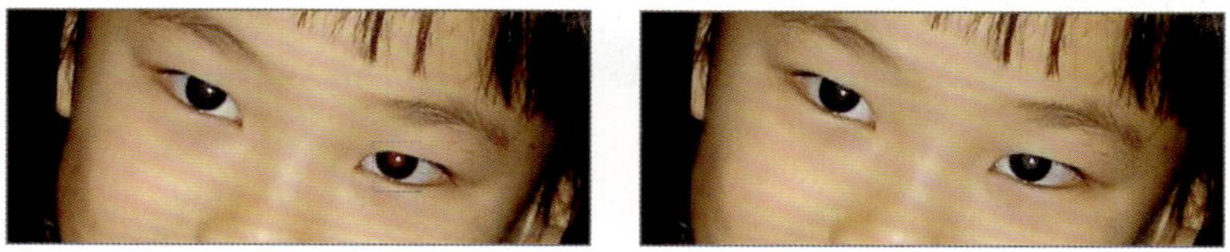

7 Although the red eyes are removed, it still looks unnatural because of the remaining gray areas. Select the Burn Tool ( ) from the tool box and set the brush size in the option bar as seen below.

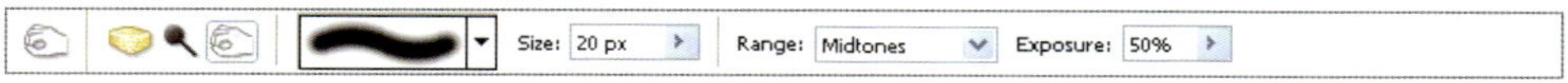

8 Click and drag on the gray eyes where the red eye has been removed. The color black will be added, giving a more natural look.

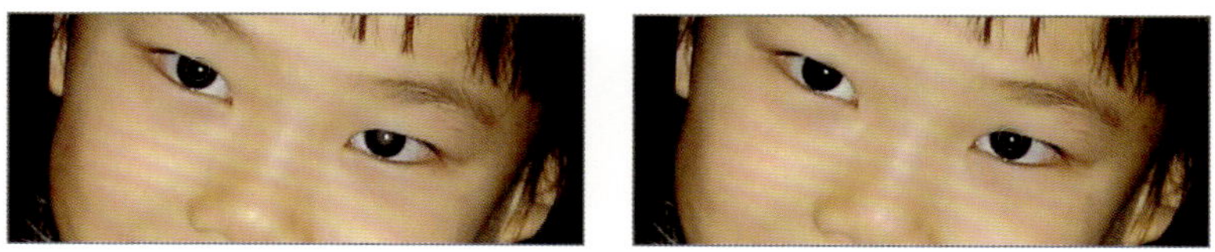

Red Eye Removal Tool Options

Pupil Size: A small pupil size will create a wider tonal range in the pupil. You will see the highlight created by the flash turning into shades of darker gray before turning completely black. A large pupil size, on the other hand, will create a smaller tonal range with fewer shades of gray so the pupil will appear to be darker. The effect of the Pupil Size setting is very subtle and you may not even notice it.

Darken Amount: Determines how dark the pupil will turn out.

15 Removing Facial Blemishes

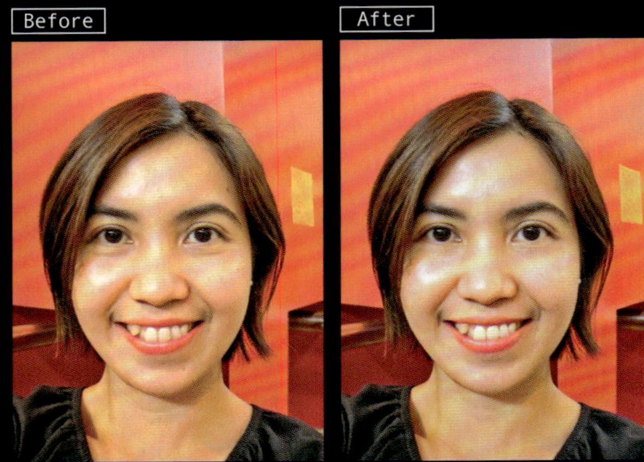

The Spot Healing Brush and Healing Brush tools are essential for removing facial blemishes such as freckles and wrinkles. The Spot Healing Brush Tool is particularly effective, as it requires only one step to remove all sorts of unwanted artifacts, such as dust and scratches. In this exercise, you will learn to use these two brushes as well as the Remove Color Cast command.

1. Select File > Open from the menu bar.

   The Open dialog box appears.

2. Open the **Sample\Chapter 3\Tech15.tif** file from the supplementary CD.

   You can see that the image has an orange color cast.

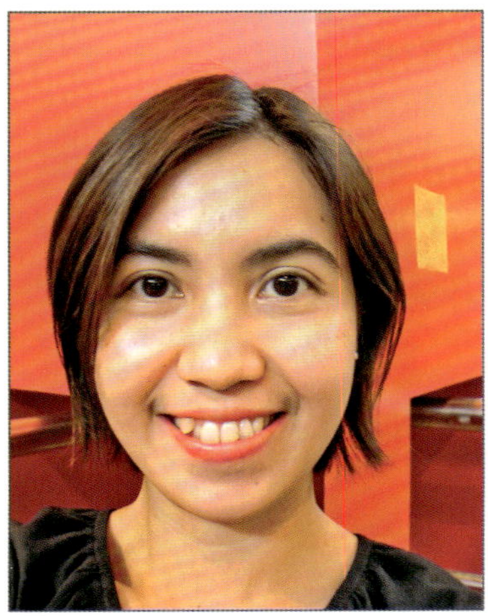

3 Select Enhance > Adjust Color > Remove Color Cast from the menu bar. When the Remove Color Cast dialog box appears, position your pointer (which has turned into an eyedropper) over the white part of the model's eyes. Click once to set this as the white point for the program to reference.

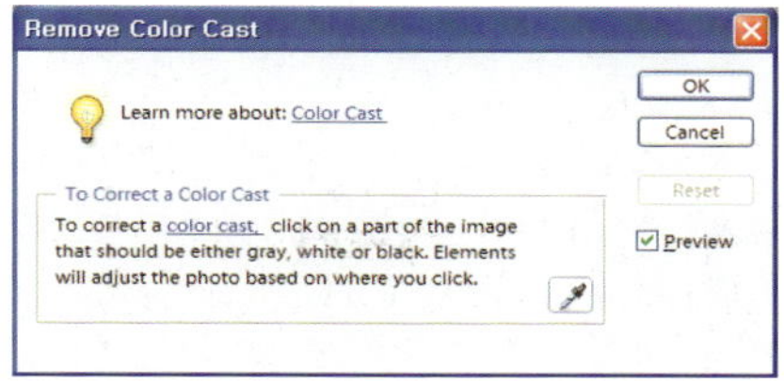

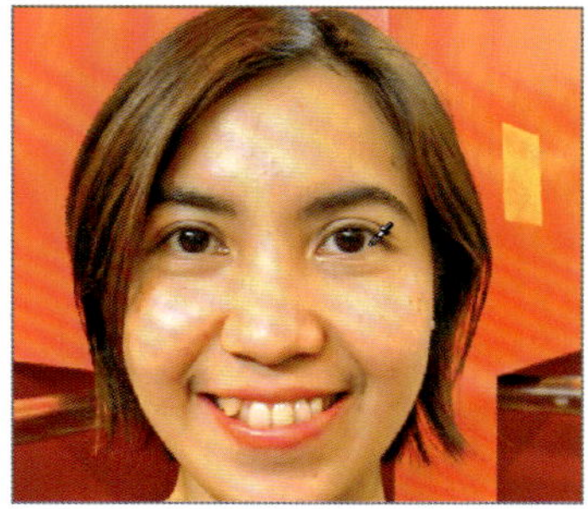

4 The image now looks less orange.

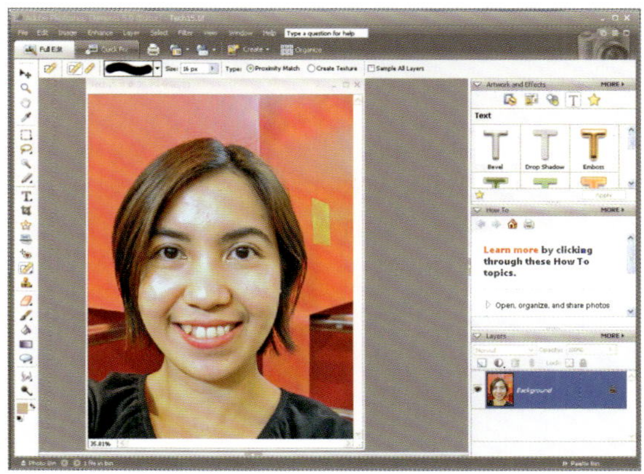

5 Next, we'll take care of the model's skin blemishes. Zoom in on the model's face. Select the Spot Healing Brush Tool ( ) from the toolbox. Set the brush size to **16 pixels** in the options bar.

(6) Position your pointer over the spot as shown and click once.

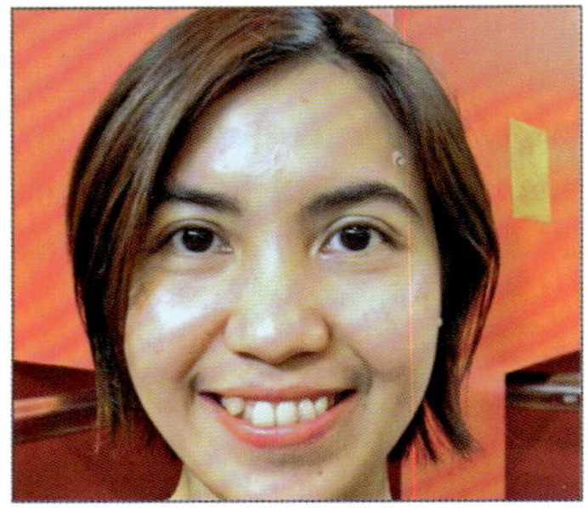

(7) Repeat step 6 on a few isolated spots.

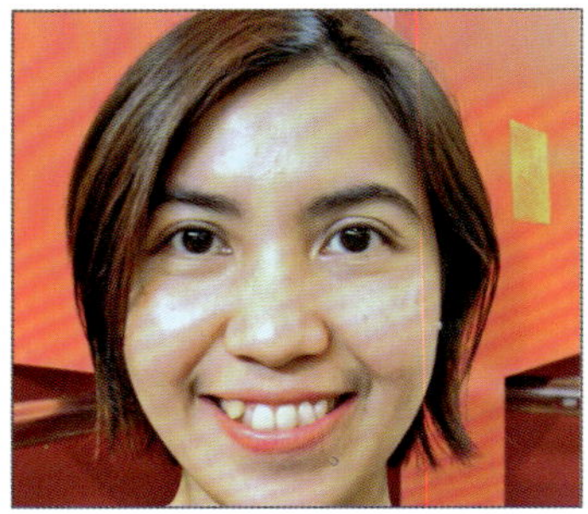

(8) To remove the group of freckles on the model's cheek, select the Healing Brush Tool (![]) from the toolbox. Hold down the [Alt] key and click on the position as shown to set a reference point for the tool.

The Healing Brush Tool works by copying and blending the area from the reference point to the area that is brushed over.

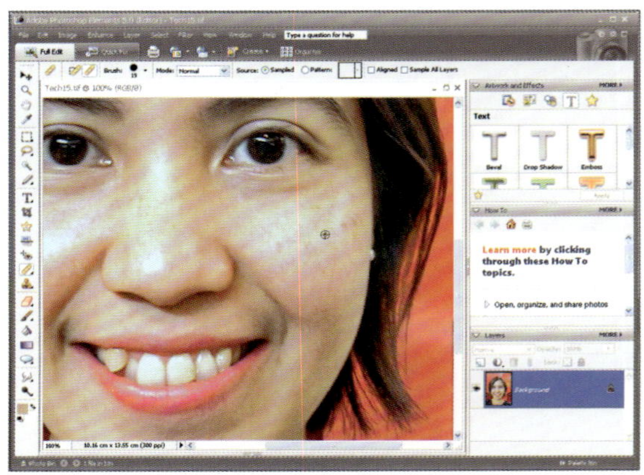

9 Check that the brush size is set to **19 pixels** and the Mode is set to **Normal** in the options bar. Brush over the group of freckles, as shown.

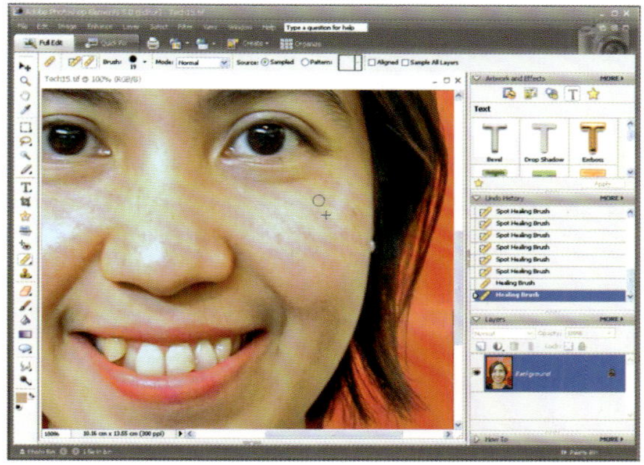

10 If you did not remove the freckles successfully, go back a few steps in the Undo History palette and try again until all the freckles are removed.

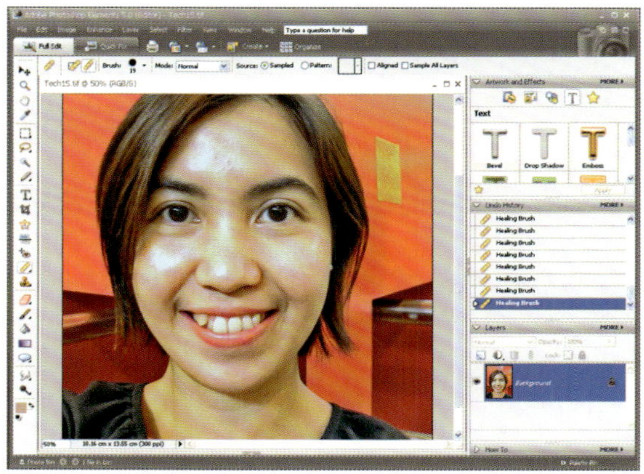

(11) Select the Spot Healing Brush Tool ( ) and drag over the lines under the right eye as shown.

(12) Repeat the step on the other eye.

Do not remove all of the lines under the eyes, as the face will look very plastic if there are no lines at all.

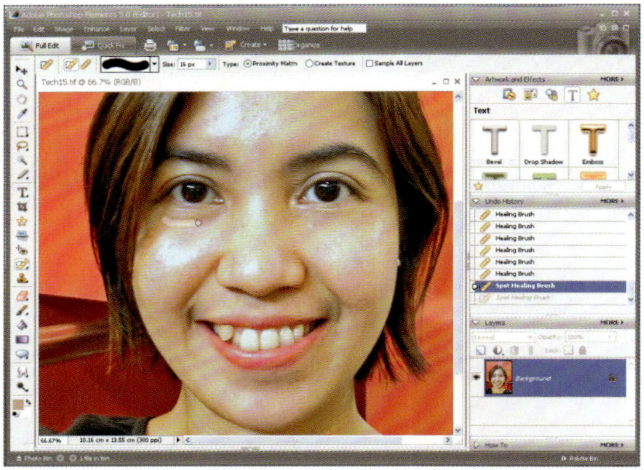

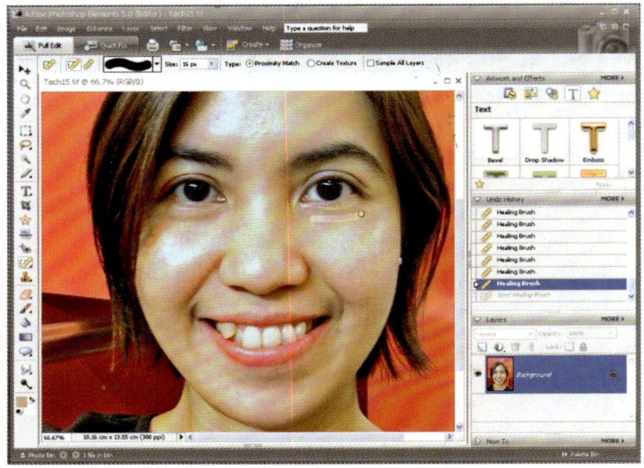

(13) In the same way, remove the lines from the neck. When you are done, save the image.

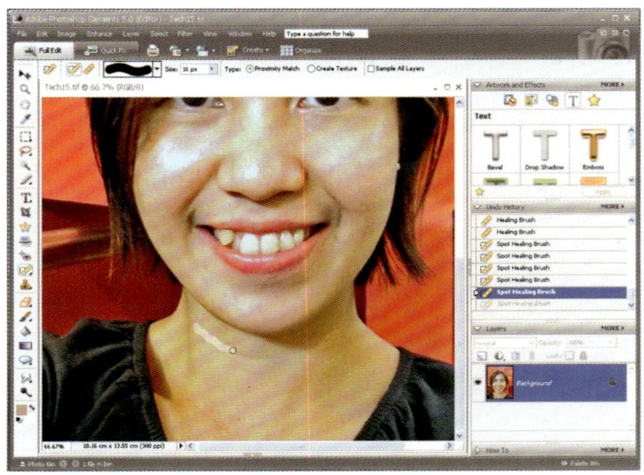

16 Applying Makeup

Some cosmetic counters or make-over studios are equipped with a computer system that captures a person's face and shows on screen the effect that their products will have on the face. By a similar process, you can change how a person looks using a computer. The most important thing you need to remember in this section is to keep the makeup natural.

Before

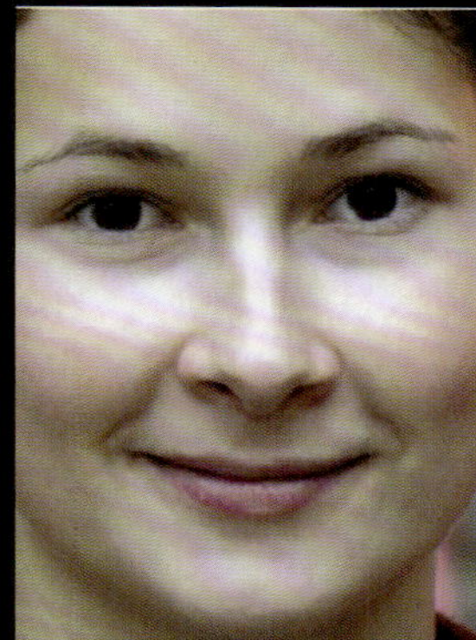

After

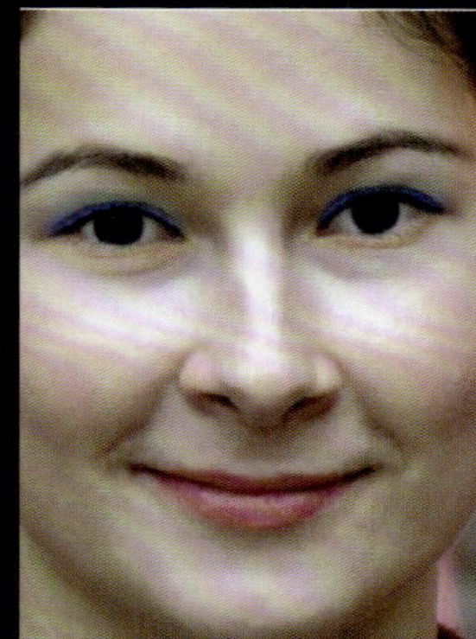

1 Select File > Open from the menu bar.

The Open dialog box appears.

2 Open the **Sample\Chapter 3\Tech16.tif** file from the supplementary CD.

3 Press Ctrl + + to zoom in on the face.

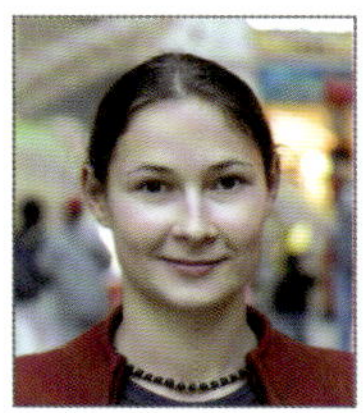

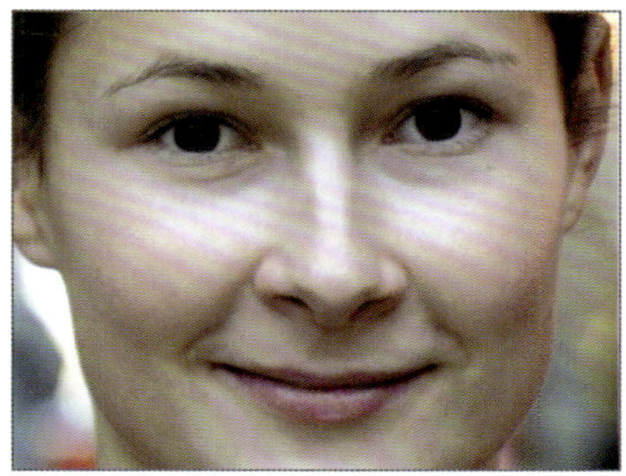

4 Select the Selection Brush Tool ( ) from the toolbox. Set Size to **5 pixels**, Mode to **Mask**, and Hardness to **100%**.

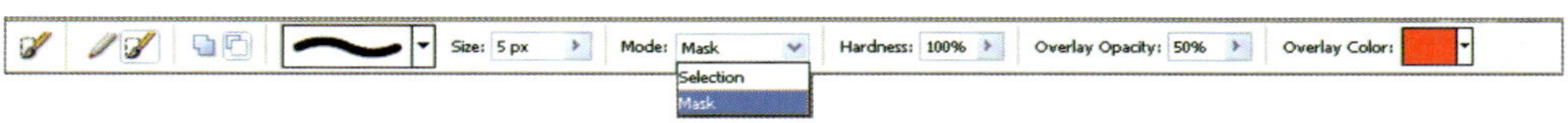

5 Click and drag over both eyes to apply a mask. With the eyes masked, you can apply eye makeup without getting any in the eyes.

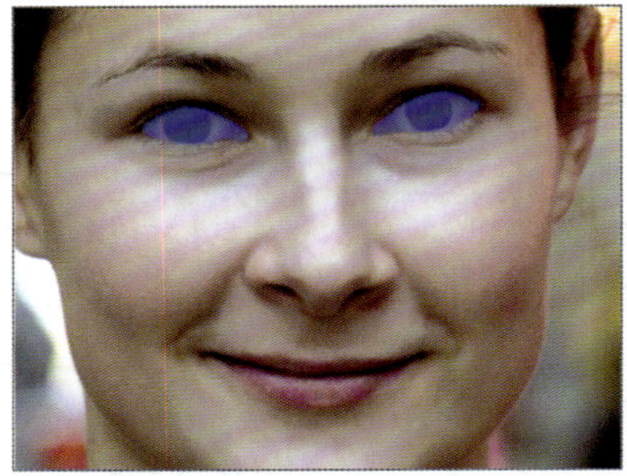

tip A masked area is protected from the changes made to the rest of the image. You can invert a masked area by clicking Select > Inverse. The previously unmasked areas will become masked instead.

6 Click the Set Foreground Color icon in the toolbox.

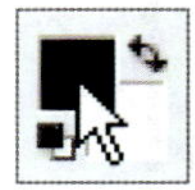

The Color Picker dialog box appears.

7 Set the RGB values to **0**, **246**, and **255**, respectively.

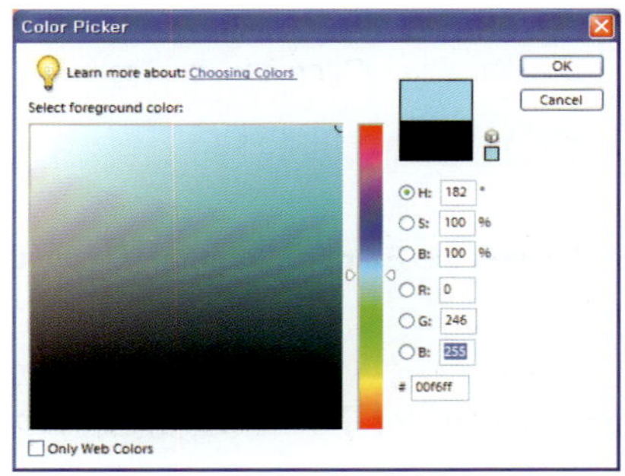

8 Click OK.

The foreground color changes, as shown.

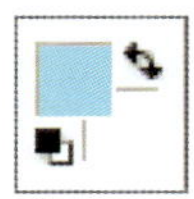

9 Select the Brush Tool () from the toolbox. In the Brush Tool options bar, set Size to **21 pixels** and Opacity to **15%**.

Reducing the opacity makes the color more transparent.

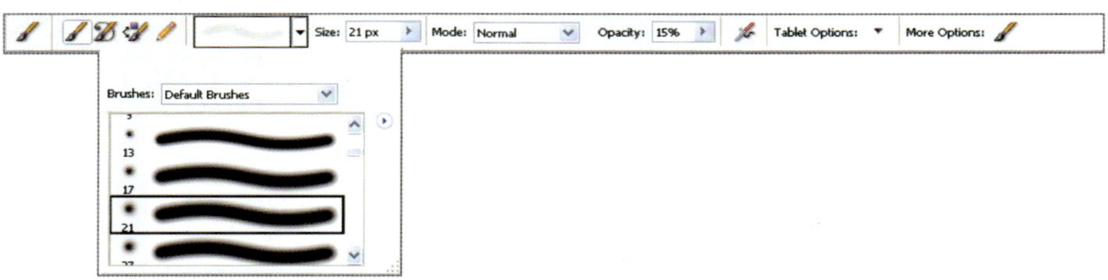

10 Click and drag the Brush Tool ( ) over the upper eyelids as if applying eye shadow.

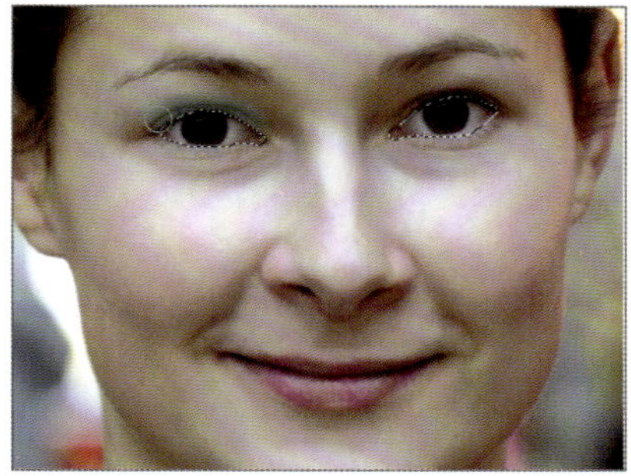

11 Click the Set Foreground Color icon in the toolbox to change to another eye shadow color. In the Color Picker dialog box, set the RGB values to **0**, **12**, and **255**, respectively. Click OK.

This darker blue will be used for the inner edges of the upper eyelids.

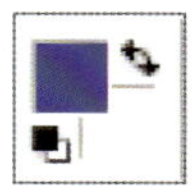

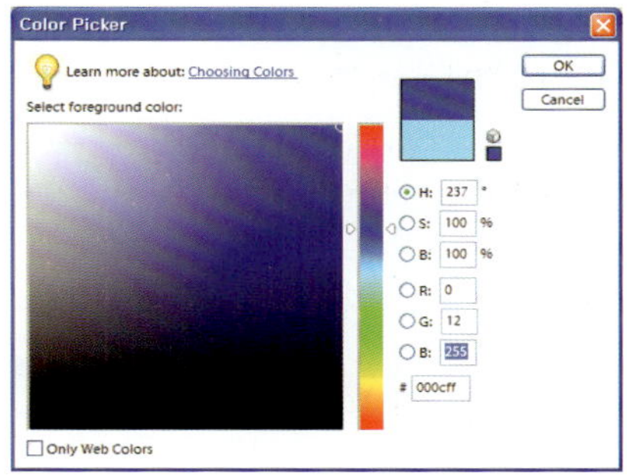

12 In the Brush Tool options bar, set Size to **12 pixels** and Opacity to **22%**.

The smaller brush size enables you to line the inner edges of the eyelids more accurately.

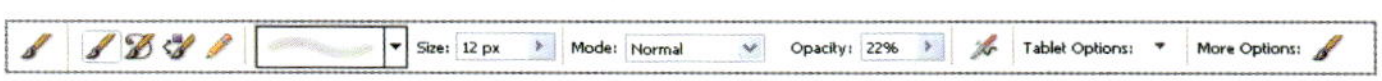

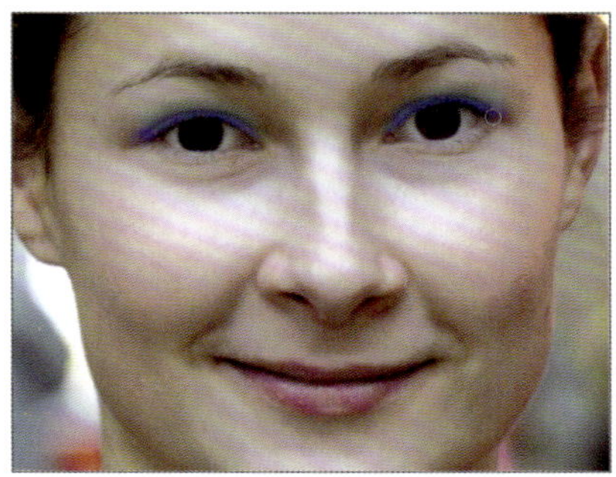

13 Click and drag along the inner edges of the upper eyelids, as shown.

This completes the makeup on the upper eyelid.

tip Pressing Ctrl + H will hide the distracting, "marching-ants" selection border. Pressing Ctrl + H again will bring it back to view.

(14) Click on the Set Foreground Color icon in the toolbox. In the Color Picker dialog box, set the RGB values to **255**, **150**, and **0**, respectively. Click OK.

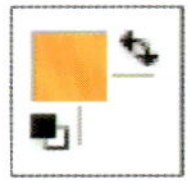

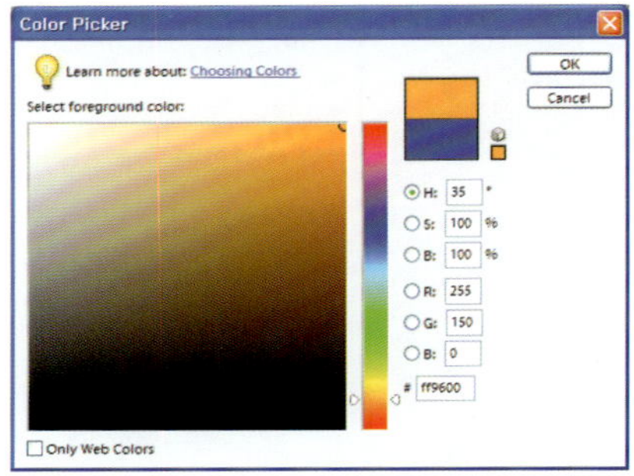

(15) In the Brush Tool options bar, set Size to **20 pixels** and Opacity to **10%**.

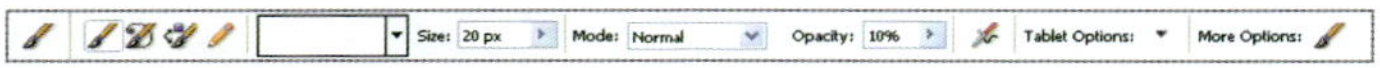

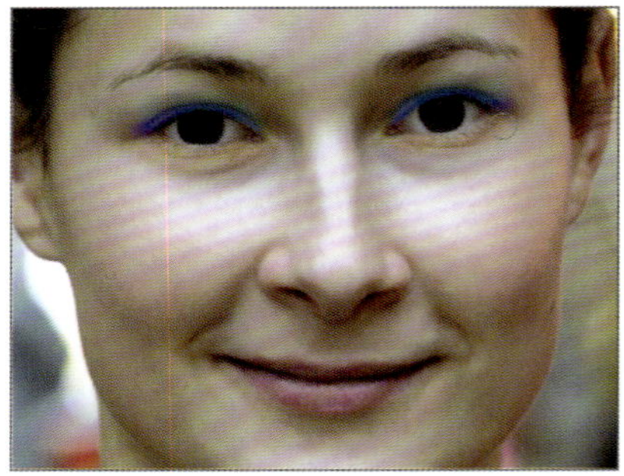

(16) Draw along the edges below the eyes.

(17) Select the Burn Tool ( ) from the toolbox. In the options bar, set Size to **5 pixels** and Exposure to **50%**.

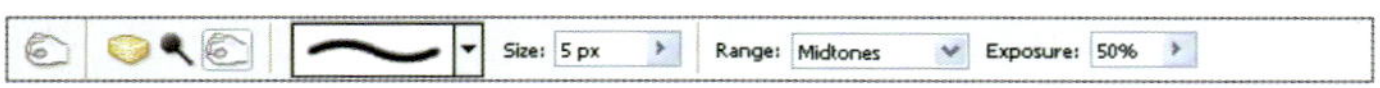

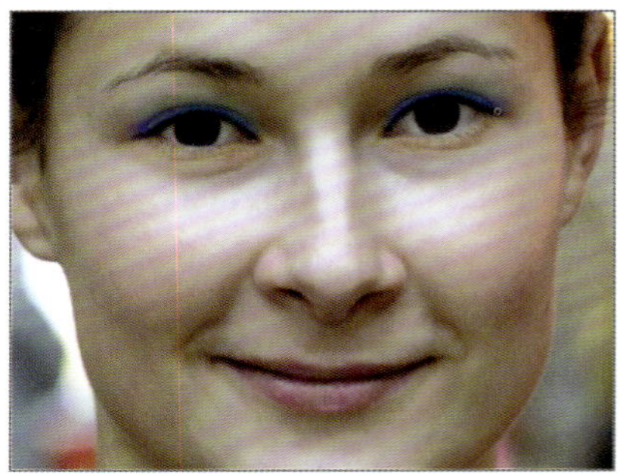

(18) Click and drag over the edge of the eyelids as if applying eyeliner.

(19) In the options bar, set Size to **15 pixels**.

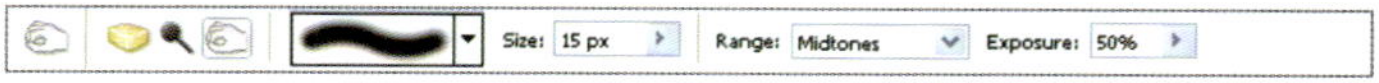

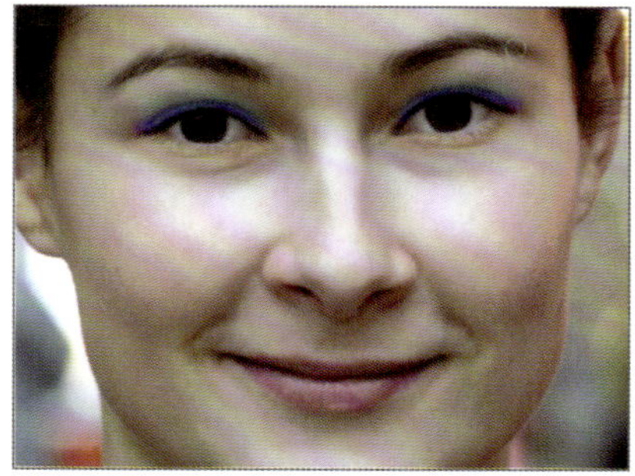

(20) Click and drag over the eyebrows to make them look more even.

(21) Note that the eye makeup has covered the eyelid lines. In the options bar, set Size to **5 pixels**. Click and drag the Burn Tool to draw the eyelid lines back in.

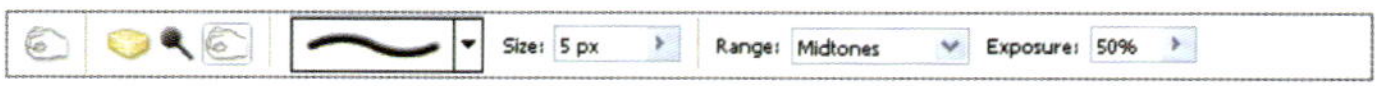

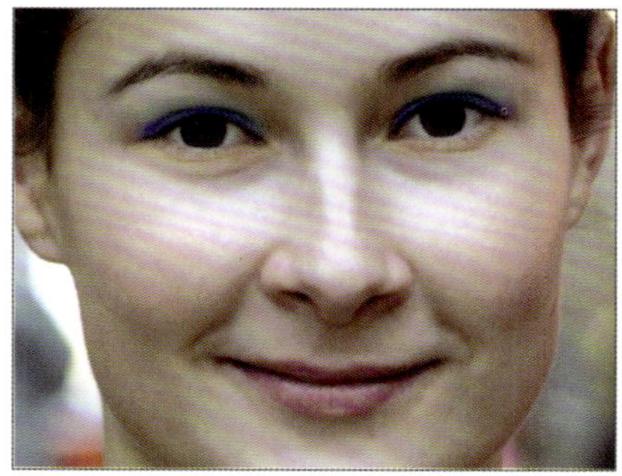

(22) In the options bar, set Size to **3 pixels**. Click and drag the Burn Tool outward from the eyes as if applying mascara.

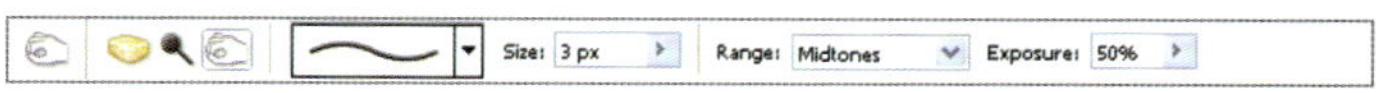

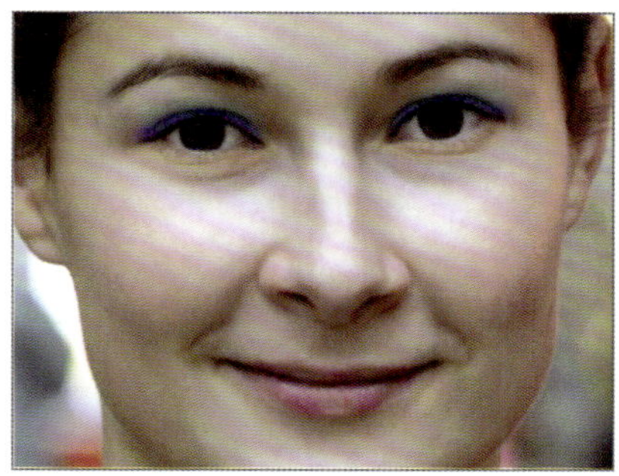

23 Click the Set Foreground Color icon in the toolbox to change to a lipstick color. In the Color Picker dialog box, set the RGB values to **251**, **6**, and **6**, respectively. Click OK.

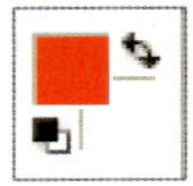

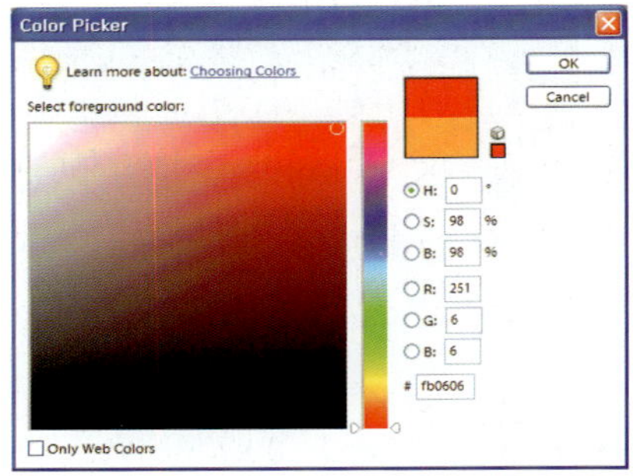

24 Select the Brush Tool ( ) from the toolbox. In the Brush Tool options bar, set Size to **15 pixels** and Opacity to **10%**.

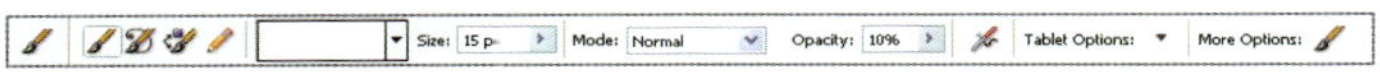

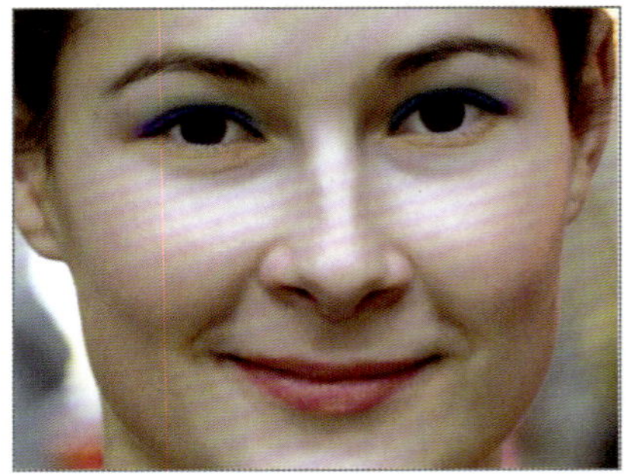

25 Draw over the lips.

26 Select the Burn Tool ( ) from the toolbox. In the options bar, set Size to **10 pixels**.

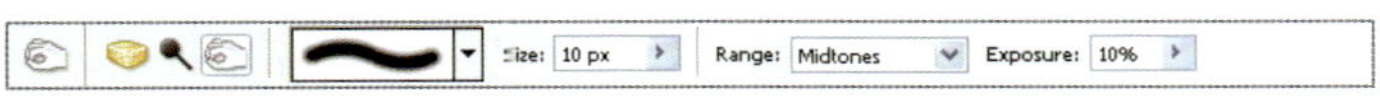

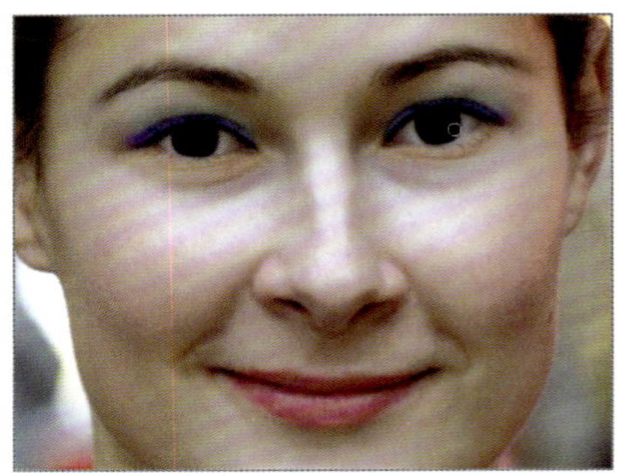

27 Click and drag the Burn Tool over the pupils in the eyes.

This darkens the pupils, making the eyes more prominent.

28 Press Ctrl + 0 to view the entire image.

17 Creating Bigger Eyes and a Sharper Chin

A major factor in physical beauty is symmetry. You may not realize it, but many of us have fairly asymmetrical faces. In this section, you will create a more symmetrical face by enlarging one or both eyes. You will also learn to use the Liquify command to make the left side of the face slimmer, with a sharper chin.

Before

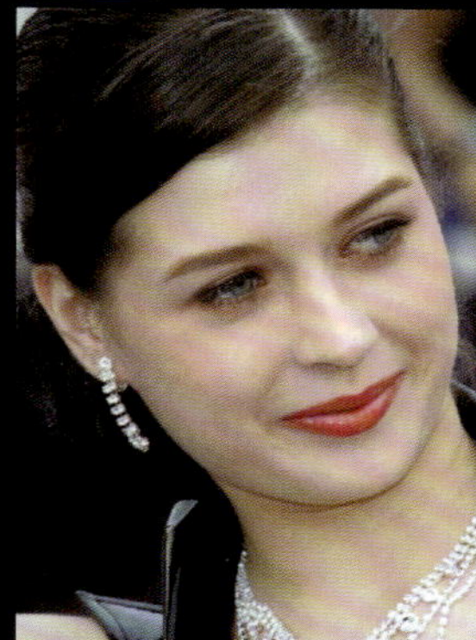

After

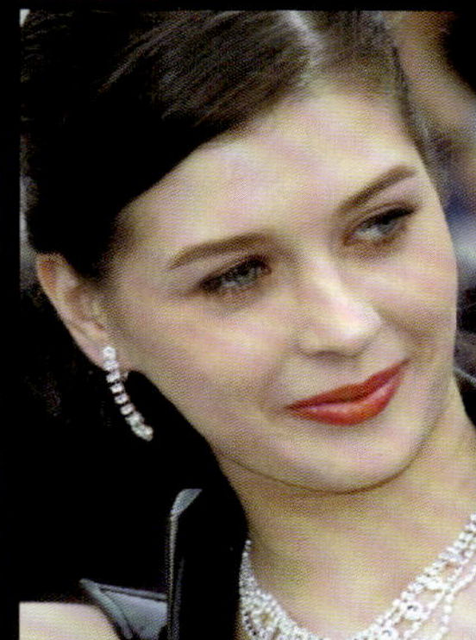

1 Select File > Open from the menu bar.

The Open dialog box appears.

2 Open the **Sample\Chapter 3\Tech17.tif** file provided on the supplementary CD.

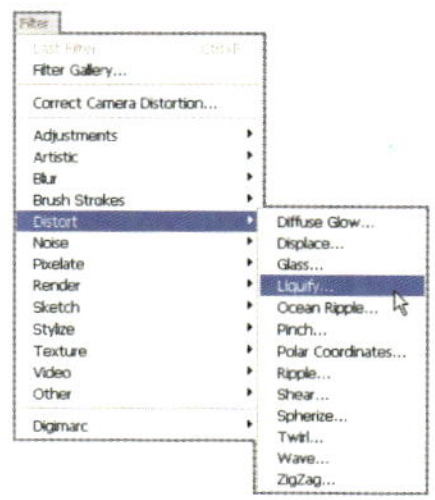

3 Select Filter > Distort > Liquify from the menu bar.

The Liquify dialog box appears.

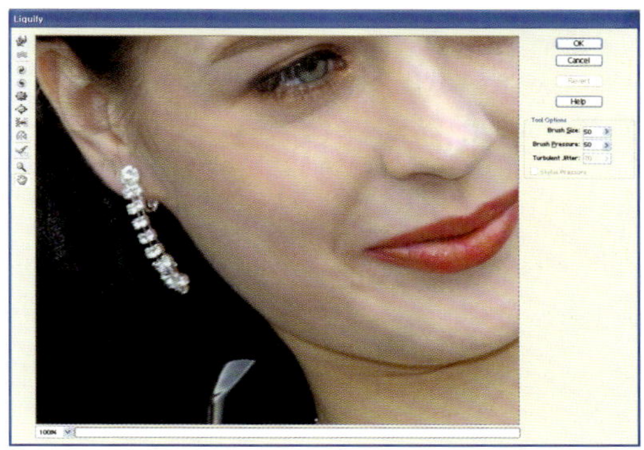

4 Select the Zoom Tool (🔍) in the Liquify dialog box. Click and drag over the right jawline for a magnified view.

5 Select the Warp Tool ( ) in the Liquify dialog box. Under Tool Options, set Brush Size and Brush Pressure to **50**.

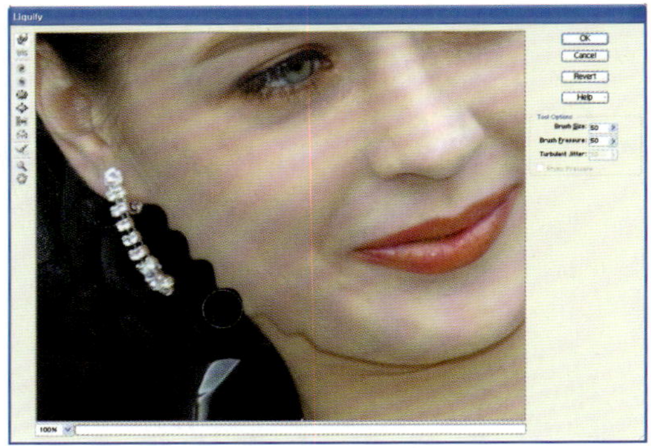

6 Click and drag the jawline inward for a sharper chin.

tip A Brush Pressure of 50%—compared to, say, 100%—will move the jawline more gradually.

7 Click and drag the tool over the jawline again to smooth out any rough edges.

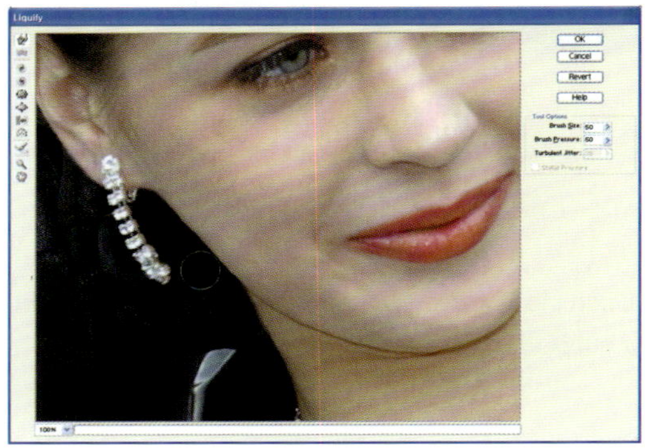

8 Select the Hand Tool ( ). Click and drag the image to move the view to the other jaw. Select the Warp Tool ( ) and repeat steps 6 and 7 on the right jawline. Click OK.

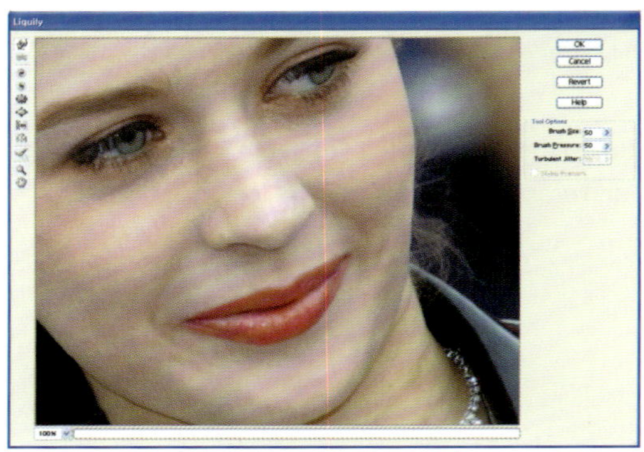

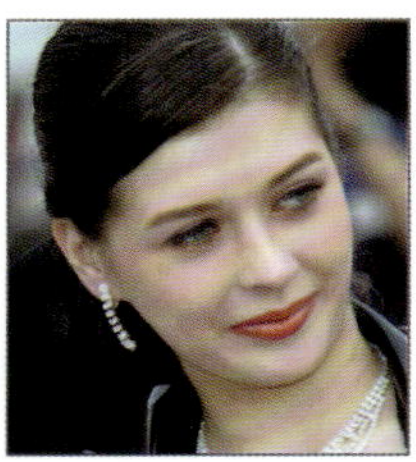

◀ A slimmer-looking face

9 Select the Zoom Tool ( ) from the toolbox. Click and drag over the eyes to zoom in on them.

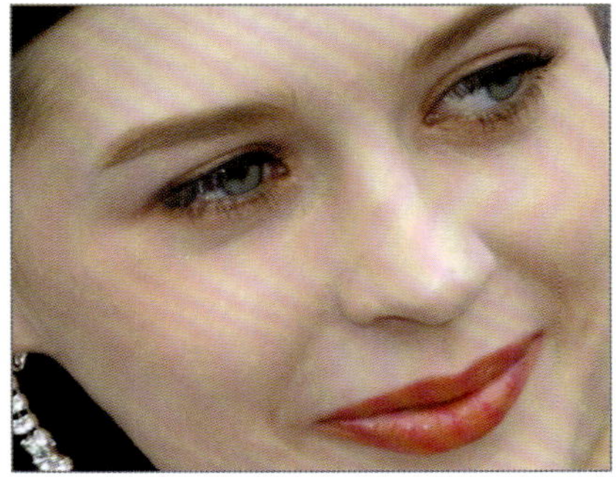

10 Select the Lasso Tool ( ) from the toolbox. In the options bar, set Feather to **12 pixels**.

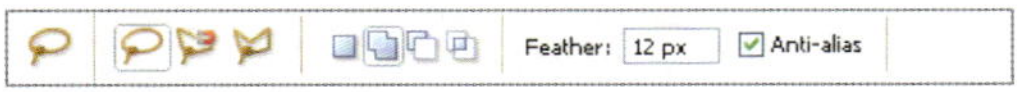

11 Click and drag over the left eye to select it. Press Ctrl + C to copy the selection.

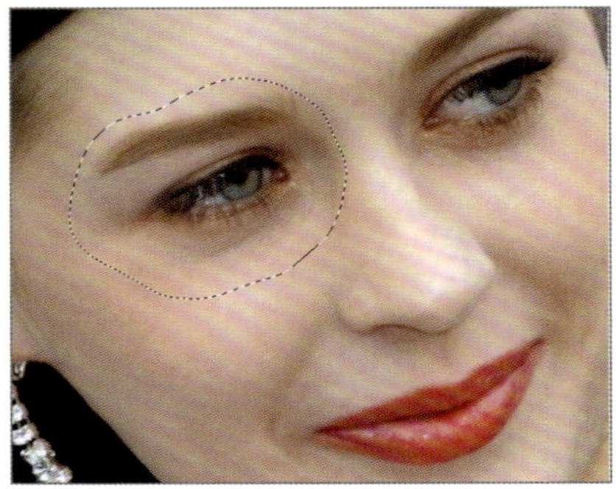

12 Press Ctrl + V to paste the copy onto the image.

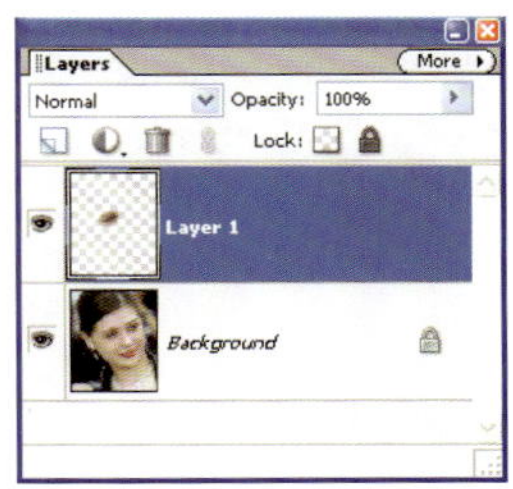

▲ Note that the copy is pasted on a new layer.

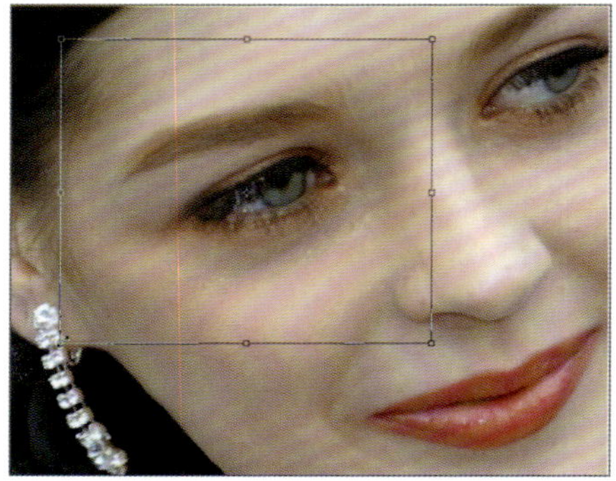

(13) Select Image > Transform > Free Transform. A bounding box with adjustment handles will appear over the selection.

(14) Hold down the Shift + Alt keys, and drag the adjustment handle on the lower-right corner slightly outward. Hit Enter .

tip The Shift key ensures that the image is resized proportionally, while the Alt key ensures that the image's center point remains unchanged. Always press the Shift key before the Alt key. Pressing the Alt key and then the Shift key will cause image distortion.

(15) Press Ctrl + - to zoom out of the image. Select the Move Tool ( ) and use the arrow keys to position the left eye to align with the right.

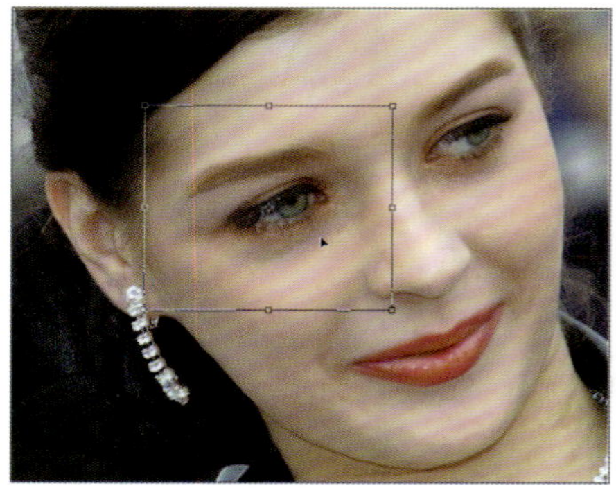

16 Press Ctrl + 0 to view the entire image.

When modifying a face, always make sure that the results look natural. Don't go overboard or you may end up with awkward and unnatural features.

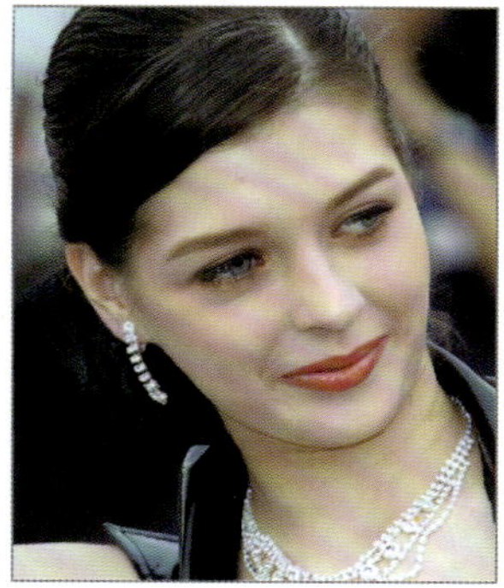

17 Select Layer > Flatten Image from the menu bar.

This combines all the layers created when you copied and pasted selections, and merges them with the Background layer.

18 Select File > Save As and save the completed image in a folder.

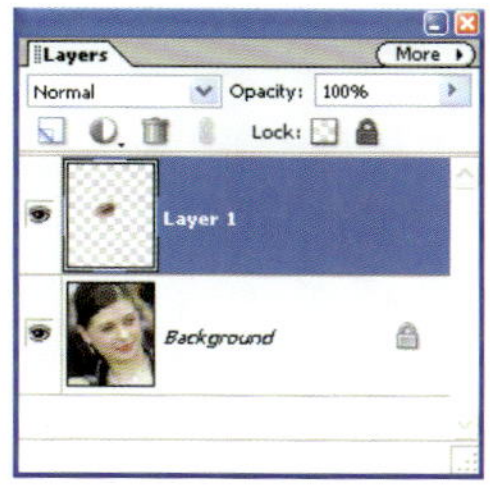

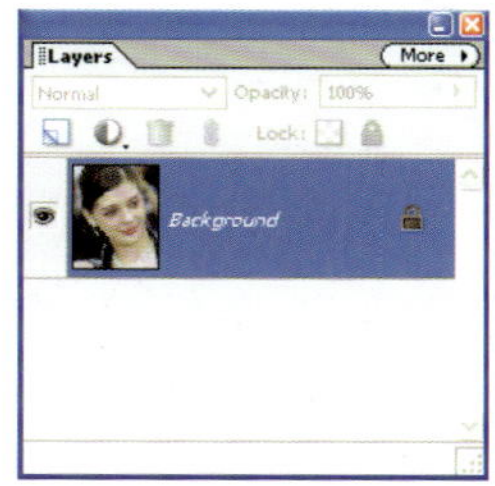

▲ Flattening the layers

The point of flattening layers is to reduce the file size—but before you do so, it is advisable to first save the image as a .PSD file, which retains layer information. If you flatten the layers without saving as a PSD file, you will not be able to access the layers again.

18 Revising a Portrait Photo Using Adjust Color for Skin Tone

Before

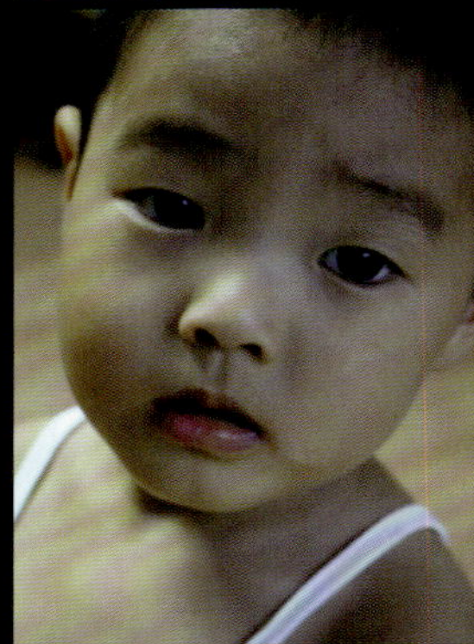

After

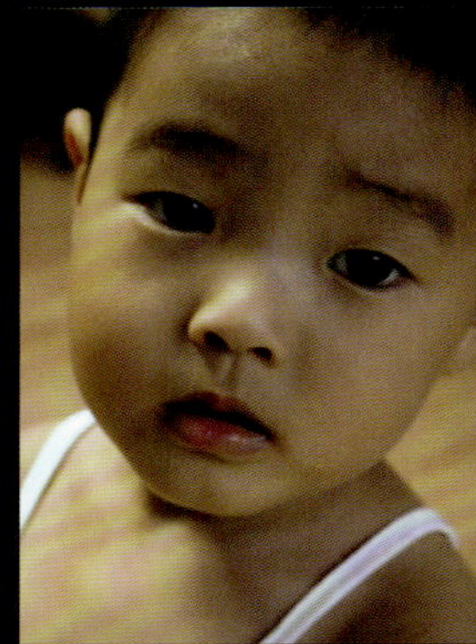

The new Adjust Color for Skin Tone feature allows you to revise the skin tone of a portrait photograph that has been taken with improper exposure or white balance to look more realistic. Furthermore, this command is useful in creating a more luxurious look for a portrait photograph.

1. Select File > Open from the menu bar.

2. Open the **Samples\Chapter 3\Tech18.jpg** file from the supplementary CD.

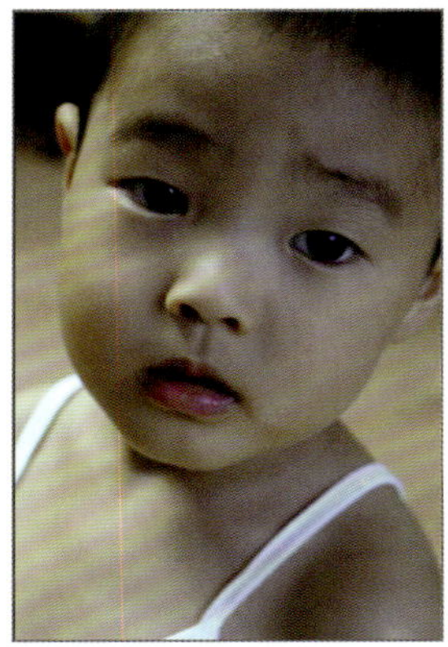

3. Click Enhance > Adjust Color > Adjust Color for Skin Tone from the Menu bar.

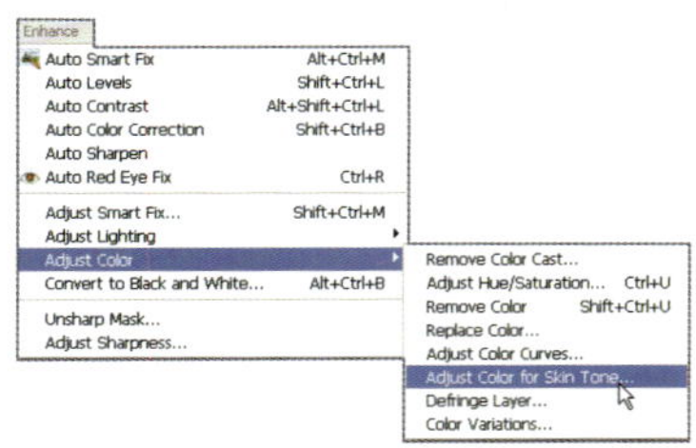

4 The Adjust Color for Skin Tone dialog box will appear. The box has directions on how to use the Adjust Color for Skin Tone feature.

5 The mouse cursor will change into an eyedropper shape once the mouse is brought to the image. Click on the cheek area as shown below.

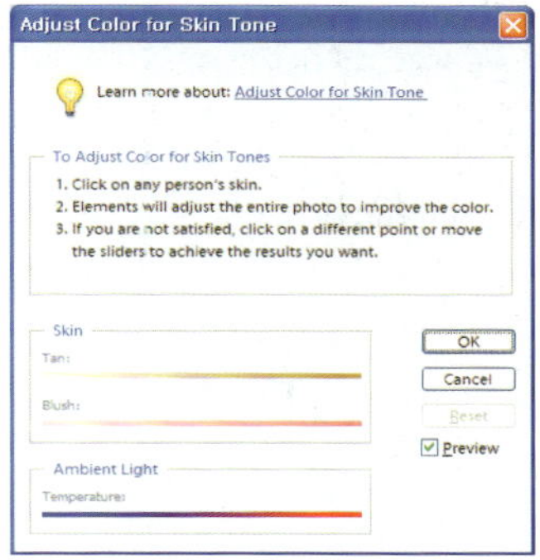

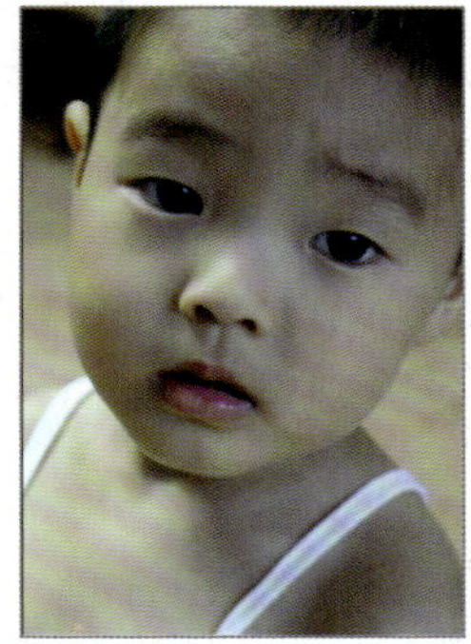

6 Once you click on the cheek, you will see a slider appear in the Adjust Color for Skin Tone dialog box, and that the general color of the Skin has changed.

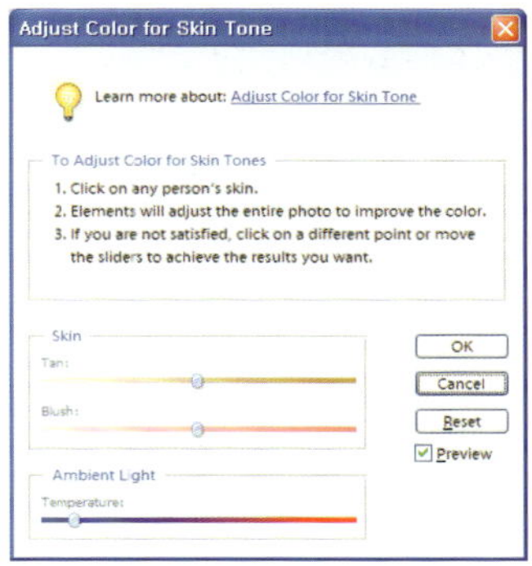

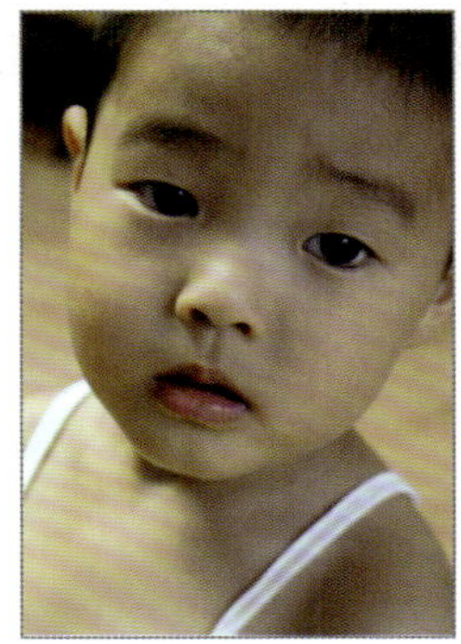

7 If you wish to make further adjustments, you can increase or decrease the Tan and Blush under Skin. Increase both the yellow and red slightly, then click the OK button.

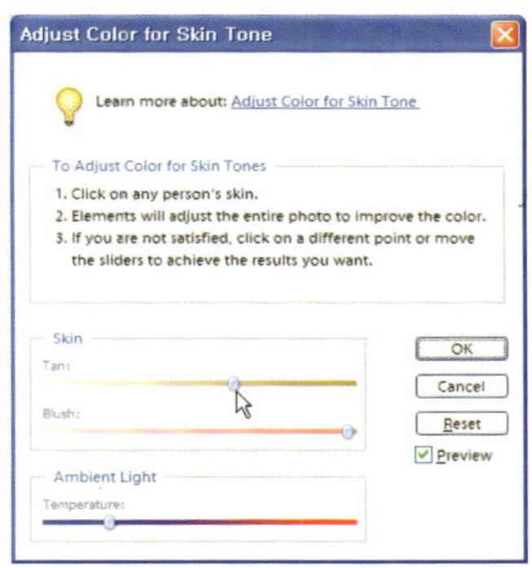

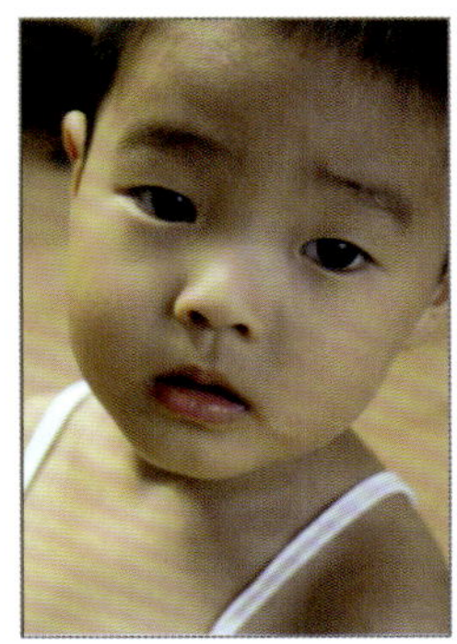

▲ Final Image

19 Opening Closed Eyes

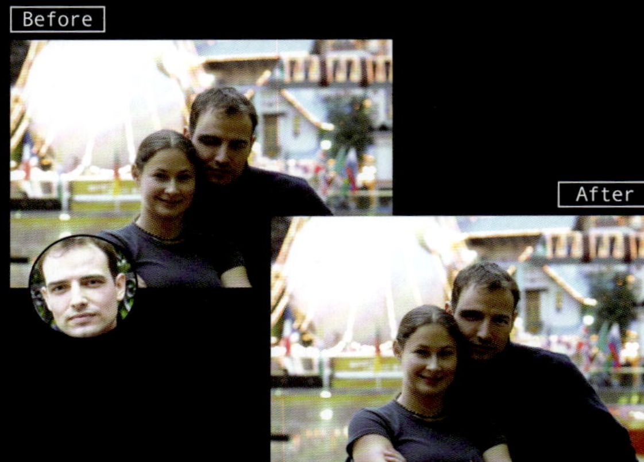

When taking group shots, the photographer cannot give everyone at the shoot his undivided attention, and so it is common to find one or two persons with their eyes closed in group photos. To make matters worse, group photos are usually taken to remember a special time or event. So if you find your subject's eyes closed in a special or important photograph, try this technique for opening closed eyes.

1. Select File > Open from the menu bar.

The Open dialog box appears.

2. Open the files **Sample\Chapter 3\Tech19.tif** and **Sample\Chapter 3\Tech19-1.tif** from the supplementary CD.

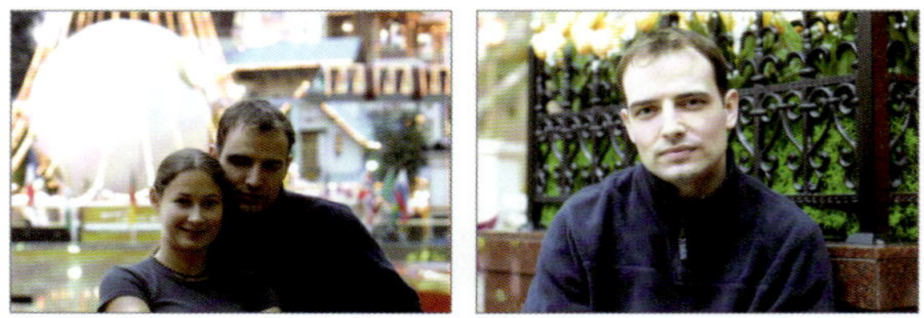

The subject's eyes are closed in the first file and opened in the second. We will use the opened eyes from the second picture to rectify the problem in the first picture.

3. Select the Lasso Tool ( ) from the toolbox. Set Feather to **7 pixels**.

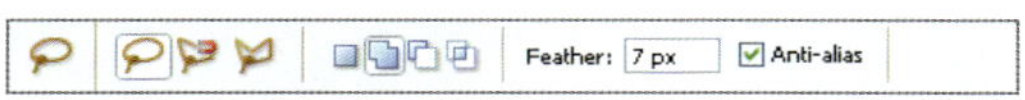

4. Select the eyes in the **Tech19-1.tif** image.

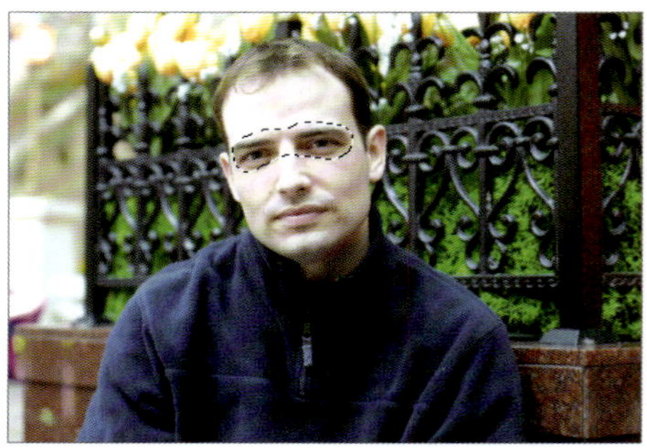

5 Select the Move Tool ([Move Tool icon]) from the toolbox. Click and drag the eyes from the **Tech19-1.tif** image to the **Tech19.tif** image.

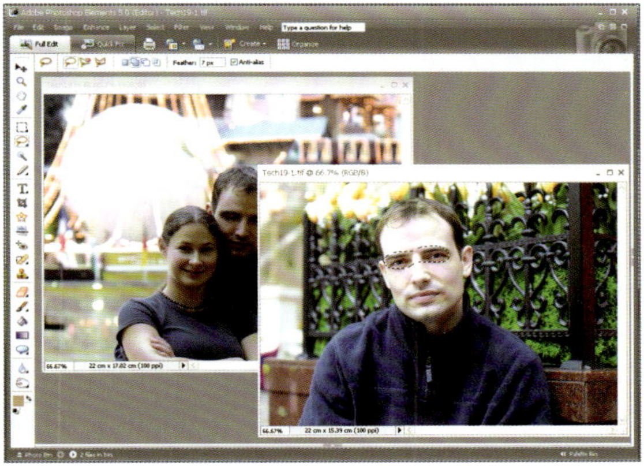

▲ Dragging the selection from one file to another

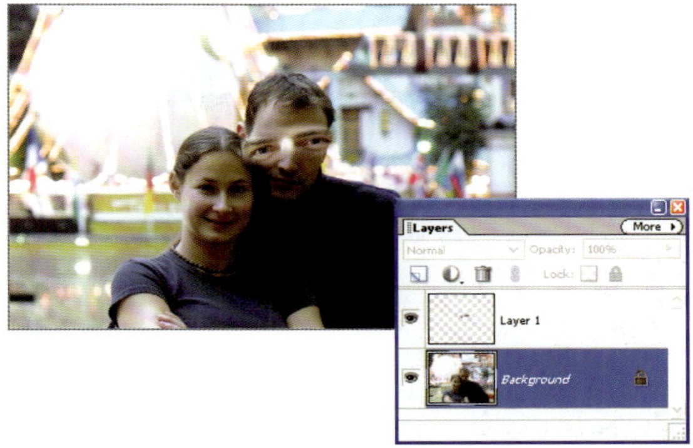

▲ The eye selection is added as a new layer.

6 Select Image > Rotate > Flip Layer Horizontal from the menu bar.

This flips the newly added eyes horizontally so that they are oriented the same way as the face.

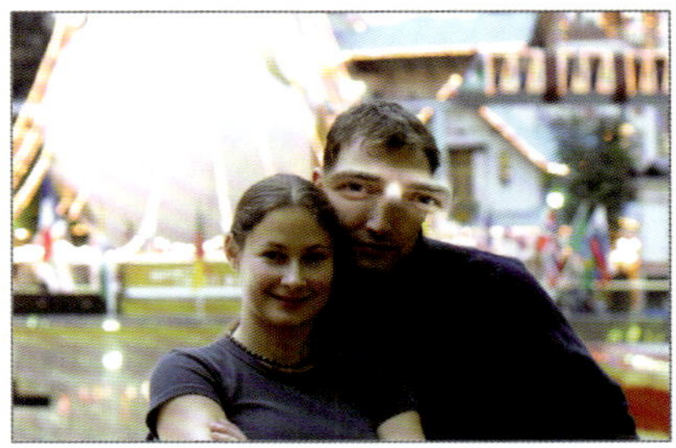

▲ Fixing the orientation of the eyes

7 Select Image > Transform > Free Transform from the menu bar or press Ctrl + T.

The Free Transform bounding box appears.

8 Place the pointer over a handle at one of the corners.

The pointer changes to a double-headed arrow.

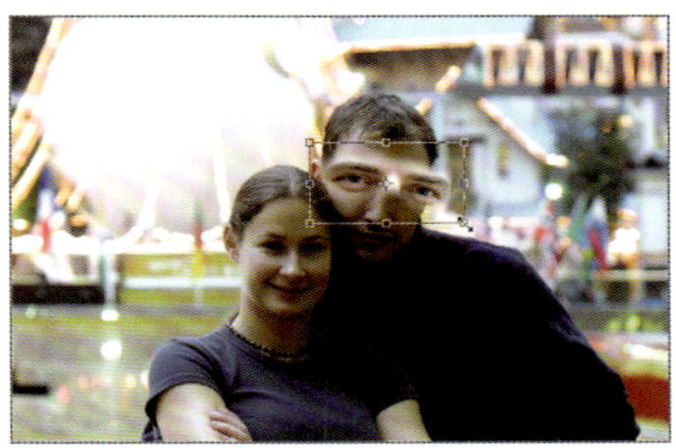

▲ Fixing the orientation of the eyes

Chapter 03

9 Hold down the Alt + Shift keys and drag the handle inward until the new set of eyes fits into the face. Press Enter.

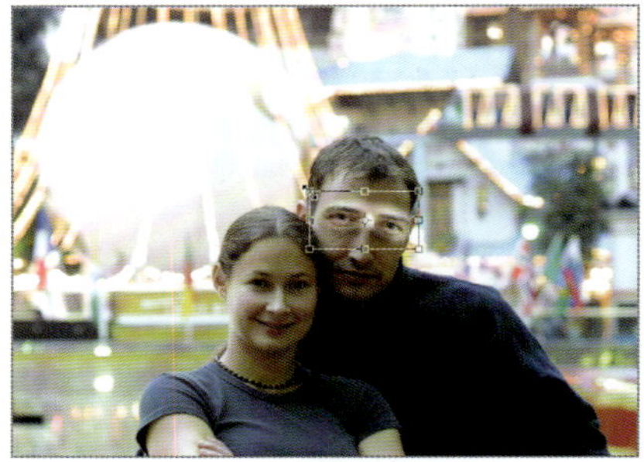

▲ Reducing the size of the eyes

10 Press Ctrl + + several times to zoom into the eyes. Select the Move Tool ( ) from the toolbox and adjust the position of the eyes.

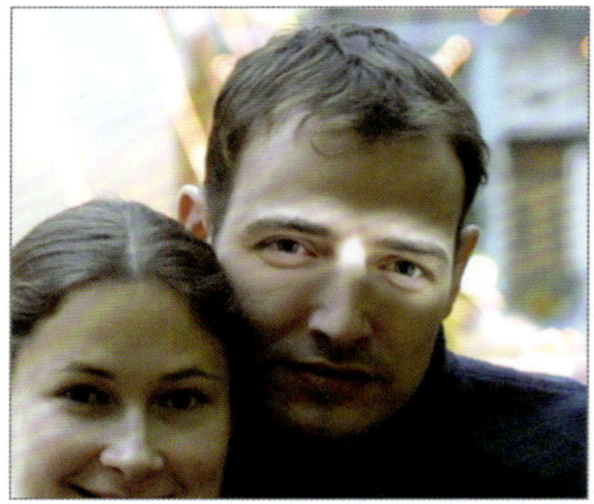

11 As you can see, the eyes are much brighter than the rest of the image. Let's fix this using the Levels command. Select Enhance > Adjust Lighting > Levels from the menu bar or press Ctrl + L. In the Levels dialog box, enter **23**, **0.77**, and **255** in the Input Levels text boxes, respectively. Click OK.

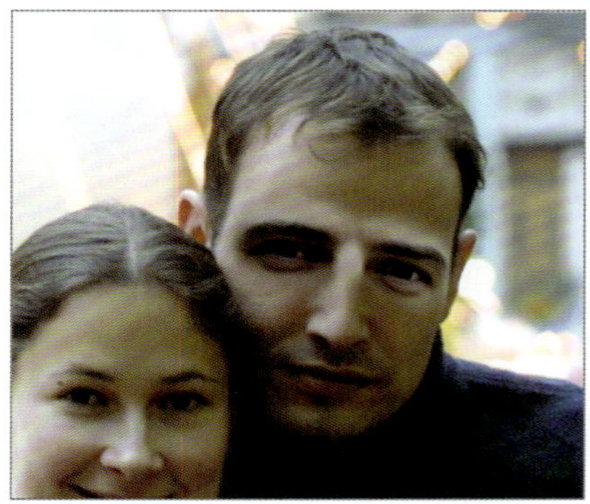

12 Select the Eraser Tool ( ) from the toolbox. In the options bar, set Size to **30 pixels** and Opacity to **50%**.

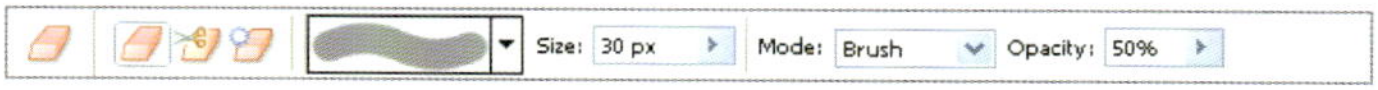

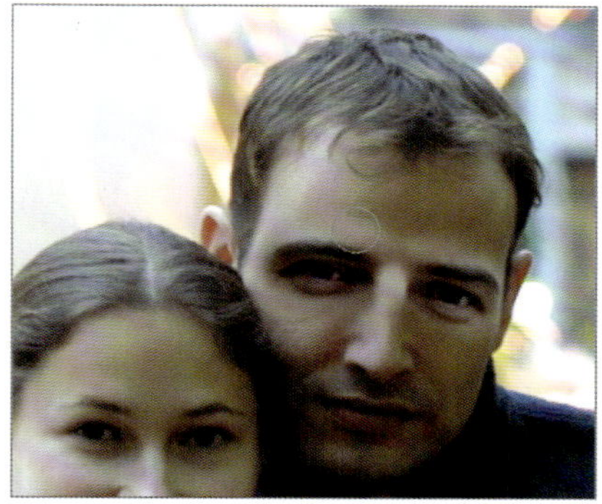

13 Use the Eraser Tool ( ) to erase as much of the skin as possible, leaving the eyes untouched.

This will minimize the difference in skin tone and make the face look more natural.

14 Press Ctrl + 0 to view the entire image.

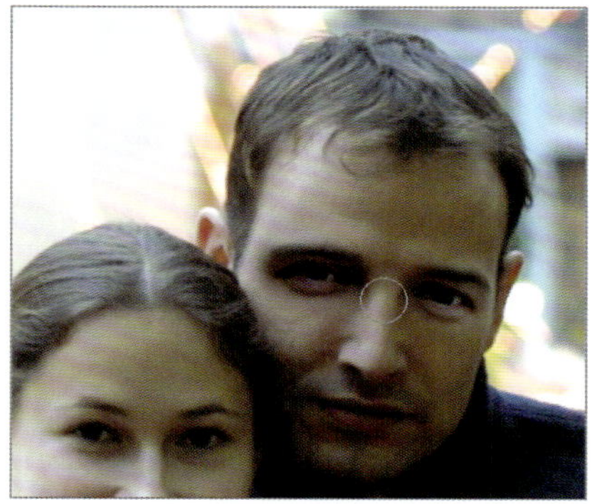

15 Select Layer > Flatten Image from the menu bar.

This combines the two layers into one.

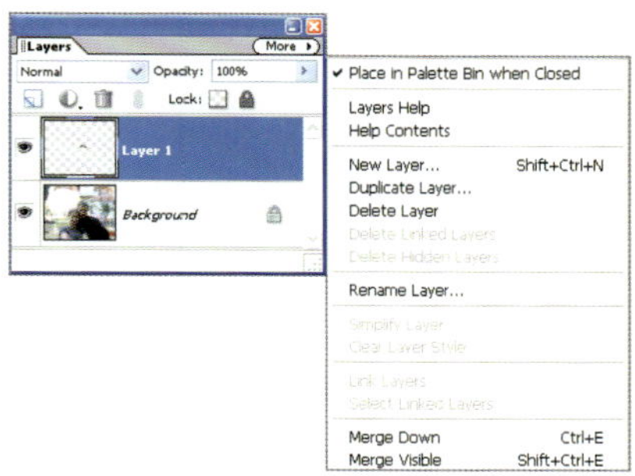

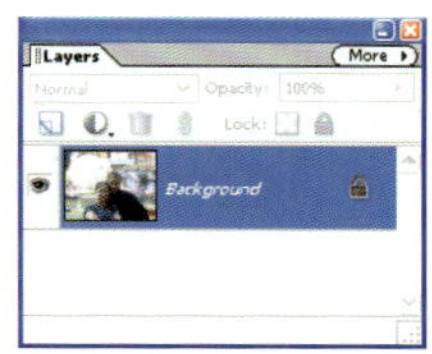

▲ Combining the two layers

20 Selective Focusing

Selective focusing is the photographic technique of keeping an area of the scene in focus while the rest of the scene is blurred. This technique has the effect of focusing the viewer's attention on a particular object or area of the image. If you are not using an SLR camera, this effect can be hard to create because the scene in your viewfinder will always look sharp. With Photoshop Elements, however, you can create such effects without the need for special lenses or equipment.

Before

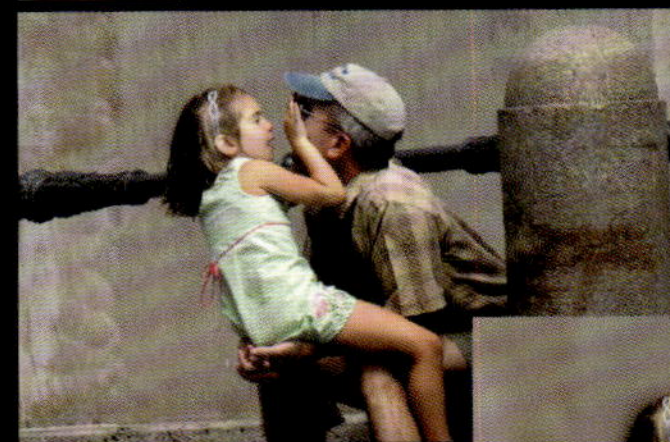

After

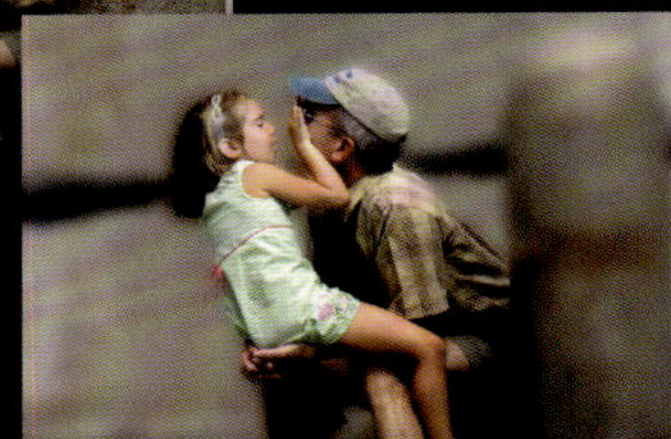

① From the menu bar, select File > Open.

The Open dialog box appears.

② Open the **Sample\Chapter 3\Tech20.jpg** file from the supplementary CD.

As you can see, the photographer has captured an intimate moment between father and child. This is a nice shot except that the background looks rather cold and drab. To fix this problem, let's blur out the background to give the image a softer feel and focus attention on the father and daughter.

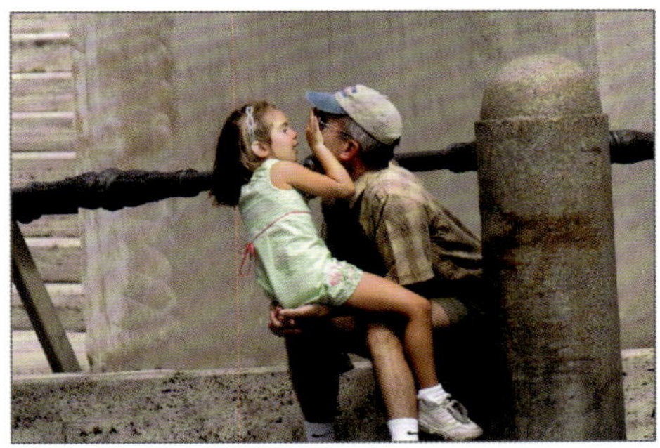

③ From the toolbox, select the Selection Brush Tool ( )and set the brush size to **35 pixels** in the options bar.

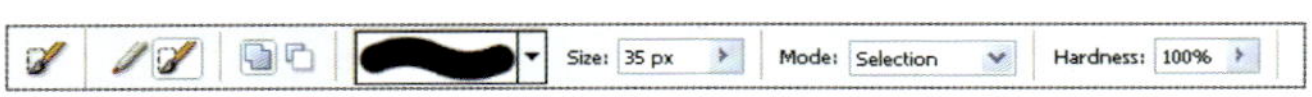

4 As shown below, drag over the subjects to select them. You may find it necessary to adjust the selection brush size as you go along.

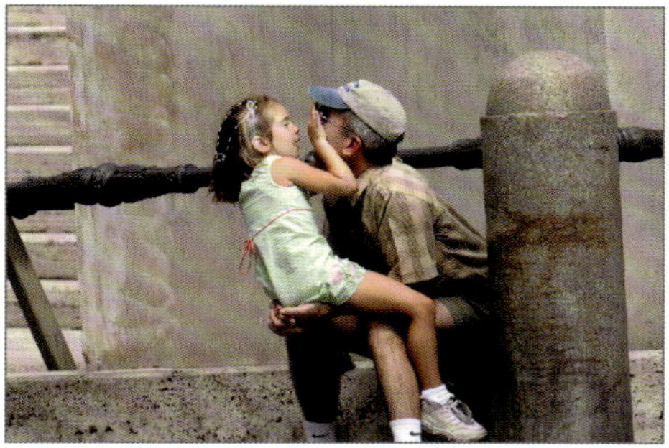

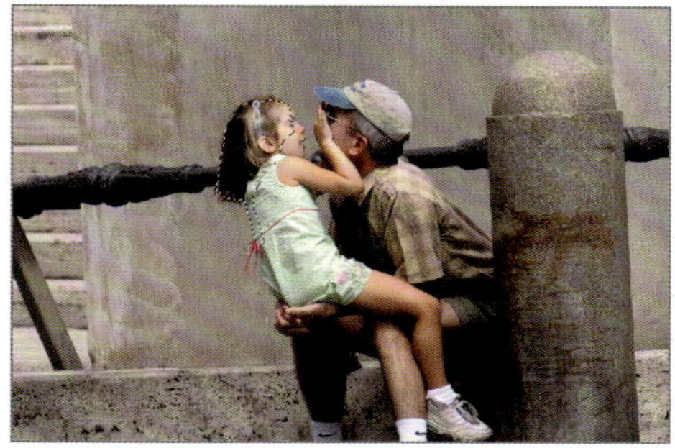

5 If you didn't select the ribbon on the girl's dress, select the Magnifying Tool ( ) from the toolbox and zoom in on the ribbon. Next, select the Selection Brush Tool ( ) and set the brush size to **6 pixels** in the options bar. Drag over the ribbon to select it.

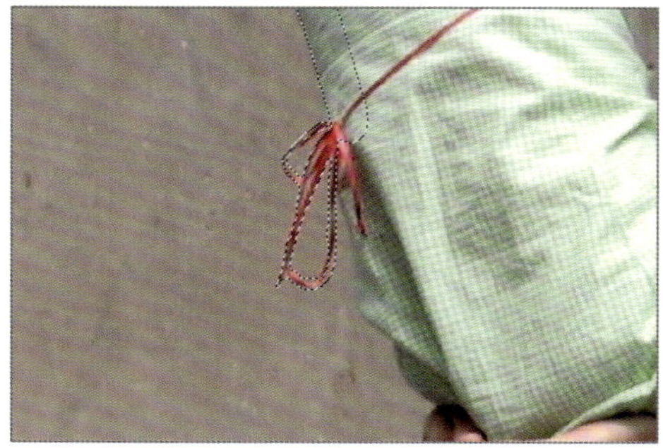

6 Let's deselect the gap between the two subjects. Holding down the Alt key, drag over the gap as shown.

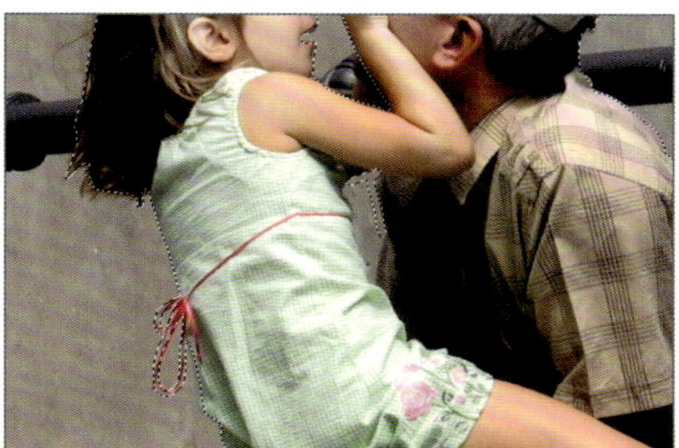

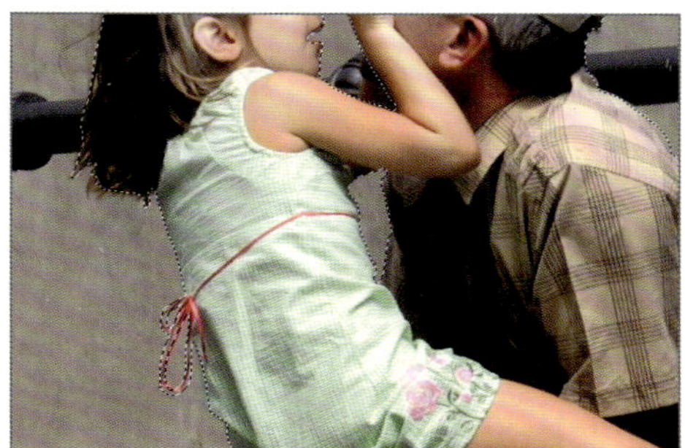

(7) On the menu bar, choose Select > Save Selection to save the selection. When the Save Selection dialog box appears, enter **People** in the Name field and click OK.

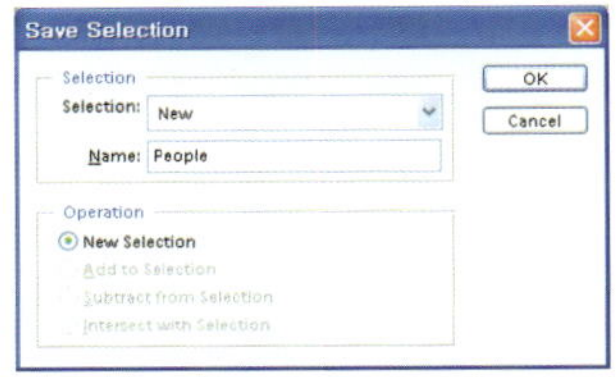

(8) In the Layers palette, click and drag the Background layer to the Create a New Layer icon ( ).

This will create a duplicate layer in the Layers palette.

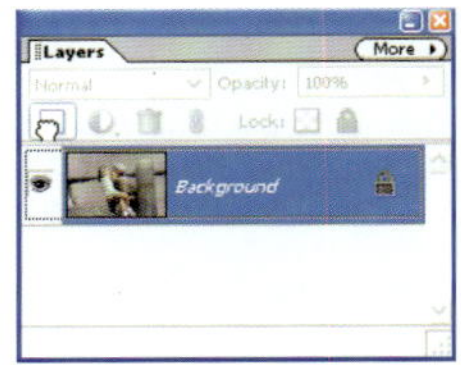

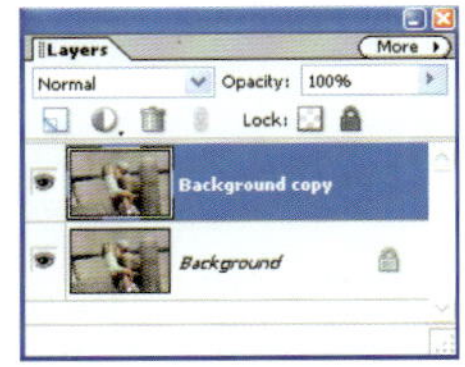

(9) Press Ctrl + D to deselect the two subjects. Select Filter > Blur > Gaussian Blur from the menu bar. In the Gaussian Blur dialog box, enter **20** in the Radius field and click OK.

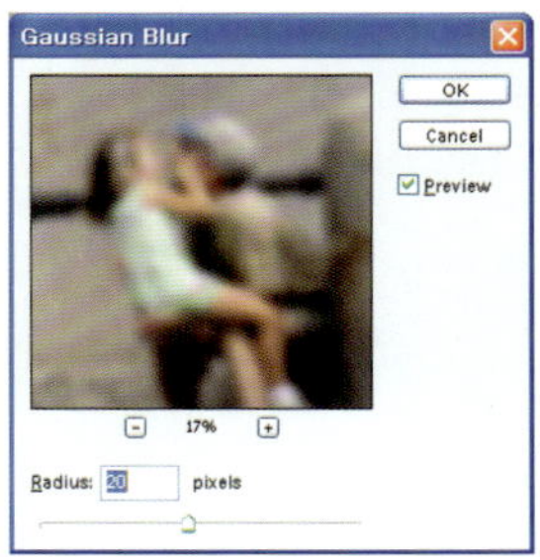

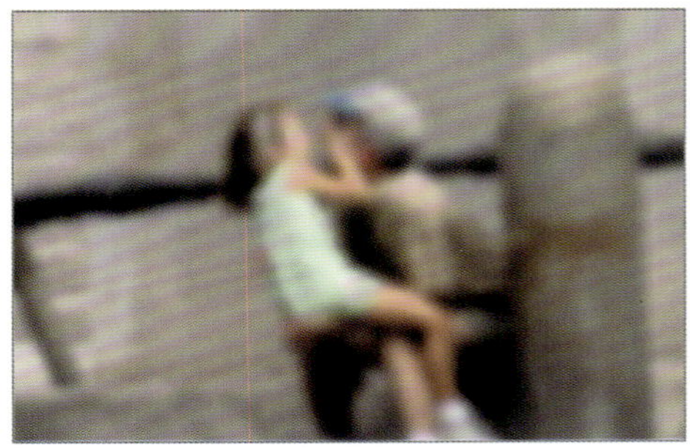

(10) Choose Select > Load Selection from the menu bar to use the selection border that you saved earlier. When the Load Selection dialog box appears, select **People** from the drop-down Selection menu and click OK.

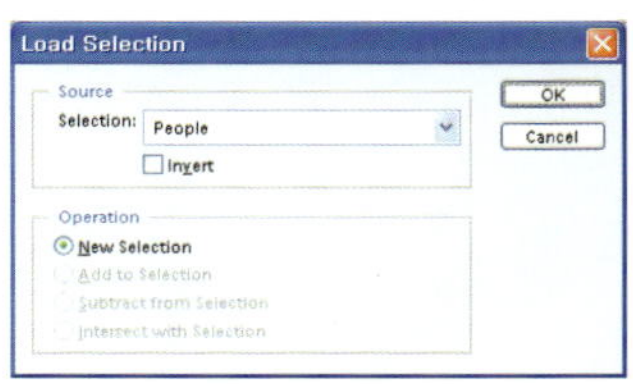

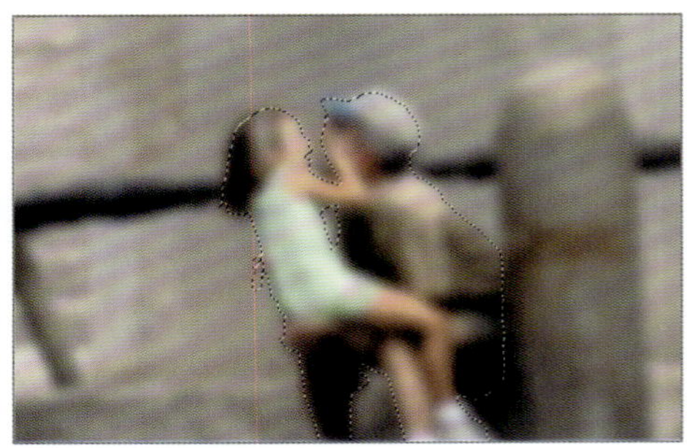

(11) On the menu bar, choose Select > Modify > Contract. In the Contract Selection dialog box, enter **3 pixels** in the Contract By field and click OK.

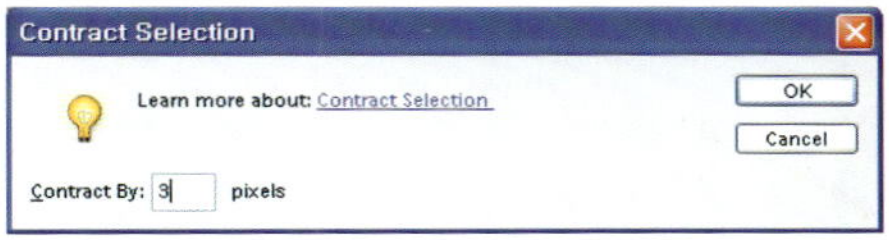

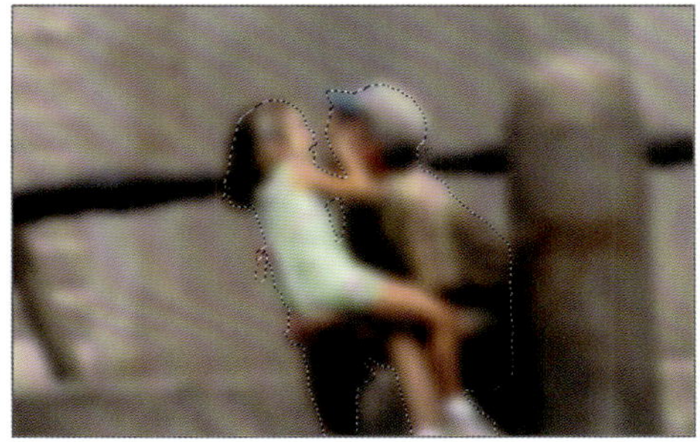

(12) Press the [Delete] key to delete the blurred subjects from the duplicate layer. This will let the subjects on the background layer show through. Press [Ctrl] + [D] to deselect the two subjects.

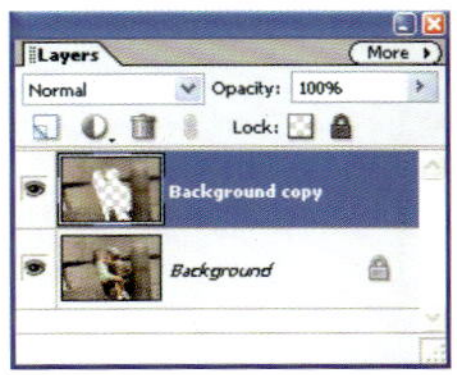

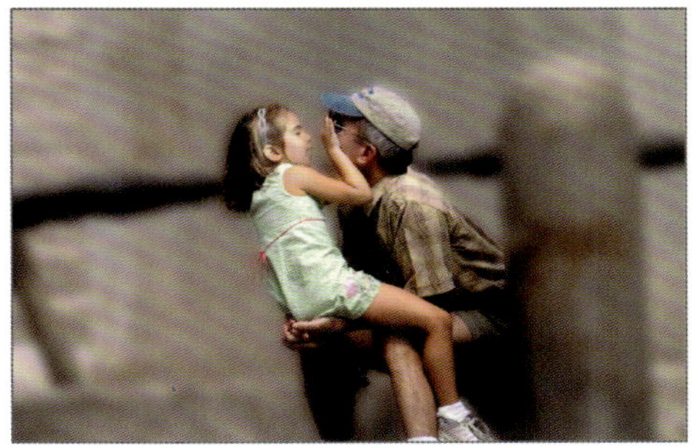

Note that the two subjects have a soft, natural-looking outline. This is the reason why the selection border had to be contracted in the previous step.

(13) In the Layers palette, click on the More icon ([More ▸]) at the top-right corner and select Flatten Image from the popup menu to merge the two layers into one.

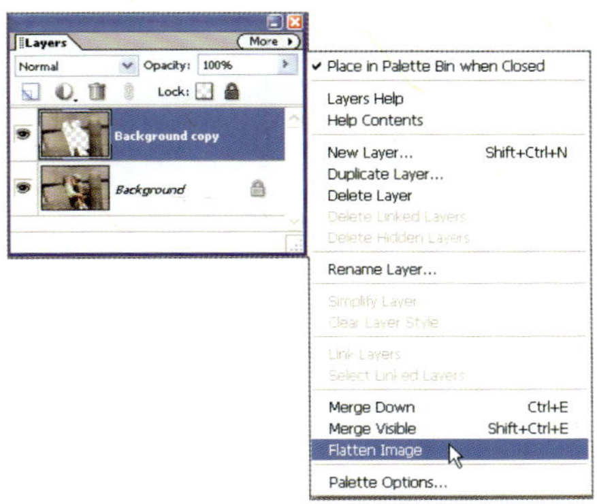

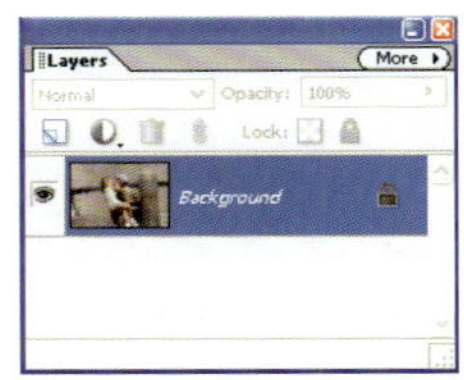

21 Creating a Studio Background and Picture Package

Before

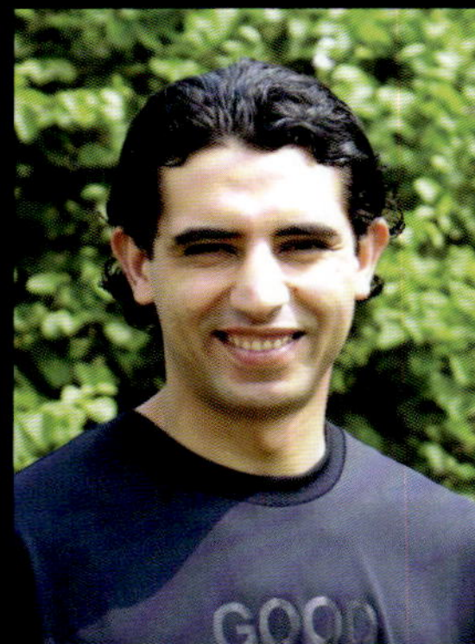

After

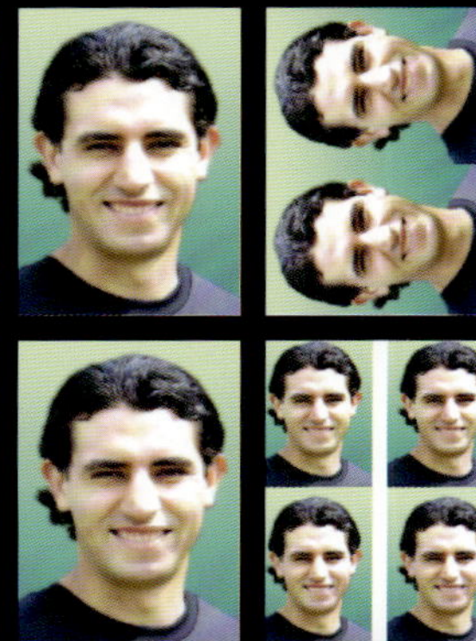

If you need a passport photo for your job application or other sorts of forms but you don't have one, you can take a good portrait shot of yourself and alter the background to make it look like a studio backdrop. With Photoshop Elements, you can even print a picture package that is a collection of the same picture in different sizes.

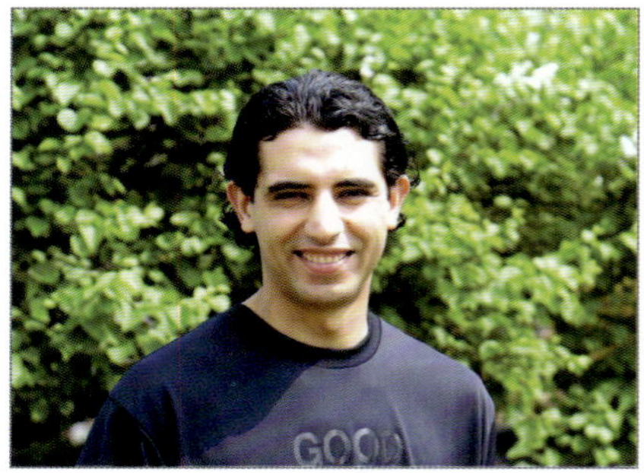

1. Select File > Open from the menu bar.

The Open dialog box appears.

2. Open the **Sample\Chapter 3\Tech21.tif** file from the supplementary CD.

tip It is best to take portraits indoors. Pictures taken outdoors are generally brighter, and the exposure is difficult to adjust when retouching.

3. Select the Crop Tool ( ) from the toolbox. In the options bar, set Width to **5 cm**, Height to **7 cm**, and Resolution to **200 pixels/inch**.

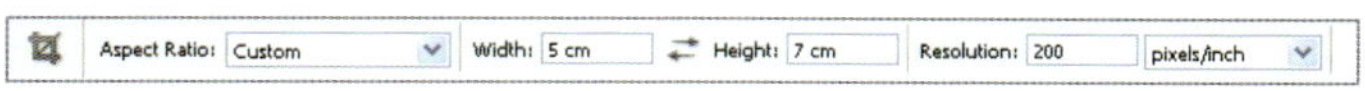

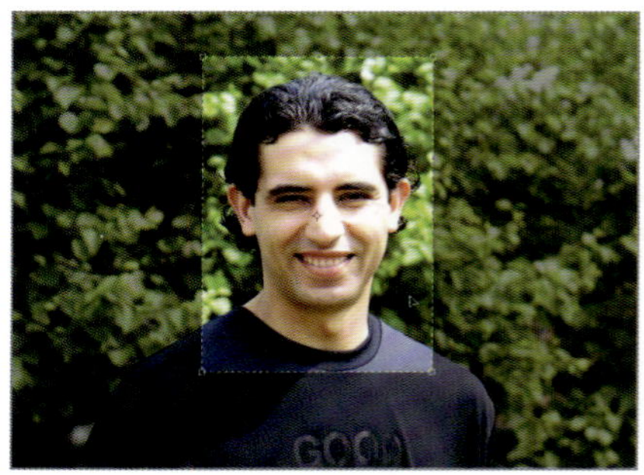

4. Click and drag over the image to produce a wallet-sized picture. Press Enter to crop the picture to the specified size.

Configuring the Crop Tool's options before cropping the image will save the settings so that the same settings can be used with the Crop Tool the next time. To clear the tool settings, click on Aspect Ratio from the Option bar, then select No Restriction.

Standard Portrait Sizes	
Half Wallet Pictures	3 cm×4 cm
Passport Pictures	3.5 cm×4.5 cm
Wallet Pictures	5 cm×7 cm

5 Now, we will remove any blemishes from the skin. Select the Clone Stamp Tool ( ) from the toolbox. In the options bar, set Size to **12 pixels**.

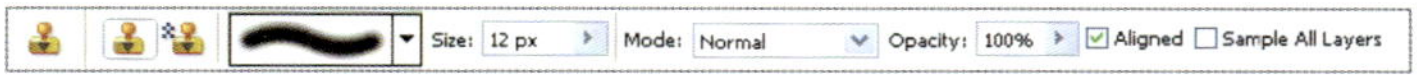

6 Hold down the Alt key and click on a patch of clear skin below the right eye to make a clone. Next, release the Alt key and stamp over the spots below the right eye.

Try to create the clone from a nearby spot for a close fit in terms of lighting and skin tone.

Zoom in on the image for delicate retouching work.

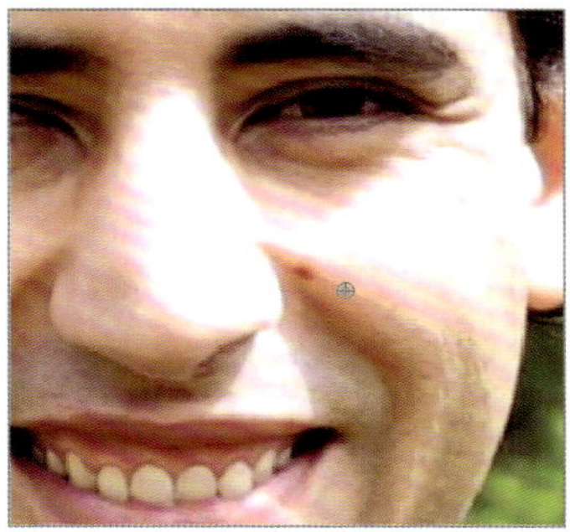

▲ Cloning a patch of skin

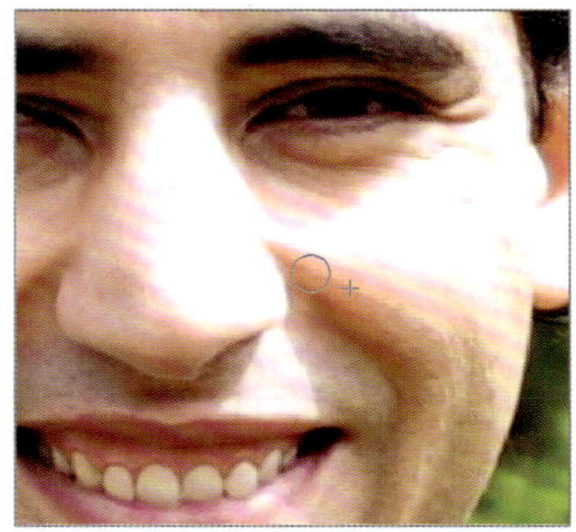

▲ Covering up a blemish

7 Hold down Spacebar to activate the Hand Tool. Move the image to see the forehead. Repeat step 6 to remove the spot on the forehead.

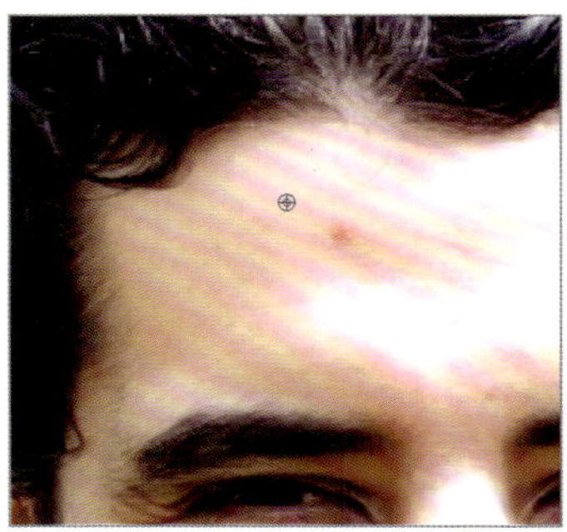

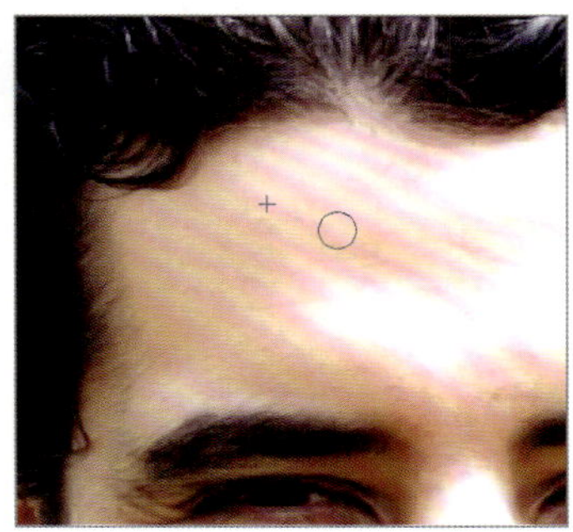

8 Repeat the previous steps until all the blemishes are removed from the face.

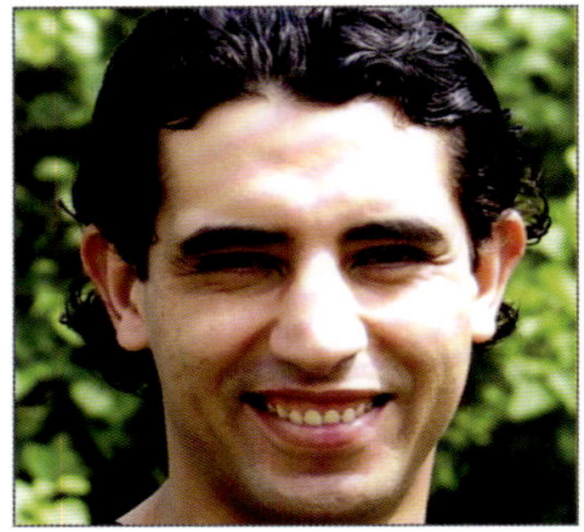

tip Avoid correcting large areas using the same clone patch. Make the changes progressively; change the brush size and use the Alt key to make a new clone each time.

9 Select the Dodge Tool ( ) from the toolbox. In the options bar, set Size to **100 pixels**.

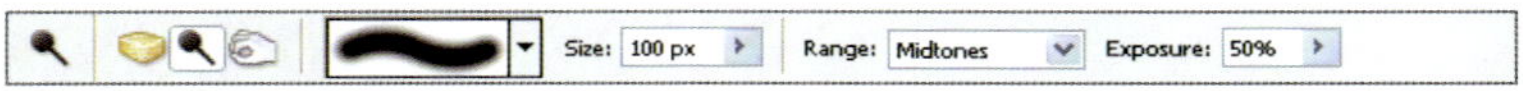

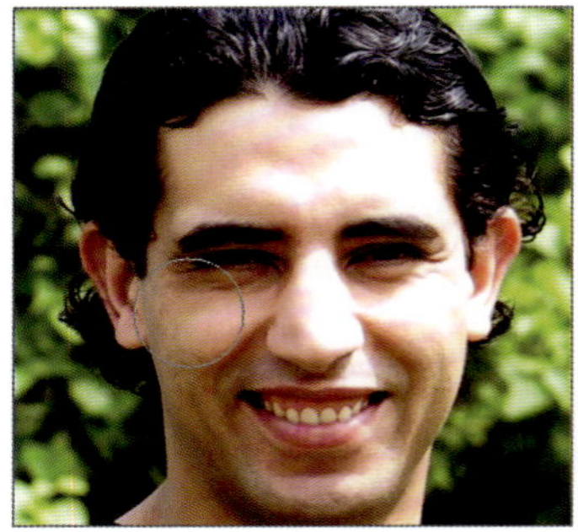

10 Click and drag the tool over the face and the hair to brighten up the entire image. As the left side of the face is darker, click and drag the tool over it a few more times to match the brightness on the right side.

tip The Dodge Tool is useful for adjusting different areas of an image to different levels of brightness, while the Levels menu applies the same brightness to the entire image.

11 Select Layer > Duplicate Layer from the menu bar to duplicate the Background layer. Click OK.

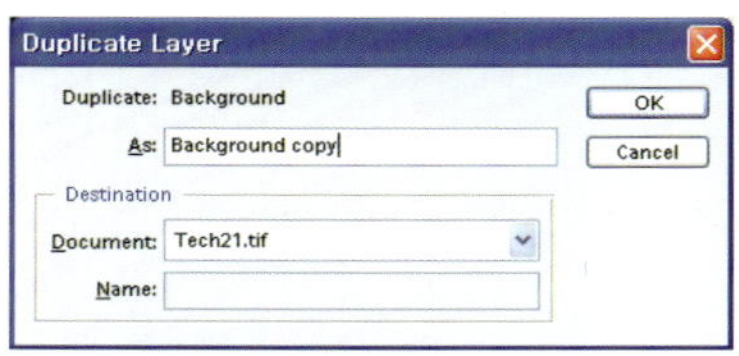

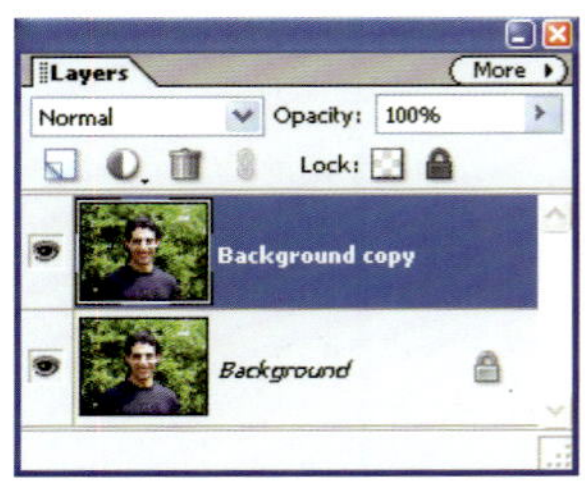

▲ The duplicate Background layer

12 Select the Smudge Tool ( ) from the toolbox. In the options bar, set Brush to **Soft Round**, Size to **70 pixels**, and Strength to **50%**.

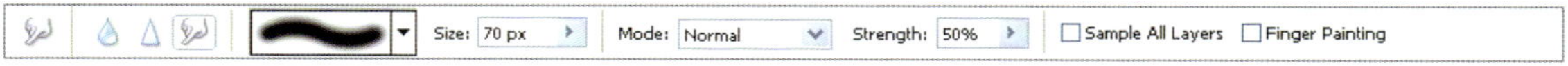

13 Click on the background some distance away from the subject, and drag outward to blur the background.

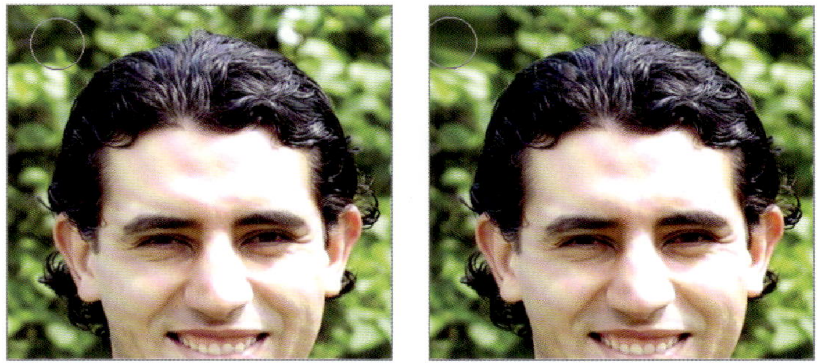

▲ Smudging the background

14 Repeat the process to smudge the area close to the subject.

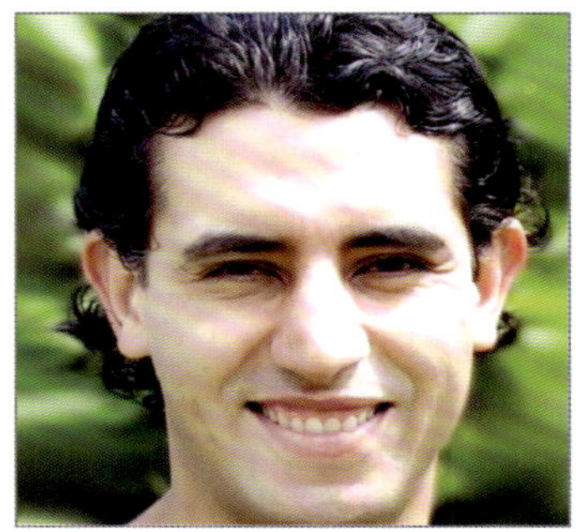

tip The Smudge Tool simplifies the background by combining surrounding pixels.

tip If you accidentally smudge the image of the subject, press Ctrl + Z to undo.

15 Now select the smudged background. First, select the Magic Wand Tool ( ) from the toolbox. In the options bar, set Tolerance to **70**.

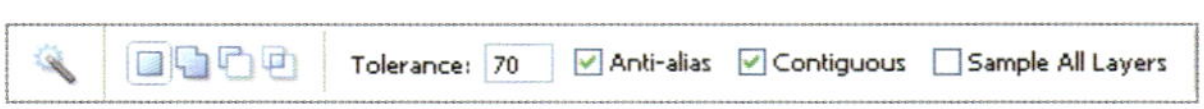

(16) Click on the background to select it.

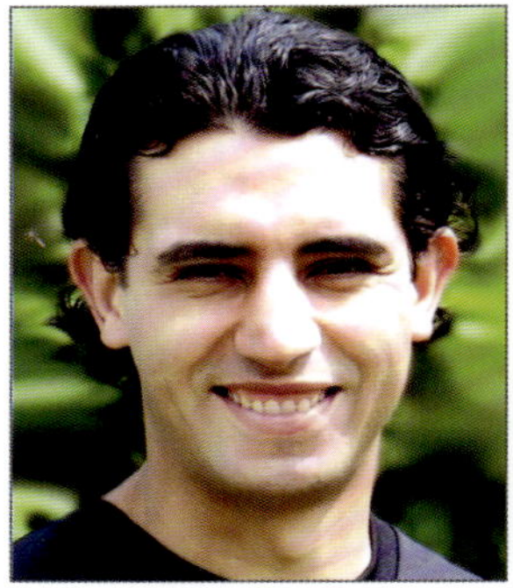

▲ Selecting the background using the Magic Wand Tool

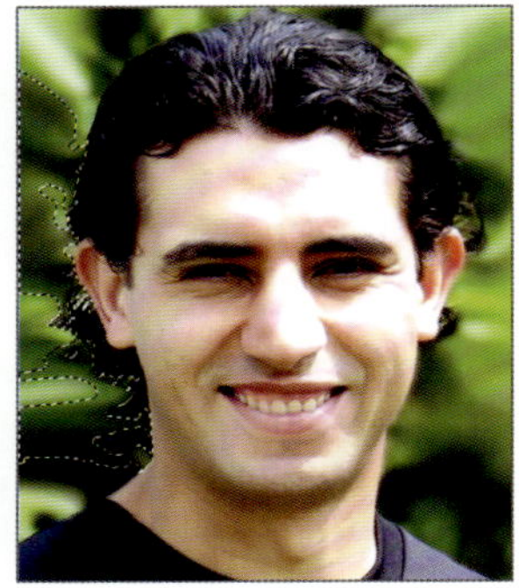

▲ The selection

(17) Hold down the Shift key and click on other parts of the background to add them to the selection.

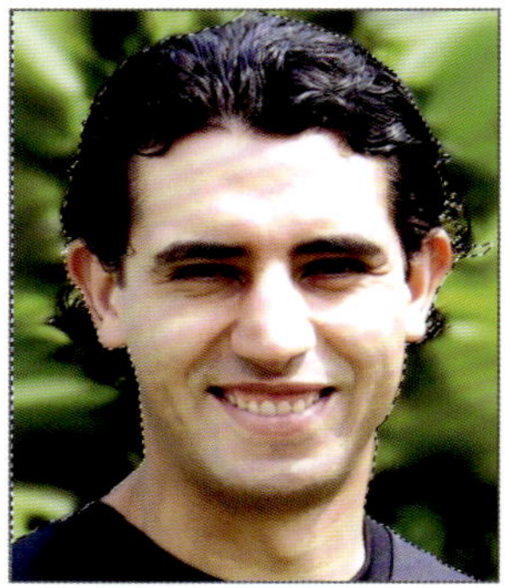

▼ Include only the background in the selection.

(18) If you accidentally select the model, remove the selection by holding down the Alt key and clicking on the image. To add more of the background, click on the desired area while holding down the Shift key. Repeat until all the background areas have been selected.

tip You should adjust the Tolerance value of the Magic Wand Tool to alter the size of the area selected (or deselected) with each click of the tool.

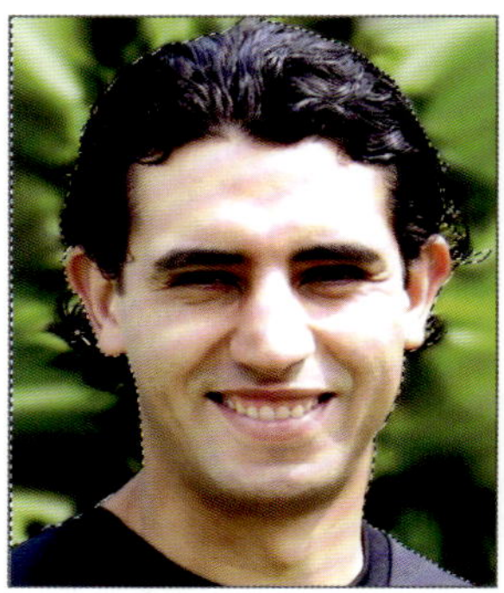

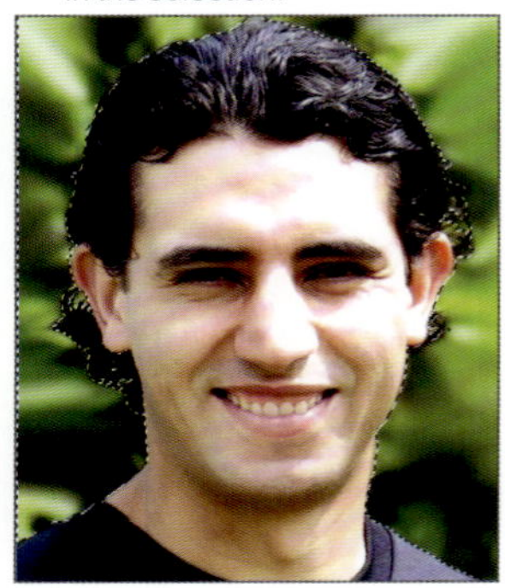

(19) Click on Select > Inverse from the menu bar to invert the selection.

Now the subject is selected instead.

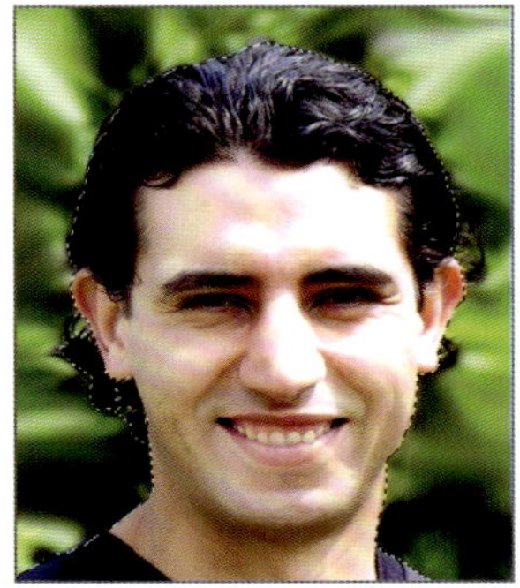

(20) Select Layer > New > Layer Via Copy from the menu bar to copy the selected image onto a new layer.

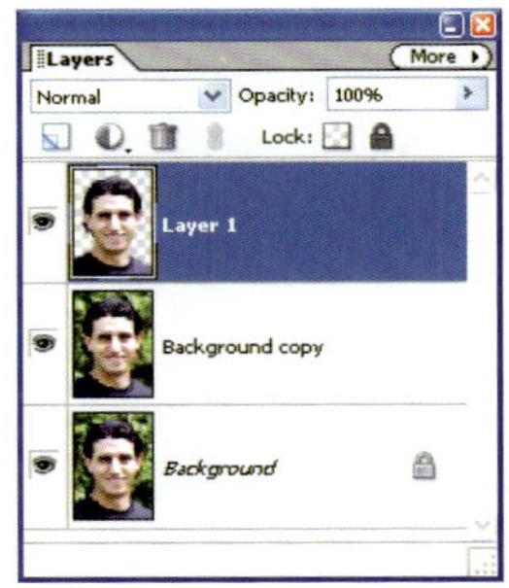

▲ Creating a new layer

(21) In the Layers palette, click the Indicate Layer Visibility option for all layers, except for Layer 1.

This hides all layers, except Layer 1.

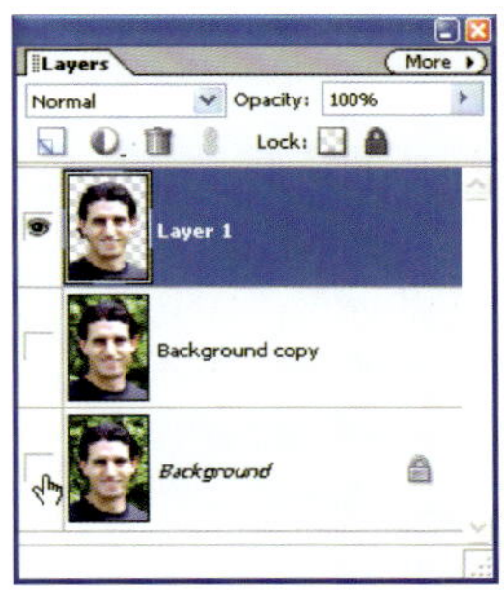

▲ Only Layer 1 is visible.

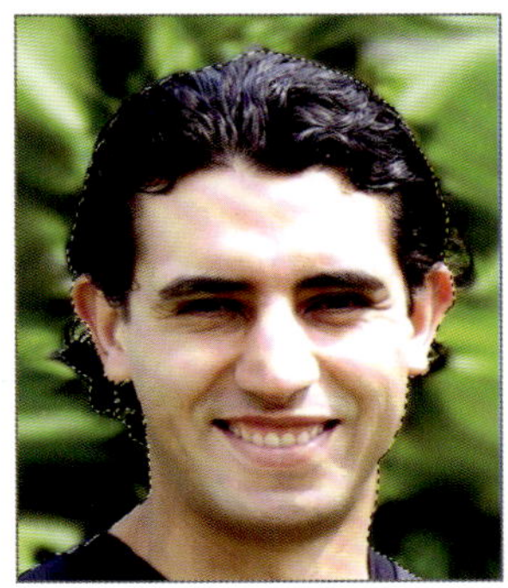

(22) Select the Eraser Tool ( ) from the toolbox. In the options bar, set Brush to **Hard Round** and Size to **20 pixels**.

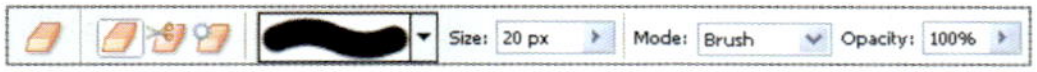

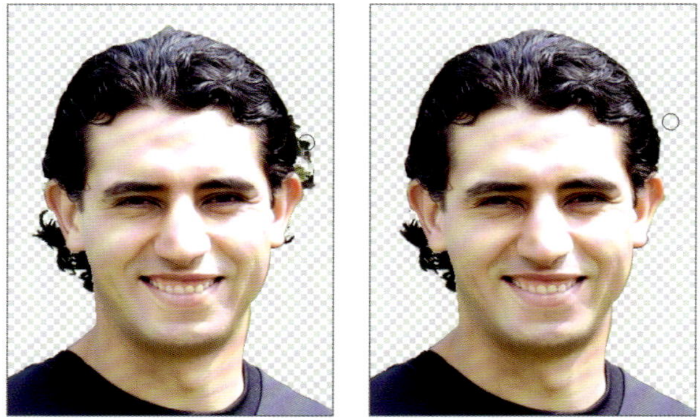

(23) Drag over the edges of the image to erase any remnants of the background. Make sure that the Eraser Tool is not applied to the face.

(24) Select the Background copy layer from the Layers palette.

(25) Click the Set Foreground Color icon in the toolbox. In the Color Picker dialog box, set the RGB values to **210**, **240**, and **180**. Click OK. Next, set the RGB values for the background color to **0**, **150**, and **150**.

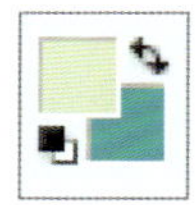

(26) Select the Gradient Tool ( ) from the toolbox. In the options bar, select **Linear Gradient** and set Opacity to **100%**.

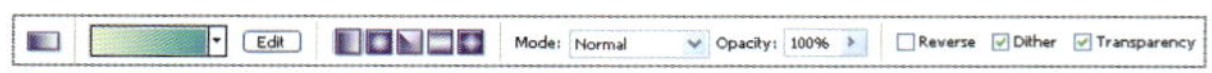

(27) Click and drag in a straight line from the top to the bottom to apply the gradient.

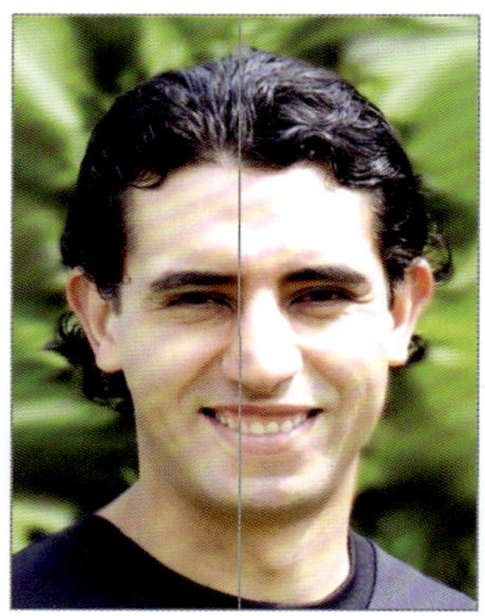

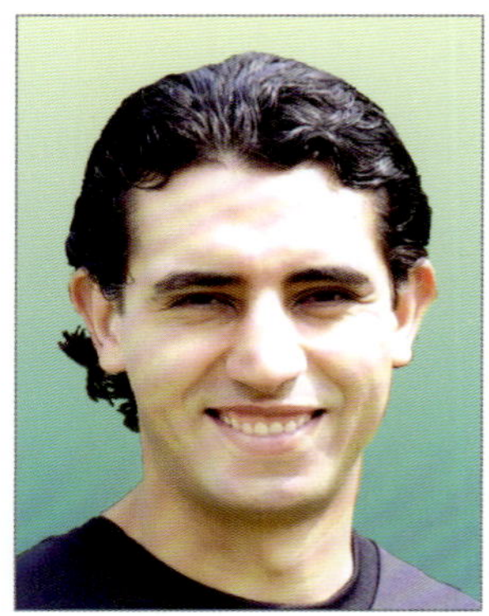

tip Check that the Background copy layer is selected in the Layers palette before applying the gradient.

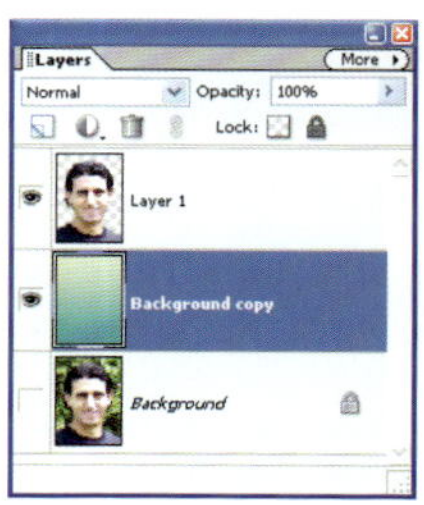

28 Next, we need to soften the edges of the face. Select Layer 1 from the Layers palette and click on the image while holding down the Ctrl key to select the face.

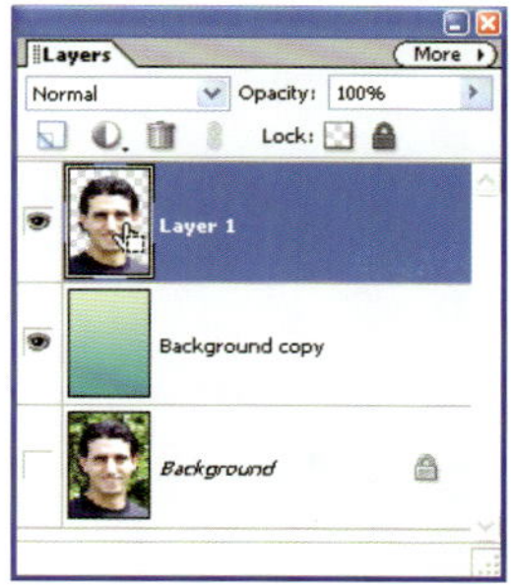

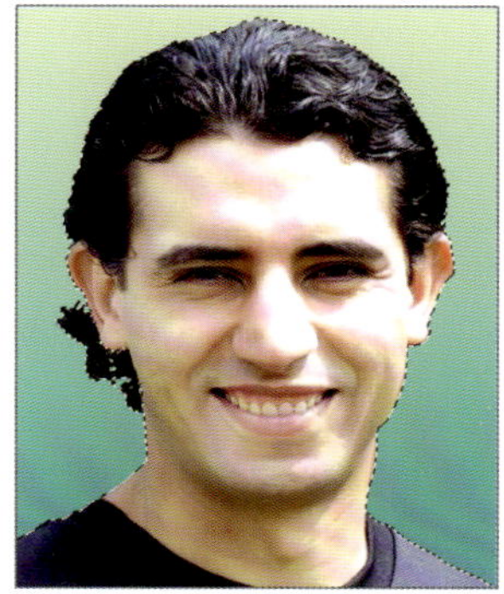

29 Click on Select > Modify > Contract from the menu bar to shrink the selection border. In the Contract Selection dialog box, set Contract By to **3**. Click OK.

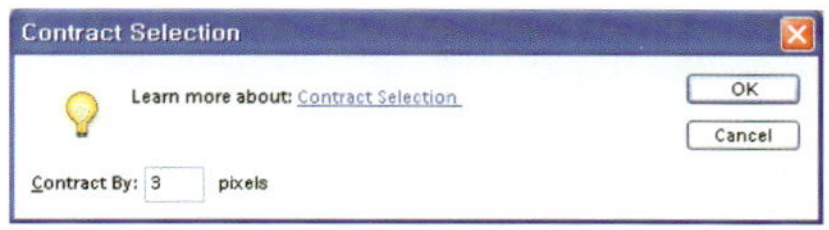

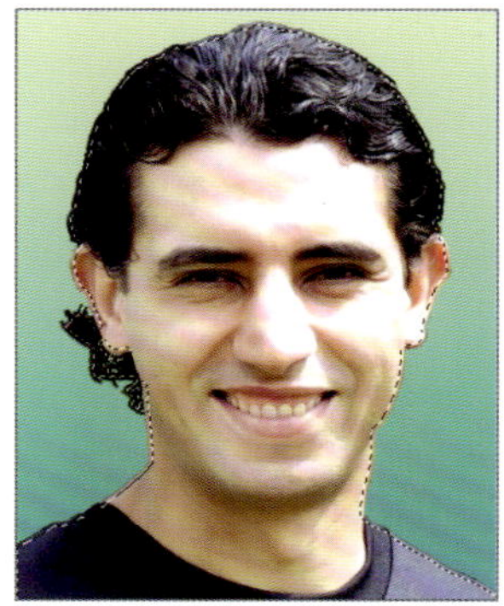

30 Choose Select > Feather from the menu bar. In the Feather Selection dialog box, set Feather Radius to **5**. Click OK.

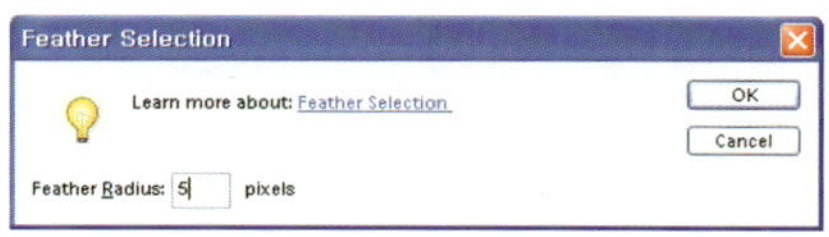

31 Choose Select > Inverse from the menu bar to invert the contracted selection border.

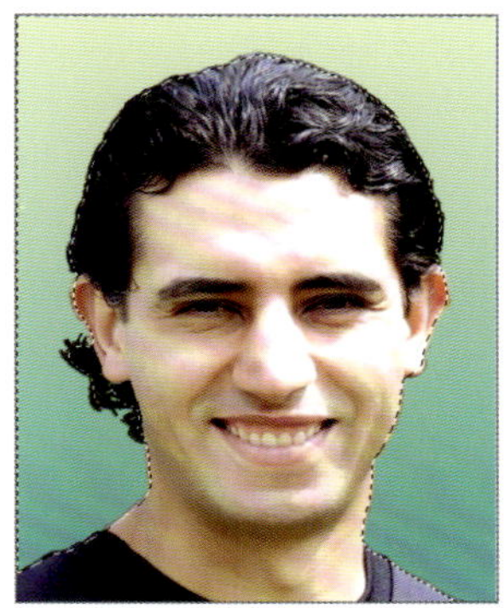

▲ Inverting the selection

(32) Click on Select > Filter > Blur > Gaussian Blur from the menu bar. The Feather Selection dialog box appears. Set Radius to **3**. Click OK.

This will blur the background.

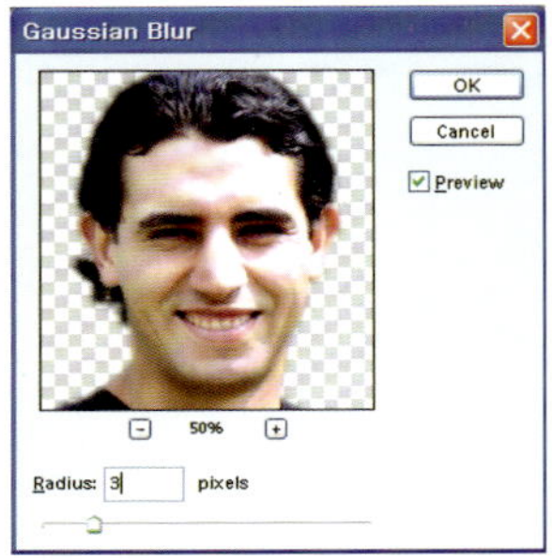

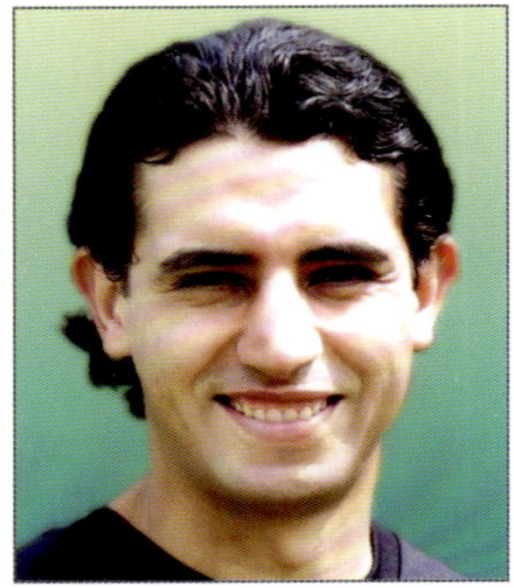

(33) Press Ctrl + D to deselect. In the Layers palette, drag Layer 1 onto the Create a New Layer button to make a copy of the layer.

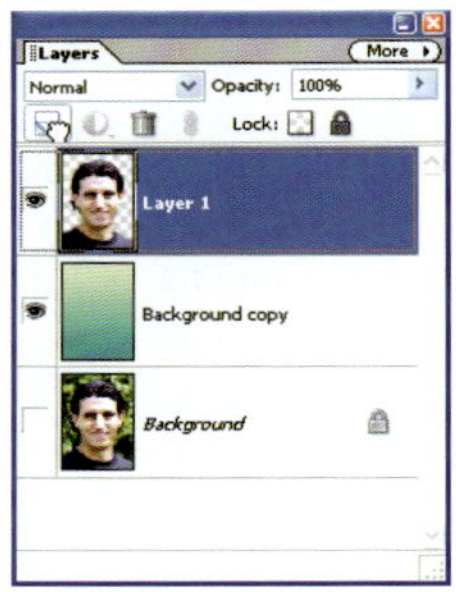

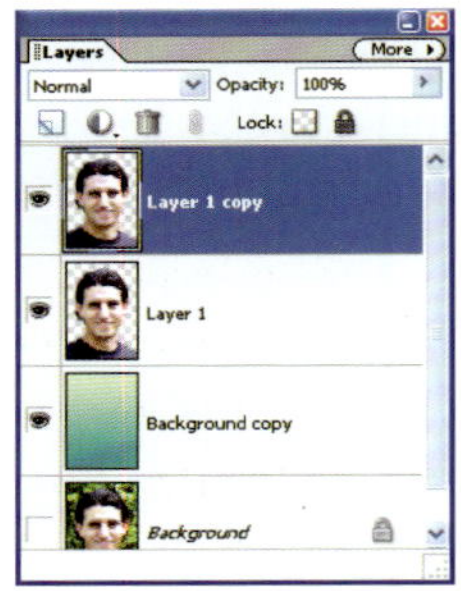

(34) Select the Layer 1 copy from the Layers palette. Click on Select > Filter > Blur > Gaussian Blur from the menu bar. In the Gaussian Blur dialog box, set the Radius to **3** and click OK.

This will blur the man.

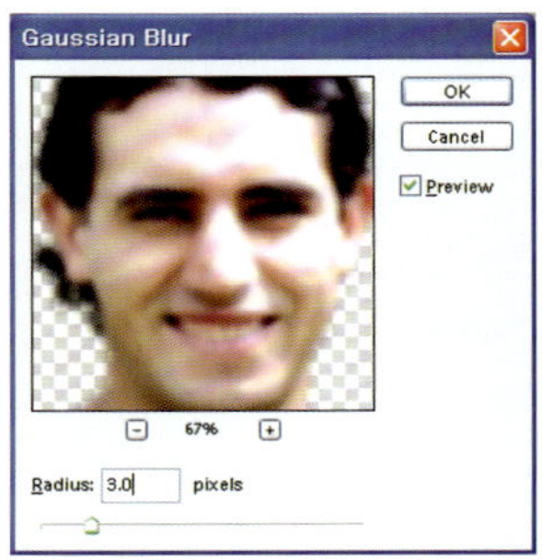

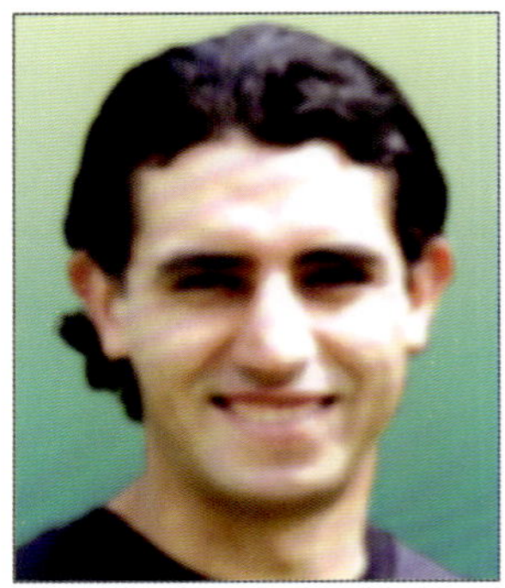

35 In the Layers palette, set Opacity to **40%** to soften the facial features.

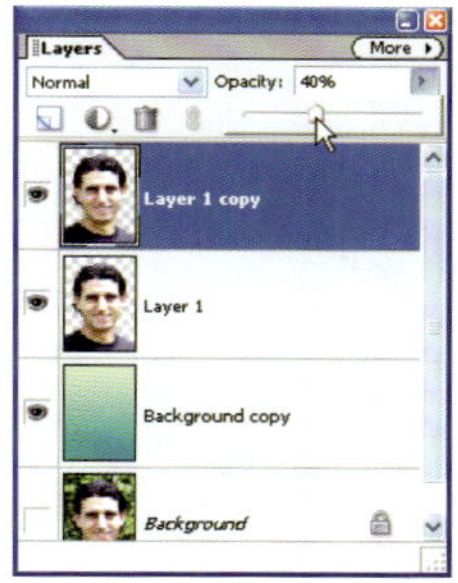

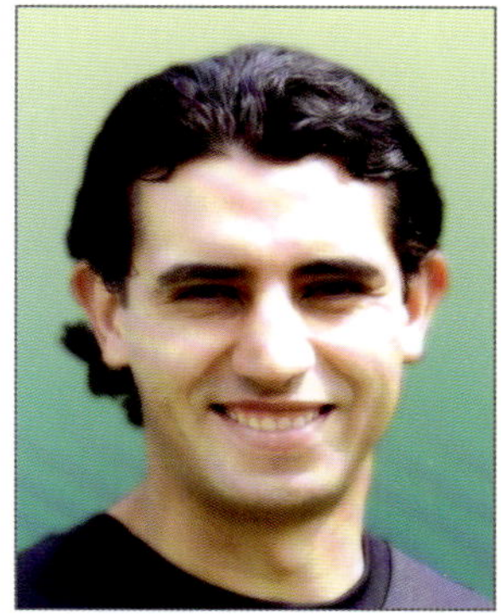

▲ The final image

36 Next, we'll print a complete set of portraits for various uses. Select File > Print Multiple Photos from the menu bar. In the Print Photos window, under Select Type of Print, click on Picture Package and match the Select a Layout selection shown in the screenshot to the right. Check the One Photo Per Page option to see many pages of images.

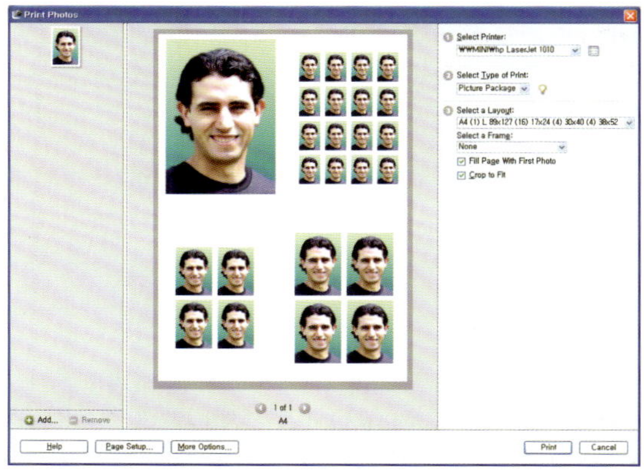

tip The Select a Frame menu offers a variety of different frames and borders to embellish images.

37 Click on Print to print out the images in various sizes.

22 Adding a Picture Frame

Before

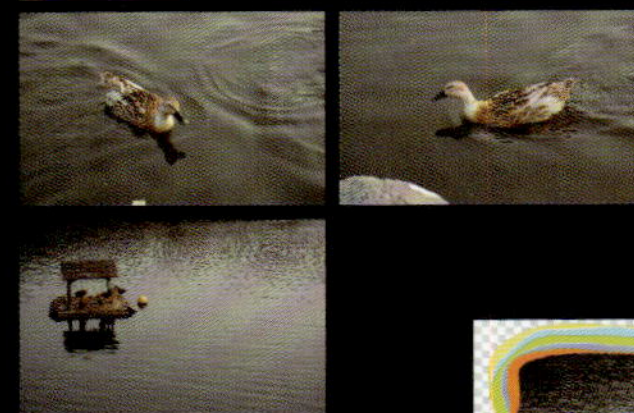

After

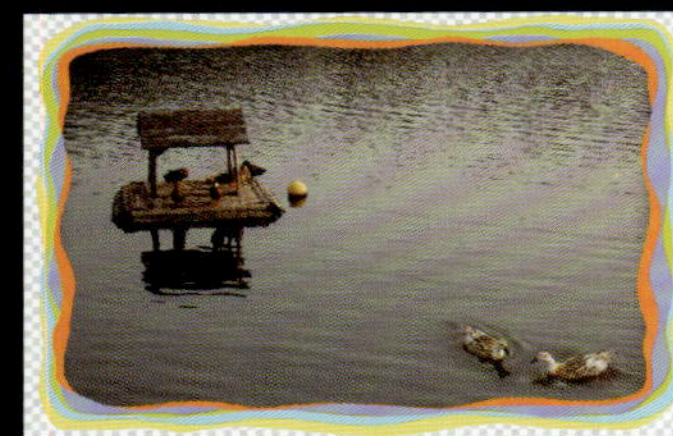

In this section, you will learn to combine images of ducks with a picture of a lake before framing it with one of the 15 default frames found in the Effects palette. You will adjust the contrast and feather the selection edges in order to blend the images together flawlessly. As you shall see, there are many interesting frames, from brushed aluminum to spatter, to choose from.

1. Open the **Sample\Chapter 3\Tech22a.tif** file from the supplementary CD.

2. Click on Selection Brush Tool ( ) from the toolbox. Set the Size to **100**, Mode to **Selection**, and Hardness to **0** in the Option bar.

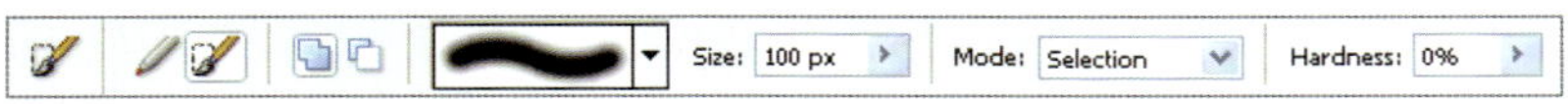

3. Now, click and drag the mouse over the duck and its shadow, including the water around the duck as shown below. Press Ctrl + C to copy the selected area.

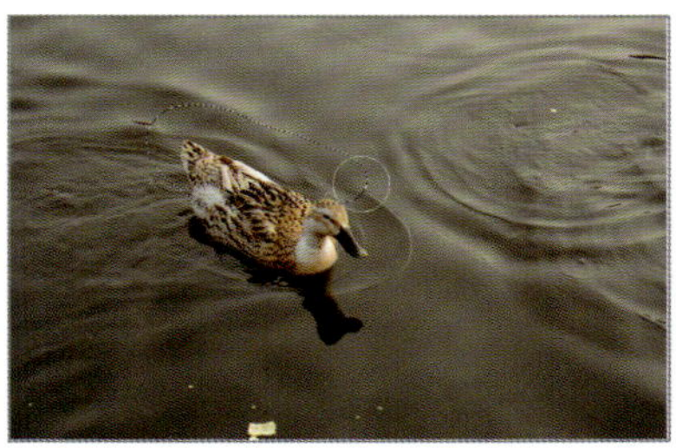

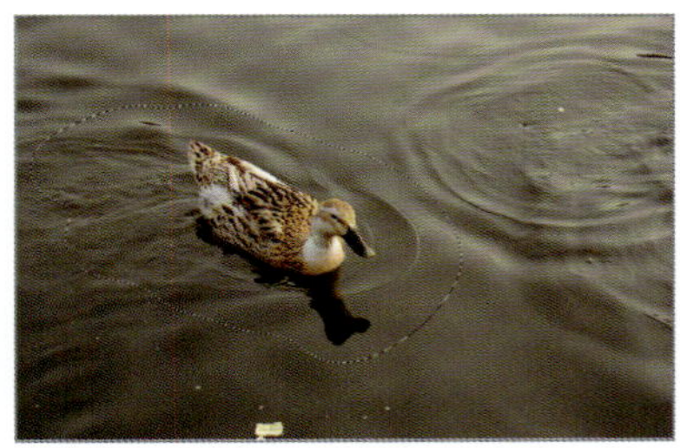

(4) **Open Sample\Chapter 3\Tech22.jpg** file from the supplementary CD. Press Ctrl + V to paste the saved selected area from step 3. You can see that a layer titled **Layer 1** has been created in the Layer Pallet for **Tech22.jpg** file.

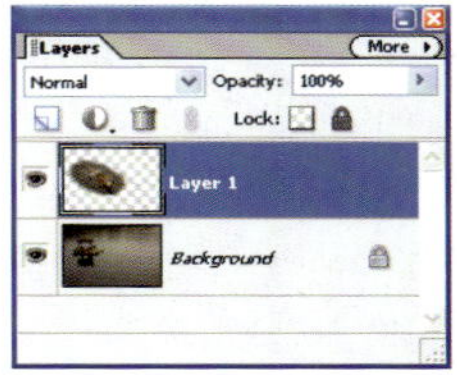

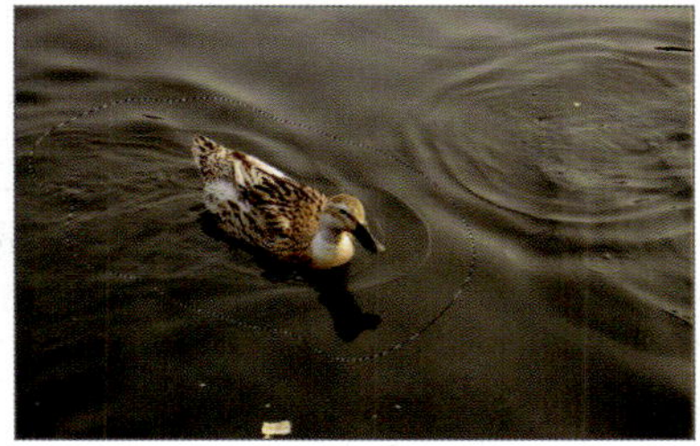

tip After copying the selected image, close the Tech22a.tif file.

(5) Open **Sample\Chapter 3\Tech22b.jpg** file from the supplementary CD and repeat step 3.

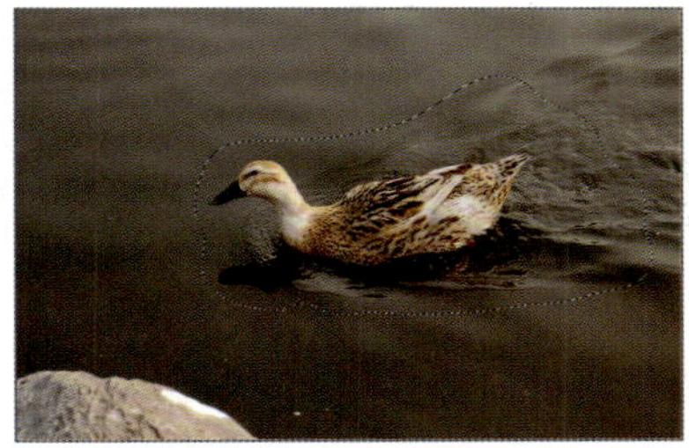

(6) Press Ctrl + V to paste the saved selected image from step 5 into **Tech22.jpg** and close the **Tech22b.jpg** file. You can see that a layer titled **Layer 2** has been created in the Layer Pallet.

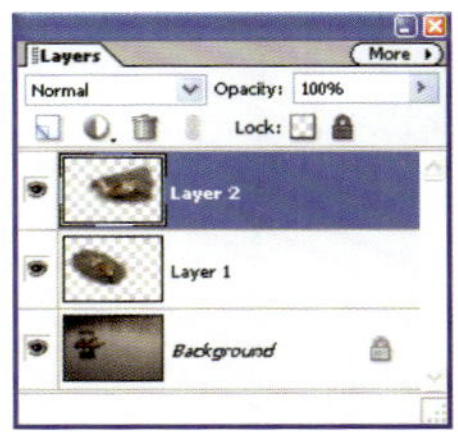

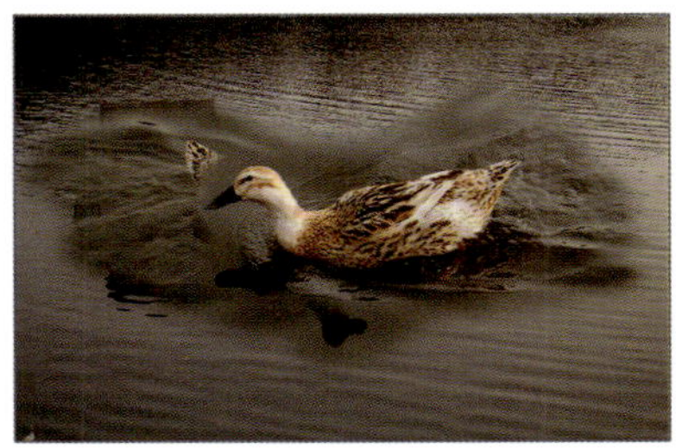

(7) While **Layer 2** is selected, hold down the Shift key and click on **Layer 1**. Now both layers are selected.

(8) Now the sizes of the copied images need to be decreased. Press Ctrl + T and a bounding box appears as seen in step 9.

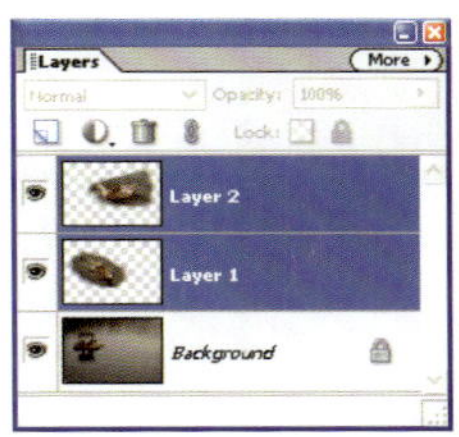

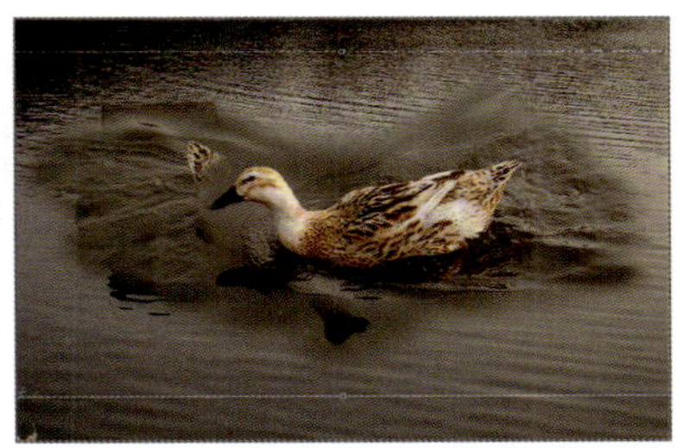

9 Bring the mouse to the corner of the bounding box. While holding down the Shift key, click and drag inward to decrease the size. Holding down the Shift key will keep the ratio of the image constant. Move the pasted images to the bottom right, as shown below, by bringing the mouse inside the bounding box, then clicking and dragging it.

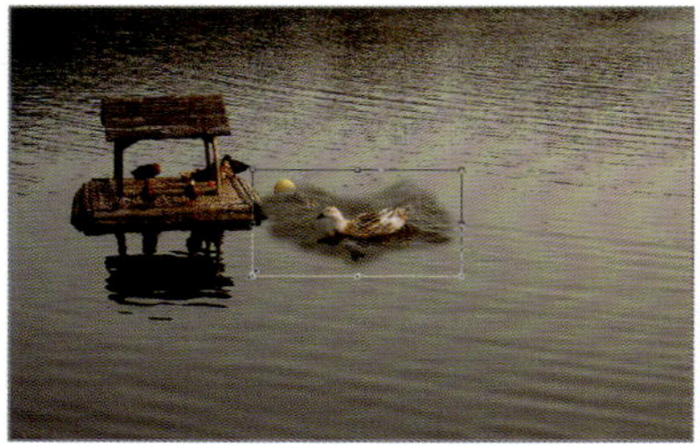

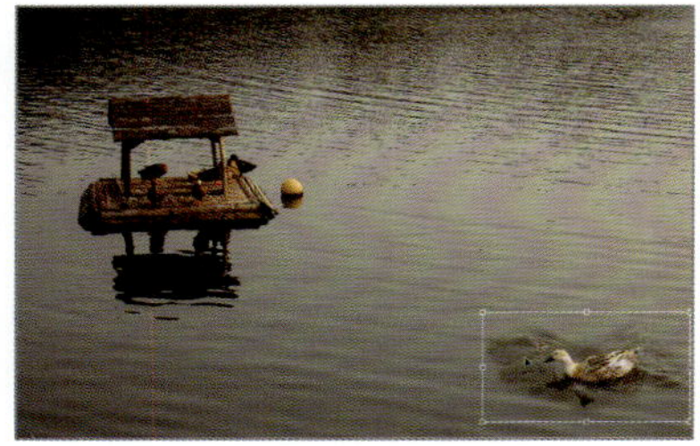

10 Click on the Move Tool ( ) in the tool box. Select one layer at a time, then position each pasted image as shown.

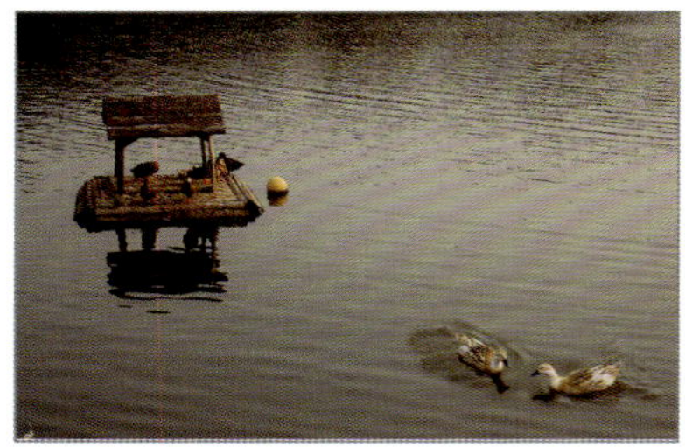

11 Click on the Eraser Tool ( ) from the tool box. As shown, click on the drop-down menu for the brush presets. Set the Brushes to **Default Brushes**, then click on the **65 Soft Round**. Now set the Opacity to **50**.

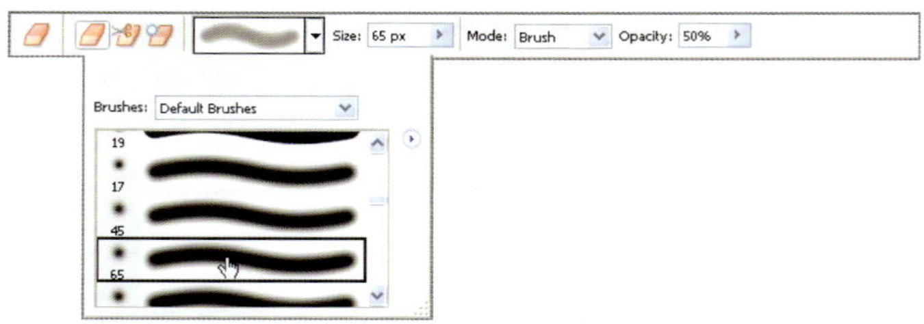

(12) Select each layer and erase the surrounding area of the selected images. The water around the ducks will look more natural.

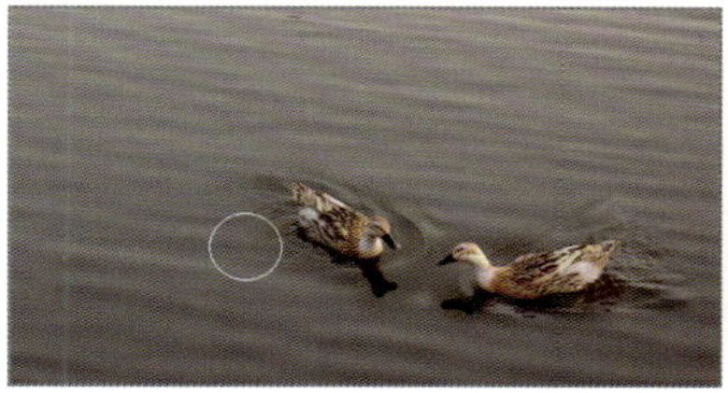

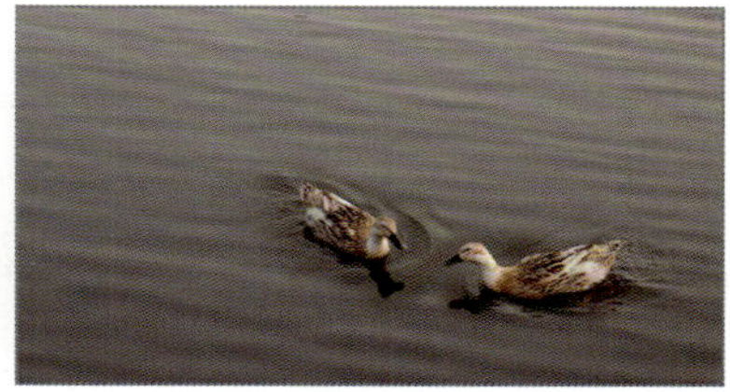

(13) Click on Window > Artwork and Effects. After selecting Artwork from the Artwork and Effects palette, select Frames from the left drop-down menu and **Colorful** from the right drop-down menu. Now double-click on **Groovy** from the list, or click once and then click on Apply.

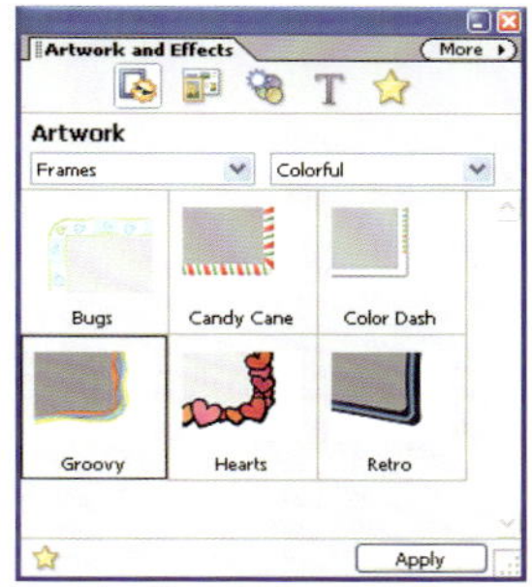

(14) The Groovy frame is applied to the image as shown here. Right-click on the image, then select **Fit frame to photo** from the Context Menu. This will automatically adjust the frame size to fit the image.

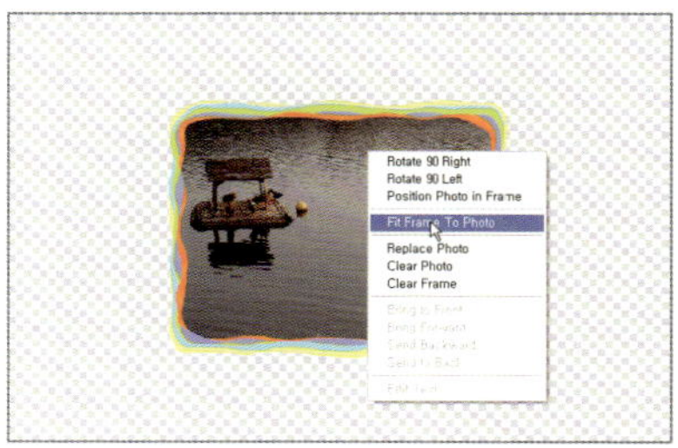

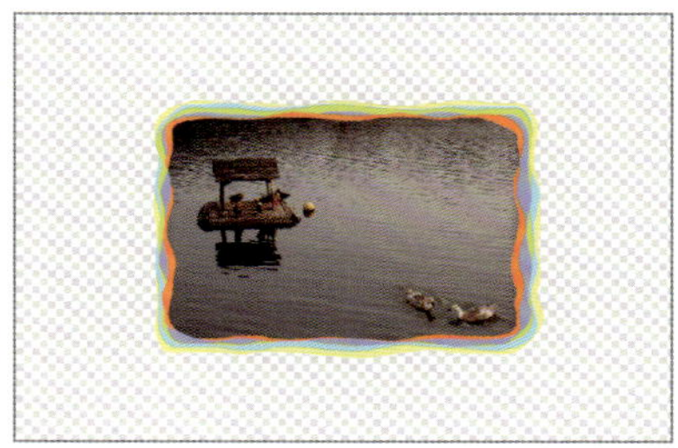

(15) You can see that the frame has resized to fit the image. By using the Free Transform tool, or Ctrl + T, you can adjust the size of the completed image by dragging on the corner handle of the bounding box.

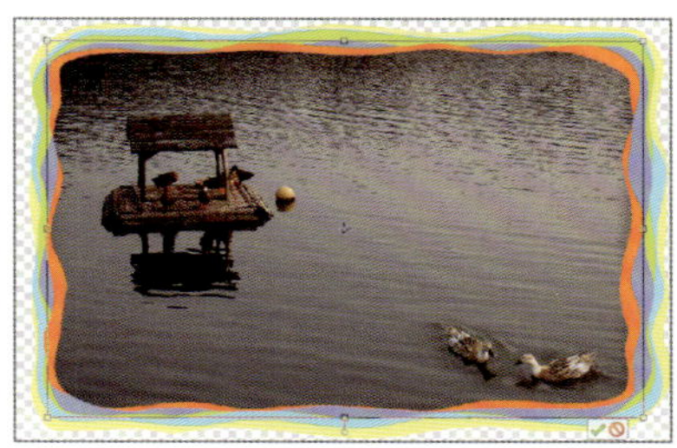

40 Digital Photo Retouching Techniques

with Photoshop Elements 5.0

Chapter 4

Editing Skills and Special Effects

In this chapter, you will learn essential editing skills for working with all kinds of images. For instance, you will see how to split a scan of multiple images into individual files. We'll also work with raw image files from digital cameras. Following that, you will learn how to adjust image size and shape, straighten distorted images, remove elements from an image, combine images, and more.

23 Automatically Separate Scanned Images

Photoshop Elements 5.0 has the wonderful new Divide Scanned Photos command, which will save you a lot of time in scanning pictures and straightening scanned images. Instead of scanning and straightening pictures one at a time, you can scan a few pictures at one go and then select the Divide Scanned Photos command to split the scanned image into individual image files. Photoshop Elements will automatically crop and straighten the images. It takes only one click!

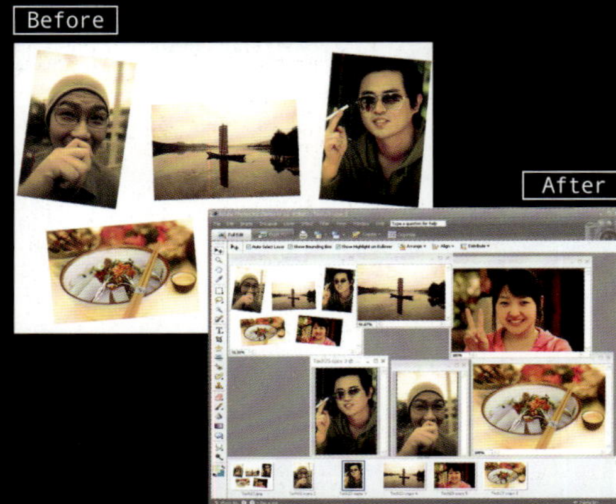

(1) Open the **Sample\Chapter 4\Tech23.jpg** file from the supplementary CD.

The image is made up of five pictures that were scanned together. Note that all of the scanned images are slanted in one way or another.

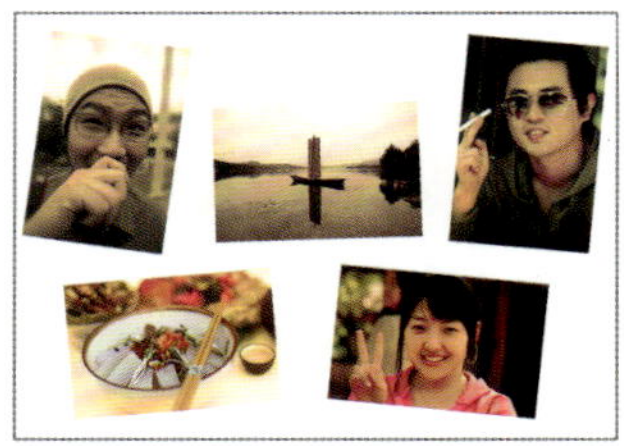

(2) Select Image > Divide Scanned Photos from the menu bar to split up the five images into individual image files.

In the Photo Bin, you can see that the scanned images have been split into individual image files. If the Photo Bin is not open, click on the Toggle Photo Bin button ( ) at the bottom of the window.

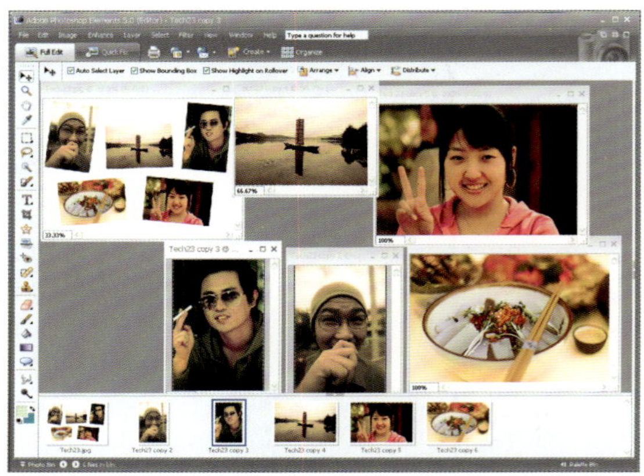

24 Opening and Processing a Camera Raw Image File

This feature is useful for photographers who use mid- to high-end camera models that record images in the raw format. Beginners should note that entry-level cameras store files of various resolutions using the JPEG format—not raw. Regardless of the camera that you use, you will learn to open and process a raw image file using the provided sample file.

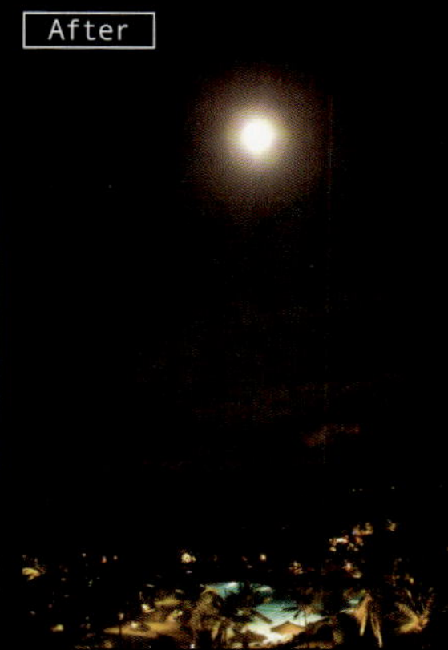

Why Use Camera Raw?

Professional photographers prefer to work in the raw format because raw files, unlike JPEG files, receive almost no processing in the camera. A raw file records an image as it was taken, without the camera automatically sharpening or adjusting the white balance, for instance. This gives the photographer greater control over the image. Another important difference is that raw files are stored in 12-bit mode, while JPEG files are only 8-bit. This essentially means that raw files are of a much higher quality than JPEG files. With the superior quality of raw images, you can do more extensive editing in Photoshop Elements because there is more data to work with. With JPEG files, you cannot edit the image as freely because an extended editing process can seriously degrade the image quality.

1. Open the **Sample\Chapter 4\Tech24.CRW** file from the supplementary CD.

2. The file will not open directly in Photoshop Elements' image window. Instead, the file will appear in the Camera Raw dialog box that opens immediately after step 1. The title bar of the dialog box contains information on the image, such as the make and model of the camera used to capture the image and the settings or conditions under which the image was taken.

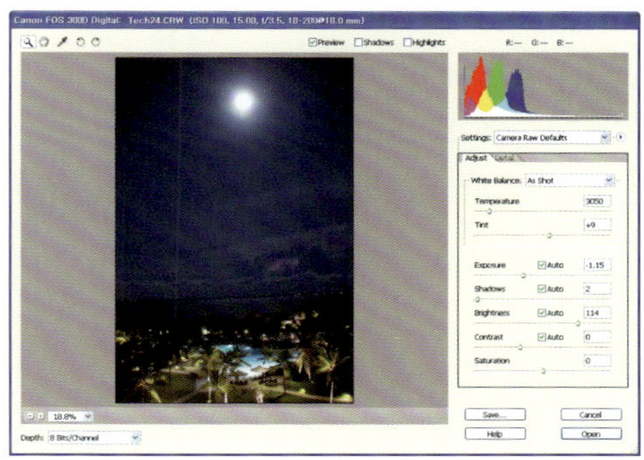

③ Because the image looks washed out, select Flash from the White Balance drop-down menu. If the Preview box is checked, you will see that the image now looks darker in the preview window.

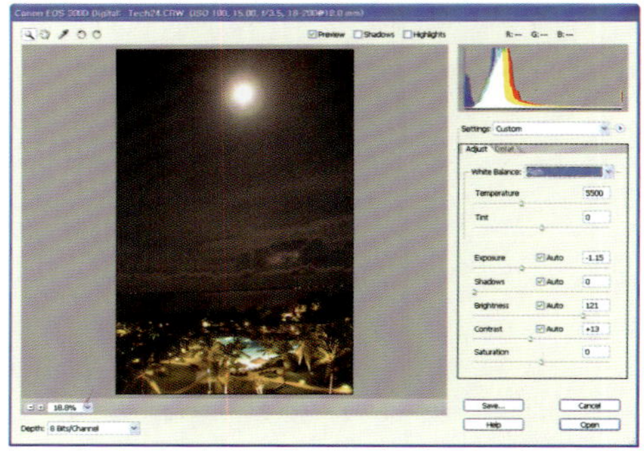

④ The image still looks a little dull. Let's increase the contrast. Set the Contrast to **50** and the Brightness to **90**. You can see in the preview window that the image appears sharper than before.

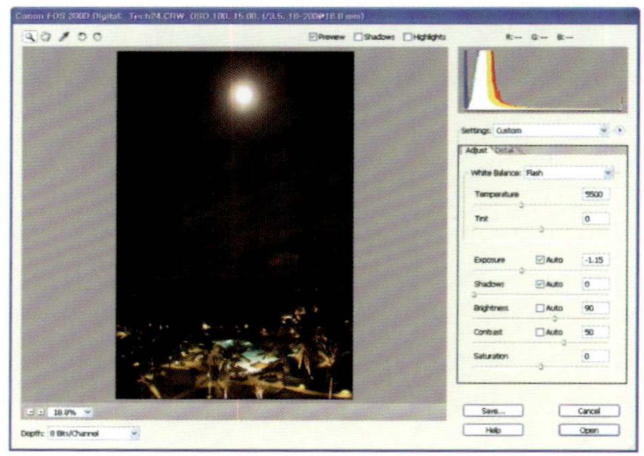

⑤ Click Open. The modified image will open in Photoshop Elements' image window. You can then edit the file as you would any other.

⑥ When you are done editing, select File > Save As from the menu bar to save the image as a JPEG or TIFF file.

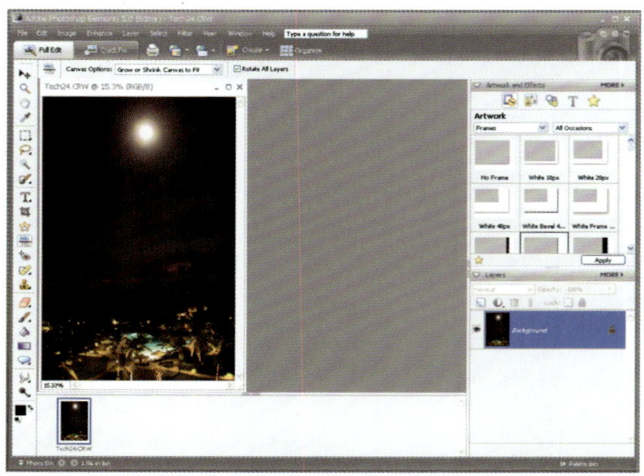

(7) To align the horizon of the photograph, click on the Straighten ( ) Tool from the toolbox. Click and drag from one end of the tilted horizon to the other. Release the mouse.

Use the Straighten Tool to correct an image horizontally and/or vertically by clicking and dragging the mouse as shown.

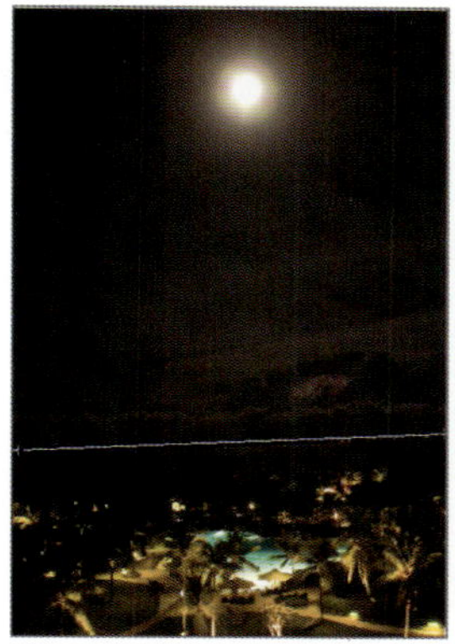

(8) The image will rotate so that the line you drew in the previous step is horizontal. Using the Crop tool ( ) from the tool box, click and drag to select the area that is to remain.

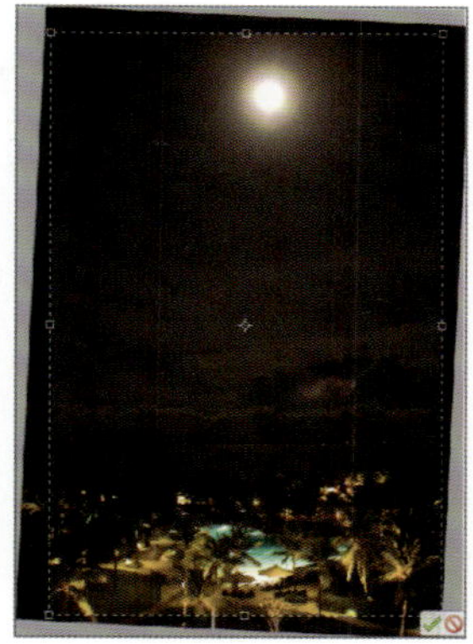

(9) Press the Enter key on your keyboard or click inside the crop box you have created.

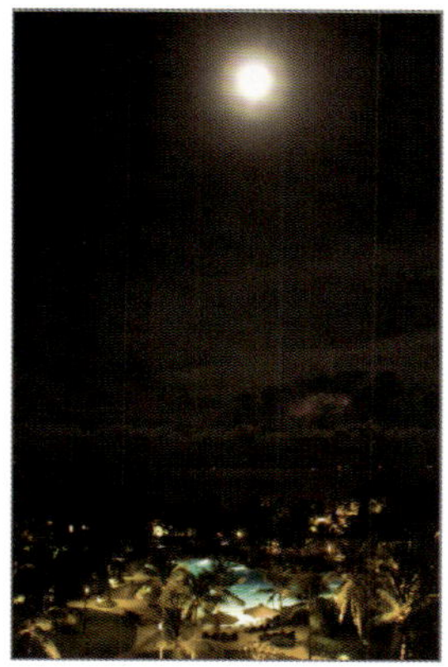

25 Adjusting Image Size and Shape

Before

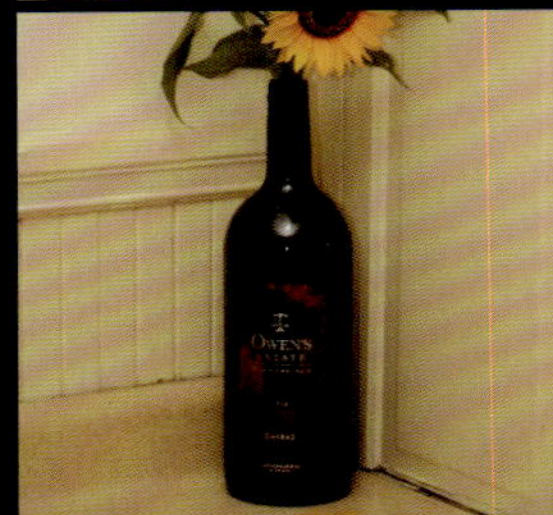

After

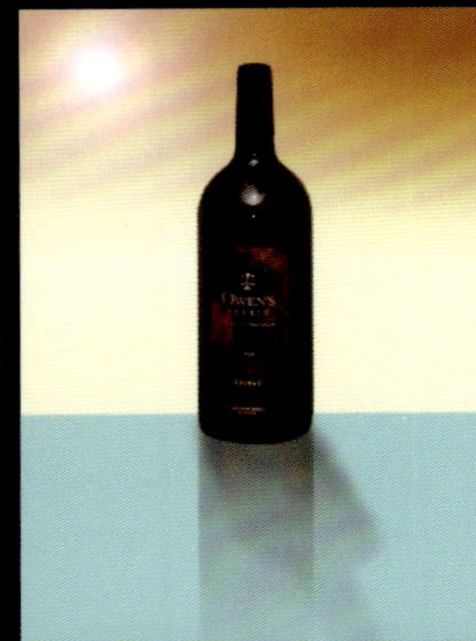

In this example, you will learn how to transform an ordinary product shot by using the Free Transform Tool to rotate, resize, and warp a copy of the image to add shadows. You will also use the Gradient Tool to create a background that has gradations in color and the Lens Flare filter to add a sparkle to the composition.

1. Open the **Sample\Chapter 4\Tech25.tif** file from the supplementary CD.

2. Select the Polygonal Lasso Tool ( ) from the toolbox. Repeatedly click and drag along the bottle's shape to select it. When you have almost outlined the entire bottle, click on the point where you started to close the selection.

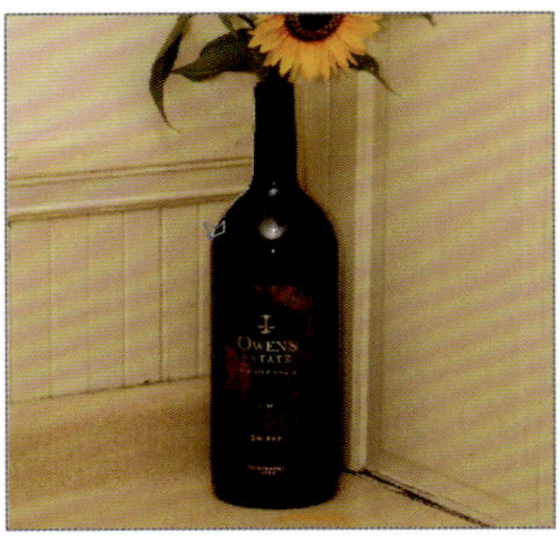

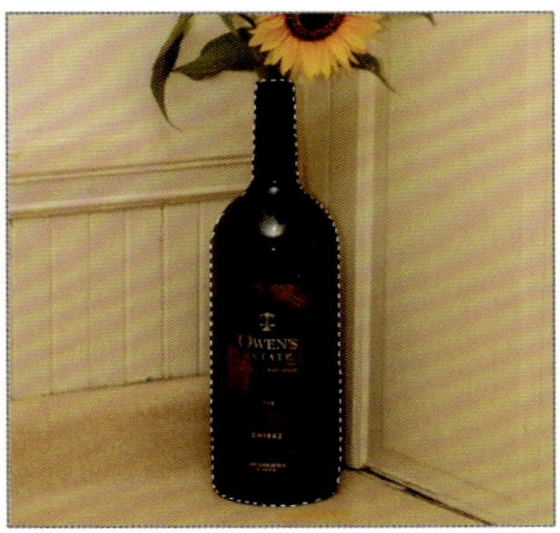

③ Double-click on the Background layer in the Layers palette to open the New Layer dialog box. The default Name is **Layer 0**. Click OK to change the Background layer into a regular layer.

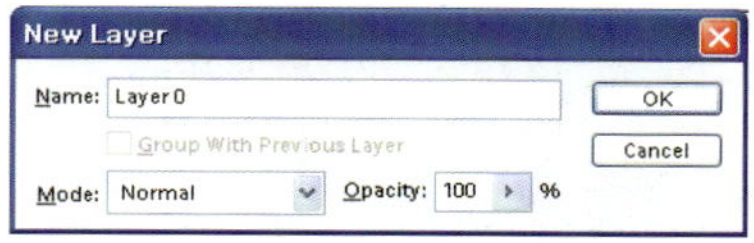

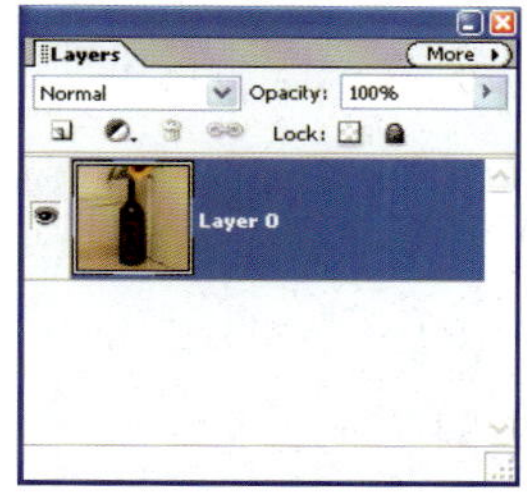

④ Choose Select > Inverse from the menu bar to select the area around the bottle instead. Press Delete to remove the background.

⑤ Press Ctrl + D to deselect.

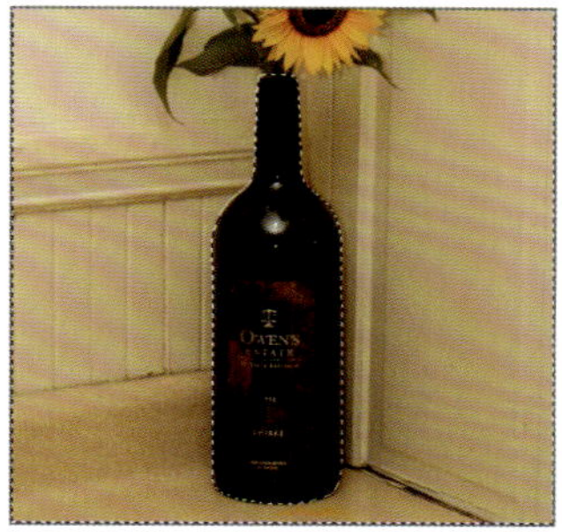

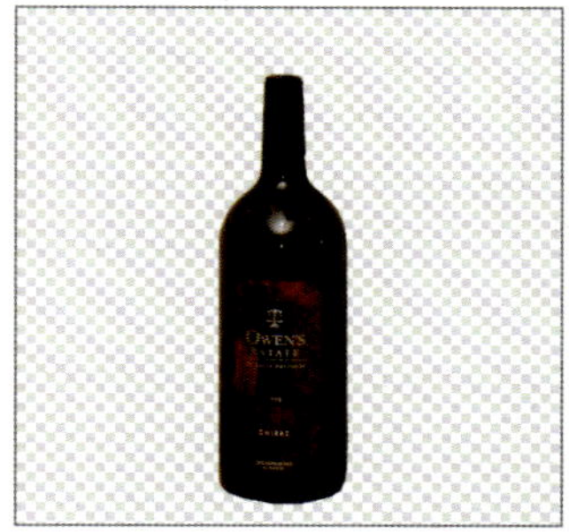

tip If you do not change the Background layer into a regular layer before deleting the selection, the deleted portion of the image will take the background color and will not be transparent.

⑥ Select Image > Resize > Canvas Size from the menu bar. In the Canvas Size dialog box, click the top-center square in the Anchor grid. This will anchor the existing image to the top-center position of the canvas. Set the Height to **20 cm**. Click OK.

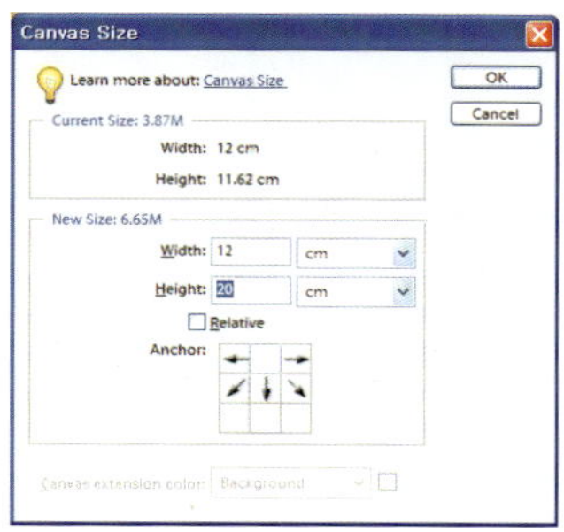

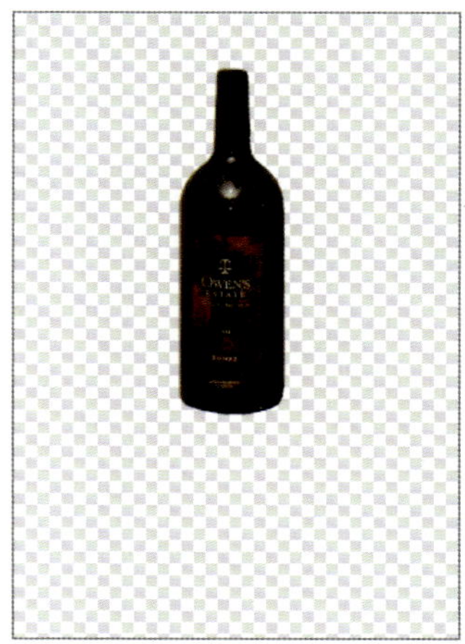

7 Click and drag Layer 0 onto the Create a New Layer icon ( ) in the Layers palette. This will create a Layer 0 copy layer above Layer 0.

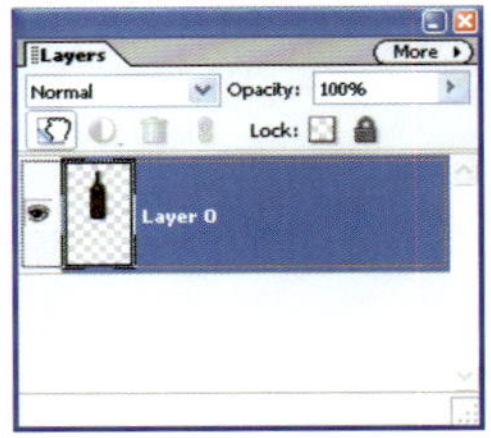

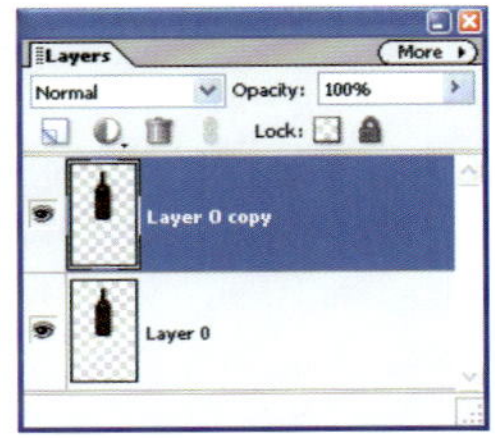

8 Select Image > Transform > Free Transform from the menu bar. The Free Transform bounding box appears around the bottle. In the options bar, set the angle to **180°** to flip the bottle upside down.

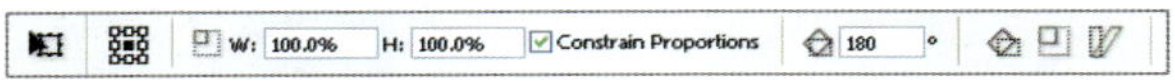

tip You can also rotate the image with your mouse. After the bounding box appears, move your pointer near one of the corner handles until you see the pointer turn into . Then click and drag the corner to rotate the image.

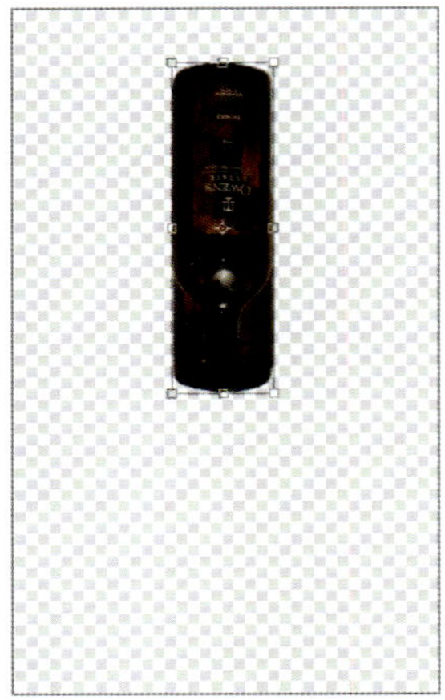

9 Click and drag the rotated image downward so that its base lines up with the bottom of the original image.

tip A better way of creating a reflection is to use the Image > Rotate > Flip Layer Vertical command from the menu bar. This will flip the image so that it looks exactly like a reflection of the original bottle. Although rotating the bottle is more troublesome and does not create an accurate reflection (the left side of the bottle is reflected on the right side), it's a good idea to become familiar with the Free Transform Tool before moving on to other techniques.

10 Move the pointer to the lower-middle handle of the reflection. The pointer changes to ↕. Click and drag the bounding box downward to make it longer. Hit Enter.

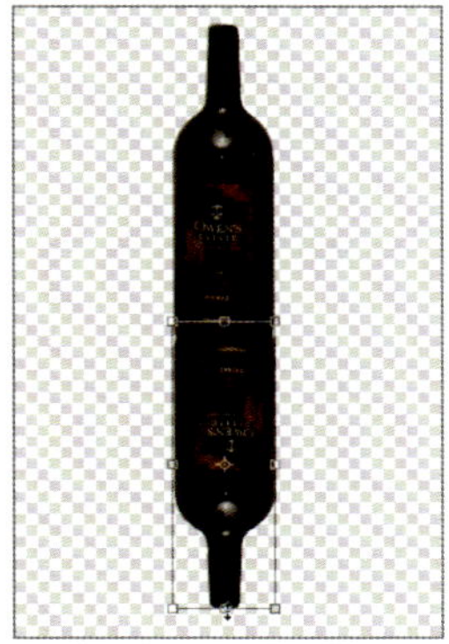

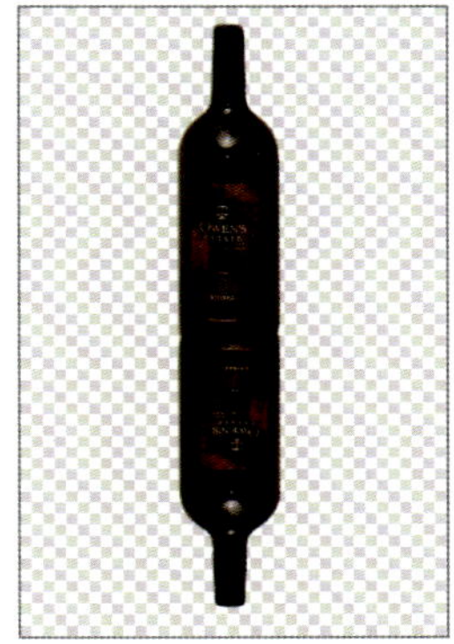

11 In the Layers palette, move Layer 0 copy below Layer 0. Click on the Create a New Layer icon ( ) in the Layers palette to create a new layer. The new Layer 1 is created above Layer 0 copy.

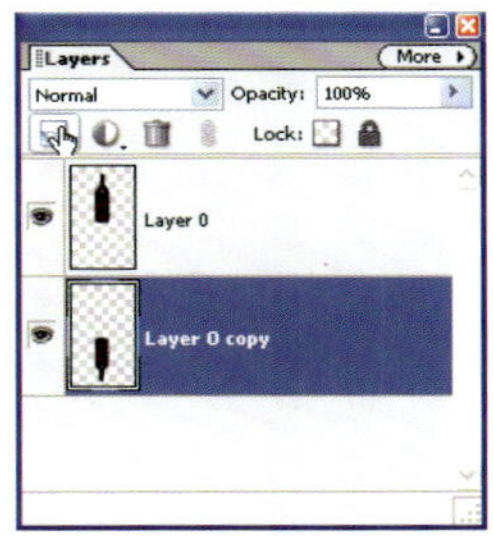

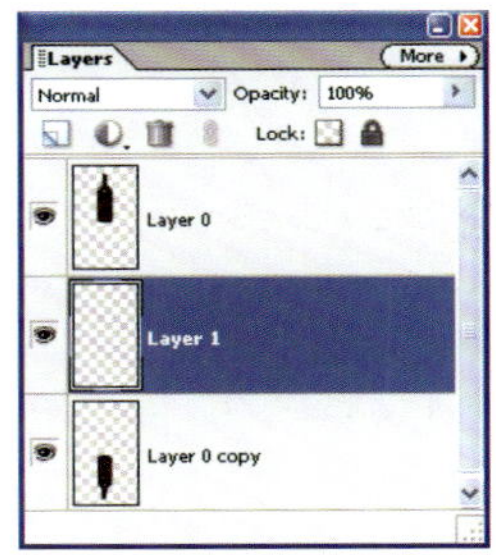

12 Click and drag Layer 1 down to the bottom of the layers list. Next, select the Rectangular Marquee Tool ( ) from the toolbox. Select the reflection, as shown.

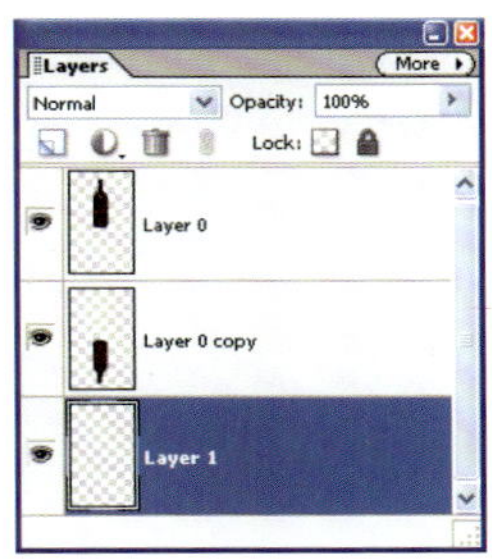

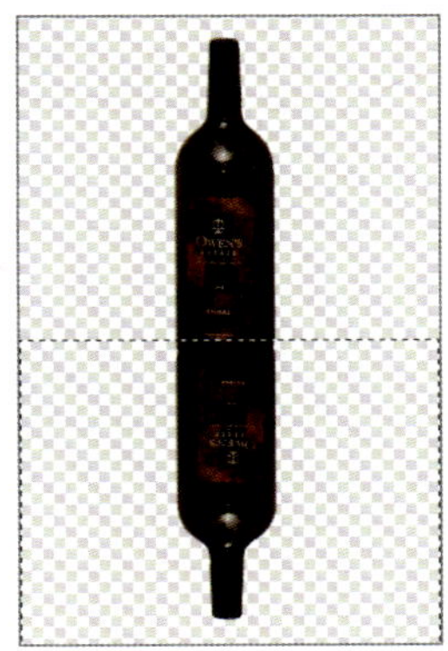

13 Click on the Set Foreground Color icon in the toolbox. In the Color Picker dialog box, set the RGB values to **140**, **200**, and **200**. Click OK to change the foreground color.

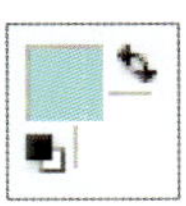

(14) Select Edit > Fill Selection from the menu bar. In the Fill dialog box, set Use to **Foreground Color**. Click OK. Press Ctrl + D to deselect the selection.

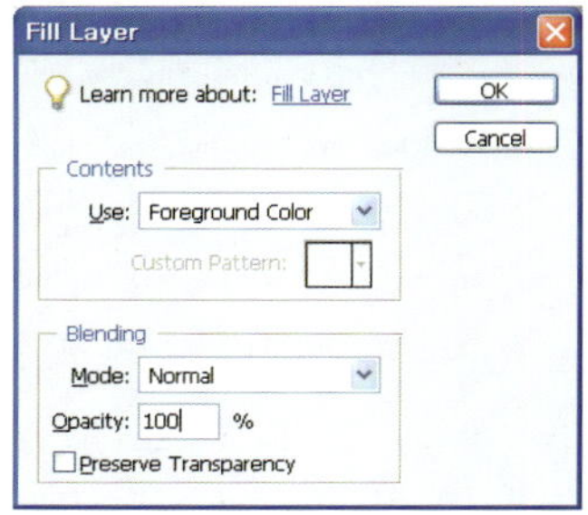

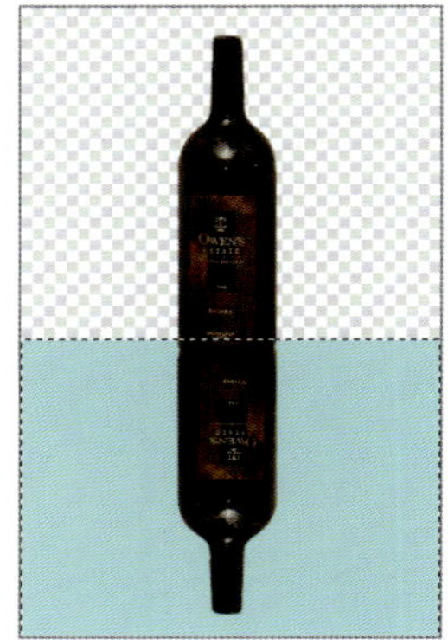

(15) Click on the Create a New Layer icon ( ) in the Layers palette to create a new layer. Click and drag the new Layer 2 below Layer 1.

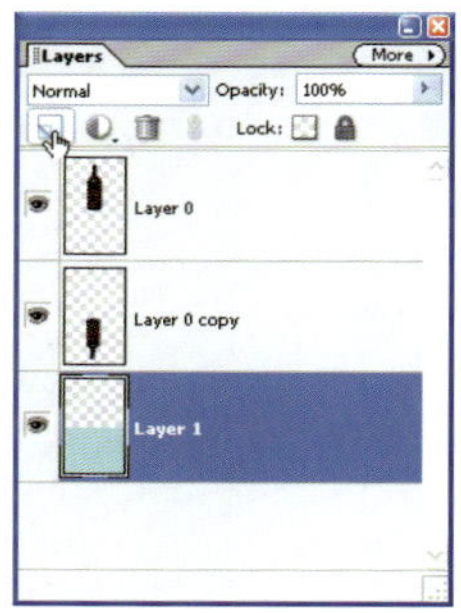

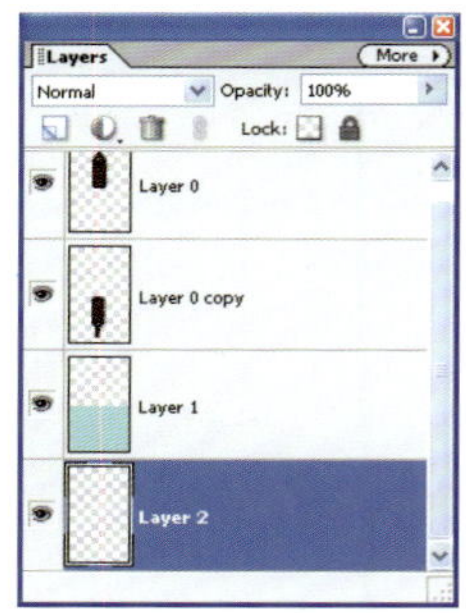

(16) Repeat steps 13 and 14 for Layer 2, using the RGB values **255**, **255**, and **200**, respectively.

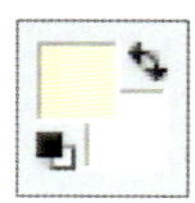

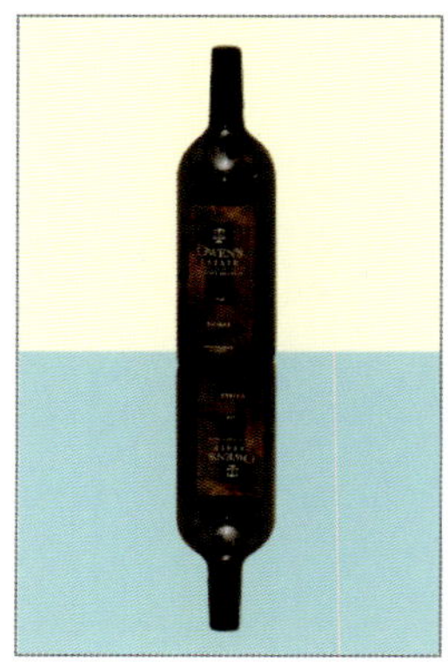

17 Select Layer 0 copy in the Layers palette. Select Filter > Blur > Motion Blur from the menu bar to blur the reflection. In the Motion Blur dialog box, set Angle to **90°** and Distance to **250 pixels**. Click OK.

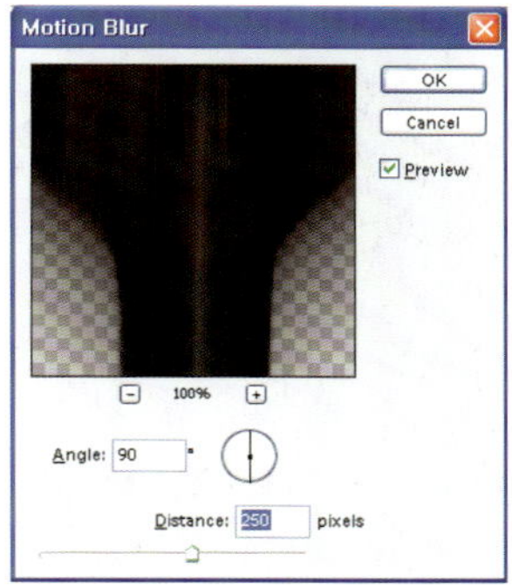

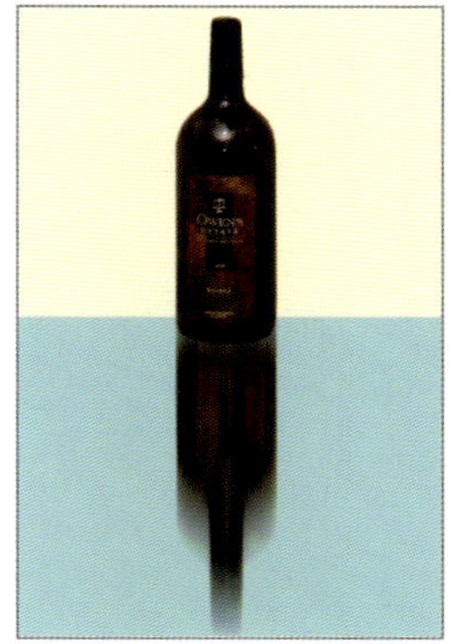

18 In the Layers palette, set the Opacity of Layer 0 copy to **50%** to lighten the reflection.

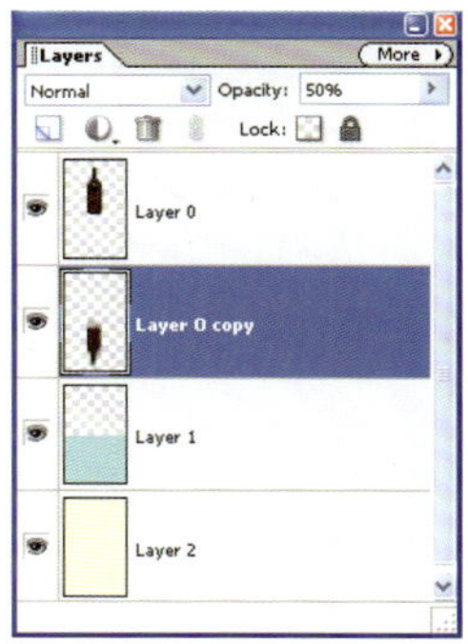

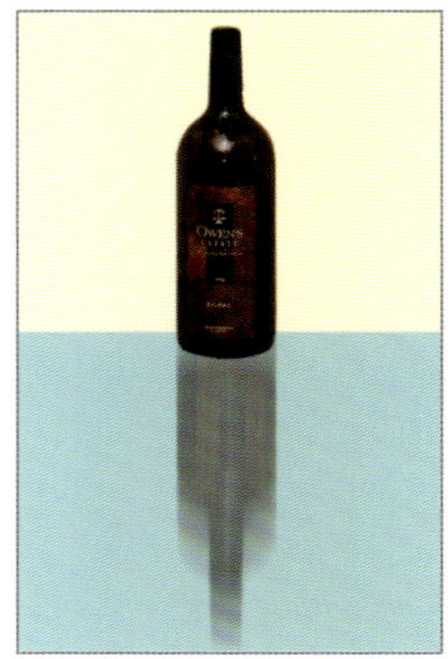

19 Select the Eraser Tool () from the toolbox. In the options bar, set Brush to **Soft Round**, Size to **500 pixels**, and Opacity to **50%**. Click and drag over the reflection so that it gets fainter toward the bottom.

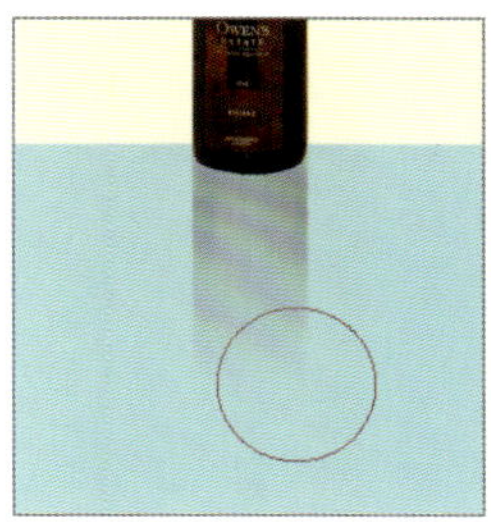

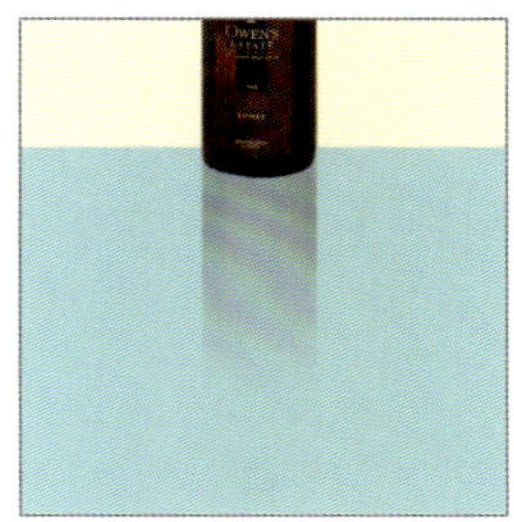

(20) In the Layers palette, click and drag Layer 0 onto the Create a New Layer icon ( ) to create a copy. Click and drag Layer 0 copy 2 below Layer 0.

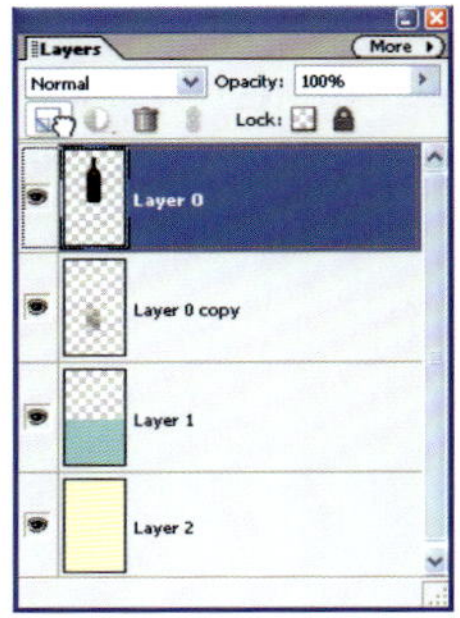

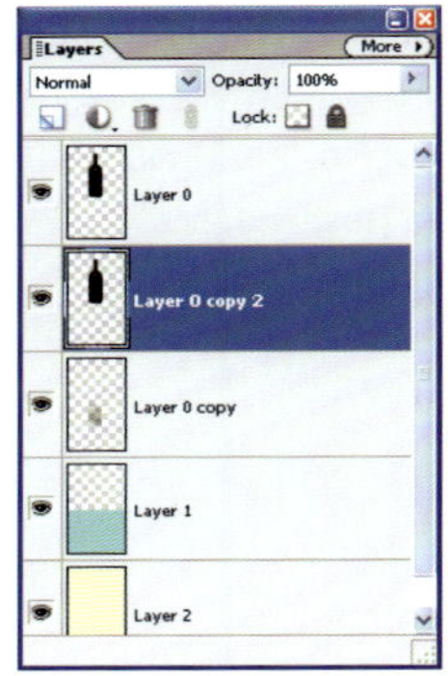

(21) Select Layer 0 copy 2. Select Image > Transform > Free Transform from the menu bar or press Ctrl + T. In the options bar, set Angle to **–180°** to rotate the bottle.

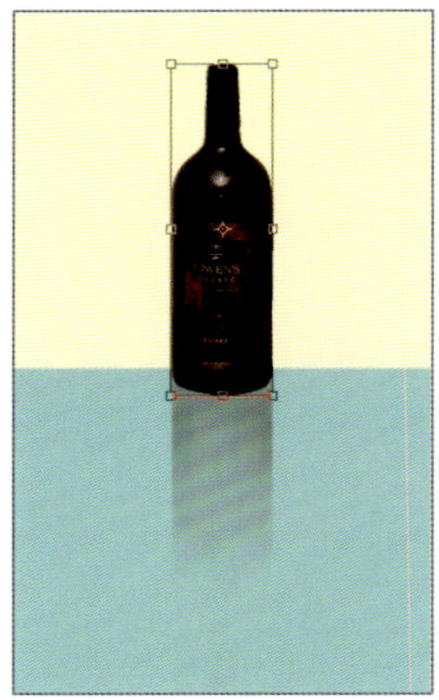

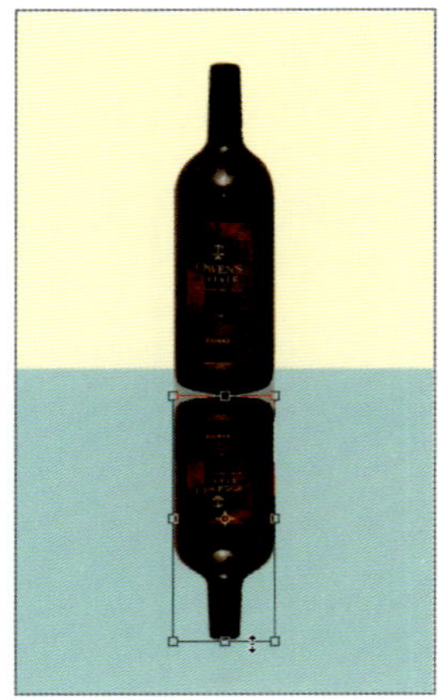

(22) Drag the reflection downward so that its base lines up with the bottom of the bottle.

(23) Hold down the Ctrl key and drag a lower-corner handle sideways. Repeat the step on the other corner until you get the result as shown. Press Enter.

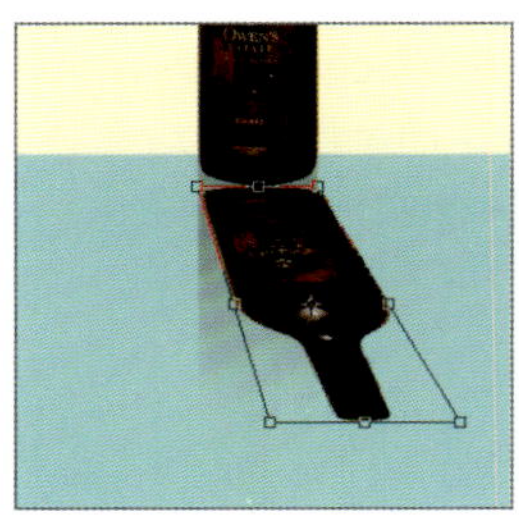

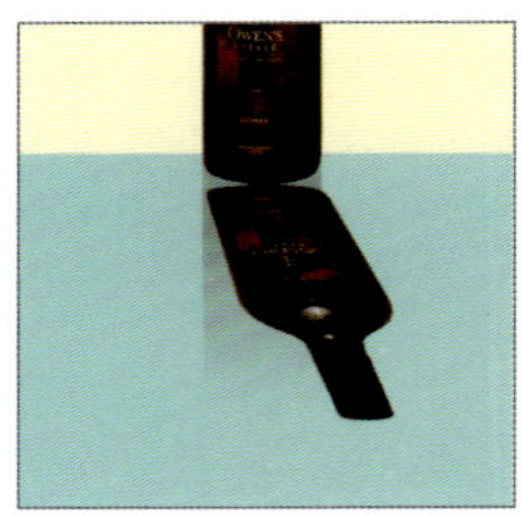

24 Select the Move Tool ( ) from the toolbox. Move the warped reflection so that its base lines up with the bottle.

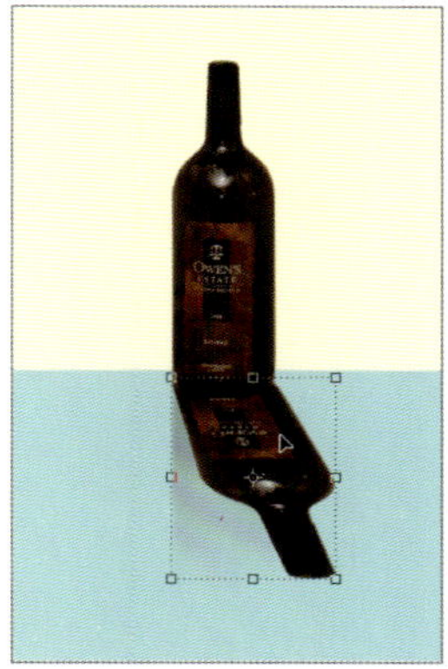

25 Select Filter > Blur > Gaussian Blur from the menu bar. In the Gaussian Blur dialog box, set Radius to **15 pixels**. Click OK to blur the reflection.

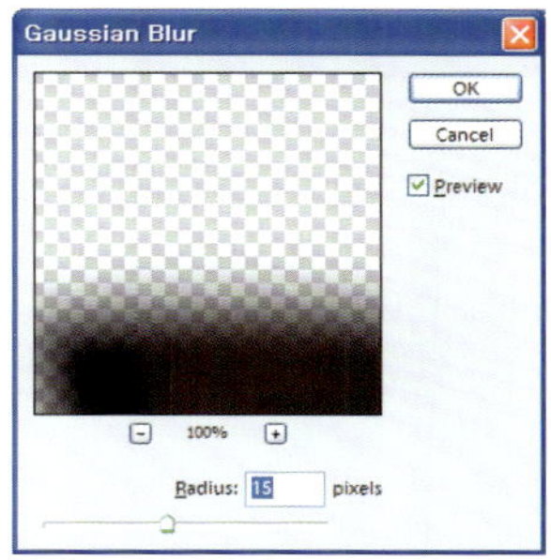

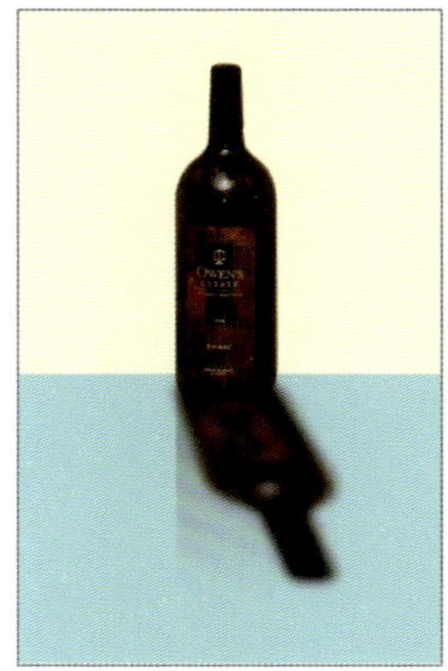

26 Select Layer 0 copy 2. Select the Eraser Tool ( ). In the options bar, set Brush to **Soft Round**, Size to **500 pixels**, and Opacity to **50%**. Drag over the reflection so that it gets fainter toward the bottom.

27 Click on the Set Foreground Color icon in the toolbox. In the Color Picker dialog box, set the RGB values to **160**, **90**, and **0**. Click OK to change the foreground color.

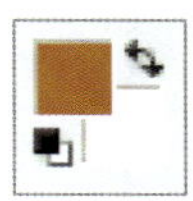

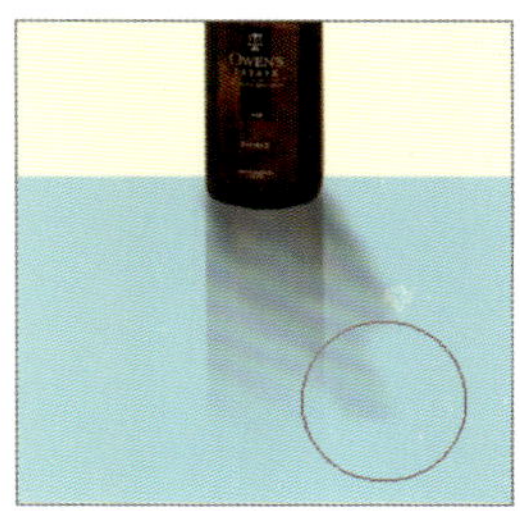

(28) Select Layer 2. Select the Gradient Tool ( ) from the toolbox. In the options bar, click on the Gradient Picker arrow to see thumbnails of available gradients. Select the **Foreground to Transparent** gradient.

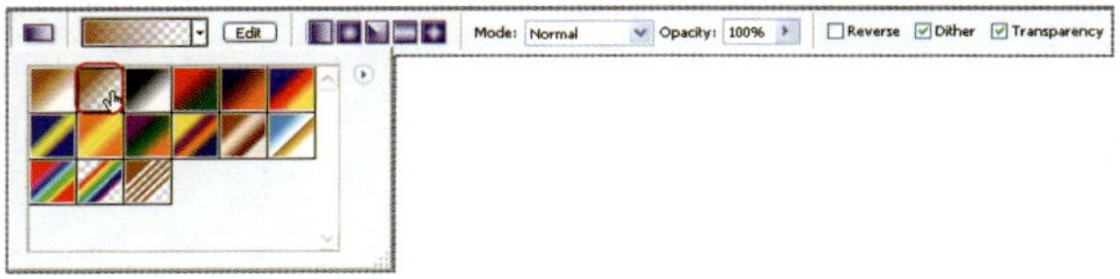

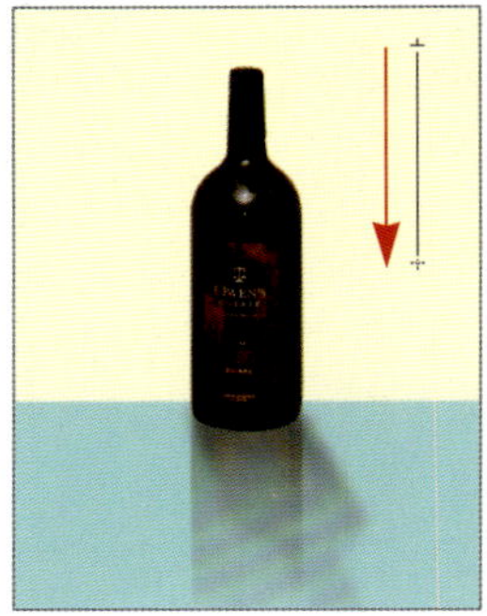

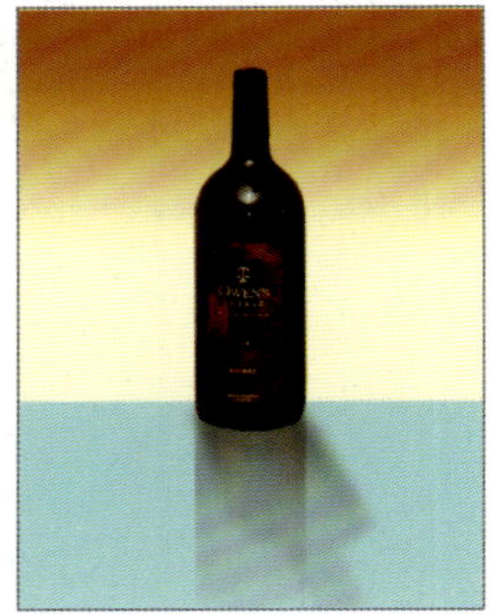

(29) To apply the gradient to Layer 2, click and drag in the top-to-bottom direction, as shown.

(30) Select Filter > Render > Lens Flare from the menu bar. In the Lens Flare dialog box, click and drag the crosshair in the preview window to the upper-left corner, as shown. Set the Brightness to **150%**. Click OK.

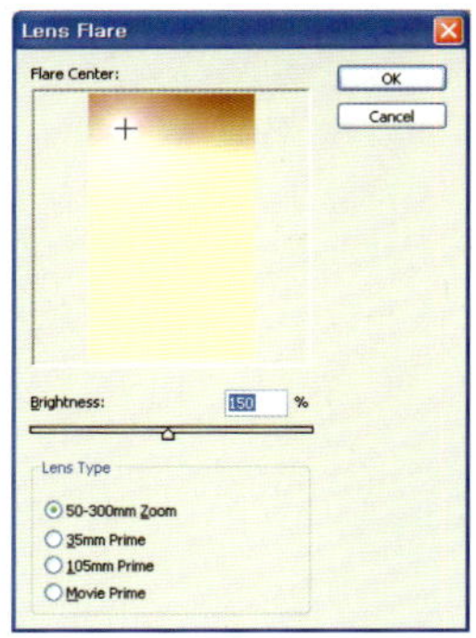

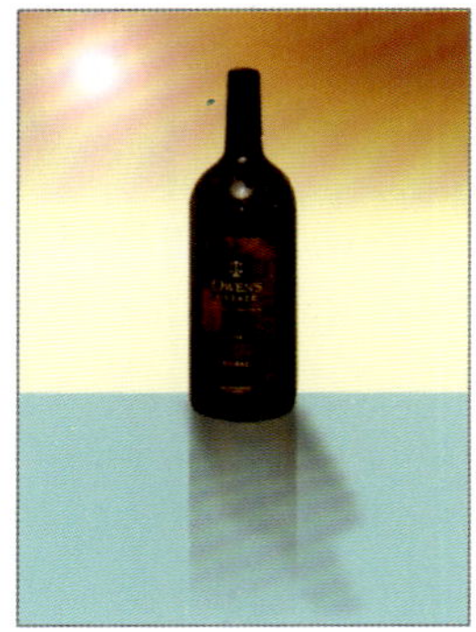

(31) Select the Crop Tool ( ) from the toolbox. Make the selection as shown. Press Enter to remove the unwanted areas.

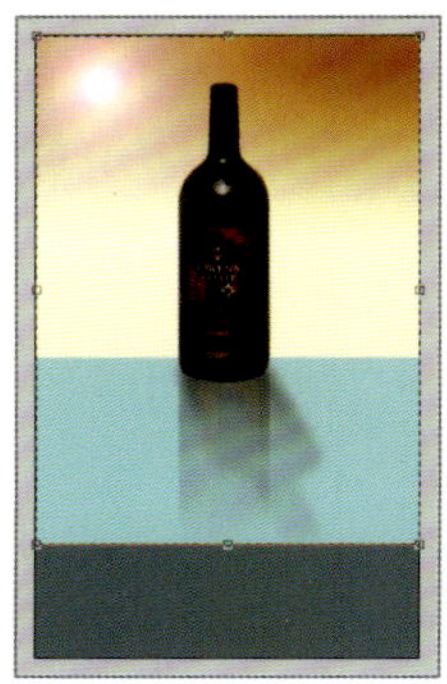

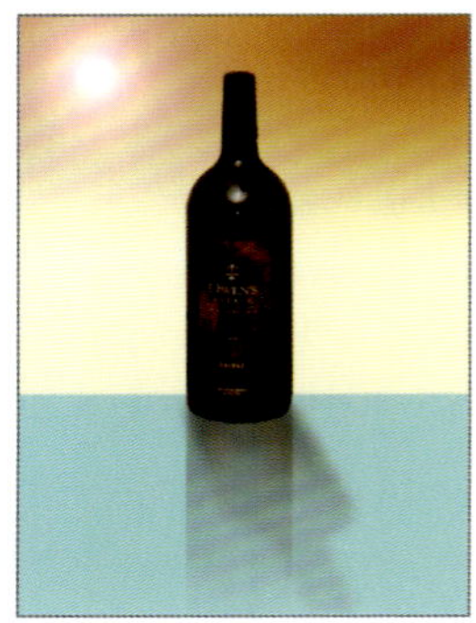

26 Cleaning Up Backgrounds

It is inevitable that unwanted people or objects will sometimes appear in the background of your pictures. This will ruin the composition of your shot and also detract attention from your main subject. A good way to solve this problem is to use the Clone Stamp Tool, which can stamp out unwanted objects easily. In this exercise, you'll use this tool to clean up a background to better isolate a photo's main subject. We'll also cover using such tools in a perfectly straight line so that you can edit images with great precision.

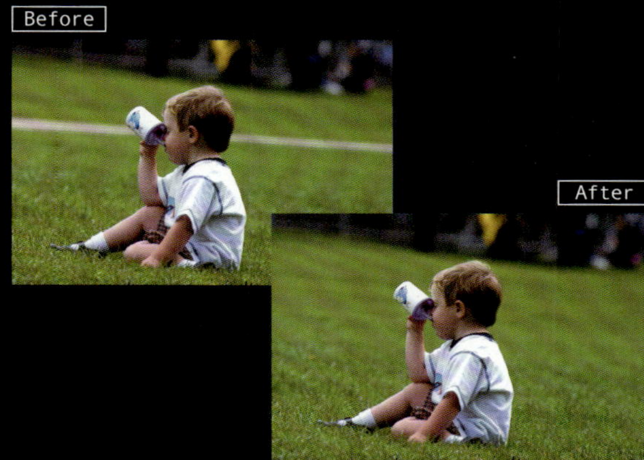

1. Open the **Sample\Chapter 4\Tech26.jpg** file from the supplementary CD.

You will be removing the footpath in the background.

2. Choose the Clone Stamp Tool ( ) from the toolbox. In the options bar, set the Size to **50 pixels**, Mode to **Normal**, and the Opacity to **100%**.

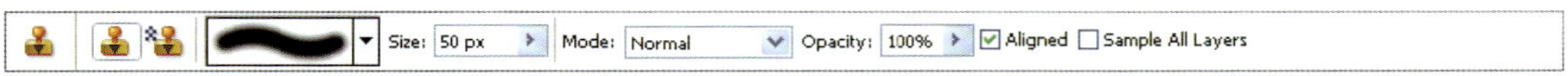

3. Holding down the Alt key, click on a patch of grass above the footpath to create a clone.

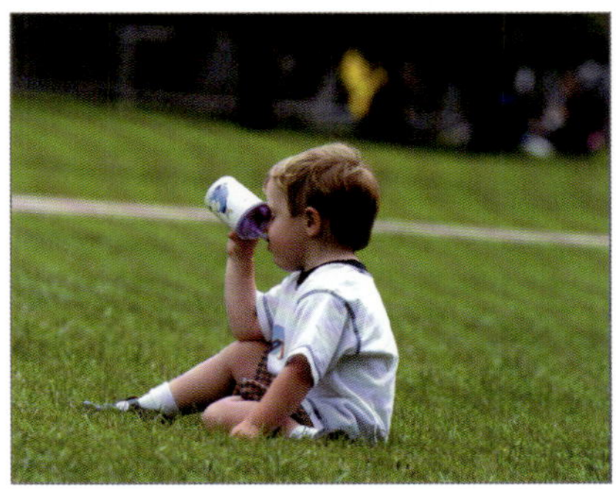

(4) Release the Alt key and drag over the footpath to cover it up with the grass patch. If you drag too far right, you will start seeing the child's image repeated in the clone. This is because the tool starts duplicating the image from the point where you created the clone. If the child's image appears in the clone, undo the step, drag in short distances, and remember to keep cloning between drags.

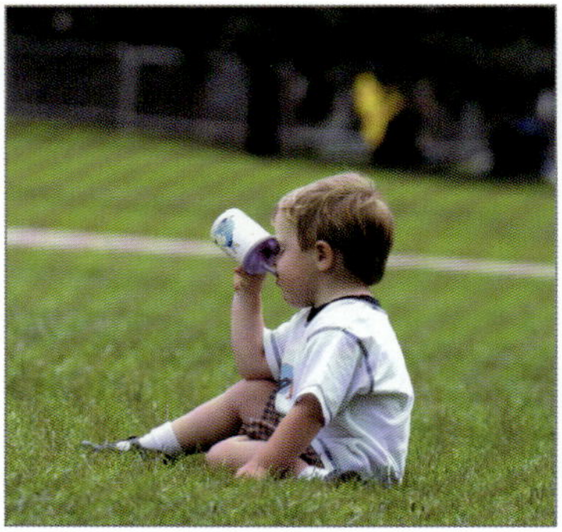

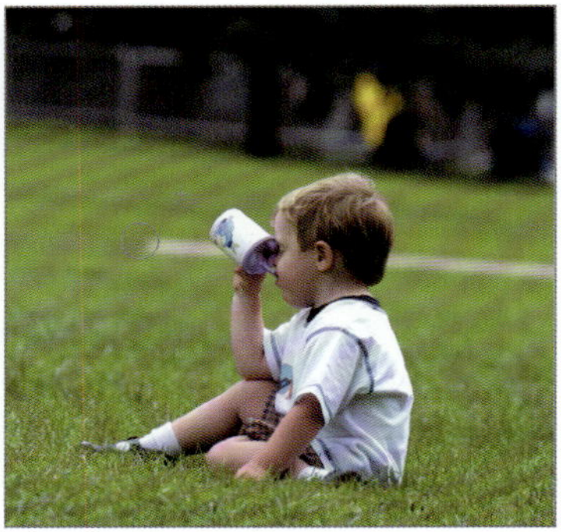

(5) As in step 4, hold down the Alt key and create a clone from above the footpath on the right side of the picture. Then, release the Alt key and drag the tool over the path on the right side. Again, be careful not to drag too far without taking another clone sample.

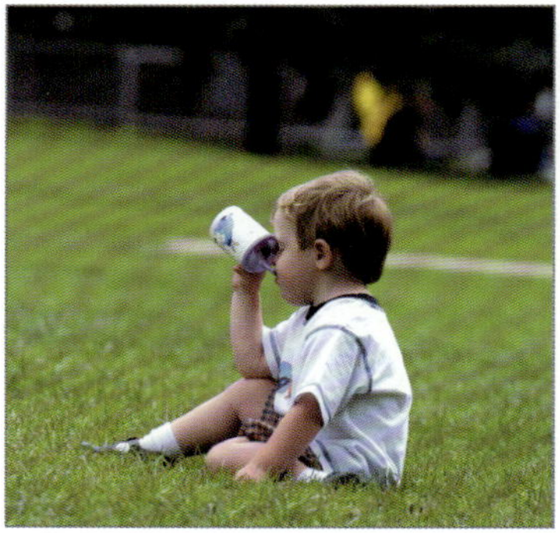

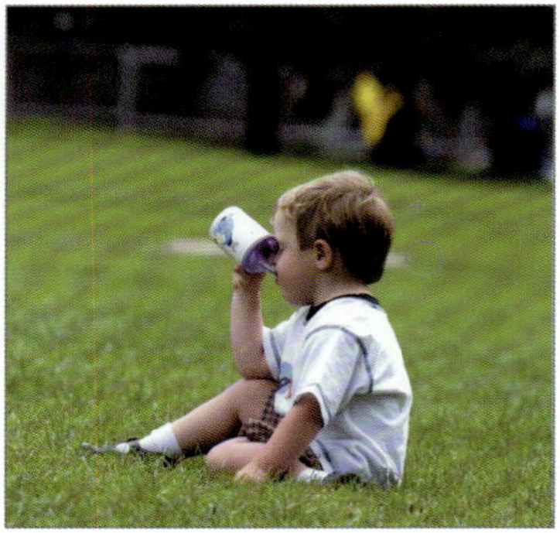

(6) With the Zoom Tool ( ) selected, click on the image to zoom in on the child's head. Select the Clone Stamp Tool ( ) and set the Size to **30 pixels** in the options bar. Hold down the Alt key and use the Clone Stamp Tool to make a new clone.

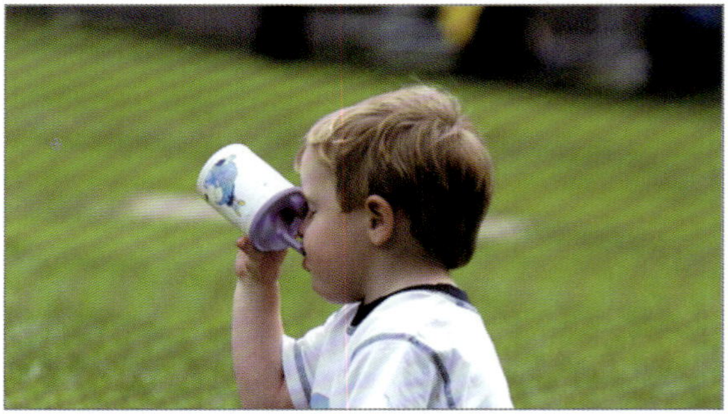

7 Release the Alt key and stamp over the footpath on the left.

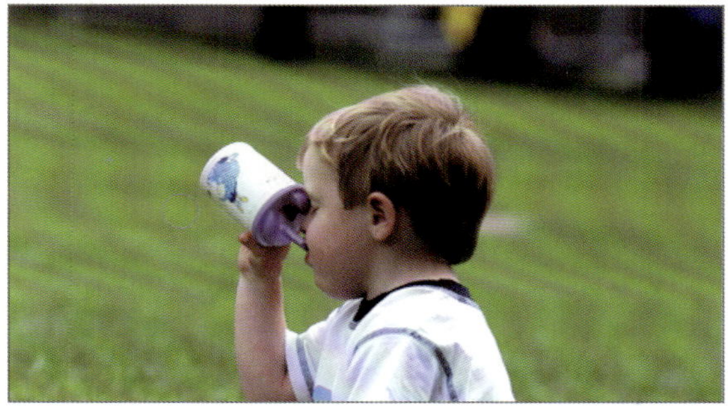

8 Repeat the previous step on the footpath on the right.

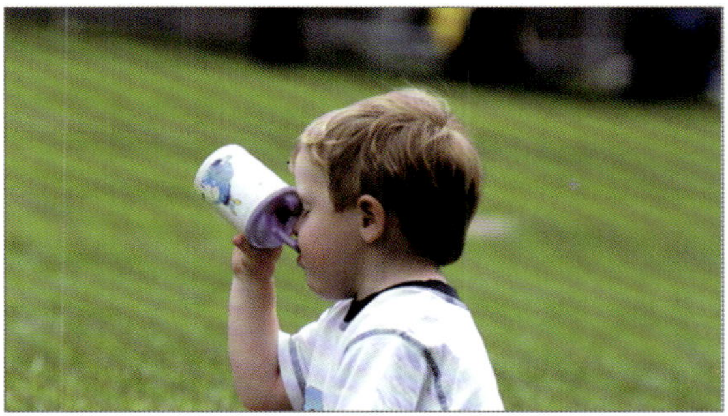

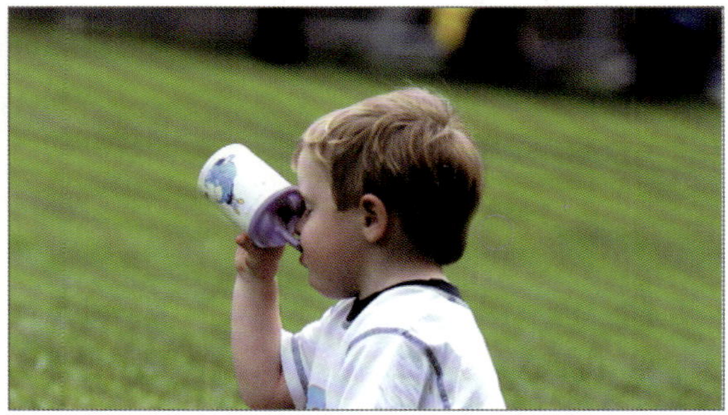

9 Press Ctrl+0 to fit the entire image in the work-space.

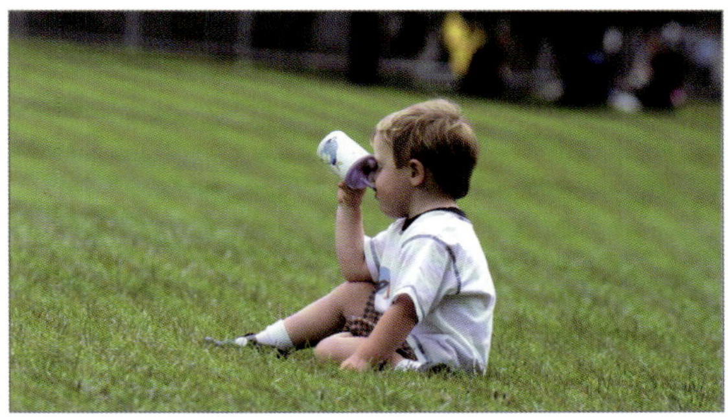

Using the Shift Key for Straight Lines

If the object that you are trying to remove has a rather straight outline, like the smokestacks in the following example, you can use the Shift key together with the Clone Stamp Tool to remove it easily.

With the Clone Stamp Tool selected, simply hold down the Shift key and click on one end of the object. Then hold down the Shift key again and click on the other end. The Clone Stamp Tool will remove the area in a straight line between the two points.

The following example can be found on the supplementary CD-ROM: **Sample\Chapter 4\Tech26-1.tif**.

1 Set the Size of the Clone Stamp Tool to **200 pixels**. Hold down the Shift key and click on the tip of the smokestack.

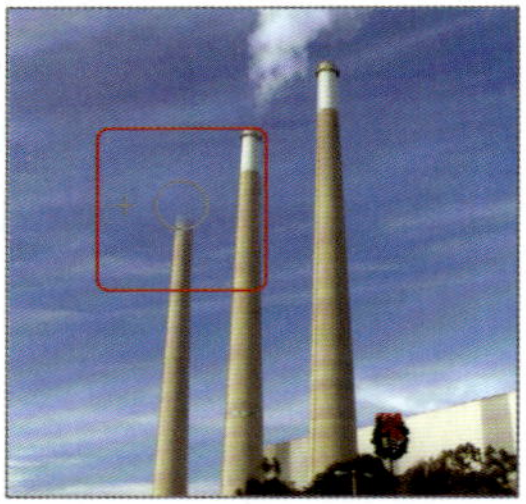

2 Hold down the Shift key and click on the smokestack's base.

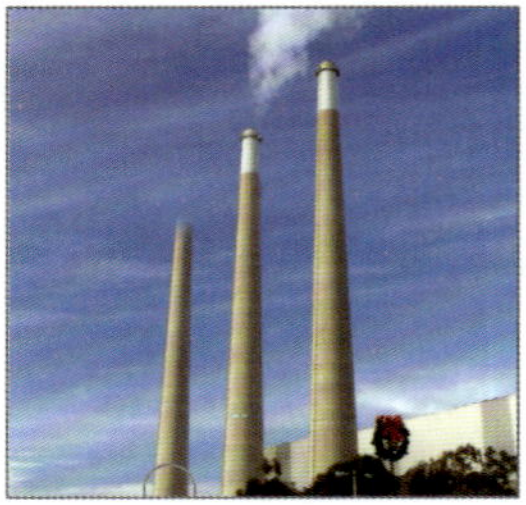

3 The Clone Stamp Tool applies the clone in a straight line between the starting and ending points.

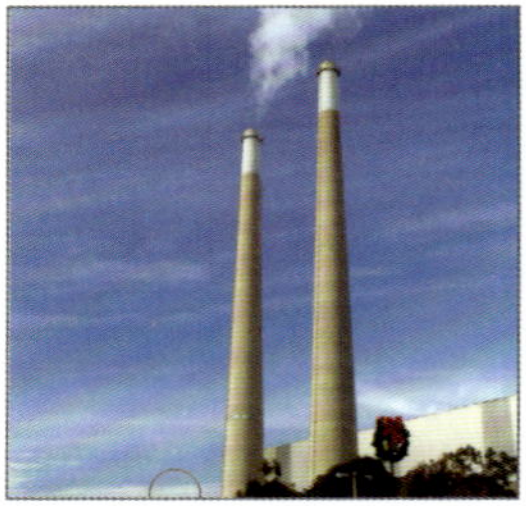

27 Creating Reflections

Before

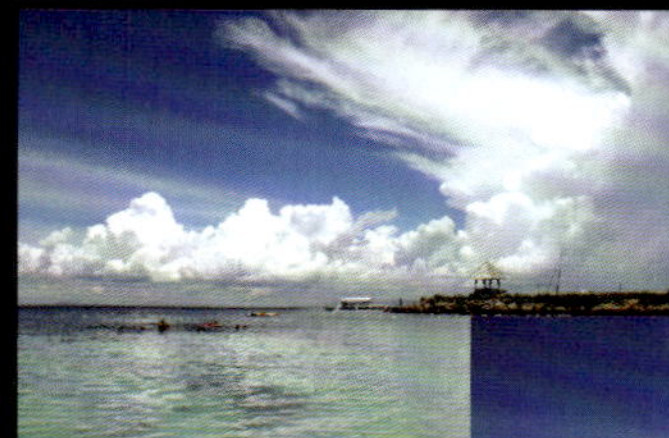

After

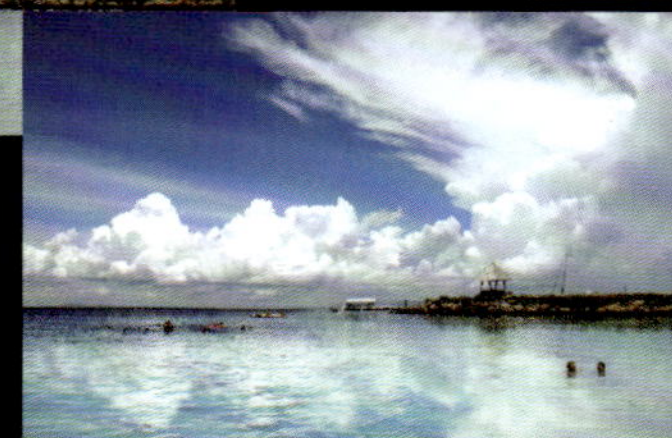

When combining images, you may have to create a new reflection for the objects that you've altered in your images. Obviously, this is necessary only if there is a reflective element in your new composition. Even if you are not combining images, you may also want to create or retouch the reflections in your images to enhance the visual effect.

(1) Open the **Sample\Chapter 4\Tech27.jpg** file from the supplementary CD.

(2) Select Image > Resize > Canvas Size from the menu bar. In the Canvas Size dialog box, click on the top-center square on the Anchor grid. This will anchor the image to the top-center position of the canvas. Increase the Height to **25 cm**. Click OK.

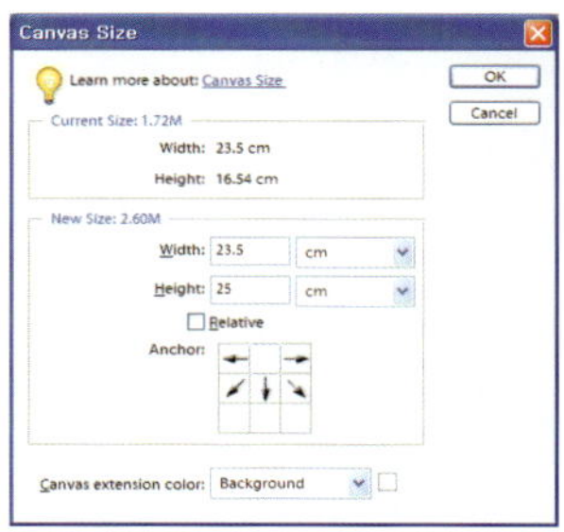

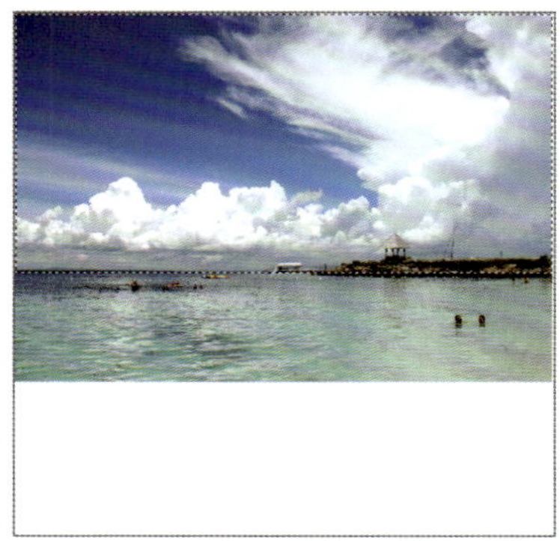

(3) Select the Rectangular Marquee Tool ( ) from the toolbox. Select the image, as shown here.

> The extra space added to the canvas will take on the background color indicated at the bottom of the toolbox. For this exercise, use a white background color.

(4) Select Layer > New > Layer via Copy from the menu bar to create a copy of the selection on a new layer. In the Layers palette, you can see that a new layer is created for the copy.

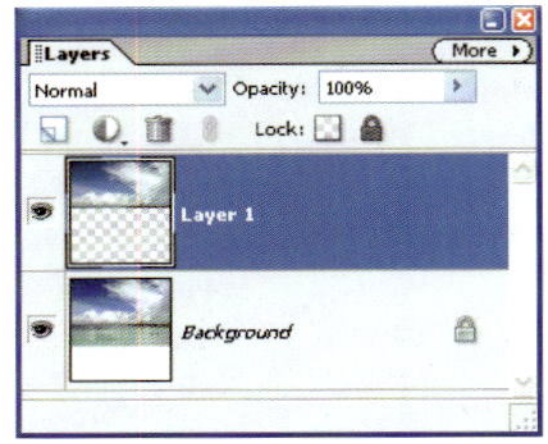

(5) Select Image > Rotate > Flip Layer Vertical from the menu bar to flip the copy vertically.

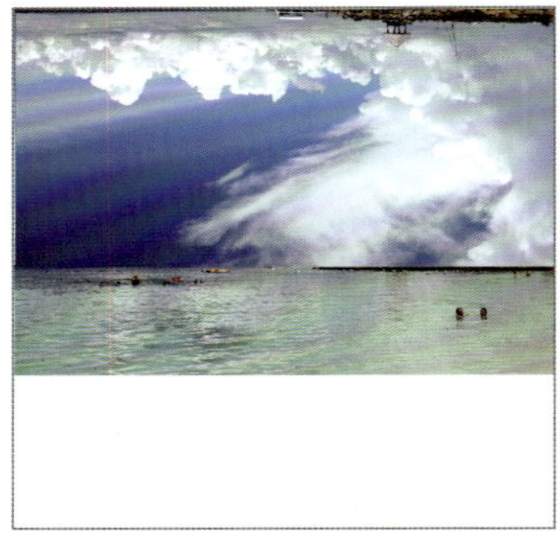

(6) Select the Move Tool () from the toolbox.

(7) Drag the copy to the bottom of the original image to use it as the reflection.

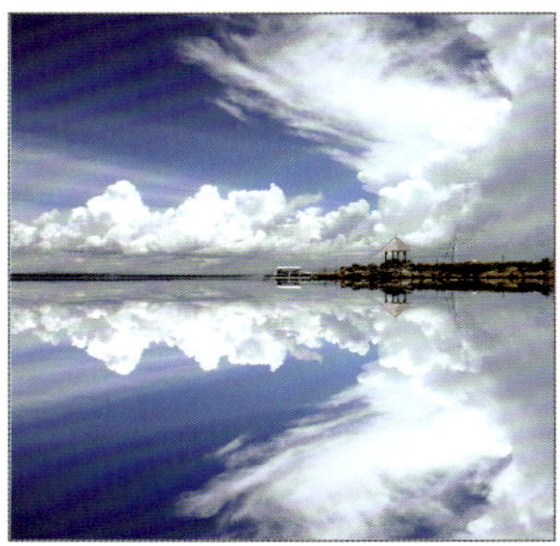

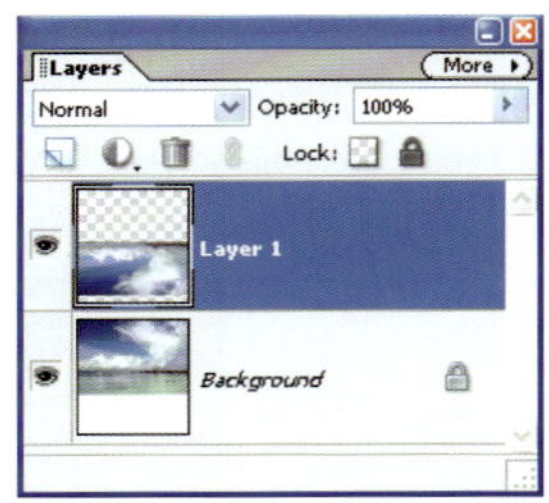

8 Select Filter > Distort > Ripple from the menu bar. In the Ripple dialog box, set Amount to **400%**, Size to **Small**. Click OK.

9 Select Filter > Blur > Gaussian Blur from the menu bar. In the Gaussian Blur dialog box, set Radius to **3 pixels** to blur the image slightly. This will make the reflection look more realistic. Click OK.

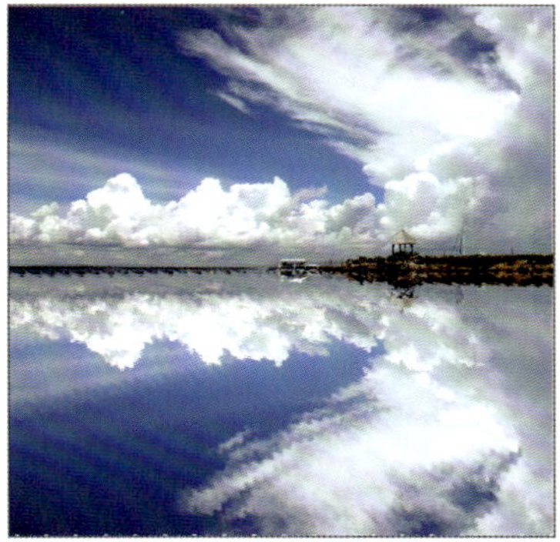

▲ Ripple

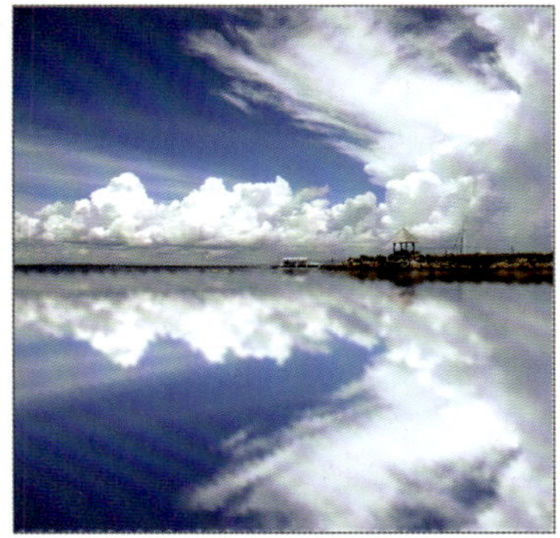

▲ Gaussian blur

10 Select **Layer 1** from the layer palette. Change the blending mode to **Overlay** and the opacity to **70**. You can see it is now more naturally combined with the Background layer.

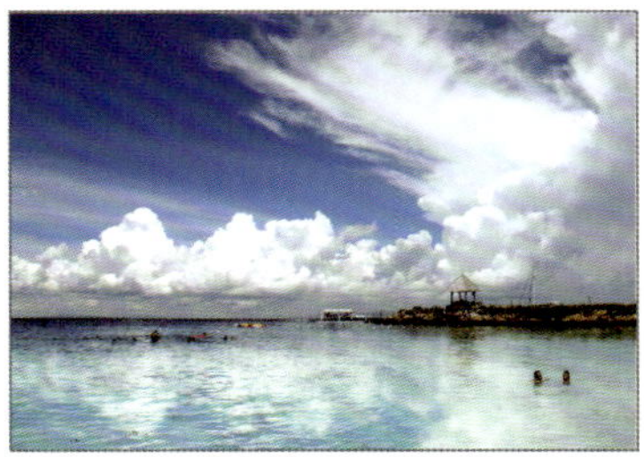

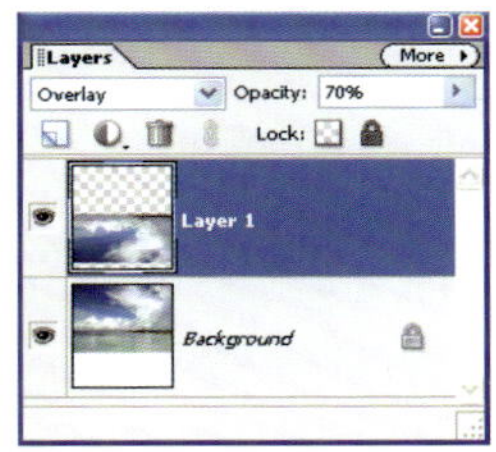

11 Cut the needed area using the Crop Tool.

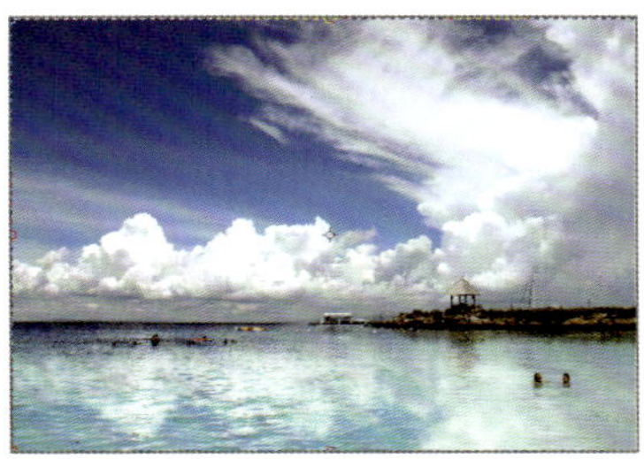

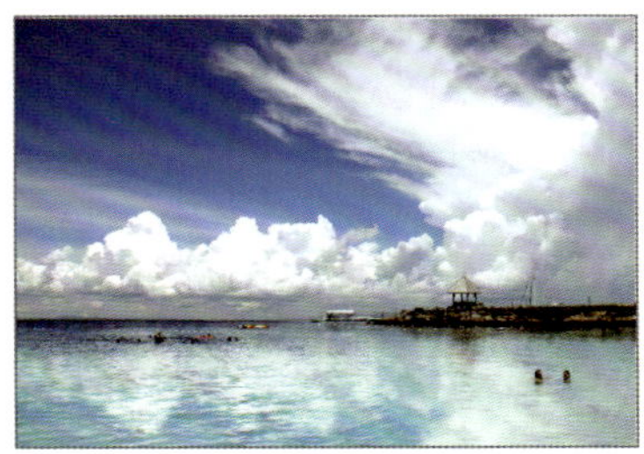

28 Adding Type Effects

In this section, you will learn how to enhance the visual appeal of text on images by using a series of blending, warping, and embossing techniques. In this exercise, we will emboss a word onto a curved surface to make it look like it is actually part of the surface.

Before

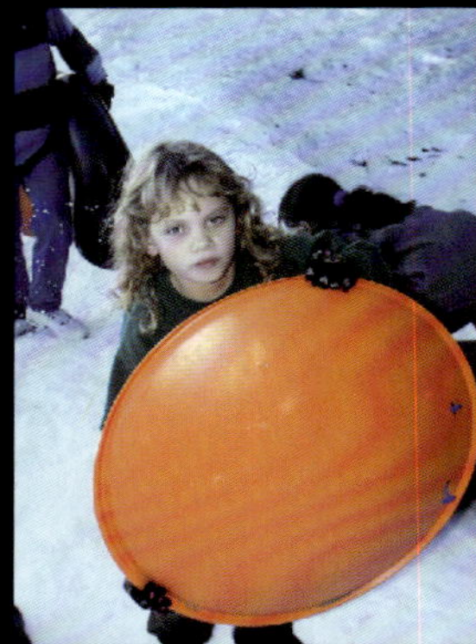

After

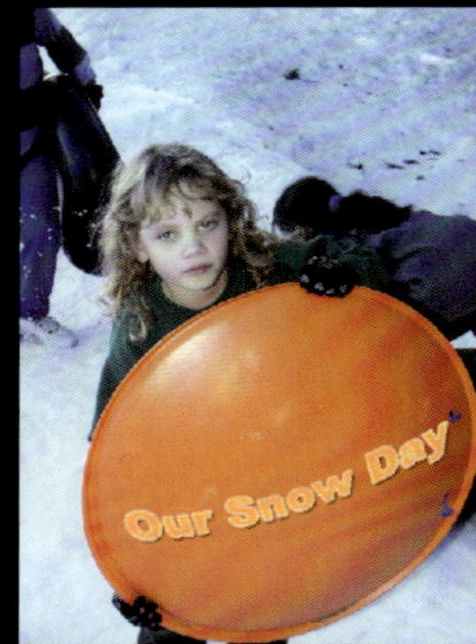

1. Open the **Sample\Chapter 4\Tech28.jpg** file from the supplementary CD.

2. Select the Horizontal Type Tool (T) from the toolbox. In the options bar, set Font to **Arial Black**, Size to **40 points**, and Color to **Black**.

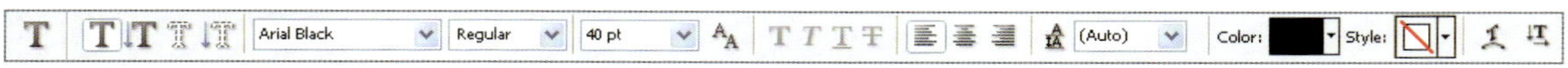

3. Click on the orange sled in the picture, and type in the words **Our Snow Day**.

4. Select Layer > Type > Warp Text from the menu bar. In the Warp Text dialog box, set the Style to Arc, Bend to **-17%**, Horizontal Distortion to **0%**, and Vertical Distortion to **-5%**. Click OK.

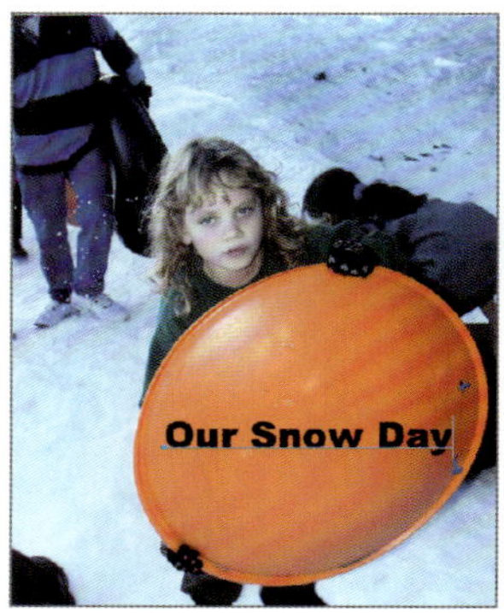

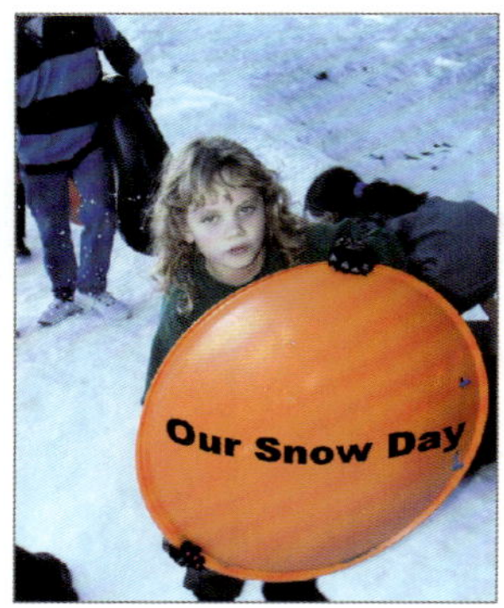

5 Press Ctrl+T to activate the Free Transform command. When the bounding box appears, move the pointer near one of the corner handles. When the pointer changes to , click and drag the box until it fits the shape of the sled. Hit Enter.

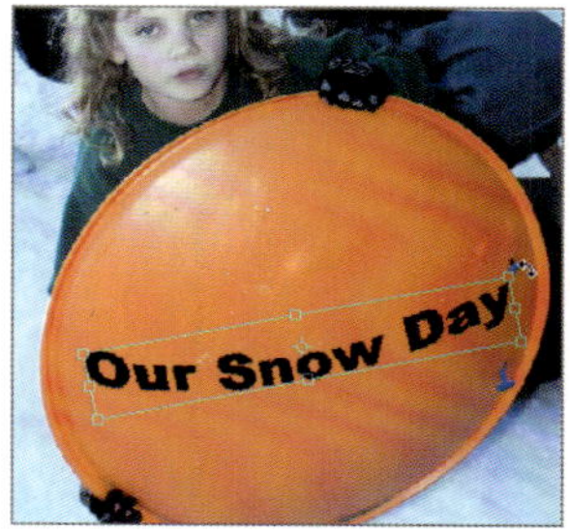

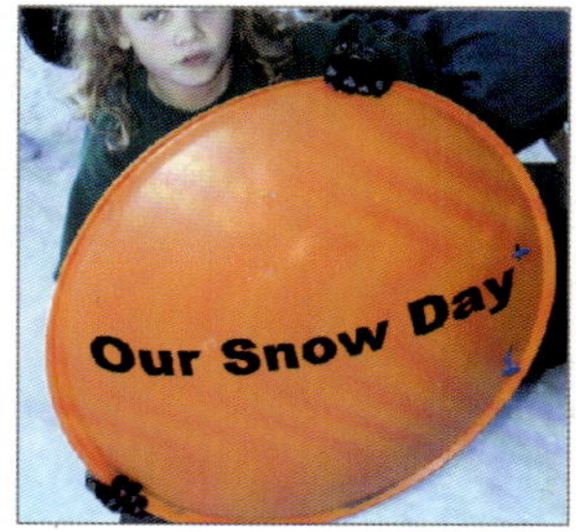

6 Click on Window > Artwork and Effects. The Artwork and Effects palette will appear. Now, click on Text from the Artwork and Effects palette, then double-click on **Inner Glow** from the list. You can see that the effect has applied to the text.

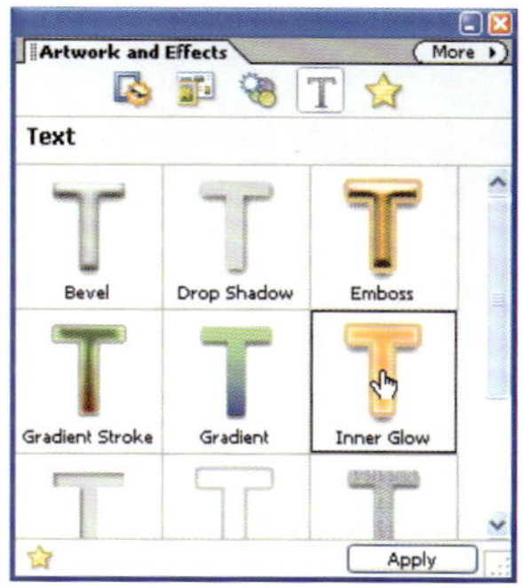

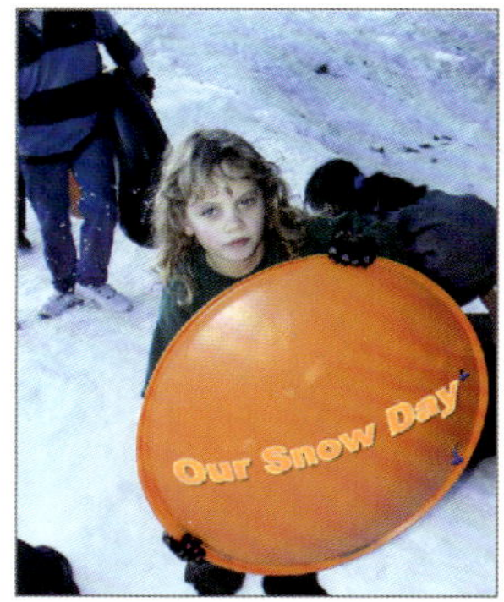

V Fine-Tuning the Effects Applied

You can fine-tune the effects you have already applied by double-clicking the symbol next to the layer to which the effects were applied. This opens up the Style Settings dialog box from which you can adjust factors such as the lighting angle, bevel size, and direction.

You can also select Layer > Layer Style > Style Settings from the menu bar to open the Style Settings dialog box.

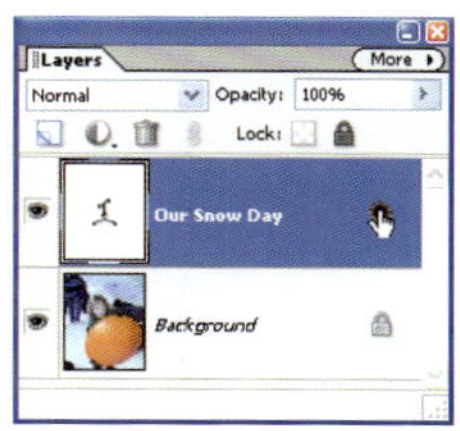

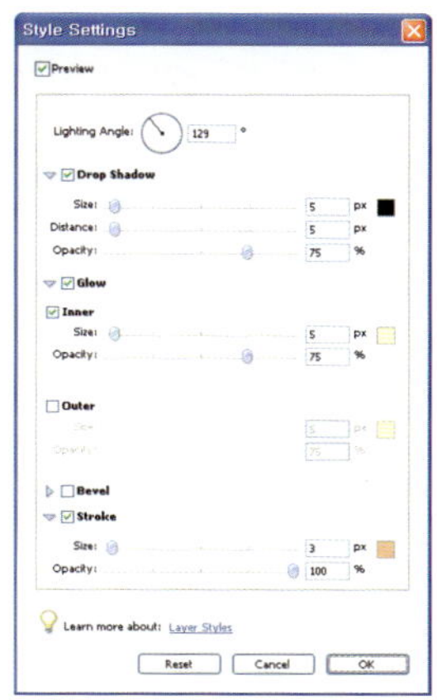

29 Altering Perspective

When a tall or wide structure is shot from the ground up, the structure seems to converge toward the sky. The only way to shoot such a picture without distortion is to take your shot from a location at half the height of the structure. You would also need to stand far enough away to fit the entire structure in the frame. Thankfully, although it is hard to get shots of giant structures without distortion, you can fix the distortion easily using the Distort command in Photoshop Elements.

Before

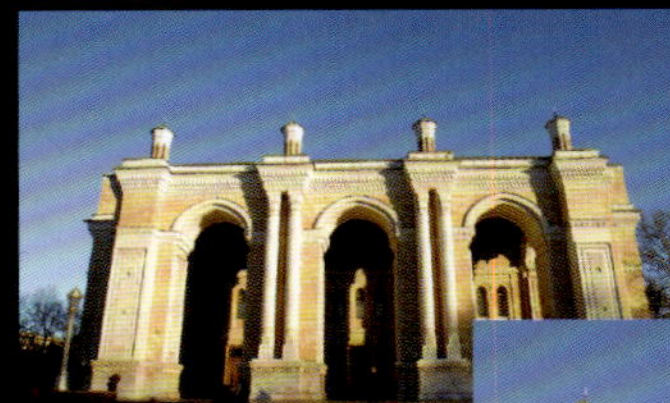

After

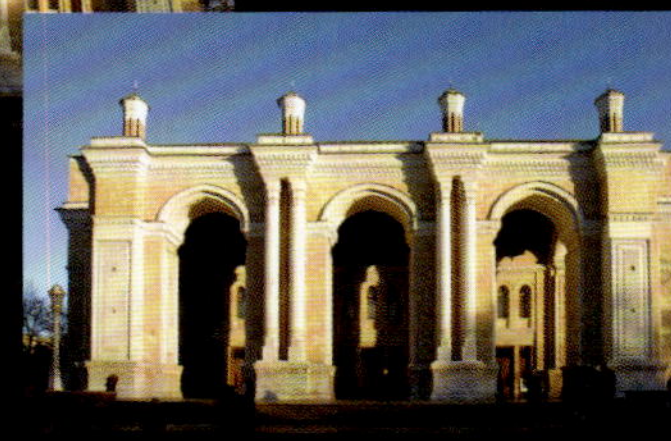

1 Open the **Sample\Chapter 4\Tech29.jpg** file from the supplementary CD.

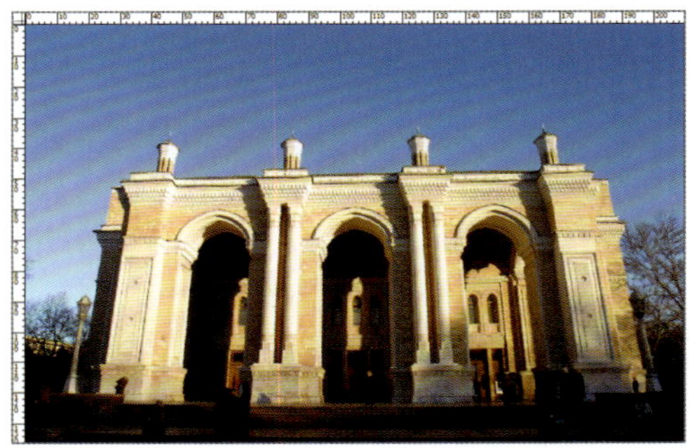

2 Hit the Shift + Ctrl + R keys to display rulers to the left and on top of the image. Another way to display the rulers is to choose View > Ruler from the menu bar.

These rulers will serve as good visual aids when you are straightening the building.

Changing the Unit of Measurement

By default, the rulers are set to measure in centimeters (cm), but the unit of measurement can be changed. To do so, select Edit > Preferences > Units & Rulers from the menu bar and, when the Preferences dialog box appears, click on the Rulers drop-down menu to choose a unit of measurement from the list.

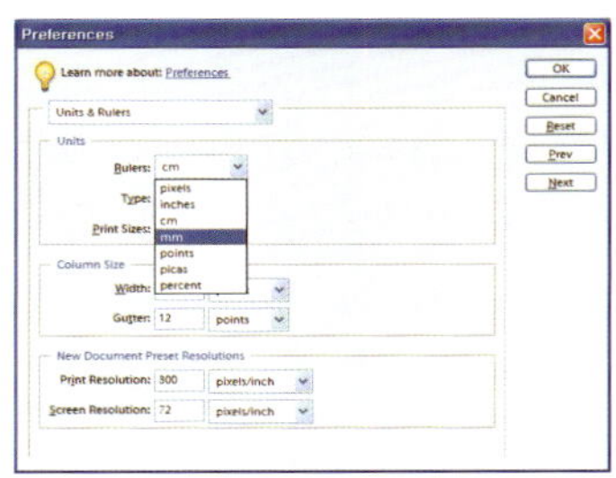

③ Select View > Grids from the menu bar. A grid will appear over the image. The grid and the rulers are visual aids that will not print with the image.

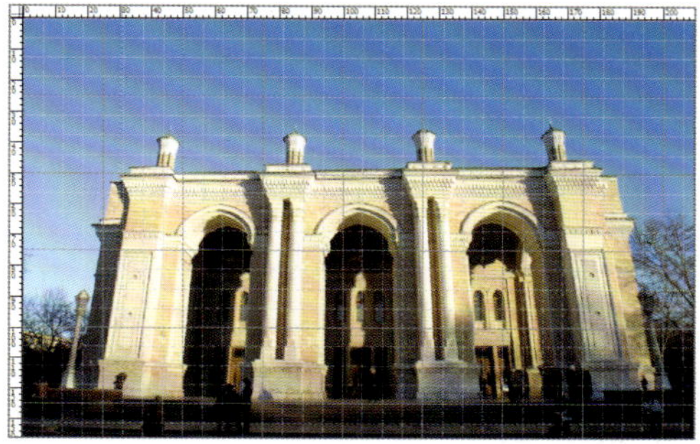

④ Press Ctrl + Alt + - to zoom out of the image.

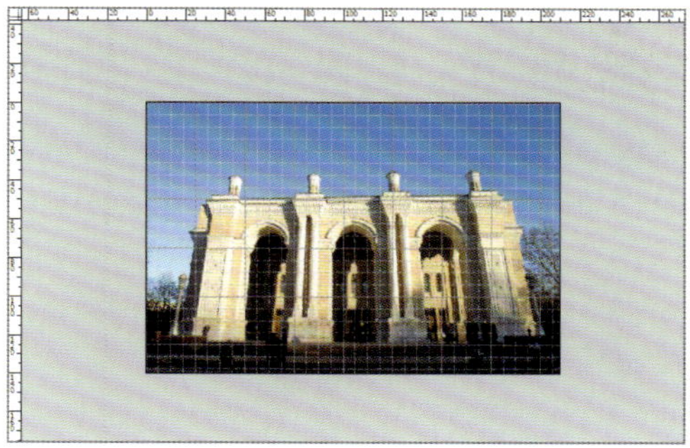

⑤ Select Image > Transform > Distort from the menu bar. You'll see a dialog box asking if you want to change the Background layer to a normal layer. Click OK.

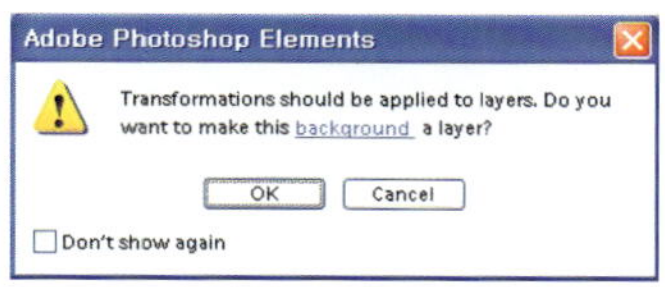

⑥ When the New Layer dialog box appears, type in a name for the layer or leave the name as Layer 0. Click OK.

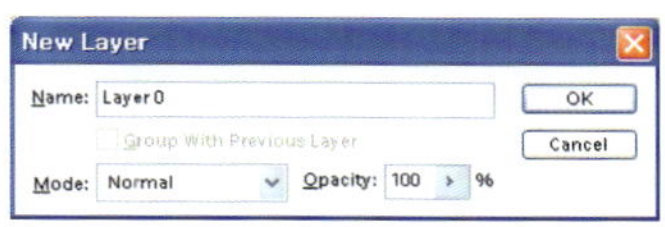

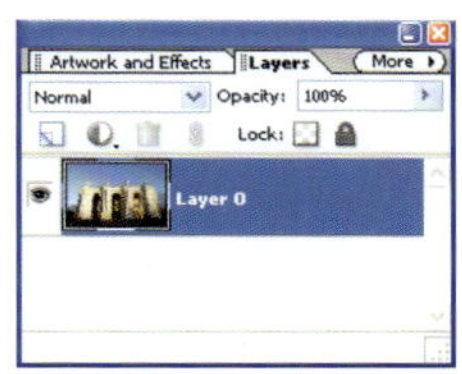

Chapter 04

7 When the image's bounding box appears, drag the top-right handle of the bounding box to the right to straighten the building.

8 Drag the top-left handle of the bounding box to the left and slightly upward.

9 After straightening the building, you will notice that the building appears shorter than it did originally. Drag the top-middle handle upward to correct this problem. Hit the Enter key to activate the transformation.

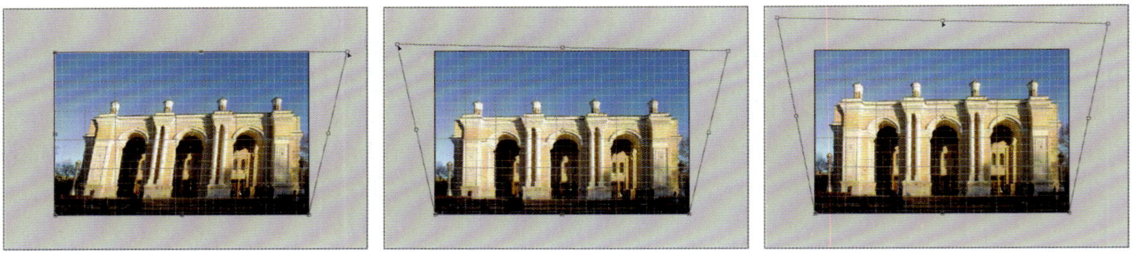

10 Choose View > Grids from the menu bar to remove the grid and hit the Shift + Ctrl + R keys to hide the rulers.

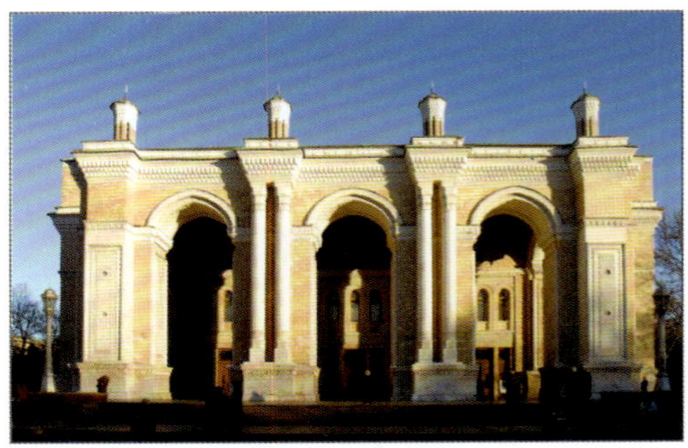

30 Combining Images

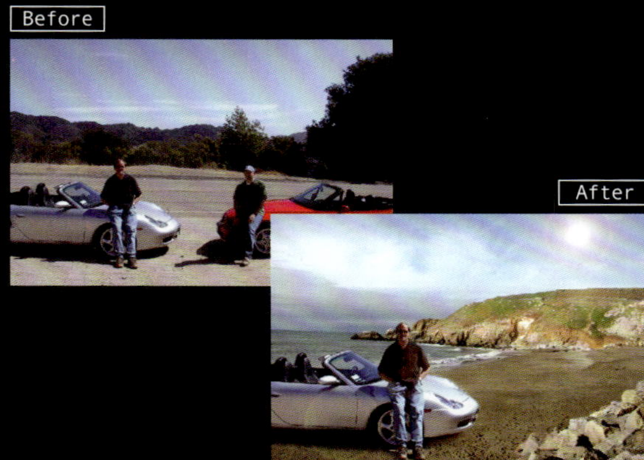

One of the easiest ways to create new and exciting compositions is to combine multiple pictures. In this section, you will learn to combine images inconspicuously by cleaning up the edges of pasted objects and adjusting the brightness and contrast so that elements taken from different sources blend together.

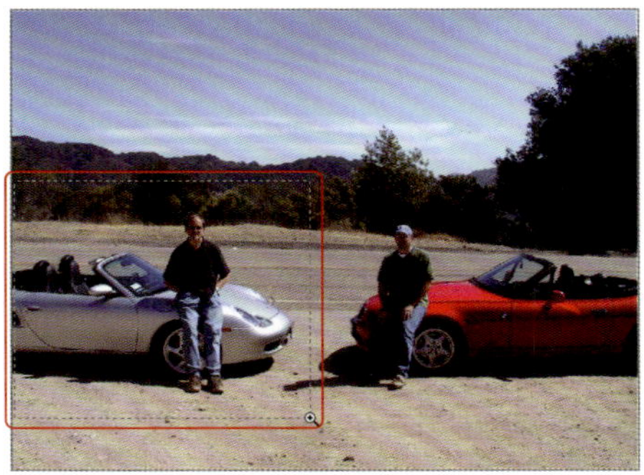

1. Open the **Sample\Chapter 4\Tech30a.tif** file from the supplementary CD.

2. Select the Zoom Tool ( ) from the toolbox. Click on the man on the left to zoom in on him.

3. Select the Selection Brush Tool ( ) from the toolbox. In the options bar, set Size to **35 pixels**, Mode to **Mask**, Hardness to **0%**, Overlay Opacity to **50%**, and Overlay Color to **Red**.

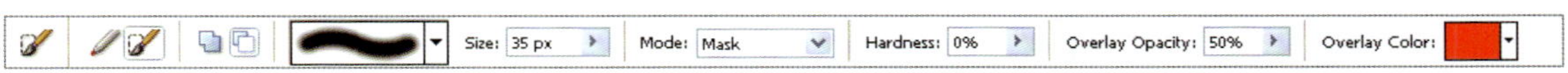

tip A Hardness of 0% makes the brush edges soft and natural. This is important in making the selection border less obvious when the image is placed into another picture.

4 Paint over the man, the silver car, and their shadows to create a mask. Change your brush size as you go along in order to cover the desired area accurately.

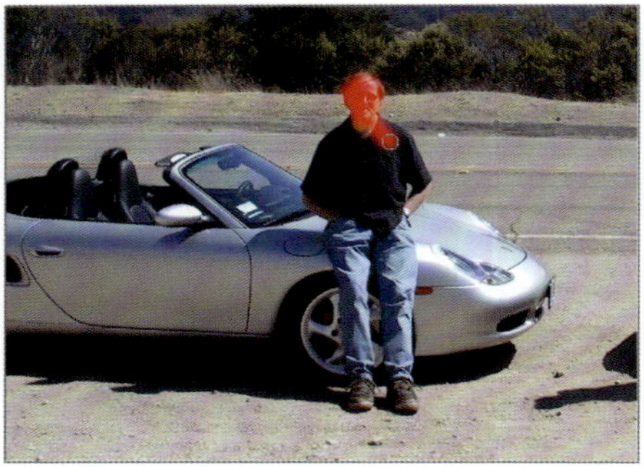

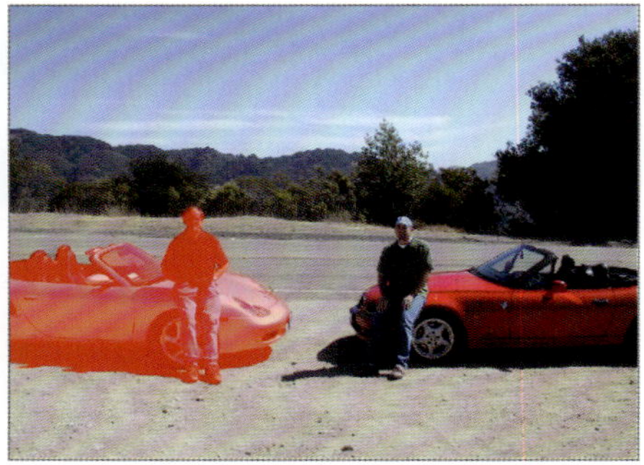

5 In the options bar, set the Mode to **Selection**. This will select the unmasked area.

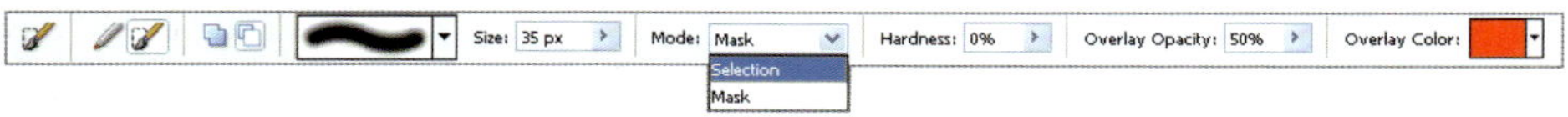

6 Choose Select > Inverse from the menu bar to invert the selection and select the masked area instead. Press Ctrl + C to copy the selection.

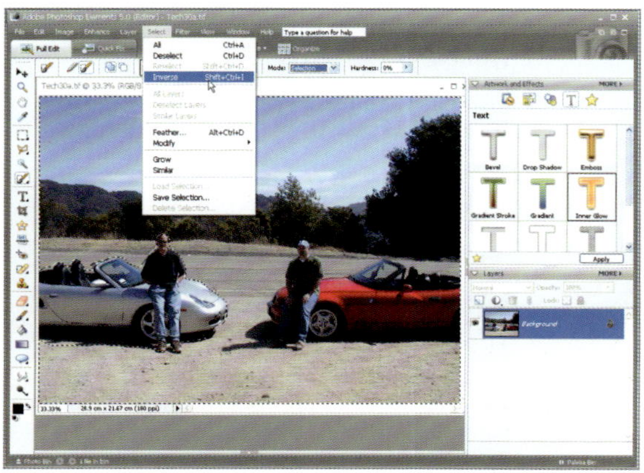

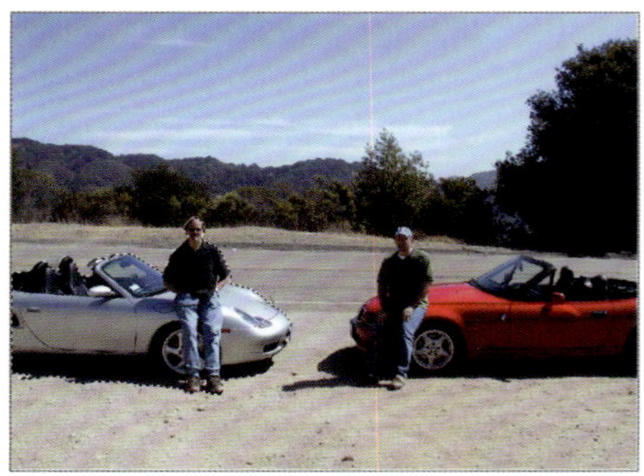

7 Open the **Sample\Chapter 4\Tech30b.tif** file from the supplementary CD.

8 Press Ctrl + V to paste the image of the man and his car onto the image of the beach.

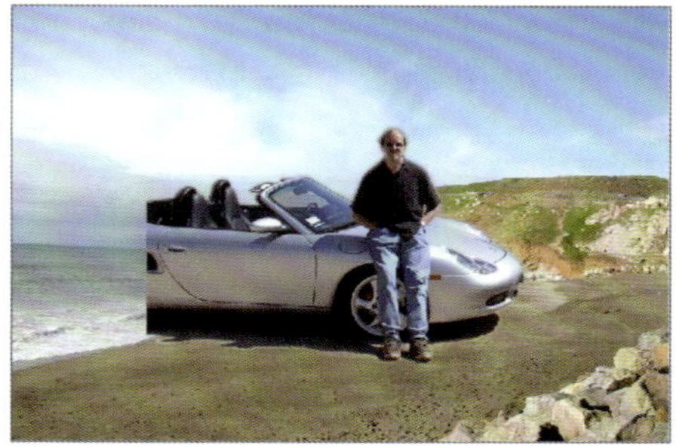

9 Select the Move Tool ( ) from the toolbox. Drag the man and his car to the position shown.

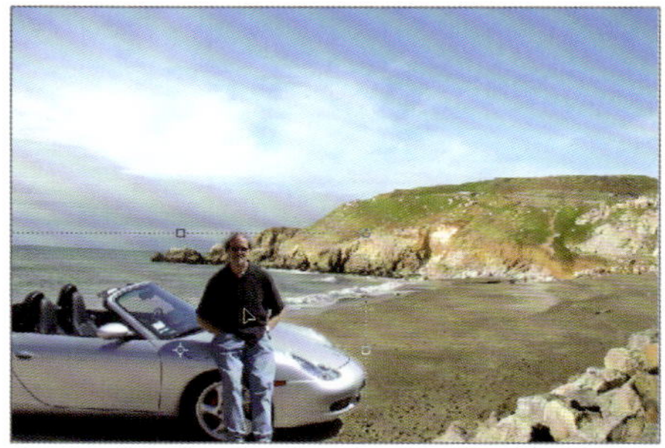

10 Select the Zoom Tool ( ) from the toolbox. Select the car to zoom in on it.

11 Select the Eraser Tool ( ) from the toolbox. In the options bar, set the Brush to **Soft Round** and Size to **9 pixels**. Use the Eraser Tool to clean up the edges of the pasted image.

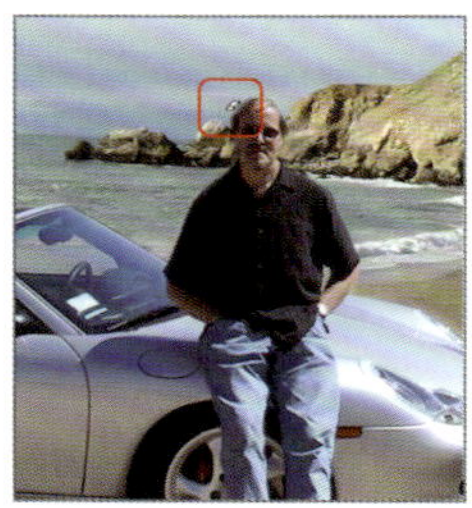

12 In the options bar, set Size to **50 pixels** and Opacity to **50%**. Use the Eraser Tool to clean up the edges of the car's shadow.

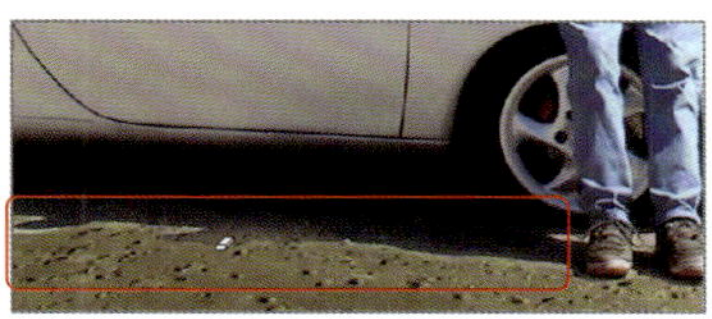

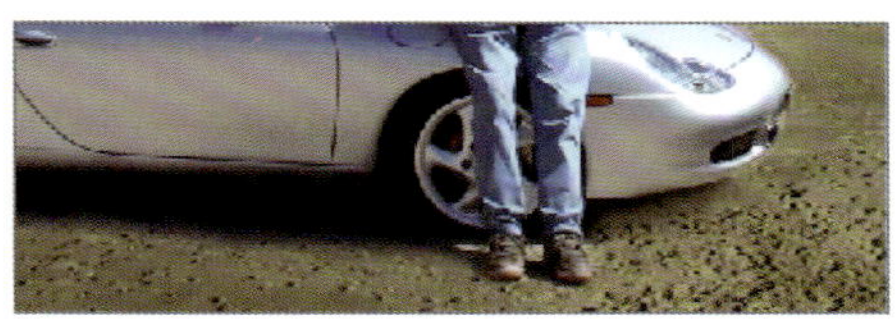

(13) Let's adjust the brightness and contrast of the pasted image to match the background. Select Enhance > Adjust Brightness/Contrast > Brightness/Contrast from the menu bar. In the Brightness/Contrast dialog box, set Brightness to **5** and Contrast to **10**. Click OK.

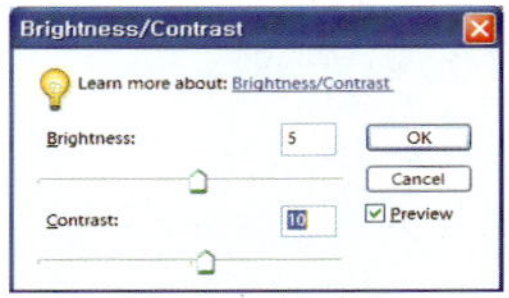

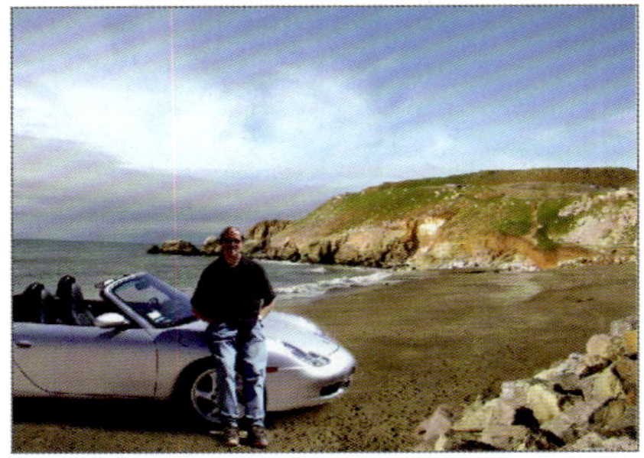

(14) Click the More button in the Layers palette. Select Flatten Image from the drop-down menu to combine the two images on one layer.

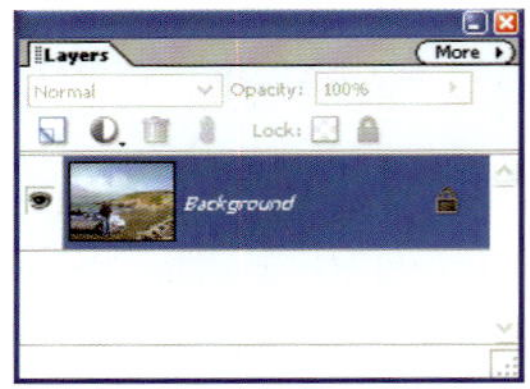

(15) Select Filter > Render > Lens Flare from the menu bar. In the Lens Flare dialog box, click in the Flare Center window to position the lens flare. Set Brightness to **100%**. Click OK.

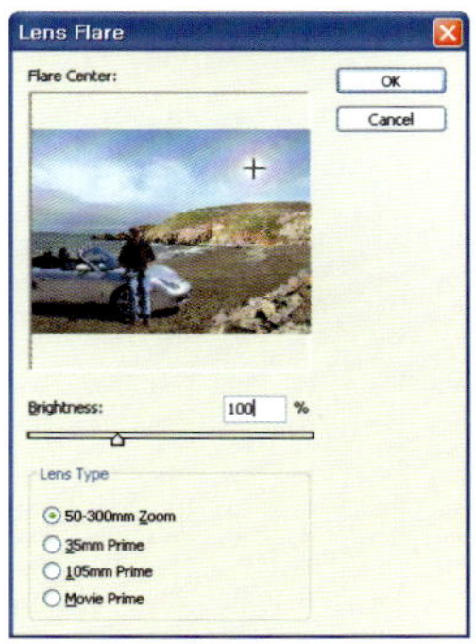

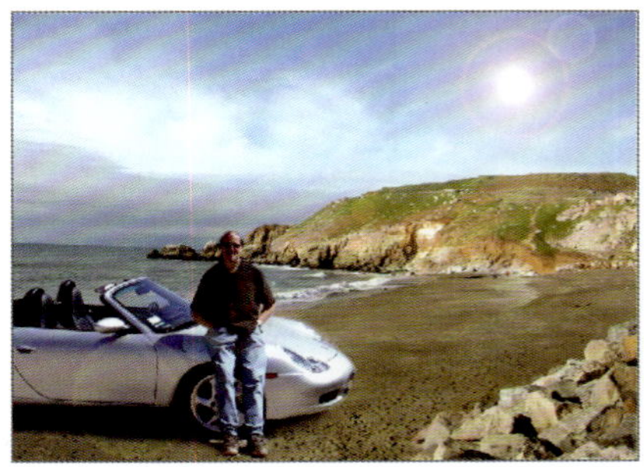

31 Defringe Layer

Before

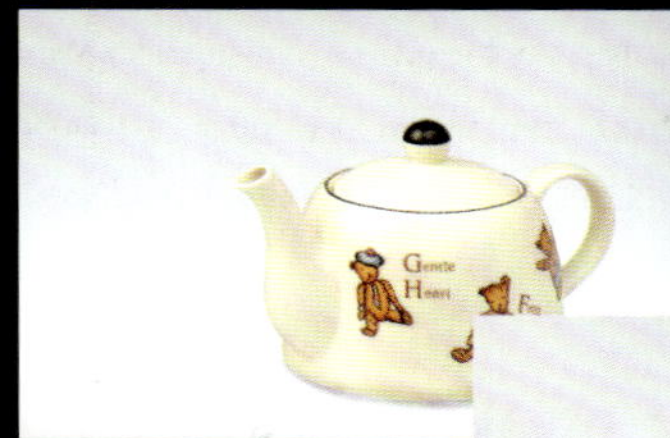

After

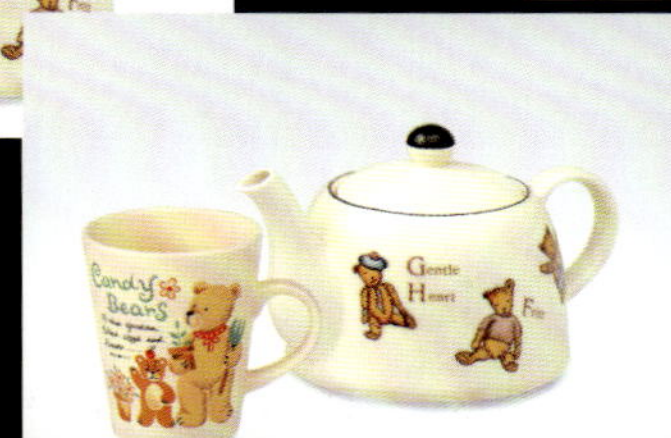

Defringe Layer is a new feature in Photoshop Elements that allows you to combine two images. This feature blurs the borders of the images to be combined, creating a more natural look. This technique will show you how to use this new feature to combine images.

① Open the **Tech31.tif** and the **Tech31a.tif** files from the **Sample\Chapter 4** folder from the supplementary CD.

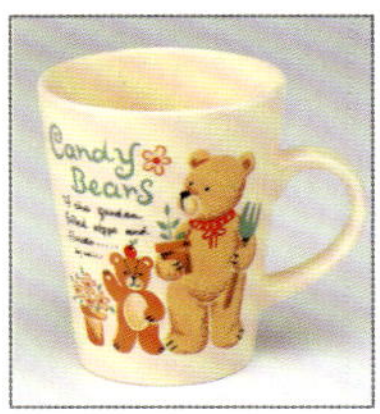

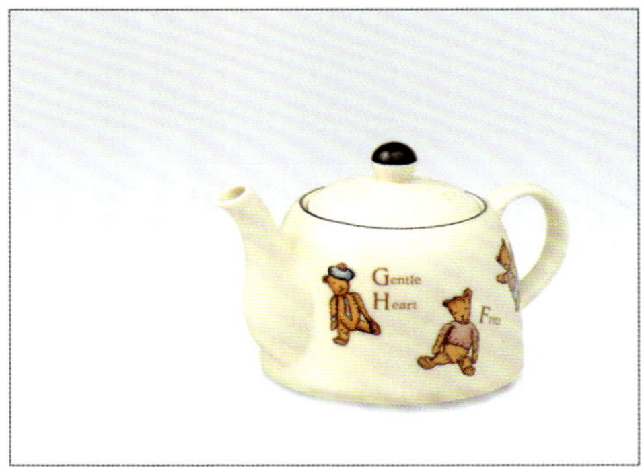

② Select the **Tech31a.tif** file, then click on Select > Load Selection from the Menu bar. The Load Selection dialog box will appear. Input **cup** for Selection and click the OK button.

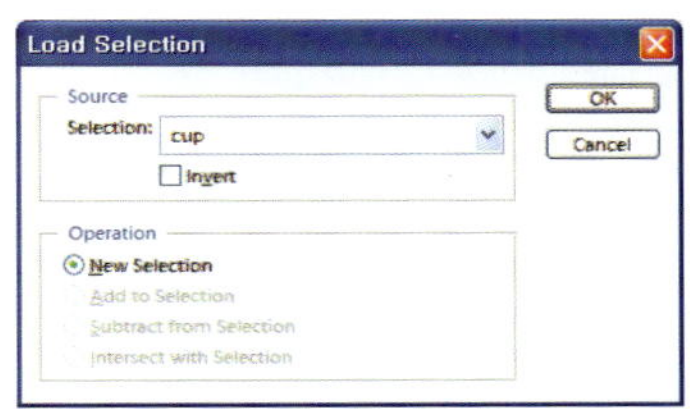

tip The shape of the cup has already been saved with the Saved selection.

(3) Once the selected area is set, press Ctrl + C to save the image inside the selected area. Close the image by pressing Ctrl + W.

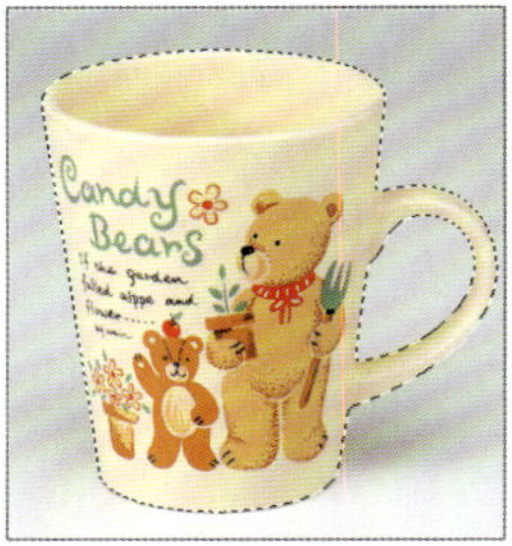

(4) With the **Tech.31.tif** file as the main file in the work window, press Ctrl + V and the mug that you selected and saved in the previous steps will be pasted as shown below.

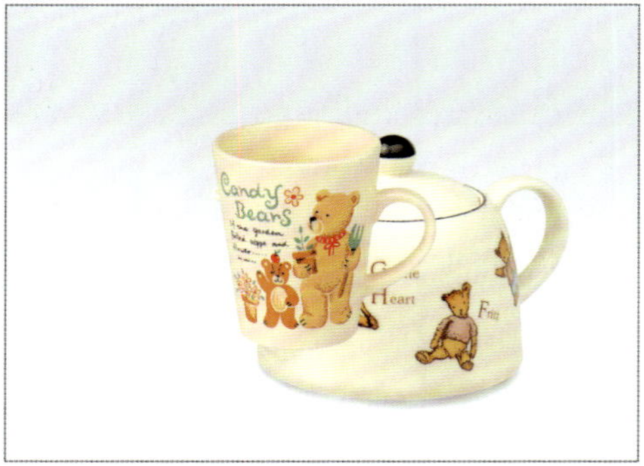

(5) Using the Move Tool ( ) in the tool box, click and drag to change the position of the mug as shown.

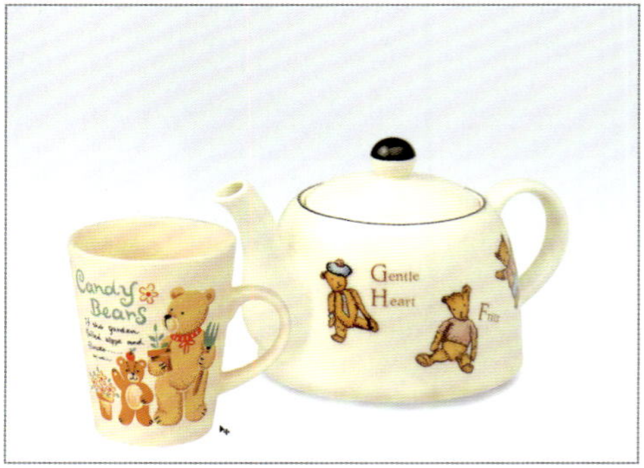

⑥ Once the image is magnified, you can see that the borders of the pasted image seem awkward because of the background from which it was selected.

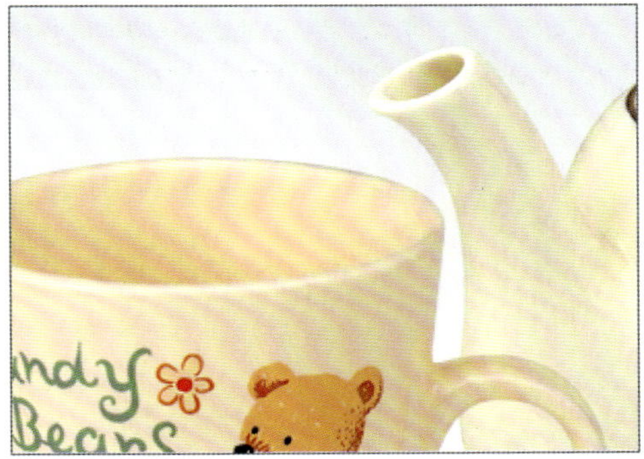

⑦ Click on Enhance > Adjust Color > Defringe Layer from the Menu bar and a Defringe dialog box will appear. Set the Width to **1**, then click the OK button.

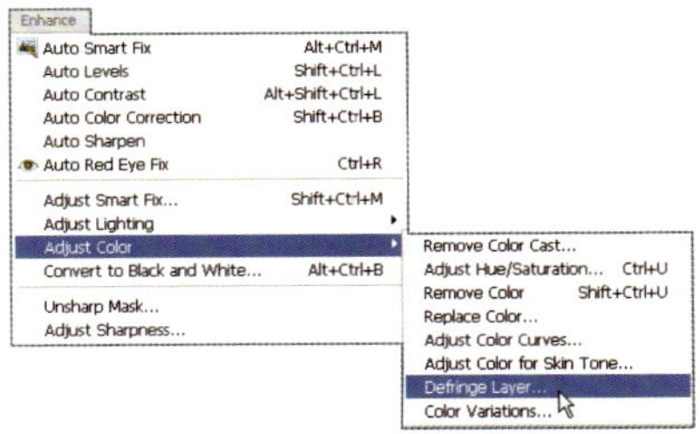

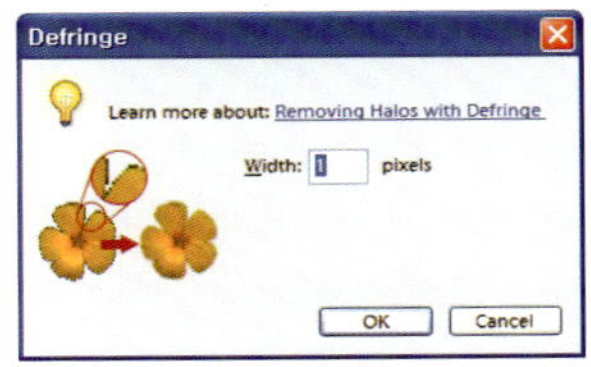

⑧ Now you can see that the border of the cup is much fainter.

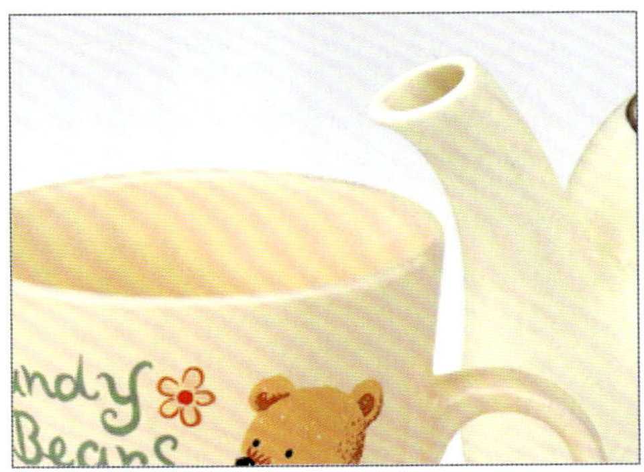

9 Type Ctrl+C to view the whole image again. You can see that the image looks more natural.

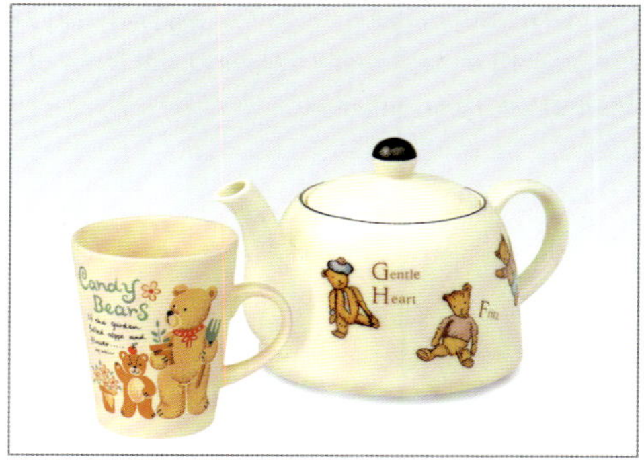

10 Now you have to create a shadow for the mug. After selecting **Layer 1**, click on the **Layer 1** layer while holding down the Ctrl key. Then click on Select > Inverse in the Menu bar to invert the selected area.

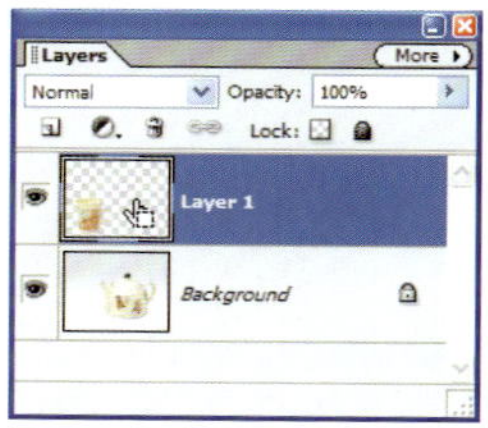

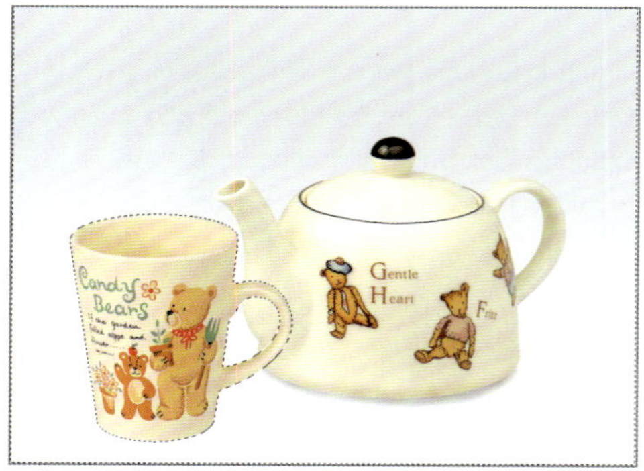

11 Now, select the Brush Tool ( ) from the tool box. Holding down the Alt key, click on the shadow of the pot. You can see that the color of the shadow has been set as the foreground.

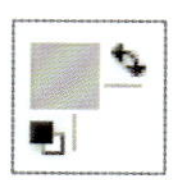

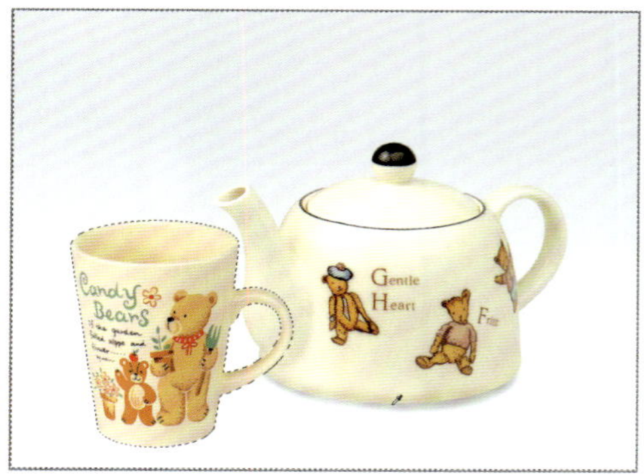

12 Set the brush size to **30** and the Opacity to **100%** in the Option bar.

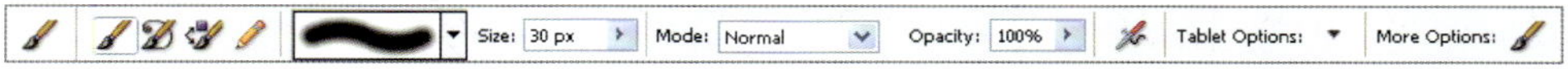

13 Create a shadow for the mug as seen below. Type Ctrl + D when finished to deselect the mug.

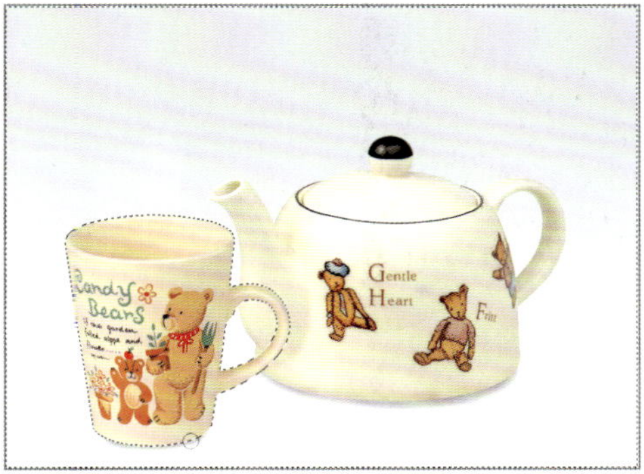

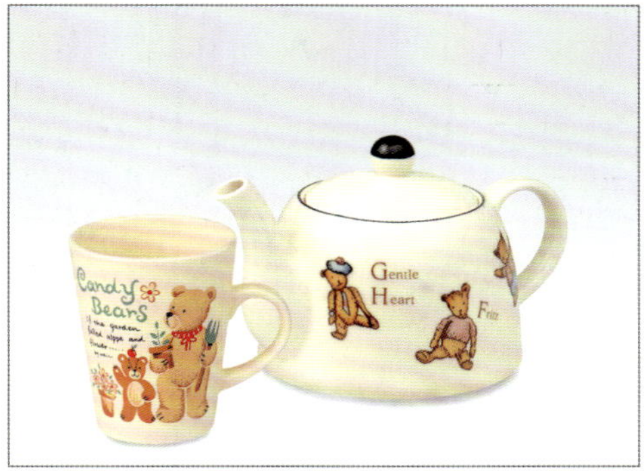

40 Digital Photo Retouching Techniques

with Photoshop Elements 5.0

Chapter 5

Very Special Effects

One feature that instantly attracts many beginners to Photoshop Elements is the Filter command. As you discovered in the previous chapters, you can create dozens, if not hundreds, of snazzy effects with this feature. This chapter will show you how to make practical and creative use of filters through a wide variety of examples. You will learn how to imitate photography techniques such as stitching images together to create a panorama, simulating motion blur, enhancing landscape pictures with snow, utilizing the Define Pattern command, and much more.

32 Stitching Panoramas

Before

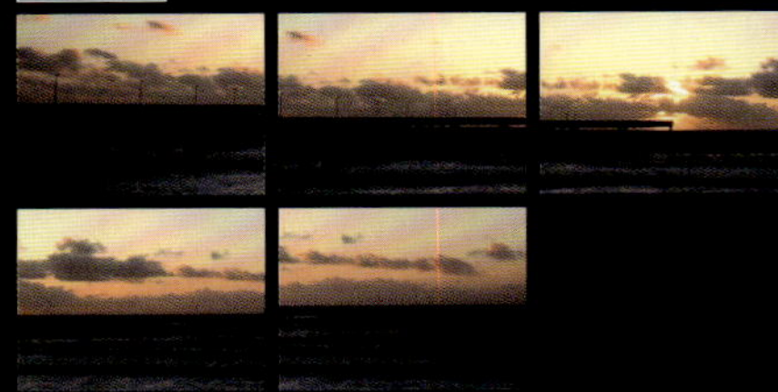

After

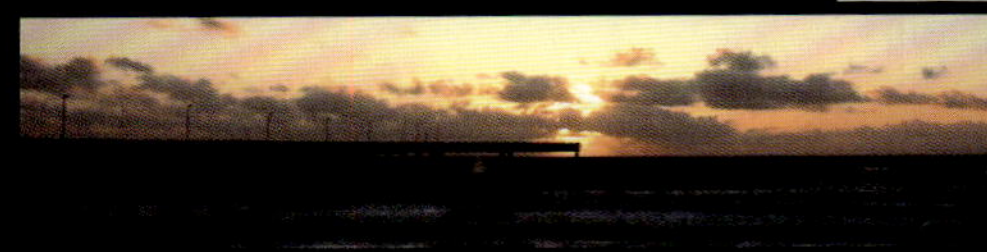

It is difficult to capture the wide expanse of a landscape in a single picture. If you stand some distance away in order to get everything in, the elements of the scene will appear too small. If you stand too close, the reverse happens. For such scenes, it is better to capture sections of the landscape in a few shots and then merge them together in Photoshop Elements.

(1) Select File > New > Photomerge Panorama from the menu bar. In the Photomerge dialog box, click on Browse.

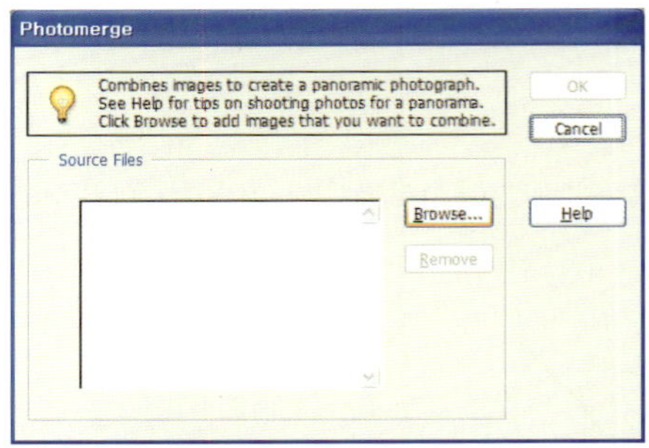

(2) When the Open dialog box appears, open the **Sample\Chapter 5\panorama** folder on the supplementary CD. Hold down the Shift key and select all the pictures in the folder.

(3) Click on Open. The files will appear in the Source Files window in the Photomerge dialog box.

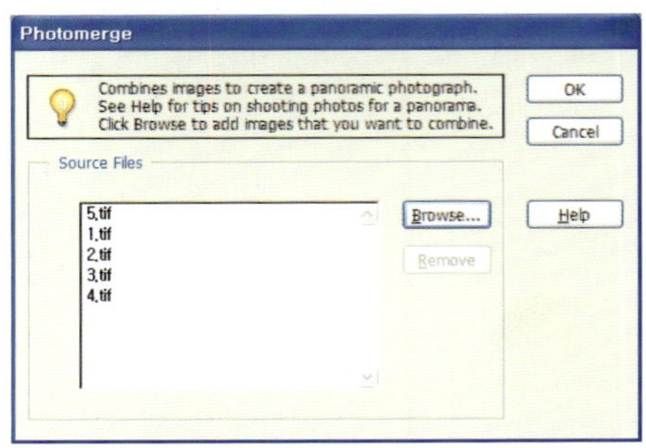

④ Click OK to open the files and execute the Photomerge command. The program will automatically analyze the image data of the overlapping areas and merge the pictures into a panorama. Note that the center piece is in the wrong position.

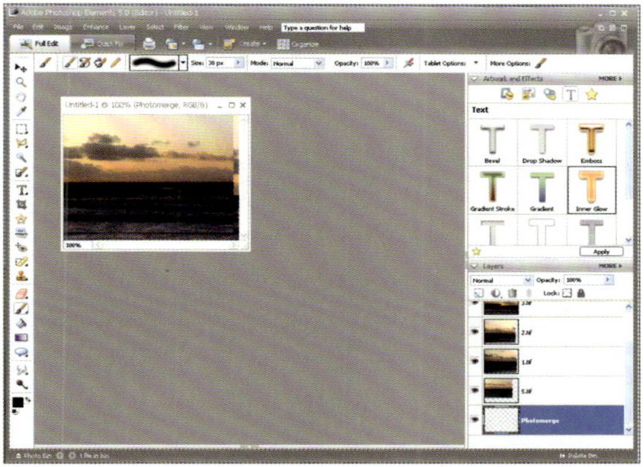

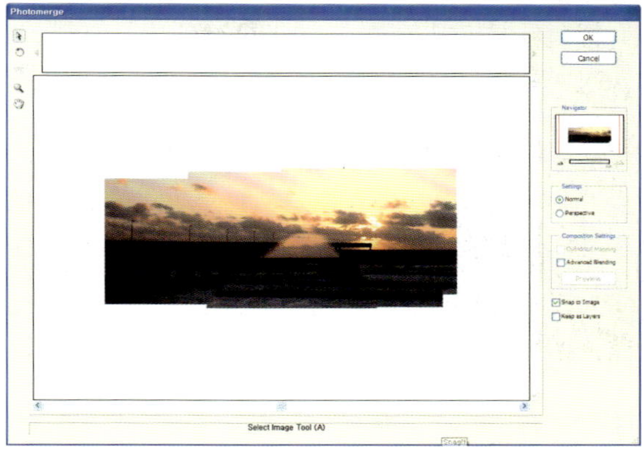

⑤ Click on the Select Image Tool ( ) in the Photomerge dialog box. Click and drag the center image to the right.

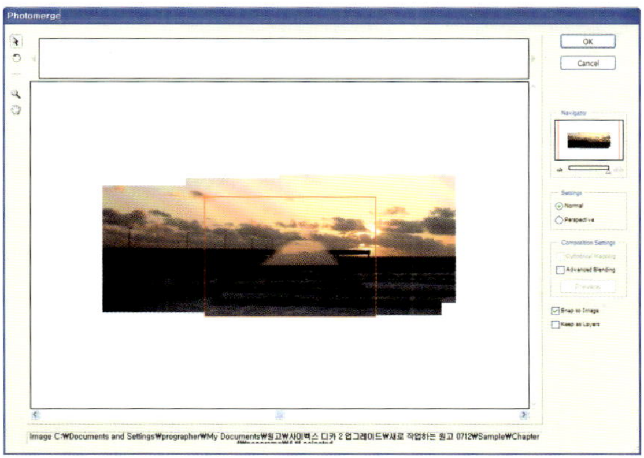

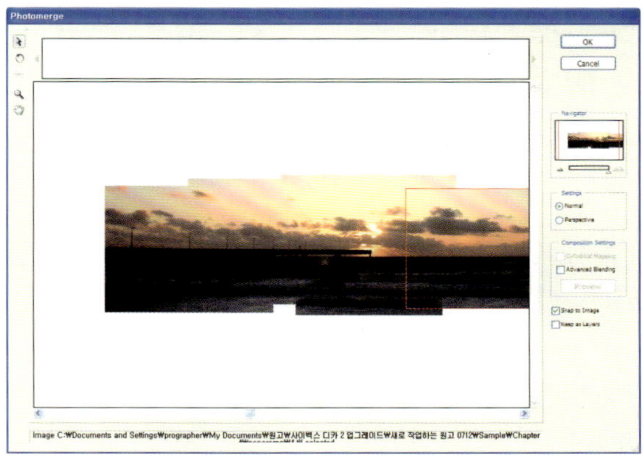

6 Check the Advanced Blending option under Composition Settings at the right of the Photomerge dialog box to blend the edges of the pictures. Click on Preview.

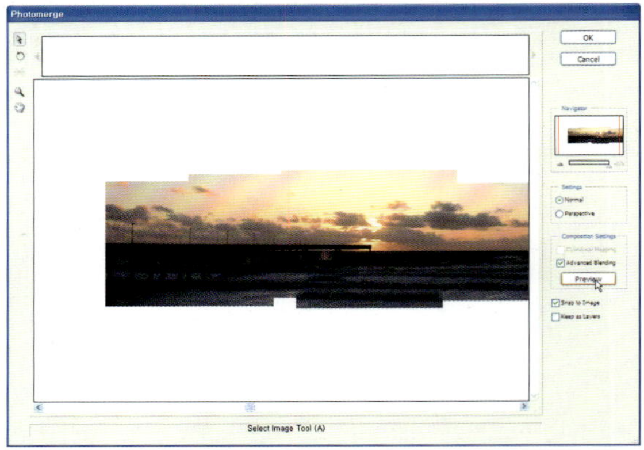

7 Click OK to complete the photomerge. The panorama appears in a new window.

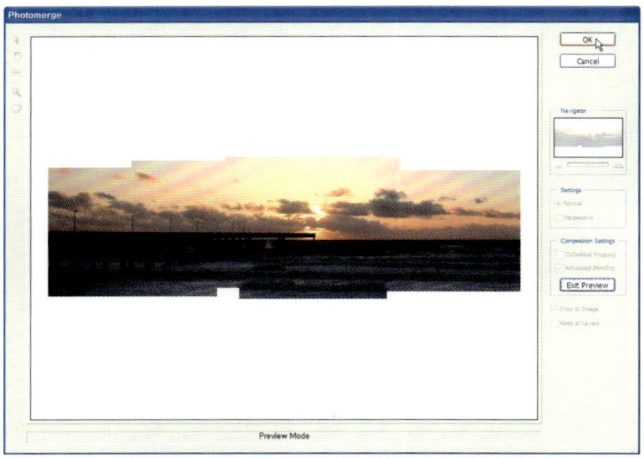

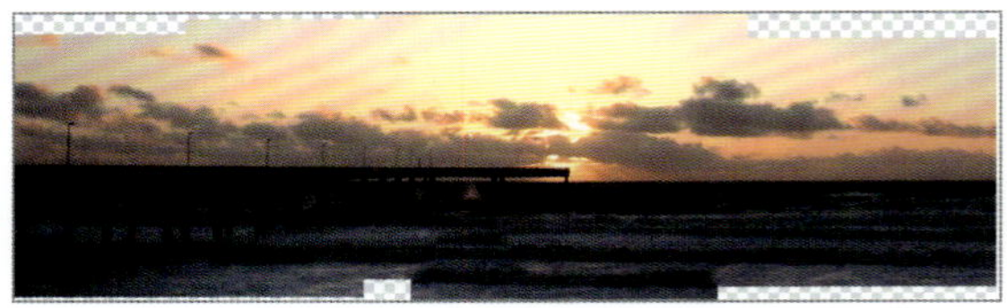

8 Select the Crop Tool ( ) from the toolbox. Select the image as shown, leaving out the jagged edges. Press Enter.

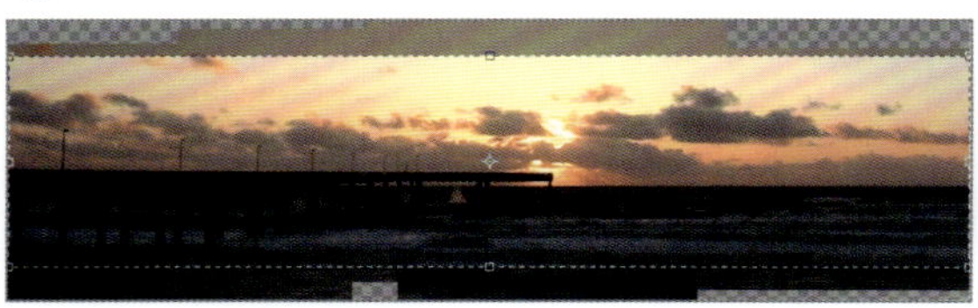

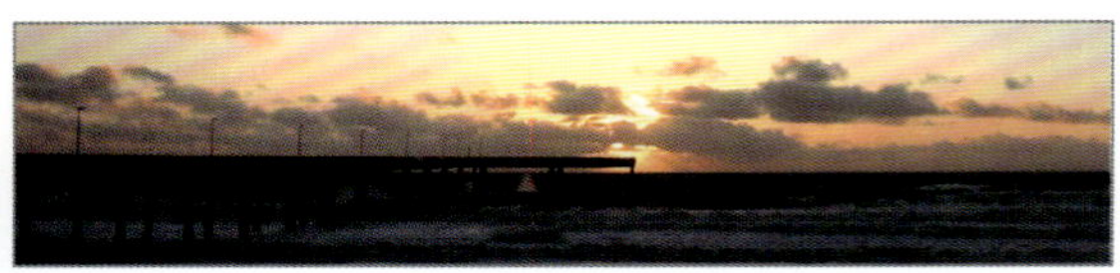

33 Adding Motion Blur

Before

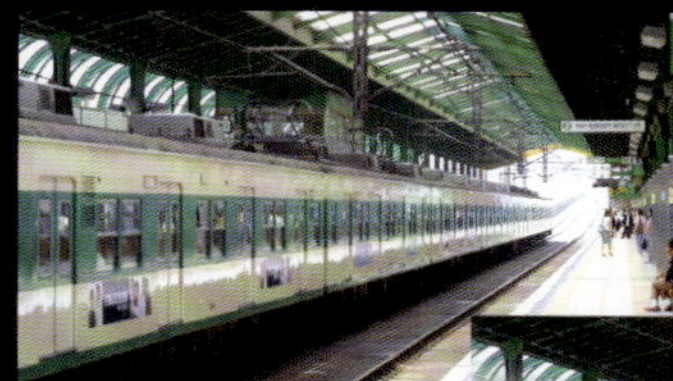

After

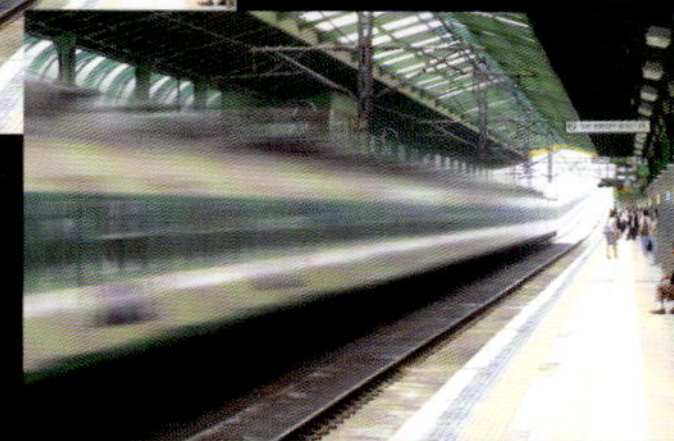

The Motion Blur filter in Photoshop Elements is great for adding motion to pictures of movable objects. It is commonly used on images of vehicles such as cars and trains. You can also use it on a shot of people walking or even on a shot of a fan.

1 Open the **Sample\Chapter 5\Tech33.tif** file from the supplementary CD.

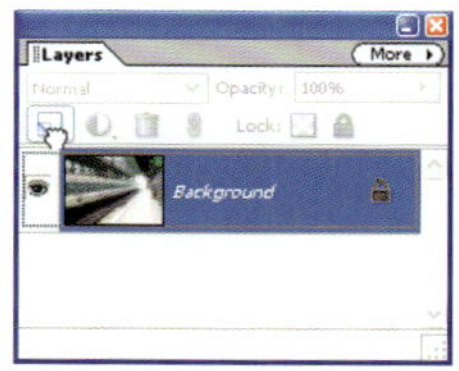

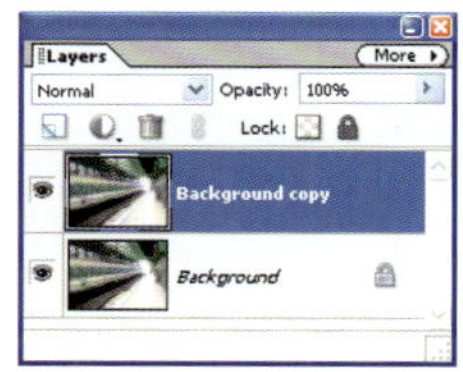

2 In the Layers palette, click and drag the Background layer onto the Create a New Layer button ( ) to make a copy of the layer. In the following steps, we will be adding motion blur effects to the copy and overlaying it onto the background.

3 Select Filter > Blur > Motion Blur from the menu bar. In the Motion Blur dialog box, set Angle to **5°** and Distance to **70 pixels**. Click OK.

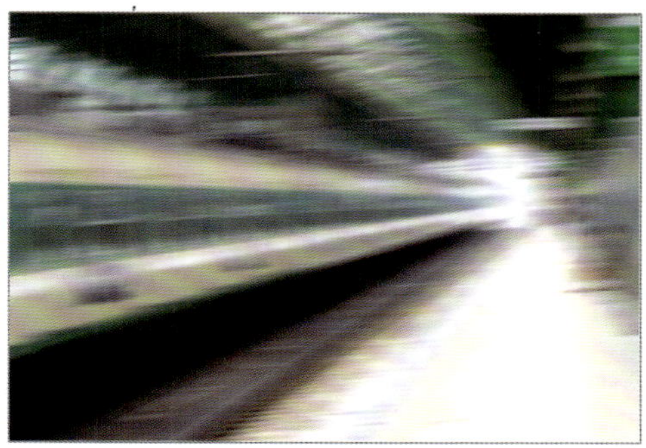

V Angle refers to the direction in which the motion blur will be applied. An angle of 0° applies the motion blur horizontally, and an angle of 90° applies it vertically. In this example, an angle of 5° applies the motion blur at a slight angle from the x-axis. Distance refers to how far the motion blur is applied.

4 Select the Eraser Tool ( ) from the toolbox. In the options bar, set Size to **300 pixels**. Erase everything in the picture but the train. This allows the background to show through areas that we want to keep in focus.

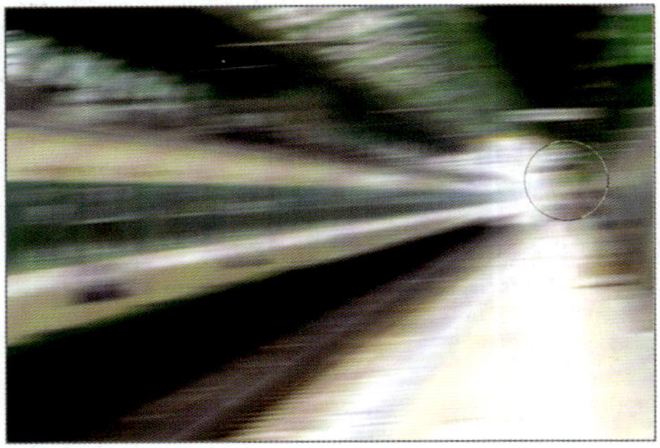

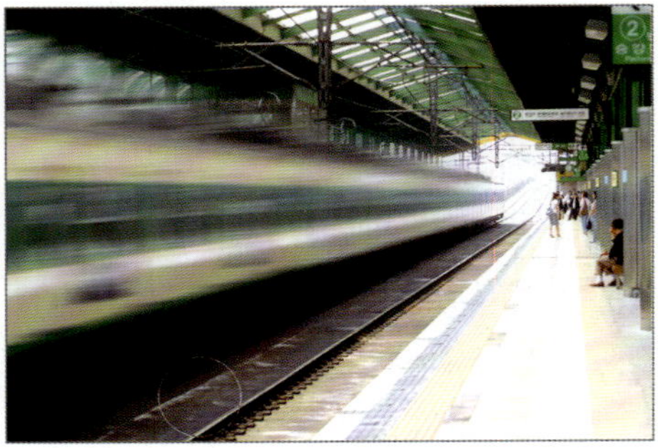

5 In the options bar, set Opacity to **30%**. Drag over the front portion of the train to reduce the motion blur. This gives the image an illusion of depth.

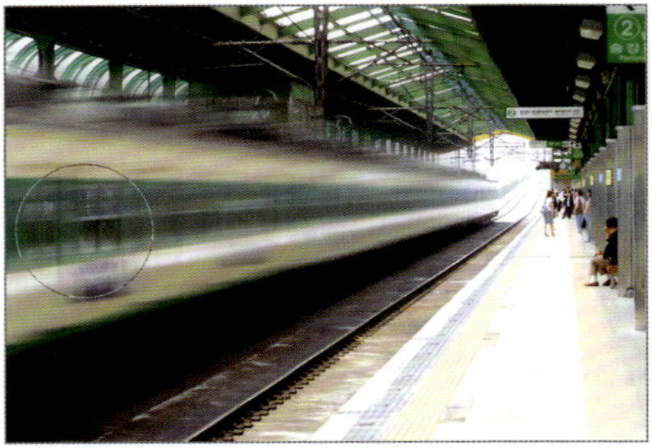

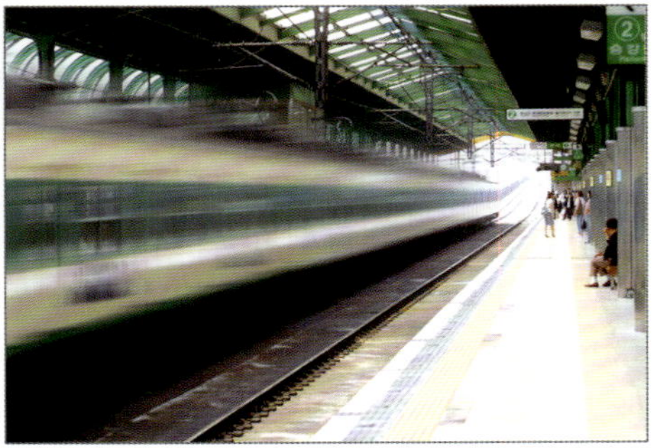

34 Giving Photos an Antiqued Look

Old photographs evoke nostalgia and seem more precious because of their fragility and the fact that the memories they capture are of a distant past. You can imitate the faded look of antiquated photos in your images by adding graininess, desaturating the colors, and adding hair and dust particles. Of course, Photoshop Elements allows you to implement and blend these effects for that perfectly aged look.

Before

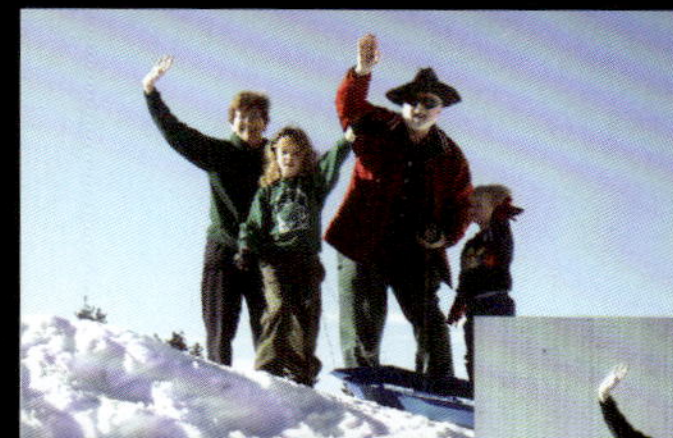

After

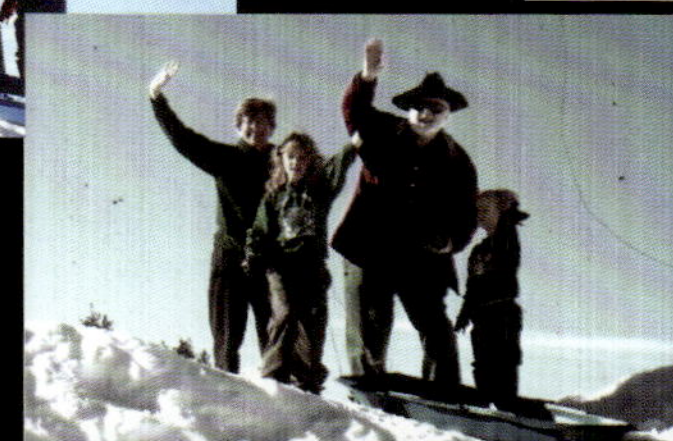

1 Open the **Sample\Chapter 5\Tech34.jpg** file from the supplementary CD.

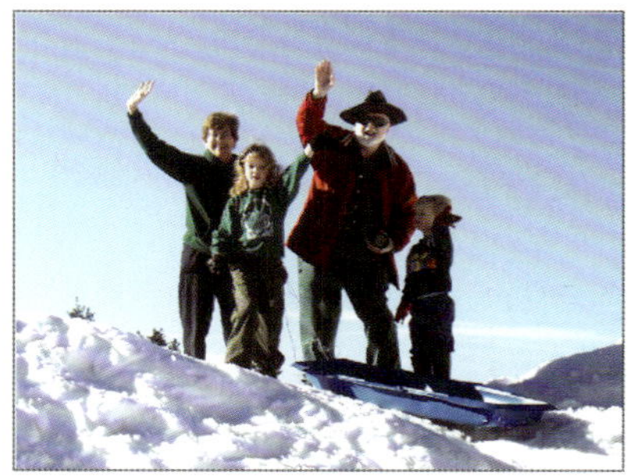

2 Select Filter > Texture > Grain from the menu bar. In the Grain dialog box, set Intensity to **12**, Contrast to **13**, and Grain Type to **Vertical**. Click OK to add fine vertical lines and a grainy texture to the picture. This will make the family portrait look as if it was shot with an old camera.

tip If you want to add horizontal lines instead of vertical ones, set Grain Type to Horizontal in the Grain dialog box.

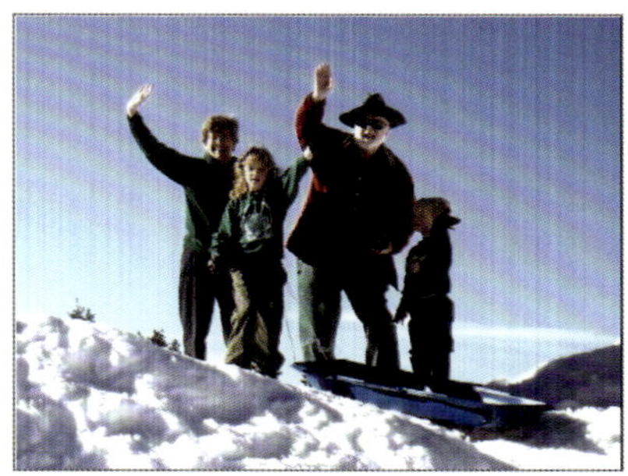

3 Select Enhance > Adjust Color > Adjust Hue/Saturation from the menu bar. In the Hue/Saturation dialog box, set Edit to **Master**, Hue to **–20**, Saturation to **–50**, and Lightness to **0**. Click OK. This will make the colors look faded.

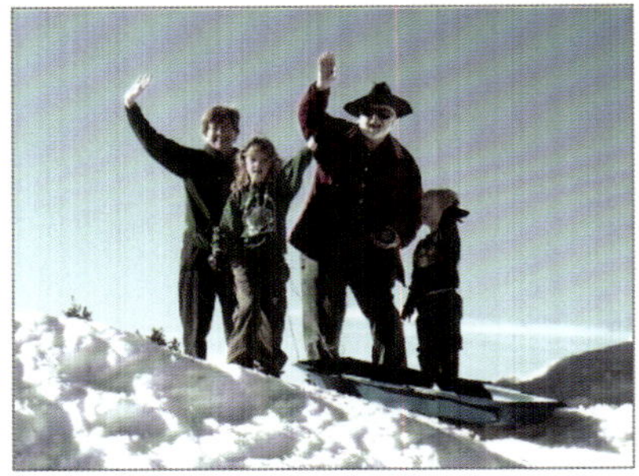

4 Select Window > Styles and Effects from the menu bar. When the Styles and Effects palette appears, double-click on the Vertical Color Fade effect. The colors in the family portrait will fade toward the top.

tip You can make the color fade across a picture by selecting the Horizontal Color Fade icon in the Styles and Effects palette.

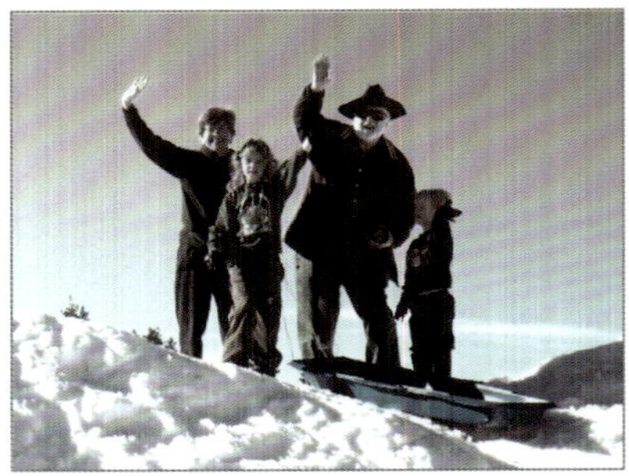

5 Open the **Sample\Chapter 5\Tech34a.jpg** file from the supplementary CD. This image was created by scanning the hair and dust particles placed on a scanner.

6 Press Ctrl + A to select the entire image and then press Ctrl + C to copy it.

7 Return to the family portrait and press Ctrl + V to paste the dust copy onto it.

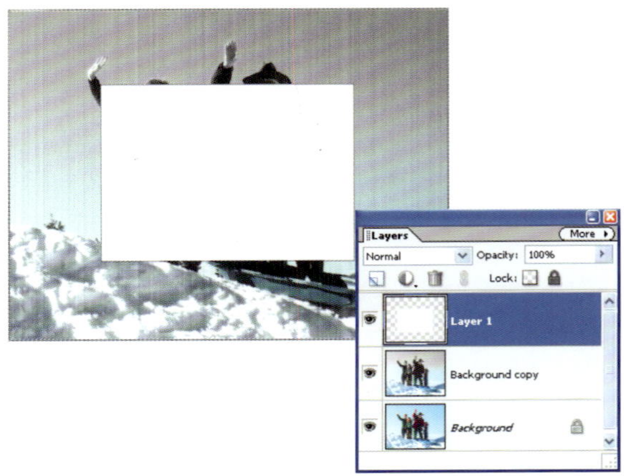

⑧ Press Ctrl+T and expand the dust image to fit the size of the picture. Press Enter or double-click inside the image when you are done.

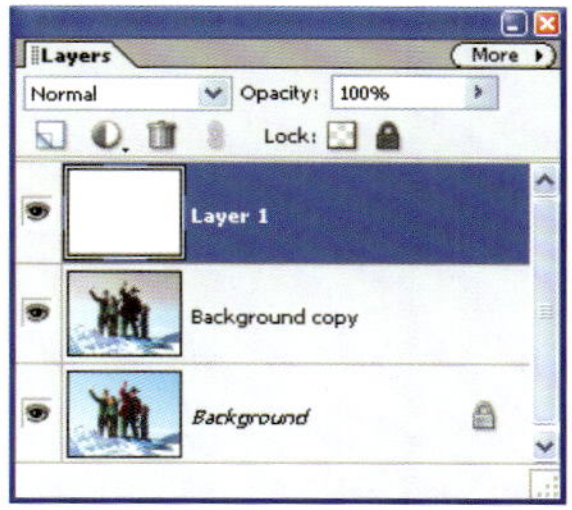

⑨ In the Layers palette, change the blending mode of Layer 1 to **Multiply**. This will allow the family portrait to show through the dust copy.

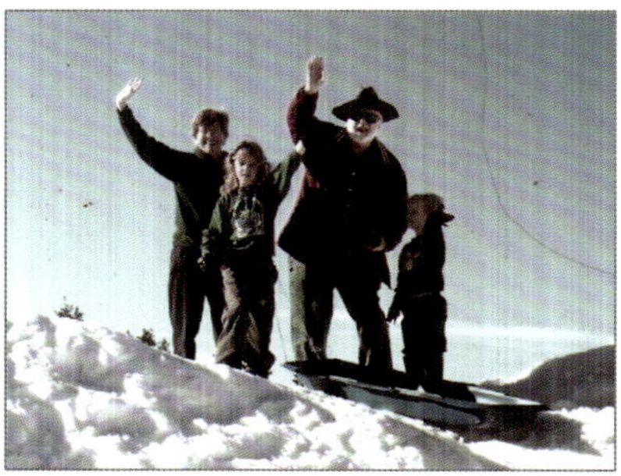

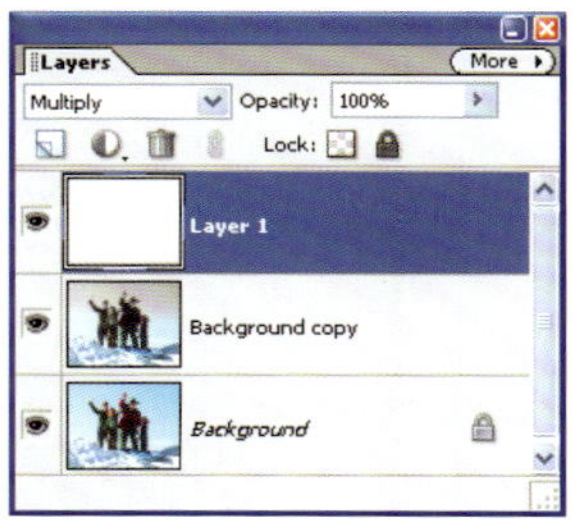

35 Maintaining Texture While Repainting an Object

Before

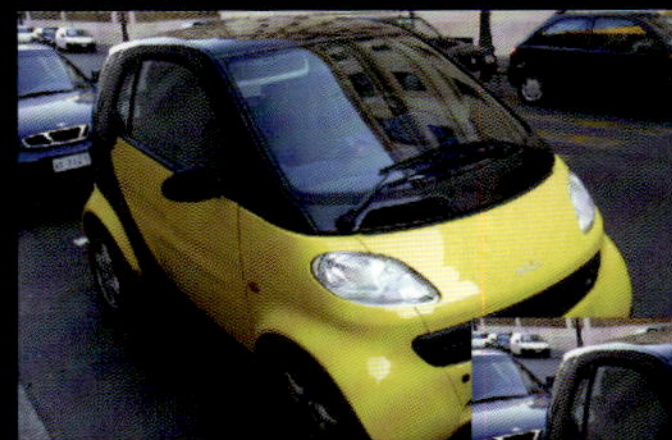

After

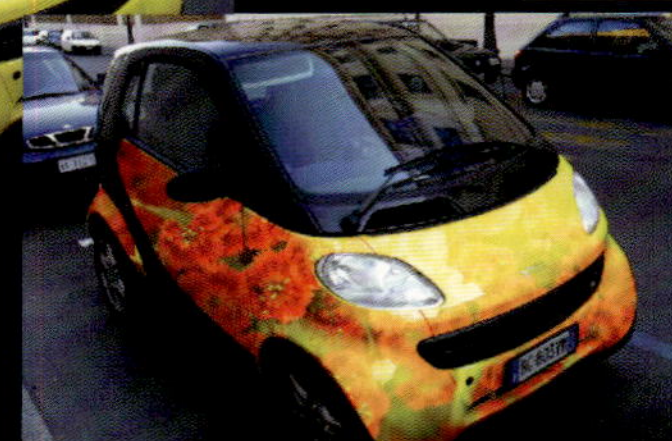

The key to keeping an object's texture intact when repainting it is the effective use of blending modes. When an image or pattern is pasted onto an object, the object will look flat and unnatural. In this exercise, you will learn to paste a flower pattern onto a car, then utilize blending modes to retain the car's original metallic texture.

(1) Open the **Sample\Chapter 5\Tech35a.jpg** and **Sample\Chapter 5\Tech35b.jpg** files from the supplementary CD.

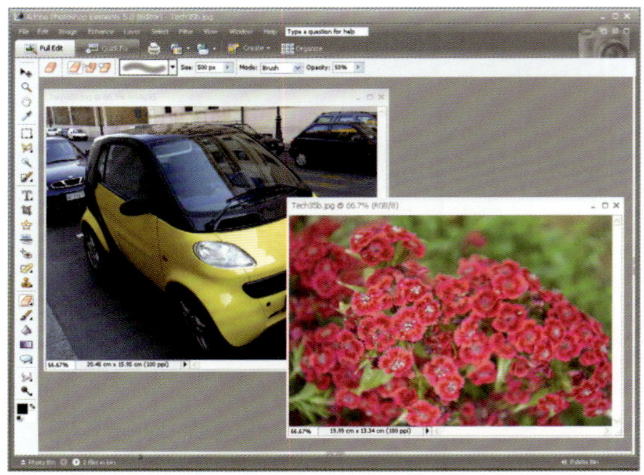

2 Select Window > Tech35b.jpg from the menu bar to bring forward the flower image. Choose Select > All from the menu bar to select the entire image. Next, select Edit > Copy from the menu bar or press Ctrl + C to copy the flower image to the clipboard.

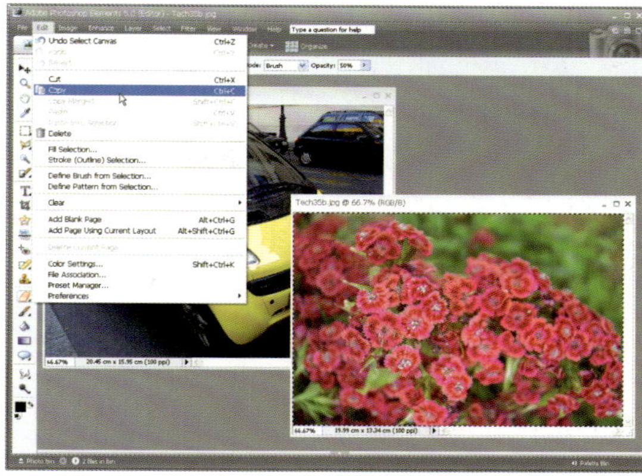

3 Select Window > Tech35a.jpg from the menu bar to bring forward the car image. Select the Magic Wand Tool ( ) from the toolbox and set the Tolerance value to **30**. Click on the hood of the car, as shown here.

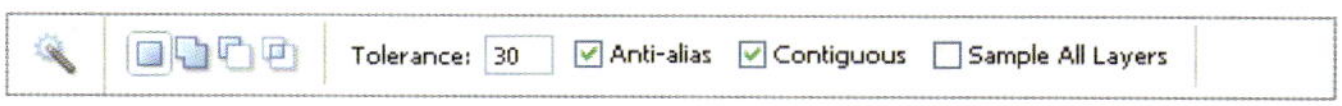

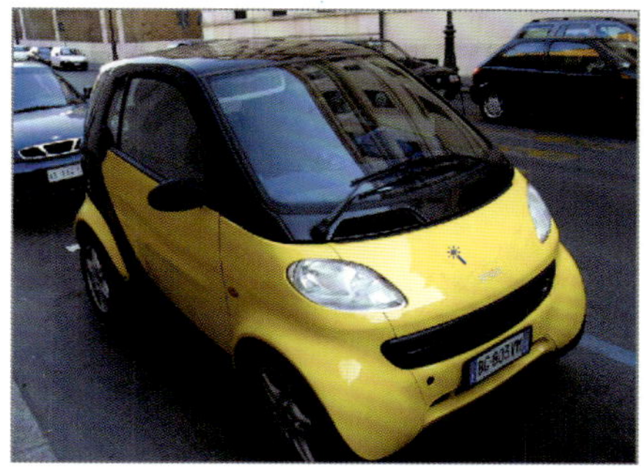

4 Click on the rest of the car's yellow body while holding down the Shift key to add to the selection.

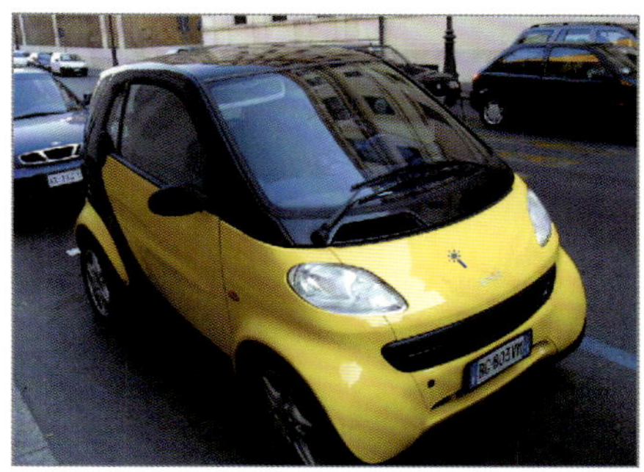

(5) Check that you have selected the car's entire yellow body, including the yellow bit on the back wheel.

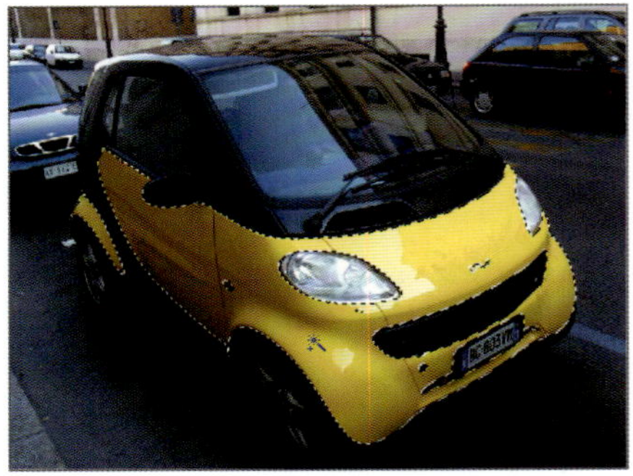

(6) Click on the Create a New Layer icon ([icon]) in the Layers palette to create a new layer.

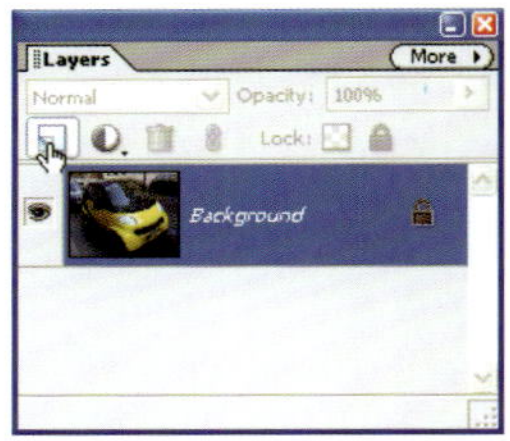

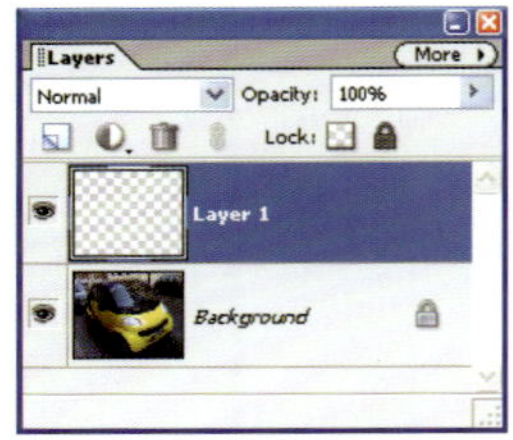

(7) Let's paste the flower image that was copied to the clipboard in step 2 onto the car's yellow body. Select Edit > Paste Into Selection from the menu bar.

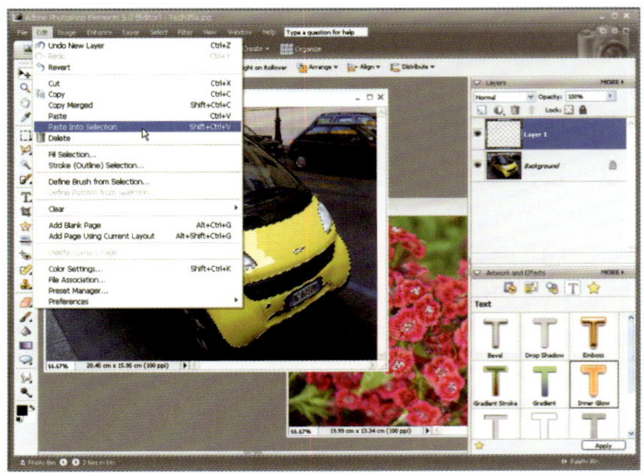

8 You can see that the car's original yellow body has been replaced with the flower image.

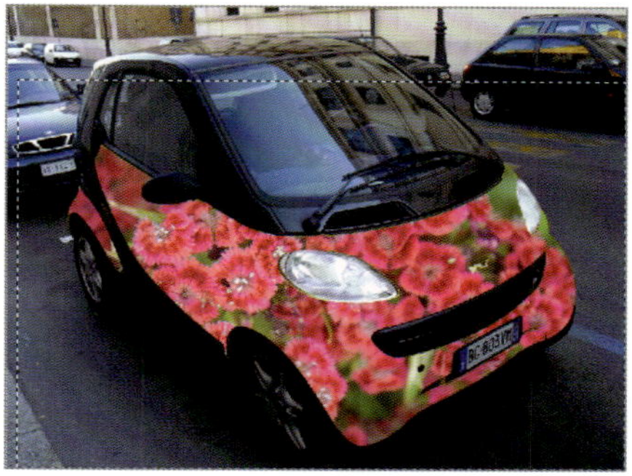

9 You may notice that the car's body now looks flat. The flower image does not have the highlights and shadows that define the car's original body. To make the body look more three-dimensional, change the blending mode to **Overlay** in the Layers palette.

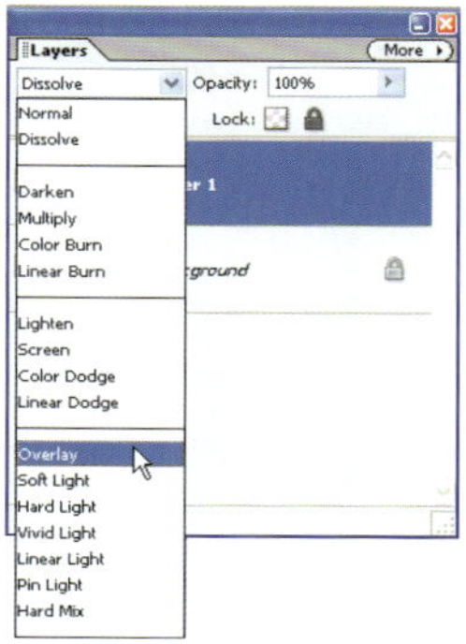

10 Changing the blending mode to Overlay blends together the car's yellow body with the flower image to create a more realistic-looking car body.

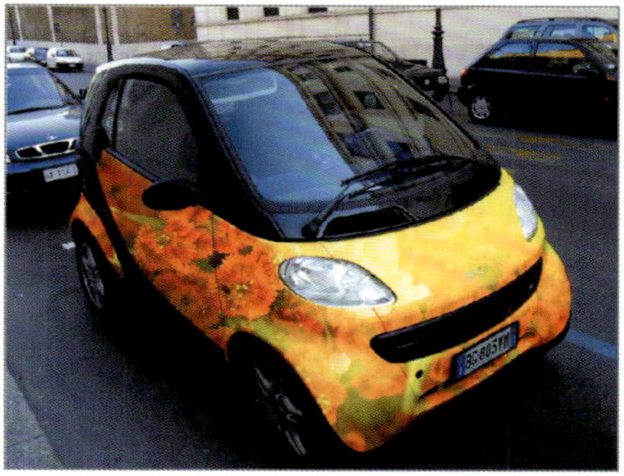

Chapter 05

(11) You can experiment with the different blending modes in the Layers palette to create a variety of new styles for the car body.

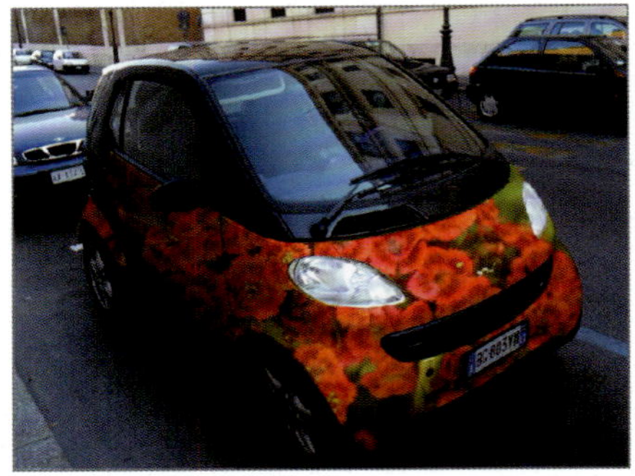

▲ Multiply

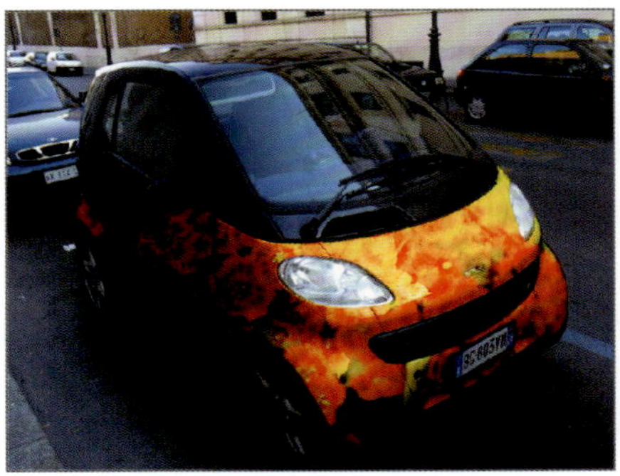

▲ Color Burn

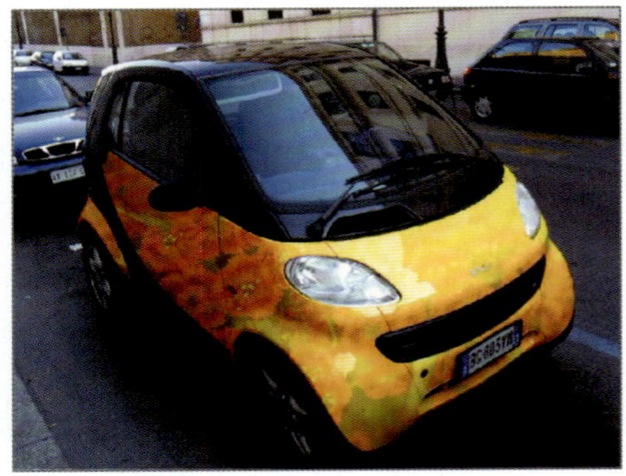

▲ Soft Light

36 Let It Snow

Before

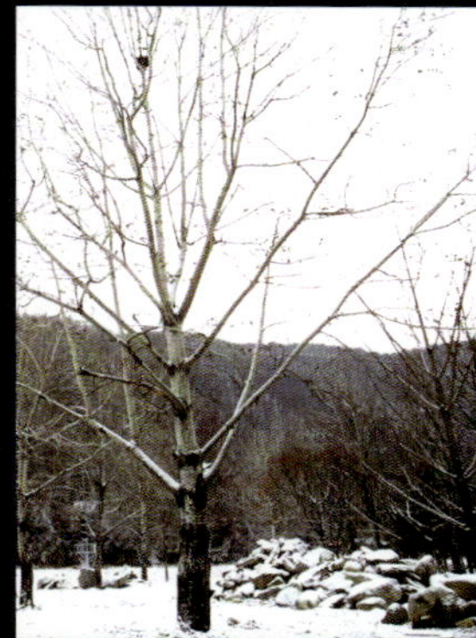

After

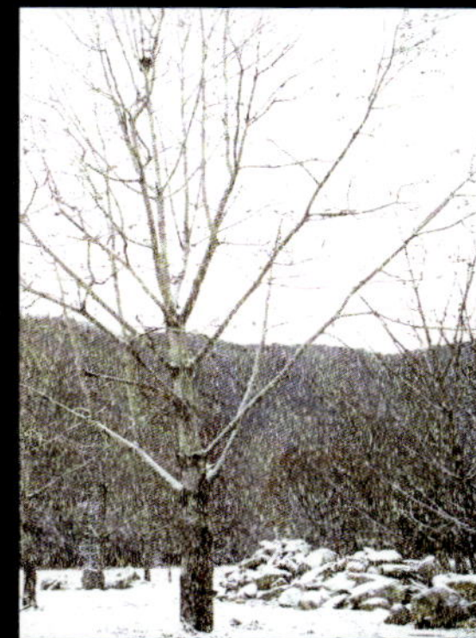

Taking pictures in subzero temperatures is hard, but getting a shot with just the right amount of snowfall is even more difficult. You need perseverance and luck to get those kinds of shots. In this section, you will make picture of snow-capped trees and mountains even more perfect by adding snowfall with the Add Noise filter.

1 Open the **Sample\Chapter 5\Tech36.tif** file from the supplementary CD.

2 Click on the Create a New Layer icon ( ) in the Layers palette to create a new layer for the snow effect.

3 Select the Rectangular Marquee Tool ( ) from the toolbox. Make the selection, as shown here.

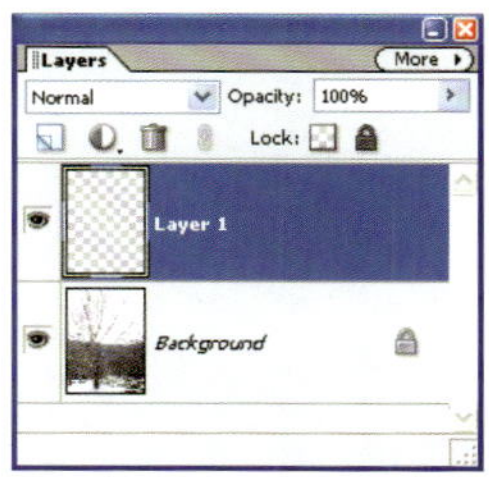

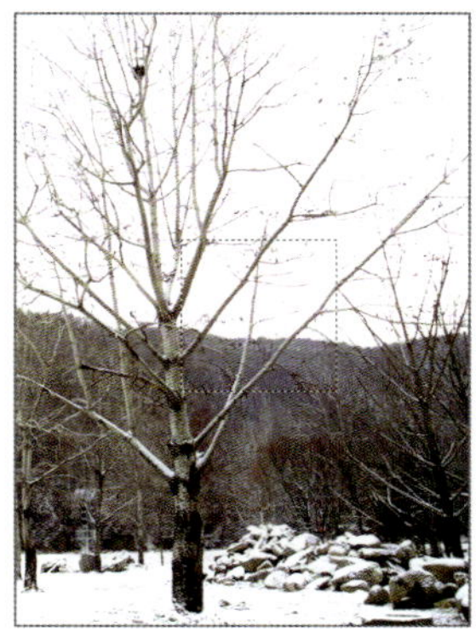

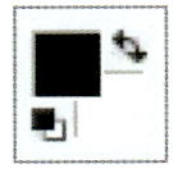

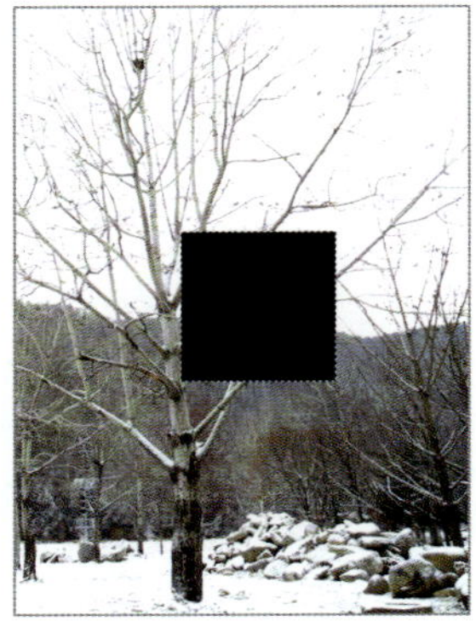

(4) Click on the Set Background Color icon in the toolbox and set the foreground color to **black**. Select Edit > Fill from the menu bar. In the Fill dialog box, set Use to **Foreground Color**. Click OK to fill the selection with black.

(5) Select Filter > Noise > Add Noise from the menu bar. In the Add Noise dialog box, set Amount to **40** and Distribution to **Gaussian**, then click the **Monochromatic** checkbox to create the effect in black and white. Click OK.

The white noise added to the picture looks like falling snow. You can increase the volume of snow by increasing the Amount in the Add Noise dialog box. If you apply too much, it will look unnatural.

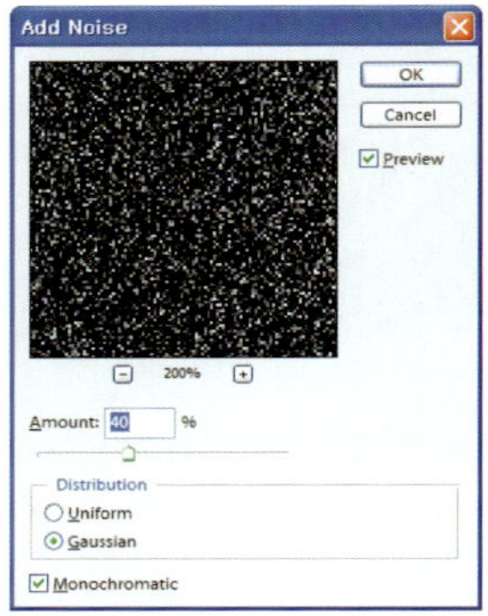

(6) Select Image > Transform > Free Transform from the menu bar. A bounding box will appear around the snowflakes. Click and drag the corner handles of the bounding box so that its height fits the image's, but its width is shortened slightly. Press Enter to apply the changes.

Adjusting the height of the selection elongates the snowflakes, which would appear round otherwise.

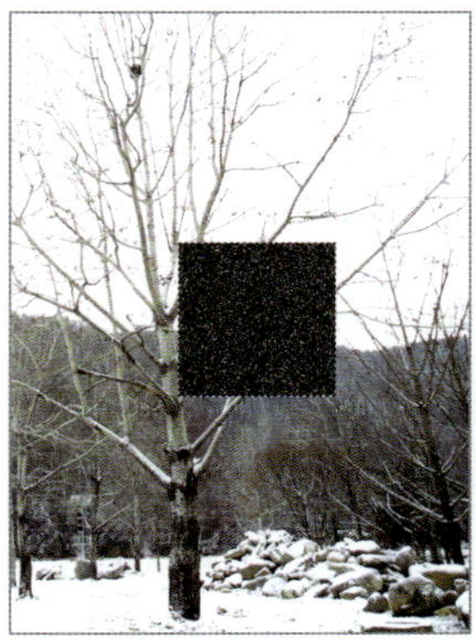

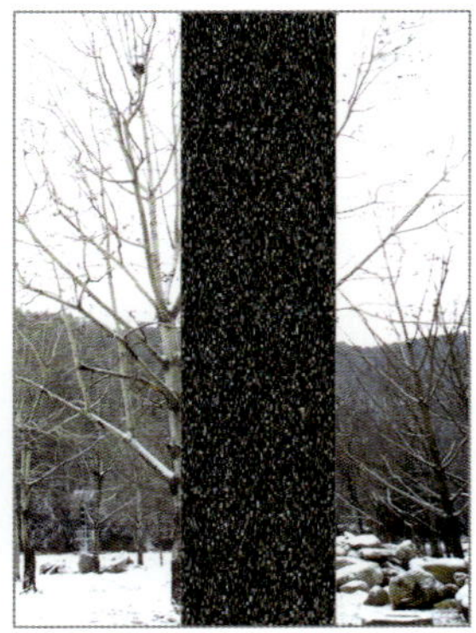

(7) Select Edit > Define Pattern from Selection from the menu bar to save the snowflakes as a pattern. In the Pattern Name dialog box, type in **Snow** for Name. Click OK.

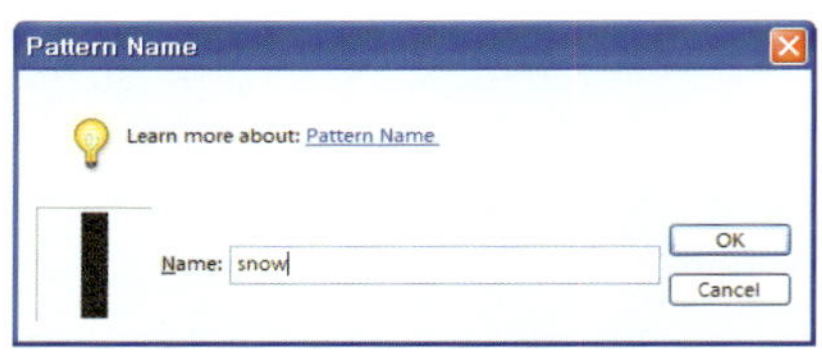

8 Press Ctrl + D to deselect the selection. Select Edit > Fill Layer from the menu bar. In the Fill dialog box, set Use to **Pattern**. Click on the Custom Pattern icon to open the Pattern Picker. Choose the Snow pattern.

9 Click OK to apply the snow pattern to the entire image.

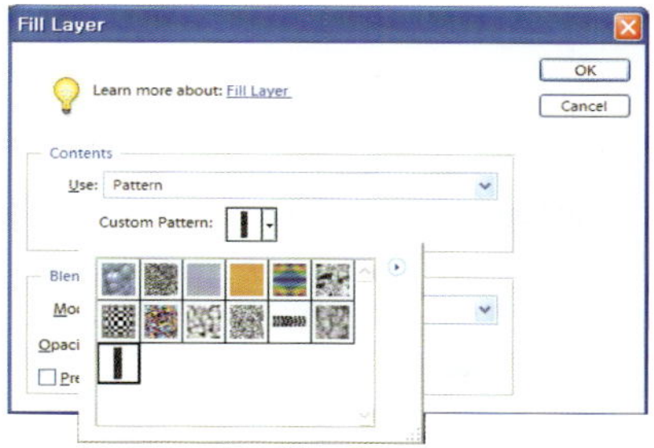

10 In the Layers palette, set the blending mode to **Screen** to let the background image show through.

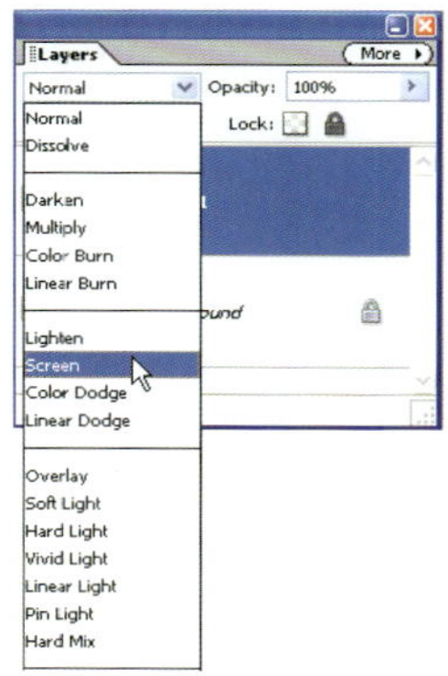

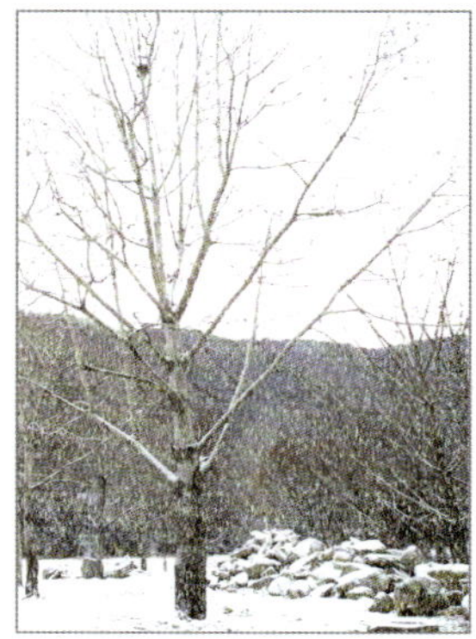

Ⅴ Creating Snow Using the Artwork and Effects Palette

By using the Artwork and Effects palette, you can create the effect of snow falling with just one click. Click on the Special Effects( ) button located on the top portion of the Artwork and Effects palette. Once you set the left drop-down menu to Photo Effects and the right drop-down menu to Image Effects, various effects will appear. Double-click on Blizzard and you can see that a blizzard effect has been applied to the image.

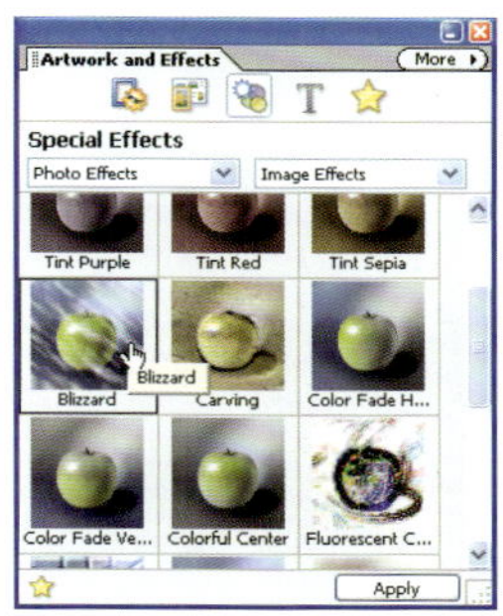

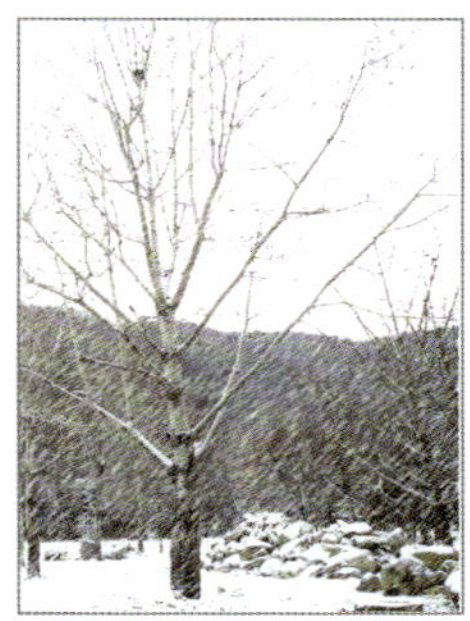

40 Digital Photo Retouching Techniques

with Photoshop Elements 5.0

Chapter 6
Using and Sharing Images

This chapter will teach you how to create postcards, multimedia slide shows, Web banners, and Web photo galleries. Although it may seem daunting to create multimedia slide shows and Web photo galleries, the Creations Wizard automates many of the steps, making the process quick and simple.

37 Making a Greeting Card

Before

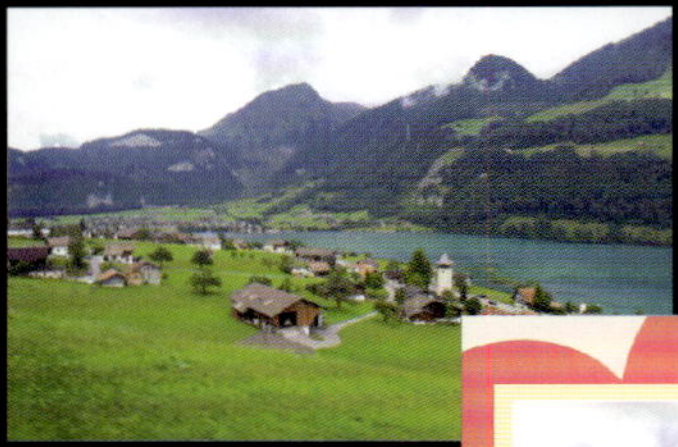

After

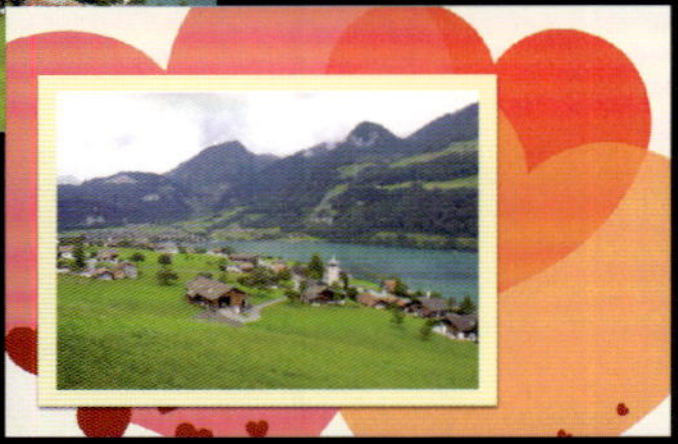

Photoshop Elements makes it easy to personalize and share images in a variety of commonly seen formats, such as postcards, slides, DVD slide shows, photo albums, and Web photo galleries.

1 Click on the Create button(Create) and select Greeting Card.

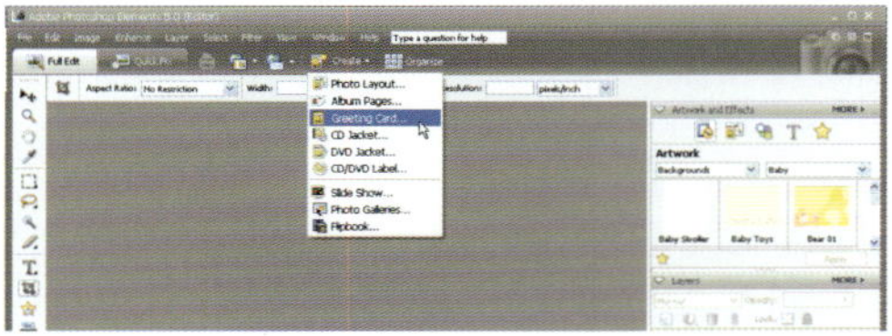

2 Once the New Greeting Card window appears, choose a size from the Select a Size drop-down menu as shown. Now select the desired style from Layout and Theme. Click the OK button.

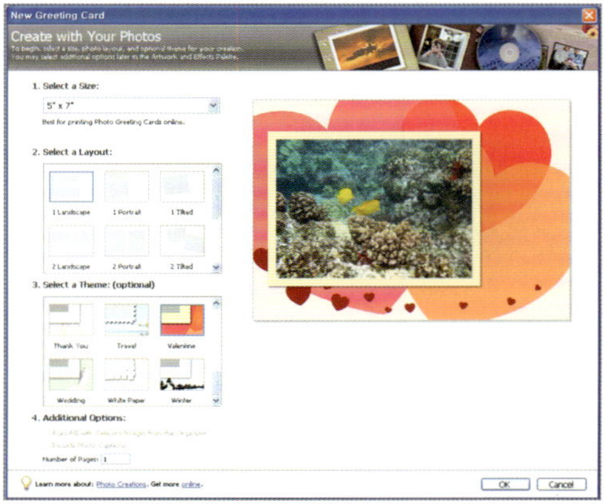

Additional Option

Auto-Fill with Selected Images from the Organizer: Activates when the image is selected from the Organizer window. Once it is checked, the selected image will automatically change size to fit the Greeting Card.

Include Photo Captions: Once it is checked, a caption can be added by double-clicking on the Greeting Card from the Organizer Window.

③ A new image window displaying the Greeting Card will appear.

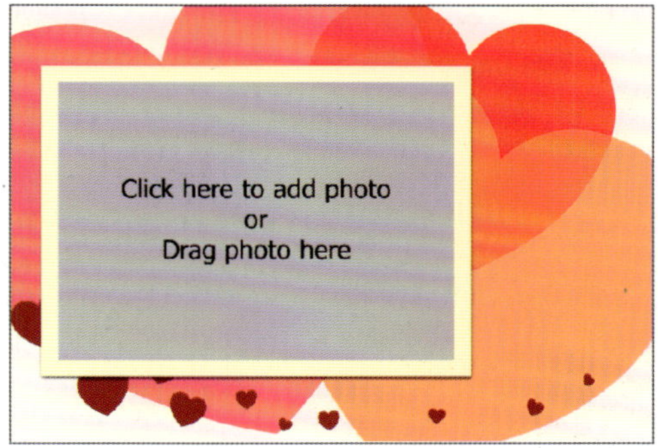

④ Click on the area that says "Click here to add photo or Drag photo here" and the Open dialog box will appear, where you can select the desired image. For this exercise, select **Sample\Chapter 6\Tech37a.jpg** from the supplementary CD.

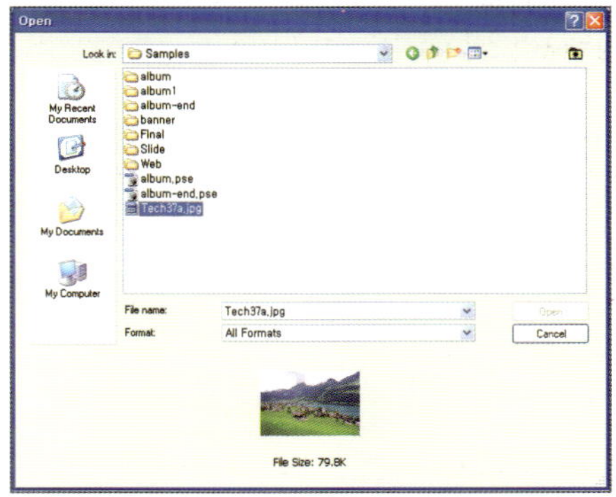

If the image to be used for the Greeting Card is already open, you can drag the image from the Tech37a.jpg window to the gray area of the newly created Greeting Card window by selecting the Move Tool from the tool box.

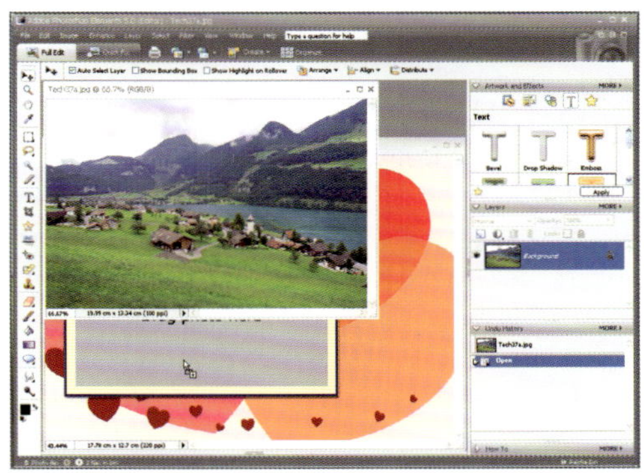

(5) You can see that the image has been inserted into the gray area. You can change the size of the photo by dragging the slide bar.

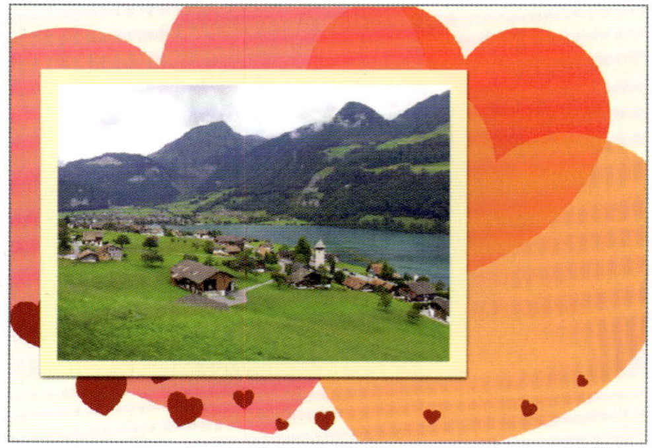

tip A convenient way to change the image size is to utilize the tool selections that appear when the image is double-clicked.

1. You can increase or decrease the size using the slide bar.
2. You can rotate the image by clicking on the Rotate the Photo button.
3. You can replace the image in the frame by clicking on the Get a New Photo to Place in Frame button.

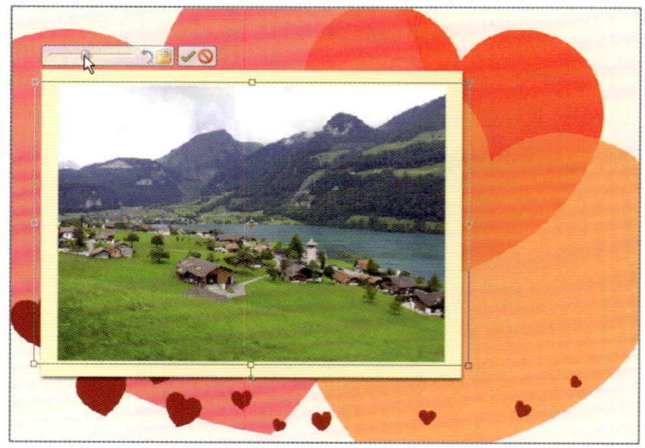

38 Maintaining Photographs with Album Pages

With the rising use of digital photography, most people choose to store and view their camera images on the computer rather than print hundreds of digital photographs. The Album Pages tool lets you create a digital album, complete with frames. You can not only create and manage several albums organized by theme, but also search and print your photographs.

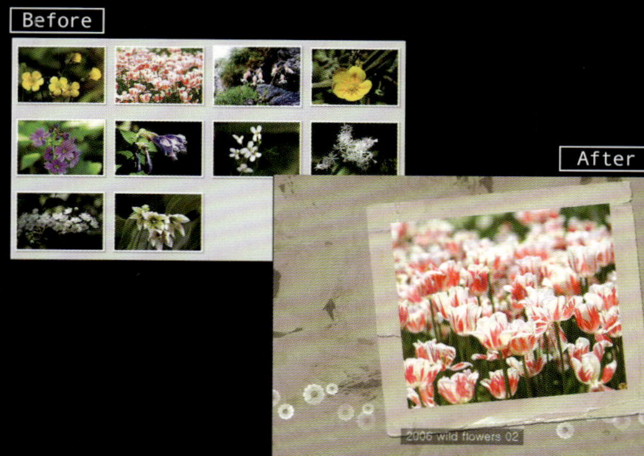

1 Run Photoshop Elements 5.0. Once the Welcome Screen window appears, click on **View and Organize Photos**.

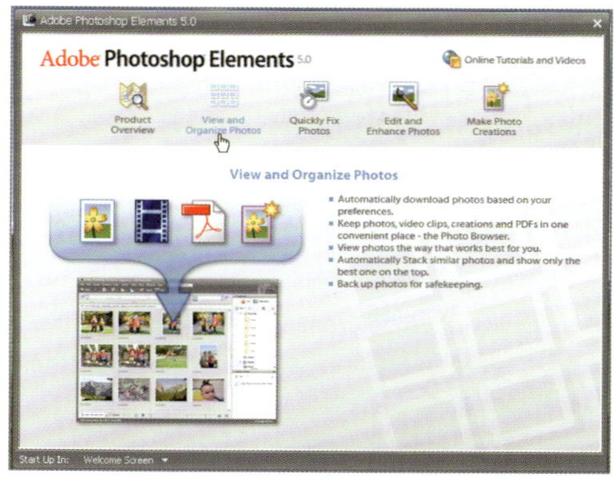

2 Once the Organize window appears, click on File > Get Photos > From Files and Folders.

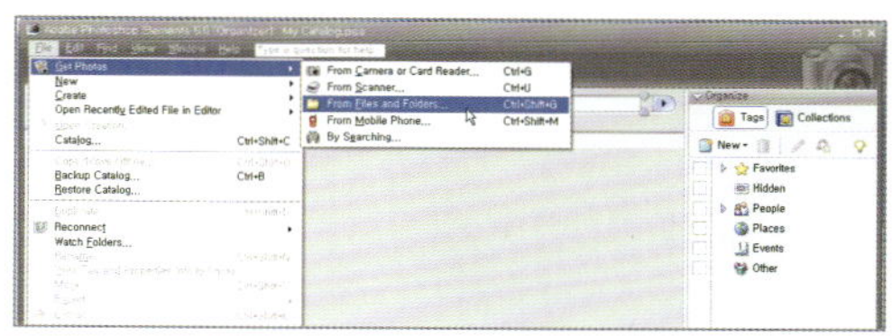

(3) Once the Get Photos From Files and Folders window appears, select all 10 image files from the **Sample\Chapter 6\Album** folder in the supplementary CD, then click on Get Photos.

tip You can select all the files by clicking on all the files while holding down the Shift key or by dragging over all the files.

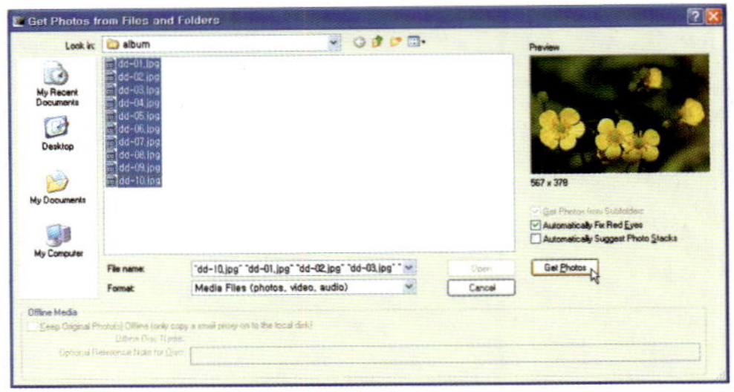

(4) The selected files will be shown in the Organize file. Now select the eight images by dragging the mouse as shown.

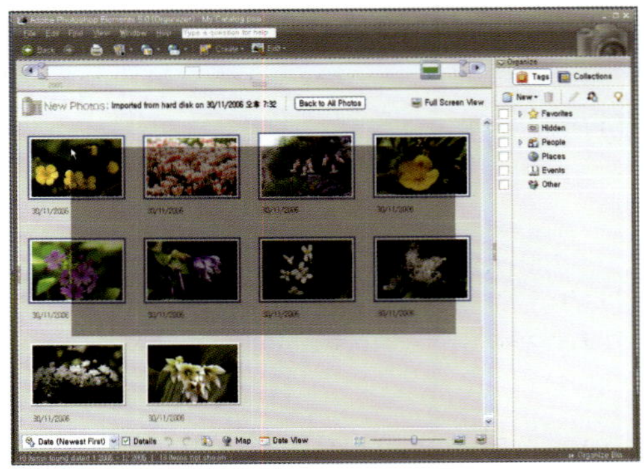

(5) Now you will be creating an album using the selected eight images. Click on the Create button from the Shortcut bar, then select Album Pages.

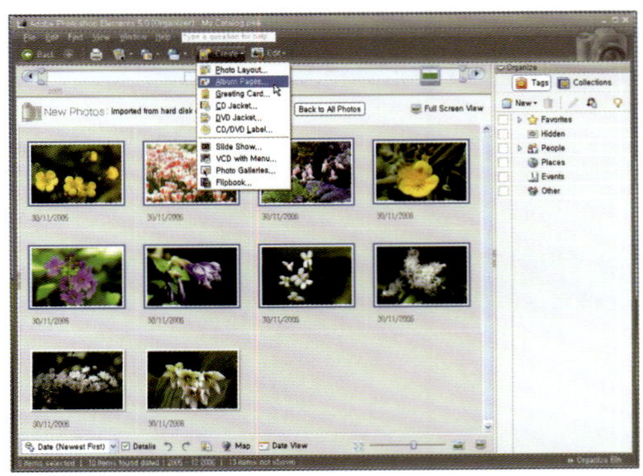

6 The Organize window has changed into the Full Edit window and a New Album Pages window will appear. Select the desired Size, Layout, and Theme, then click the OK button.

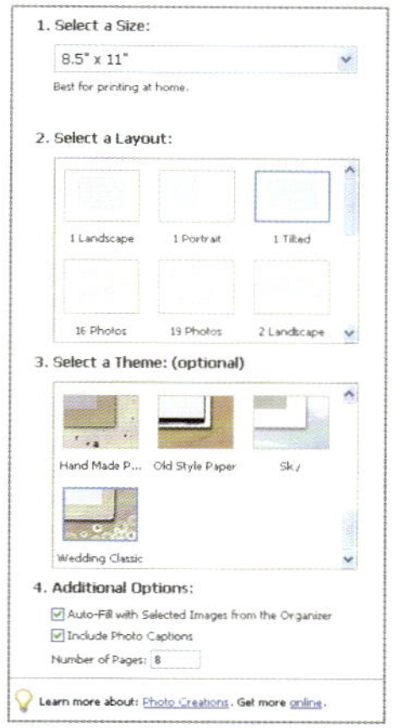

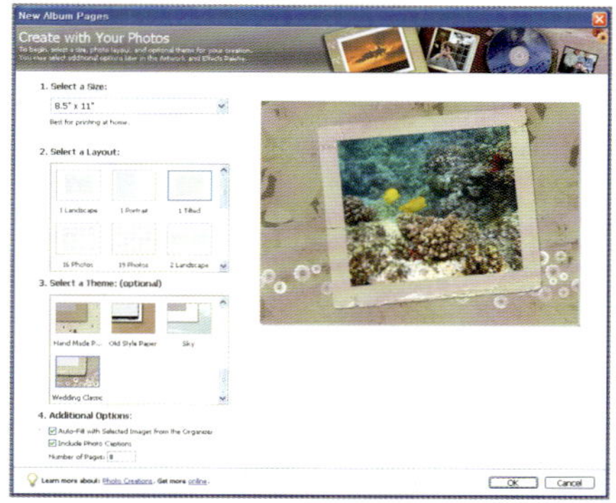

7 As shown, a new image window will automatically be created according to the selected size, layout, and theme. All eight images will also automatically have the same frame around them.

You can see on the bottom of the window that 8 has been set automatically for Number of Pages. This is because you have set the option that shows one image per page in the layout category. If you had chosen the layout option to show three images per page, the Number of Pages would be 3.

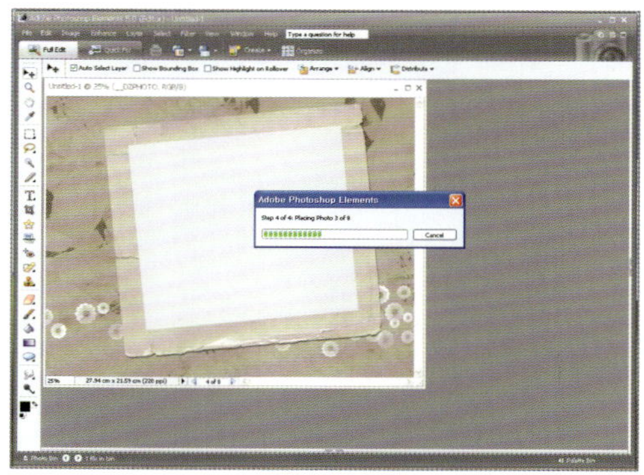

⑧ From the image window for the first page of the album, right-click your mouse, then click on **Fit Frame to Photo**. The size of the frame will automatically adjust to the size of the image.

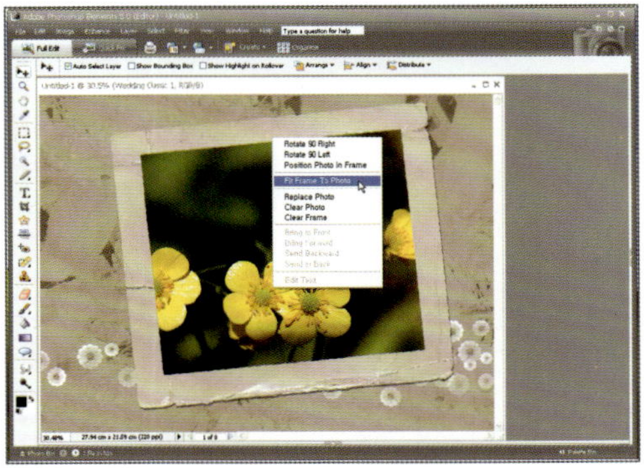

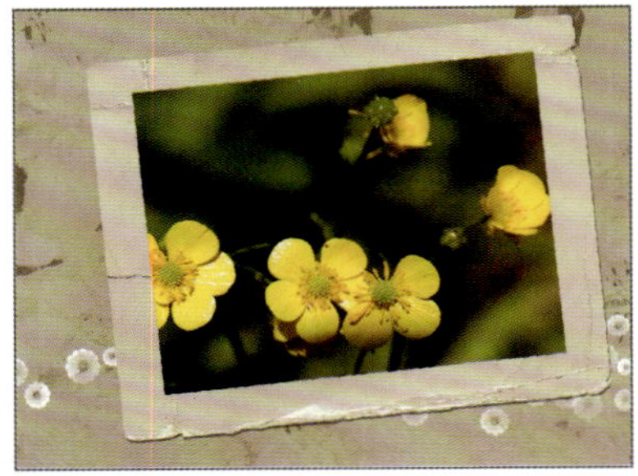

⑨ Now move to the second page of your album by clicking on the arrow(1 of 8) at the bottom of the image window.

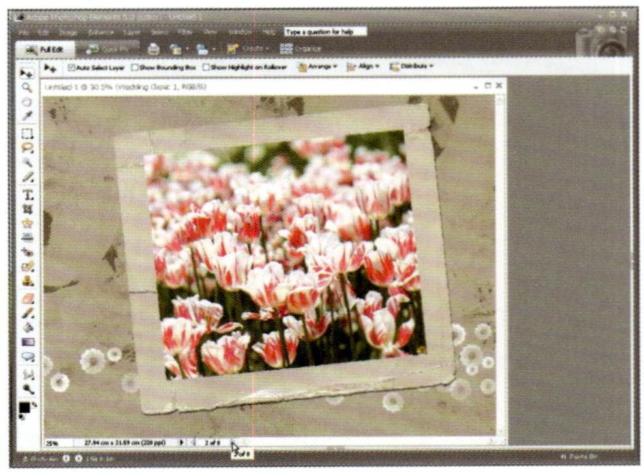

(10) By using the Move tool( ), you can change the position of the image by dragging on the frame.

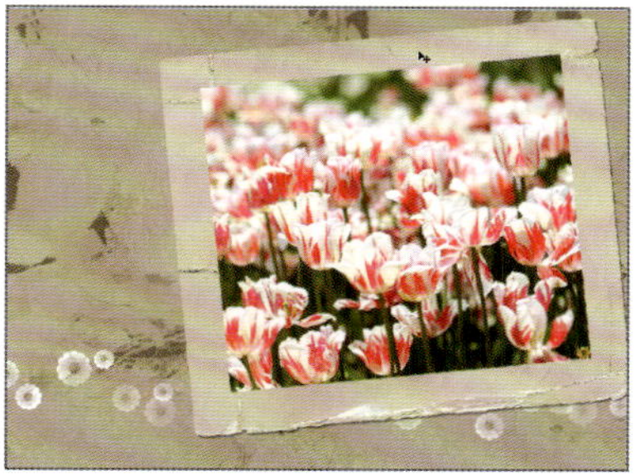

(11) Now move to the third page of your album by clicking on the arrow at the bottom right of the image window. You can remove the frame only from the third page of your album if you right-click on the inside of the frame, then select **Clear Frame**.

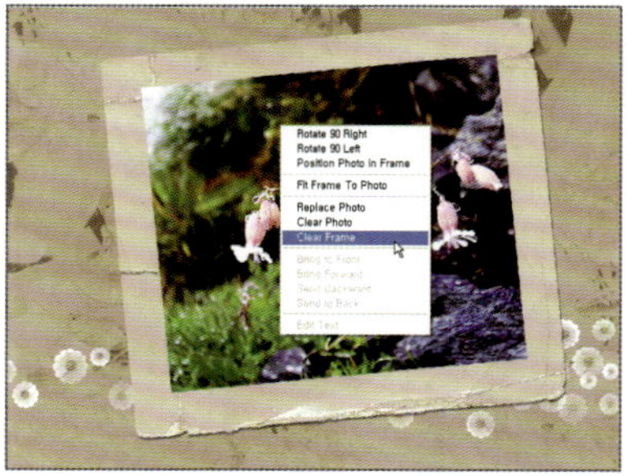

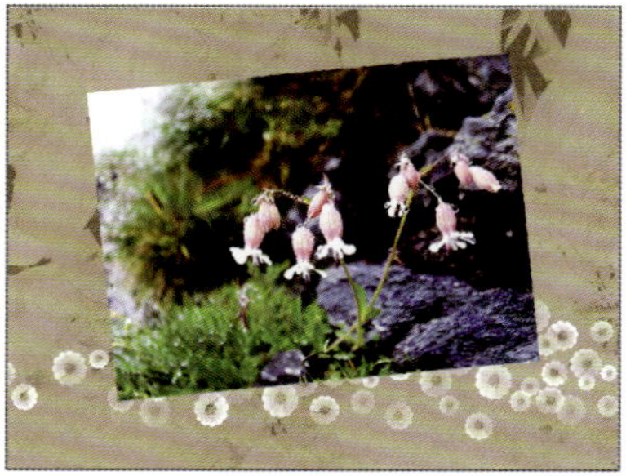

(12) Now move to the fourth page of your album. If you want to change the photo in the frame, right-click inside the frame, then select **Replace Photo**. Select the **dd-09.jpg** file, and then click the OK button once the Open window appears.

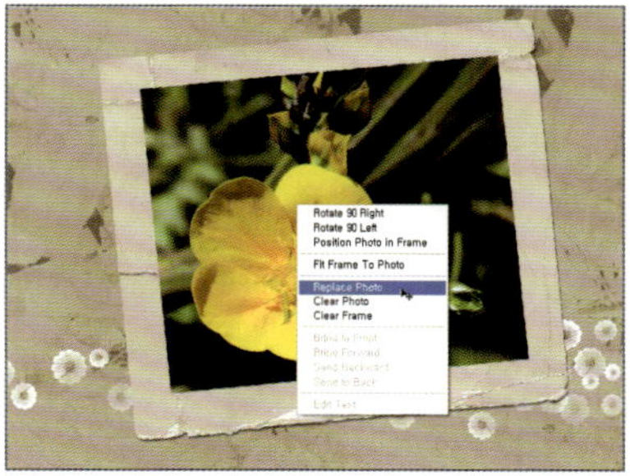

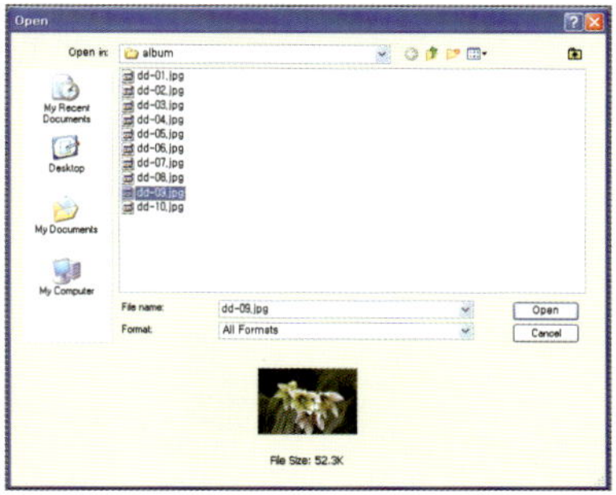

(13) You can see that the image in the frame has changed. You can adjust the size of the image using the slide bar.

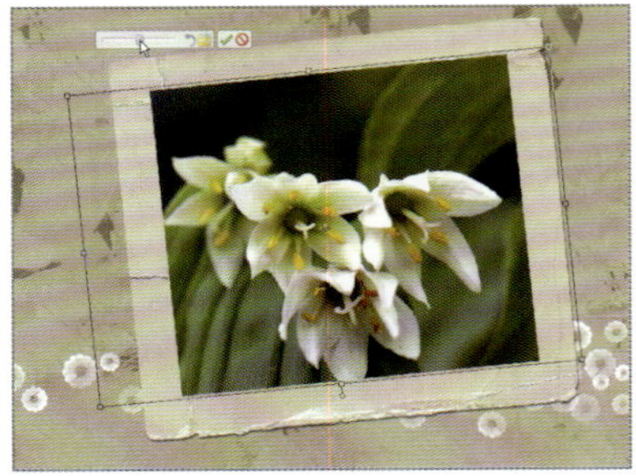

(14) Now move to the fifth page of your album. Click on Window > Artwork and Effects. You will see that the Artwork and Effects palette will appear on the right side of the work window. From the Artwork and Effects palette, set the Select a Category to **Backgrounds** and View a SubCategory to **Baby**, then double-click on **Bear 01** from the list.

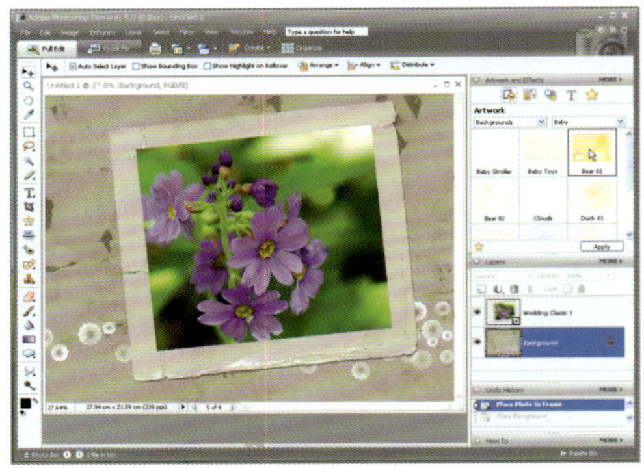

(15) You can see that the background of the fifth page has changed.

You can make changes and adjustments to the photos on each page by using the various tools and menus in the toolbox.

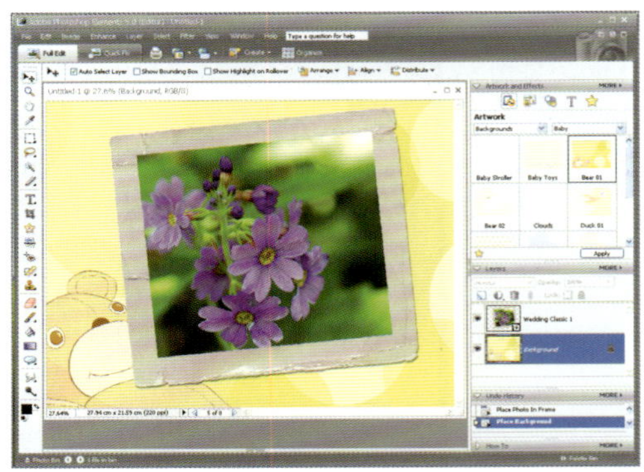

(16) After you are done modifying all pages using the tools, functions, and menus mentioned previously, click on File > Save As. When the Save As window appears, select the folder in which you would like to save the file and input the name of the file. Click on the Save button.

You can see that the file type has automatically been set to PSE. This Photo Creation Format is unique to Photoshop Elements 5.0.

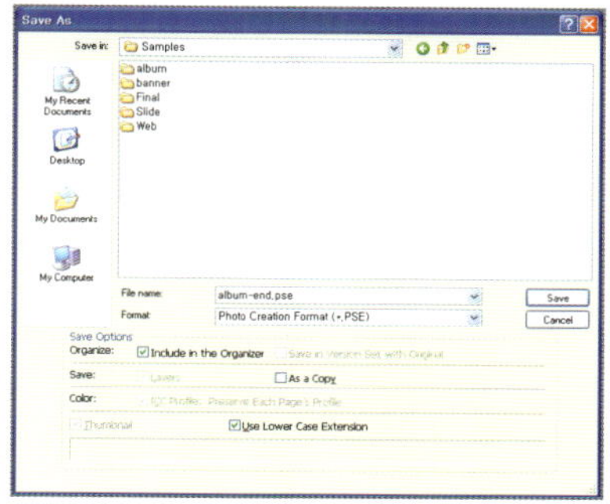

(17) After you have saved the file, move to the Organize window. Your new album is created. If you look at the thumbnail of the newly created album, you will notice a red line across the width of the thumbnail and an icon of a lock. This is because the files that you worked on previously in the Full Edit window are still open. Double-click on the Album thumbnail after closing the .PSE files that you saved in the Full Edit window, or completely close the Full Edit window.

If you do not close the .PSE files that were saved in the Full Edit window or completely close the Full Edit window, you cannot make changes in the Organize window.

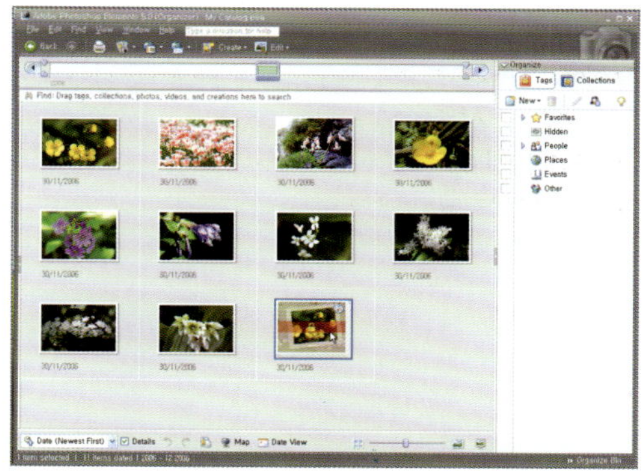

(18) When the work window is in the Single View mode, you will be able to see a Click Here to Add Captions option at the bottom of the window. Click on this text to input the title and/or description of the photograph.

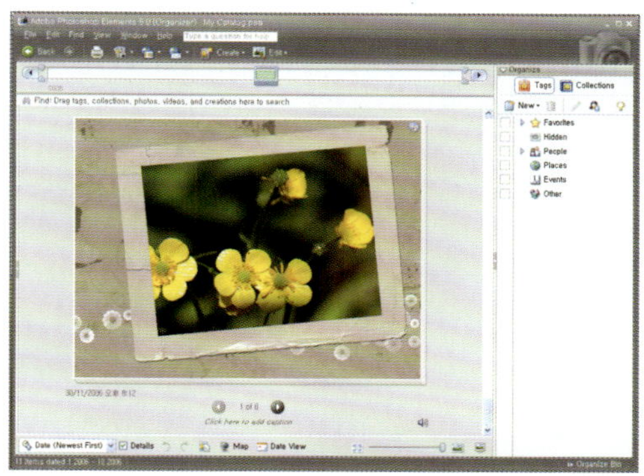

(19) To confirm the creation of your album, click on the Full Screen View button( ) at the bottom right of the window.

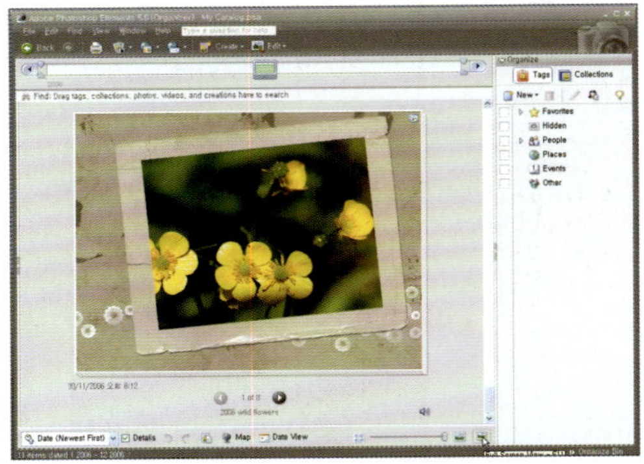

(20) Once the Full Screen View Options window appears, set the settings as shown here, then click the OK button.

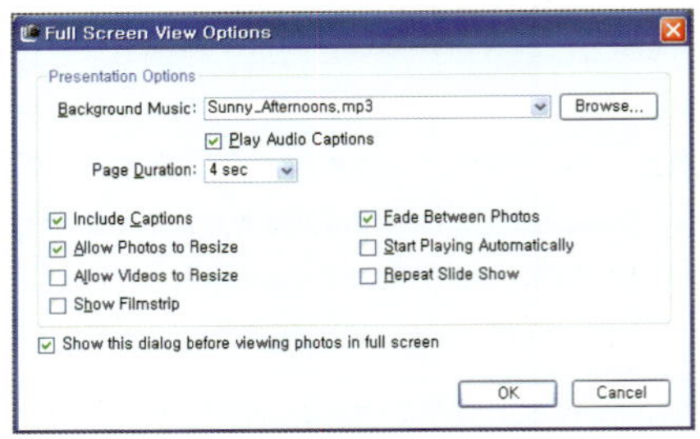

(21) Now your Photo Page project is displayed in full screen mode and there is a tool bar at the top of your screen. Once you click the Play button, you will be able to hear the music and view your album, including the captions.

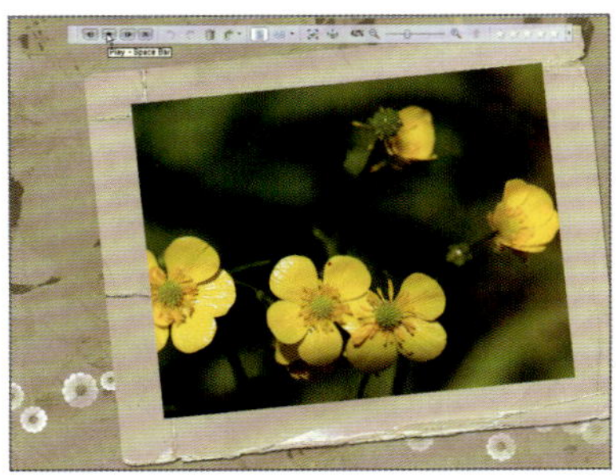

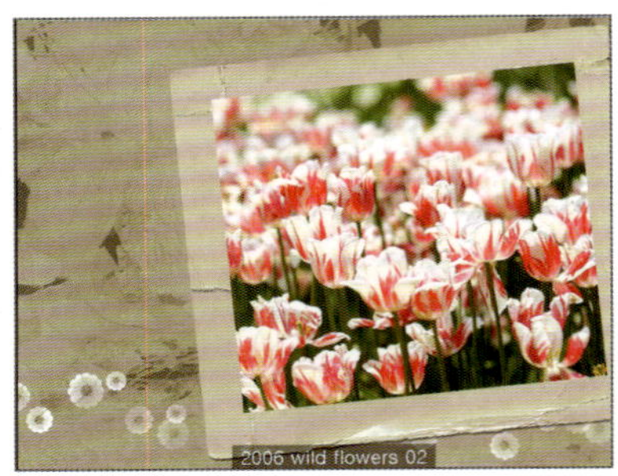

39 Making a Web Banner

Before

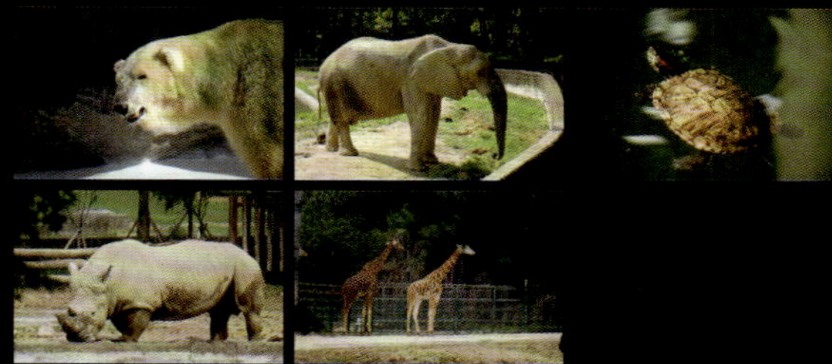

After

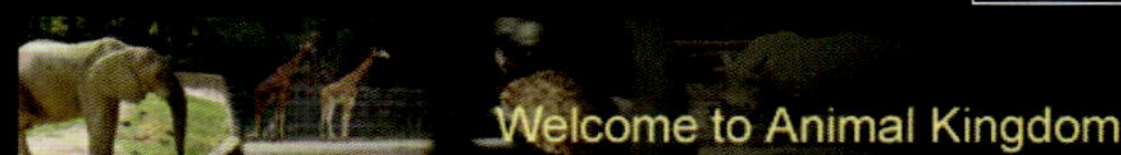

You can use Photoshop Elements to create images that are optimized for the Web, and then use those images as part of a Web site. In this section, you will learn to use the Gradient Map command together with the Photomerge command to make a Web banner.

1 Select File > New > Photomerge Panorama from the menu bar. When the Photomerge dialog box appears, click on Browse.

2 Select the **Sample\Chapter 6\banner folder** on the supplementary CD. Hold down the Shift key and click on each of the pictures in the folder to select all of them. Click on Open. This will add the selected pictures to the Photomerge dialog box.

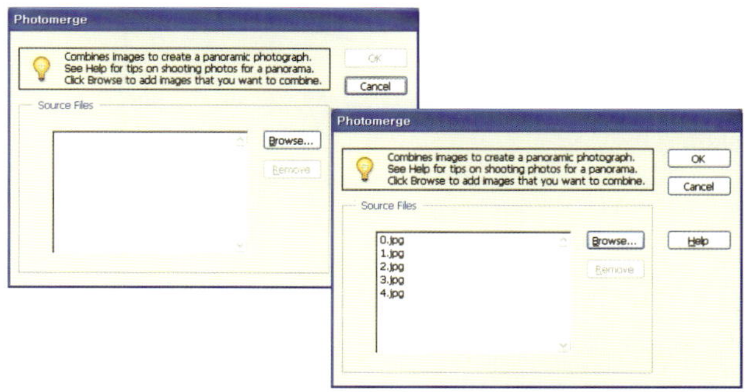

3 Click OK. A warning message appears saying that Photomerge is unable to merge the images to form a panorama. Click OK to close the message box.

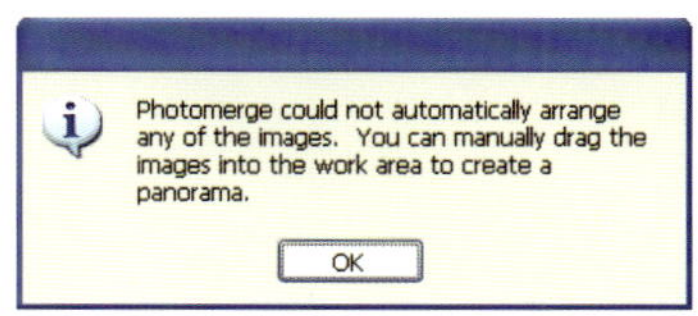

tip When using Photomerge to make a panorama, the source images must overlap between 15% and 40%. Otherwise, Photomerge may not be able to assemble the images. When making a Web banner, the images to be merged may be entirely different, and Photomerge won't be able to automatically align them. In such cases, you'll have to manually arrange the images instead.

4 In the Photomerge dialog box, drag an image from the lightbox onto the work area, as shown. The overlapping edge between the images is blended automatically.

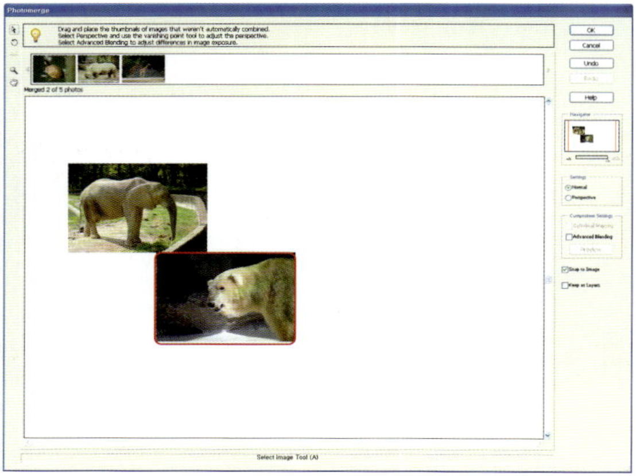

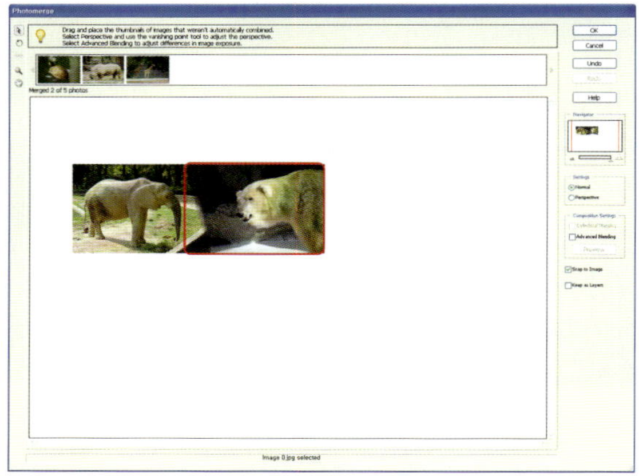

5 Repeat step 4 on all the other images on the lightbox. Remember to position them with the edges overlapping, as shown.

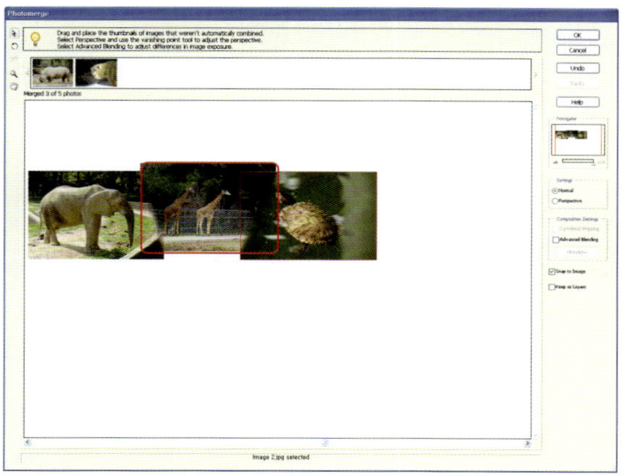

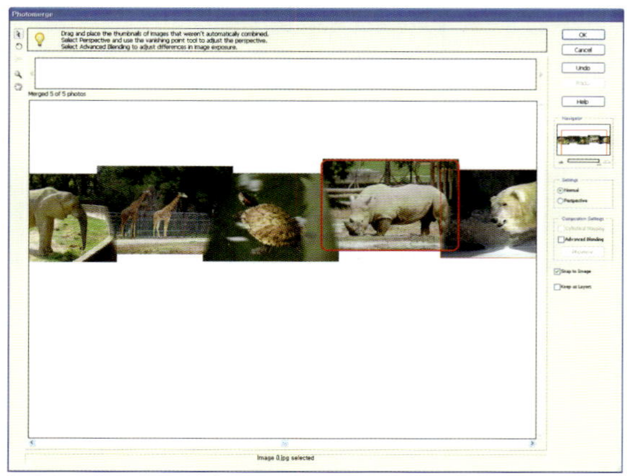

tip To blend edges seamlessly, you need to move the image around until you find the perfect position.

⑥ Check the Advanced Blending option under Composite Settings on the right of the Photomerge dialog box. Click on Preview.

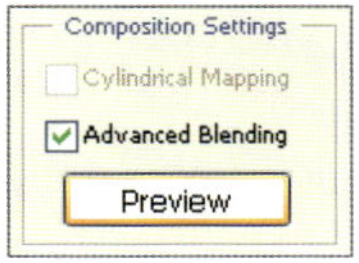

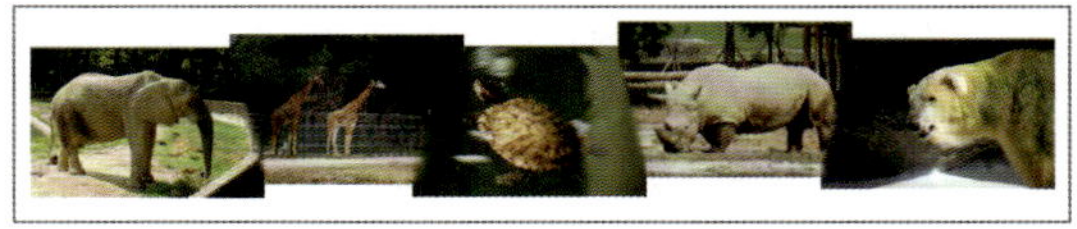

If you are not satisfied with the panorama, click the Exit Preview button and reposition the images.

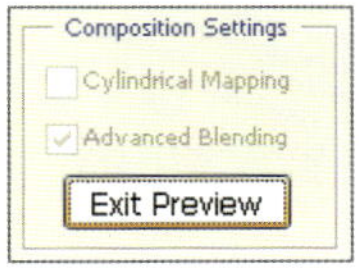

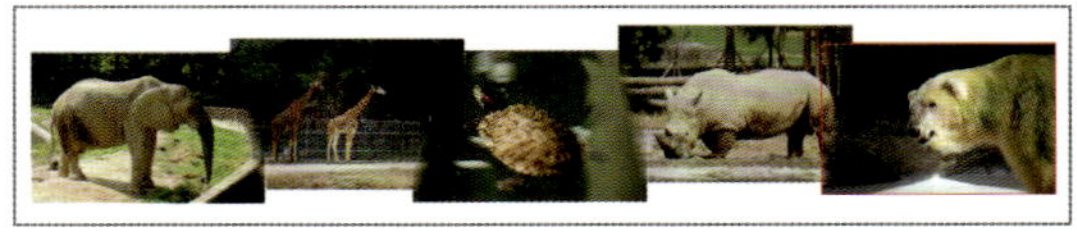

⑦ Click OK to merge the photos. The panorama will appear in a new window.

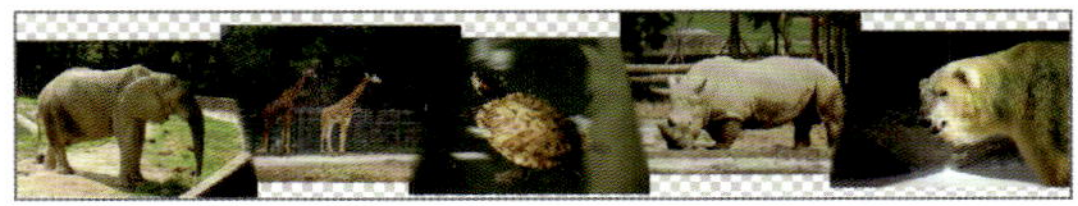

⑧ Select the Crop Tool ( ) from the toolbox. Set Width to **468 pixels**, Height to **60 pixels**, and Resolution to **72 pixels/inch**.

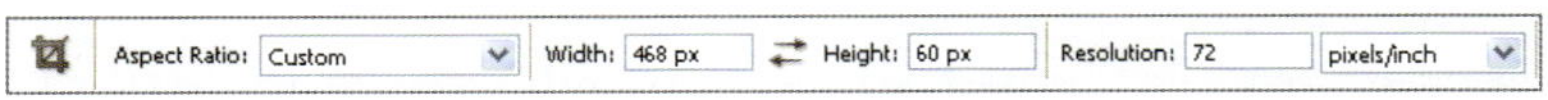

The Crop tool's default unit of measurement for width and height is centimeters. If you type **468**, it will be interpreted as **468 cm**. To use a different unit of measurement, you need to include the unit as well (i.e., **468 pixels**).

⑨ Select the part of the image to be used as the Web banner. Hit **Enter** to crop off the unwanted areas.

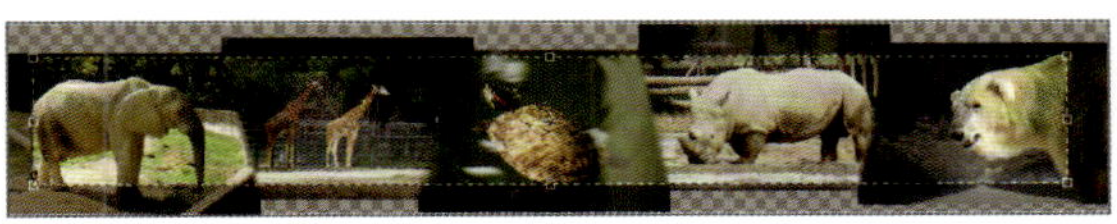

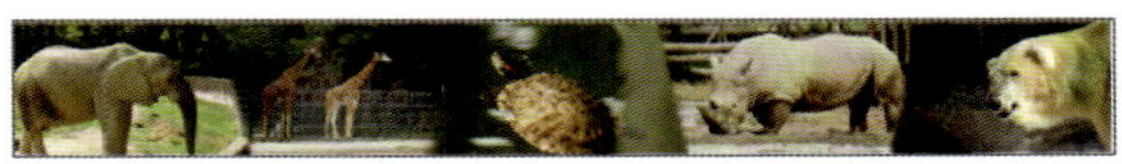

(10) Select Layer > Duplicate Layer from the menu bar. When the Duplicate Layer dialog box appears, click OK to make a copy.

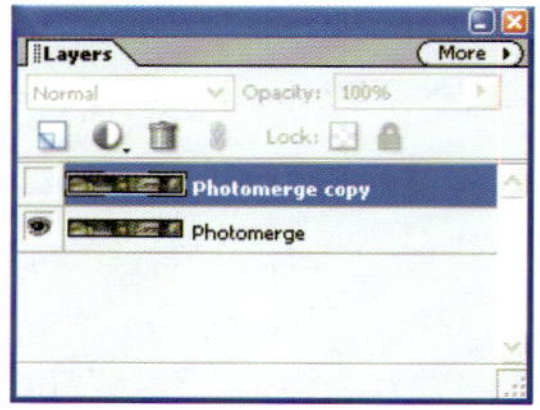

(11) Click on Create Adjustment Layer button (◐) from the layer palette, then click on Hue/Saturation. Once the Hue/Saturation dialog box appears, check the Colorize box, then set the Hue at **124**, Saturation at **25**, and Lightness at **–80**. Click the OK button.

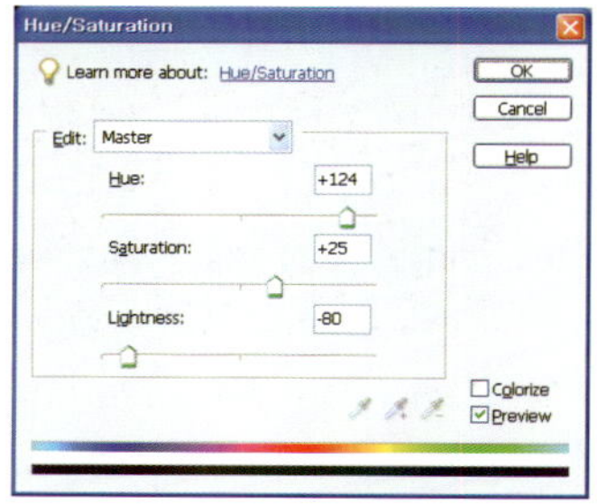

(12) You can see that an Adjustment Layer has been created in the layer palette and the tone of image window has turned a dark green.

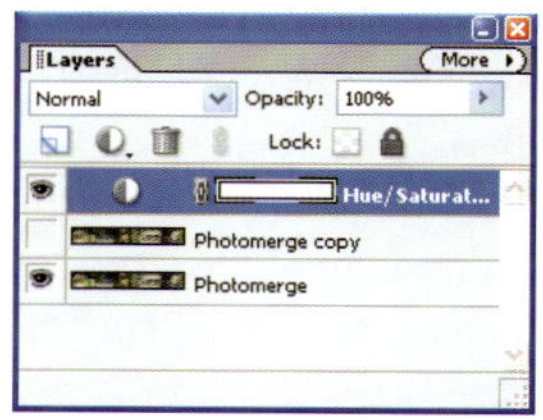

(13) Select the Rectangular Marquee Tool ([ ]) from the toolbox. Make the selection, as shown here.

(14) Choose Select > Feather from the menu bar. In the Feather Selection dialog box, set Feather Radius to **100 pixels**. Click OK to soften the edges of the selection.

(15) Press Delete to remove the gradient map and reveal the color image in the selection. Press Ctrl + D to deselect.

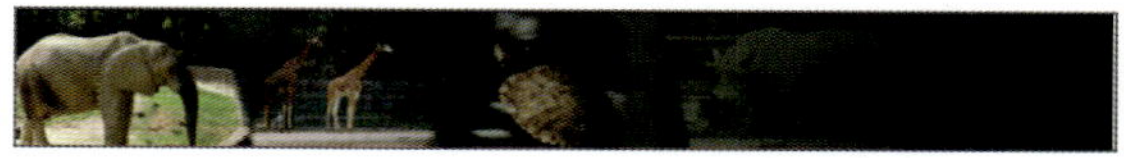

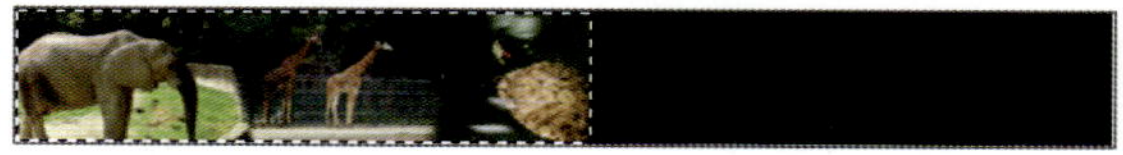

tip If you do not apply feathering to the selection border, the edges will be distinct without a gradual transition between the colored and black-and-white sections of the image.

(16) Select the Horizontal Type Tool (T) from the toolbox. In the options bar, set Font to **Arial** and Size to **20 pt**.

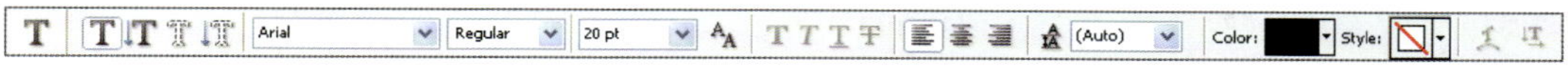

(17) Click on the Set The Text Color swatch in the options bar. When the Color Picker dialog box appears, click the Only Web Colors checkbox. This ensures that the Web banner uses only Web-safe colors or colors that will display accurately on computer screens. Set the hexadecimal color value to **ffff99**.

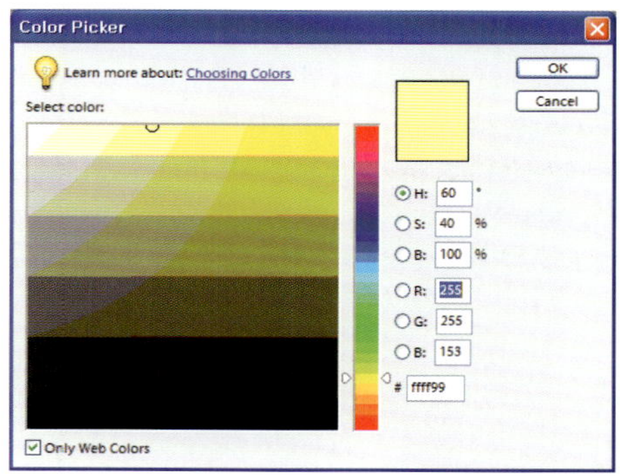

(18) Complete the Web banner by typing in the text as shown.

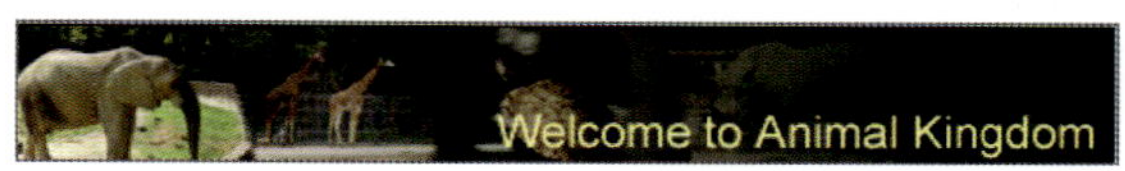

(19) Select File > Save For Web from the menu bar and save the image as a GIF or JPEG file.

40 Making a Web Photo Gallery

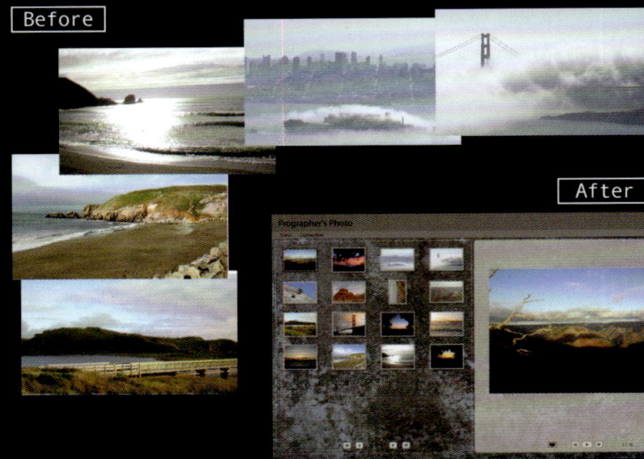

These days, most professional photographers have a Web photo gallery where they display their pictures on the Internet. A Web photo gallery is a simple site consisting of a home page with thumbnails of images that you can click to see full-sized versions. In Photoshop Elements, creating a Web photo gallery is very simple. You will only need to enter some information and make some selections, and the program will do the rest for you.

1 Click on Organize (Organize) in the main menu. In the Organizer window, select File > Get Photos > From File and Folders to load the images that will be used in the Web photo gallery.

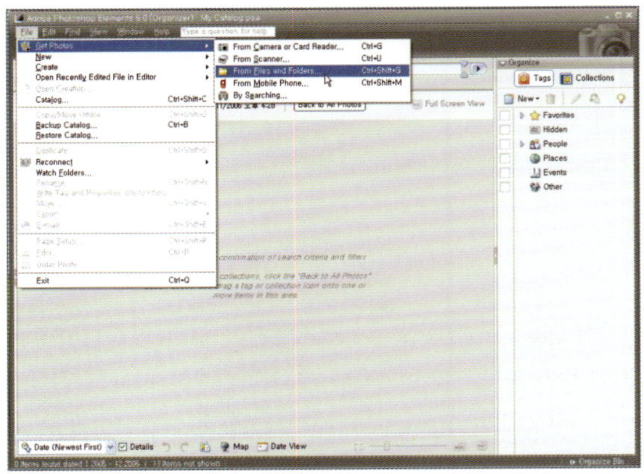

2 When the Get Photos from File and Folders window appears, choose all the images in the **Sample\Chapter 6\Web** folder on the supplementary CD and then click on the Get Photos button.

③ As we can see here, the selected images will appear as thumbnails in the Organizer window. To create the Web photo gallery, click on the Create button, then select Photo Galleries.

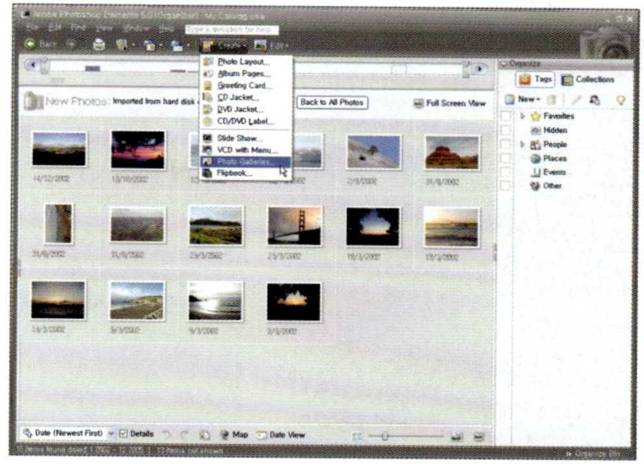

④ The Photo Galleries Wizard window will appear. Confirm that the Type is set to Web Galleries, then select a layout.

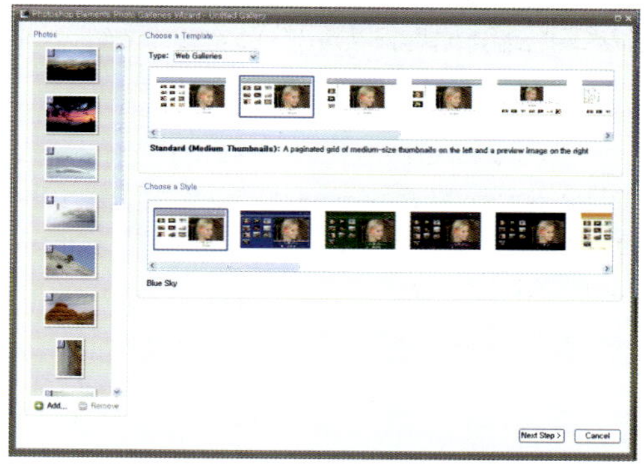

⑤ Slide the slide bar under Choose a Style to the right, and then select Patina Style as shown in the image. Click on the Next Step button.

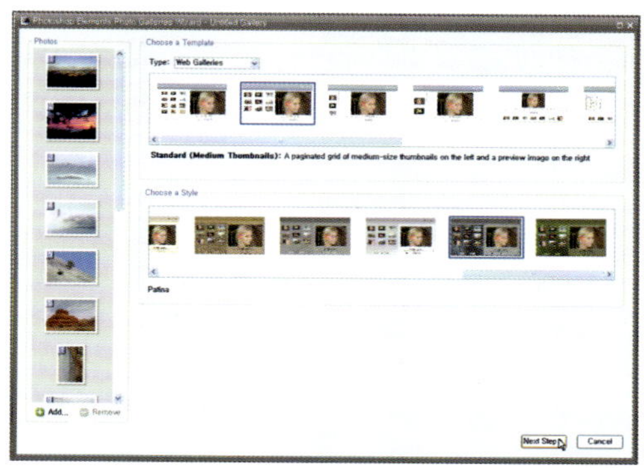

⑥ When the window appears, input the data on the left part of the window.

If you drag the scroll bar down, there are options where you can change the color of the background, title bar, etc.

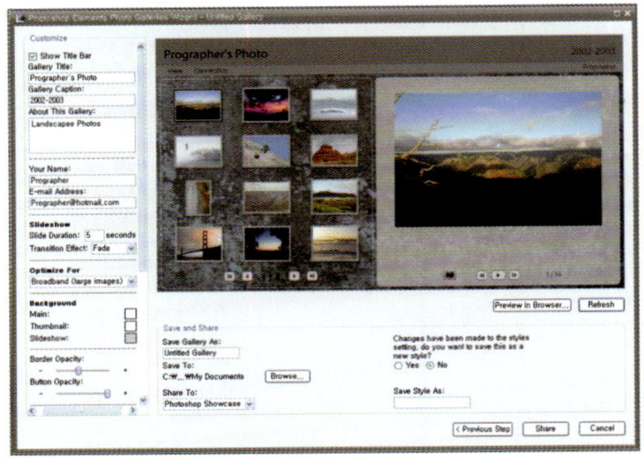

⑦ To designate a folder in which the photo gallery is to be saved, click on the Browse button from the Save and Share option.

tip You can preview the photo gallery that you have created using Internet Explorer or another Web browser by clicking on the Preview in Browser button.

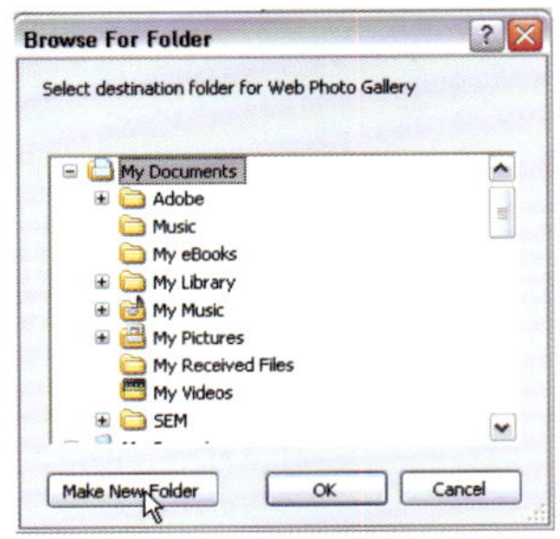

⑧ Once all the options have been set, click on the Share button. The Share Photo Gallery window will appear. Input your data to create an account, then click on the Next button.

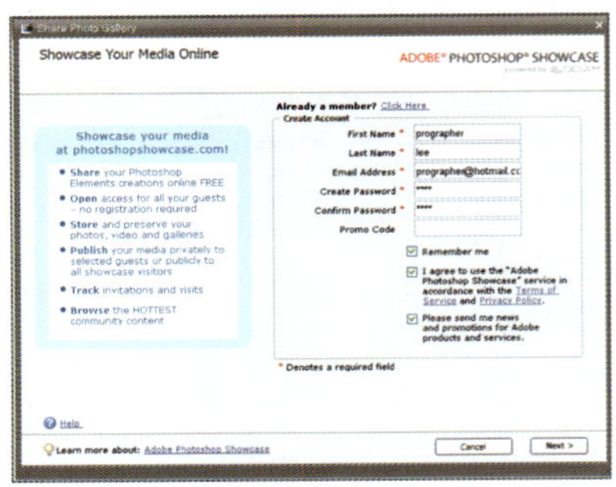

9 Input the desired name for your gallery for Name Your Gallery, then click Next. When the Invite window appears, input a message you'd like to leave in the Message option, then click Next.

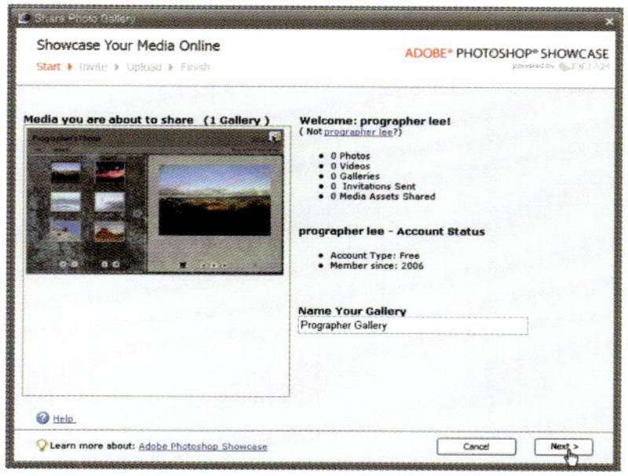

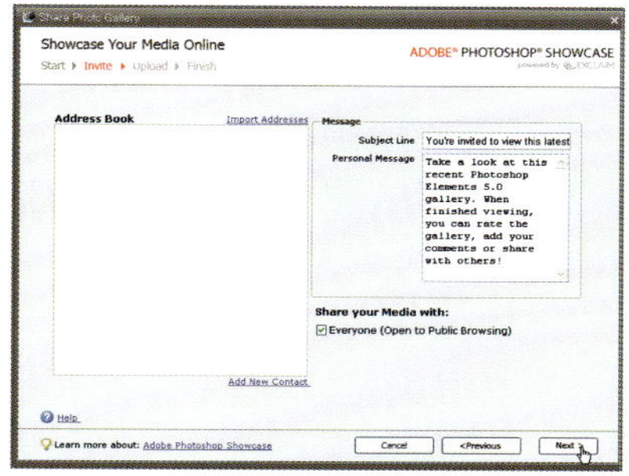

10 If your computer is online, your photo gallery will begin uploading. Once uploading is complete, a confirmation window will appear. Click on the View This Gallery button.

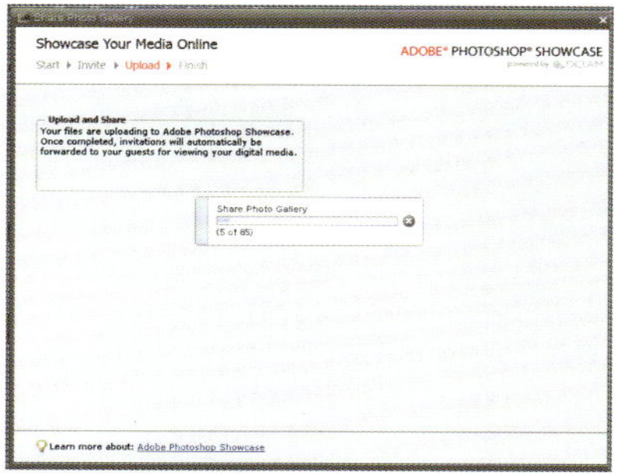

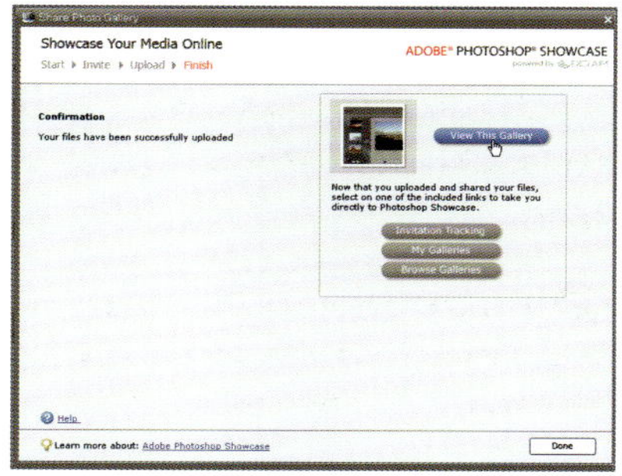

11 Internet Explorer or your Web browser will appear. You can view your photo gallery by clicking on the Project Thumb.

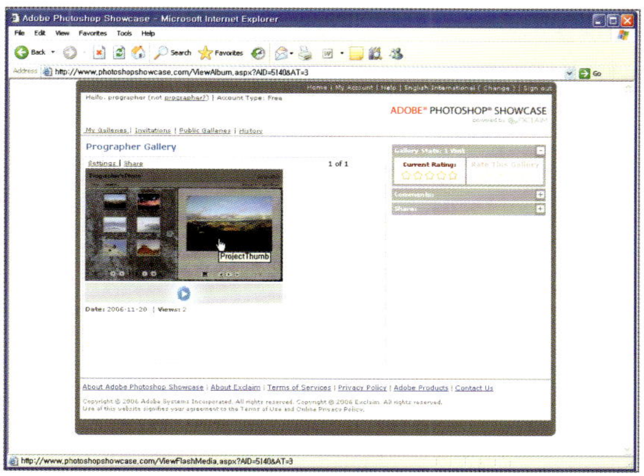

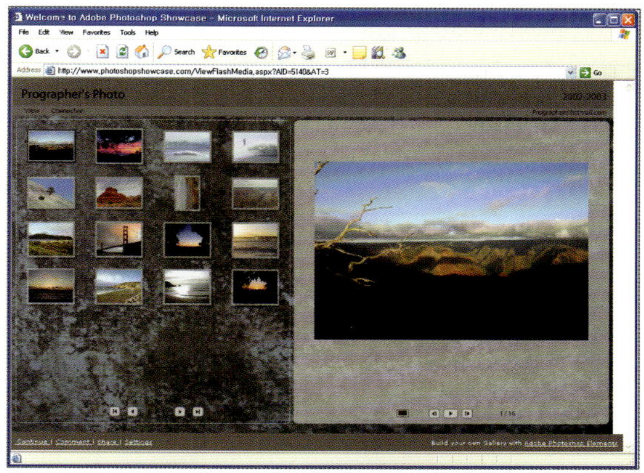

Contents of the Supplementary CD

Insert the supplementary CD-ROM into your CD-ROM drive. You should see these two folders.

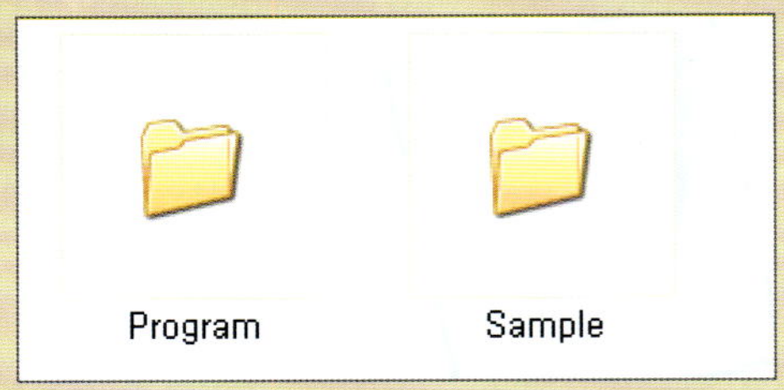

Program Folder

This folder includes a 30-day trial version of Photoshop Elements 5.0. The trial version will automatically be unzipped once you double-click on the PSE_5.0_WIN_TRYBUY_ENG.exe file. Follow the dialog boxes for installation instructions.

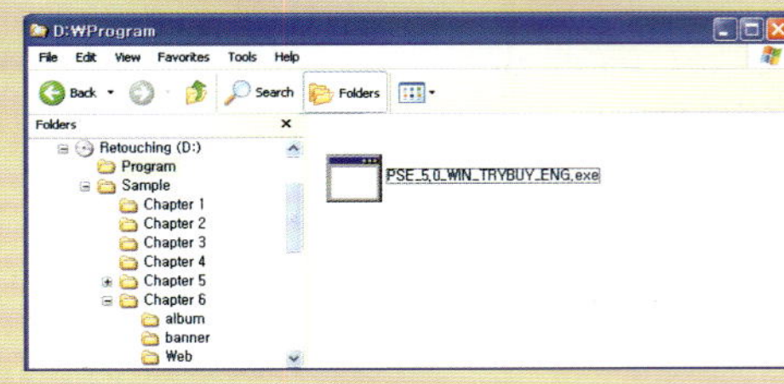

Sample Folder

This folder contains the sample images used in this book, organized by chapter. Each chapter folder contains example files used in the corresponding techniques.

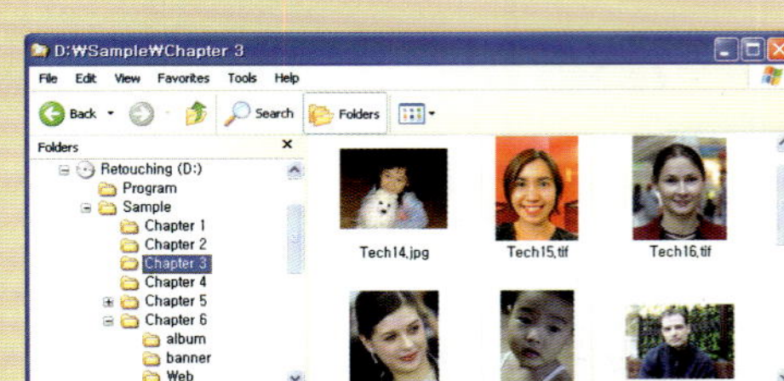

Index

A

Active image area, 22
Add Noise filter, 172
Adjust Smart Fix command, 65
Adobe Acrobat, 14
Artist's color wheel, 67

B

Backlighting, 43–45
Black-and-white image
  removing color, 59–61
  coloring, 62–64
Blending colors, 67
Blending modes
  Multiply, 165
  Overlay, 61, 169
  Screen, 173
Blur (correcting), 38–39
Brightness/Contrast command, 40
Brightness/Contrast dialog box, 38–39
Brush tool, 85–90
Burn tool, 88

C

Camera Raw dialog box, 123–125
Clone Stamp tool, 135–137
  and shift key, 138
CMYK color model, 67
Color, 49-75
  Color Picker, 73–74
  color wheel, 67
  Replace Color command, 53
Color Curves, 58
Color Replacement tool, 72–75
Color Variations command, 55–58
Color Variations dialog box, 47, 58
Contrast (correcting), 35–47
  adjusting with Levels command, 40–42
  adjusting with Shadows/Highlights command, 43–45
  analyzing with Histogram command, 36–37
  brightening a specific spot, 46–47
  Brightness/Contrast command, 38–39
Convert to Black and White, 61
Copying
  Copy command, 93
  duplicate layer, 104
  Layer Via Copy command, 111
Creation Setup dialog box, 176–195
Crop tool, 106–107, 189

D

Define Pattern command, 172
Deselect command, 47
Dialog boxes
  Brightness/Contrast, 38–39
  Color Variations, 67
  Feather Selection, 47
  Histogram, 36–37
  Hue/Saturation, 52
  Levels, 42
  Liquify, 91–92
  Motion Blur, 161
  Photomerge Panorama, 158–160
  Replace Color, 53
  Save As, 30
  Save for Web, 31
  Welcome Screen, 17–20
Distort command, 144–146
Divide Scanned Photos command, 122
Dodge tool, 108
Dots per inch (dpi), 12
Dpi (dots per inch), 12

E

Editor window, 21–23
  active image area, 22
  Menu bar, 21
  Options bar, 22
  Palette Bin, 23
  Photo Bin, 23, 122
  Shortcuts bar, 22
  Status bar, 23
  Title bar, 21
  Toolbox, 22
Eraser tool, 101
Exposure (analyzing), 36–37
Eyedropper tool, 53

F

Feathering, 69
Feather Selection dialog box, 47
File Formats, 14–16
  BMP format, 15
  CompuServe GIF format, 14
  GIF format, 14
  JPEG format, 15
  PCX format, 16
  PDF format, 14
  PDP format, 14
  Photoshop EPS format, 15
  Photoshop PSE format, 185

PICT format, 15
PIXAR format, 16
PNG format, 15
PSD format, 14, 95
PXR format, 16
RAW format, 16, 123
TGA format, 16
TIFF format, 16
File size, 11
Fill command, 130, 173
Filters
Add Noise, 172
Gaussian Blur, 133
Grain, 163
Lens Flare, 134
Liquify, 91
Motion Blur, 161
Photo Filter, 66
Ripple, 141
Threshold, 60
Flatten Image command, 95
Free Transform command, 94, 128, 143

G

Gradient map, 187
Gradients
Foreground to Transparent gradient, 134
Linear gradient, 112
Greeting card (making), 176–177
Grid, 145

H

Hand tool, 33, 92
Handles, 94
Healing Brush tool, 80–84
Histogram command, 36–37
Histogram dialog box, 37
Hue/Saturation command, 64
Hue/Saturation dialog box, 52

L

Lasso tool, 46
Layers
changing background layer into normal layer, 127
Create a New Layer button, 161
create new fill or adjustment layer, 66, 190
duplicate layer, 108
Layer Via Copy command, 111
opacity, 131
style settings, 143
Levels command, 40–41
Levels dialog box, 42
Liquify command, 91–92

M

Magic Wand tool, 110
Masking
adjustment layer, 66
Selection Brush tool, 86
Menu bar, 21
Move tool, 94,99
Moving
Hand tool, 33, 92

O

Opening files, 24–26
Options bar, 22
Organizer window, 27–28
date view, 28
find bar, 27
main window, 27
Photo Browser Arrangement, 28
tags and collections panes, 28
thumbnail size slider, 28
timeline, 27

P

Panorama (stitching), 158–160, 187–191
Paste command, 93
Pattern (see define pattern command)
Perspective (altering), 144–146
Photo bin, 23, 122
Photo Browser button, 176
Photomerge Panorama command, 158–160, 187–191
Photoshop Elements interface
Editor window, 21–23
Organizer window, 27–28
Welcome screen, 17–20
Picture Package command, 115
Pixels, 10
Pixels per inch (ppi), 10
Polygonal Lasso tool, 126
Portrait sizes, 107
Portraits (enhancing), 77–119
Ppi (pixels per inch), 10–11
Product pictures, 151

R

Raw image file, 123–125
Red Eye Removal tool, 78–79
Reflections (creating), 139–141
Remove Color Cast command, 80–81
Resizing
canvas size, 127, 139
image, 12–13
Resolution, 10–13
file size, 11

pixels, 10
ppi, 11, 13
RGB color wheel, 67
Rotating
Flip Layer Horizontal command, 99
Flip Layer Vertical command, 128
Ruler, 144

S

Saving files, 29–31
Save As dialog box, 30
Save For Web dialog box, 31
Selecting
add to selection, 69
brush size, 63
contract selection, 105
Deselect command, 47
feather, 68
invert, 111
Lasso tool, 46
load selection, 104
Magic Wand tool, 110
Polygonal Lasso tool, 126
Rectangular Marquee tool, 129
save selection, 104
Selection Brush tool, 85
Selective focusing, 102–105
Sepia-toned image, 65-66
Shadows/Highlights command, 43–45
Shortcuts bar, 22
Slide show (making), 179–186
Smudge tool, 109
Snow (creating), 171–173
Spot Healing Brush tool, 80–84
Status bar, 22
Studio background (creating), 106–115
Styles and Effects palette, 129
Blizzard, 173
Clear Emboss (type), 143
Vertical Color Fade, 164

T

Text, 142
adding text to photo, 142
Horizontal Type tool, 142, 144
merging text and image, 130
Warp Text command, 142
Threshold command, 60–61
Title bar, 21
Toolbox, 22
Tools
Brush tool, 86–90
Burn tool, 86–90
Clone Stamp tool, 135–138
Color Replacement tool, 72–75
Crop tool, 106–107, 189
Dodge tool, 108
Eraser tool, 101
Eyedropper tool, 53
Hand tool, 33, 92
Healing Brush tool, 80–84
Horizontal Type tool, 142, 144
Lasso tool, 46
Magic Wand tool, 110
Move tool, 94, 99
Polygonal Lasso tool, 126
Rectangular Marquee tool, 129
Red Eye Removal tool, 78–79
Selection Brush tool, 104
Smudge tool, 109
Spot Healing Brush tool, 80–84
Zoom tool, 32–33
Type (see text)

V

Viewing tools, 32–33
grid, 145
ruler, 144

W

Web, 187–195
Web banner, 187–191
Web photo gallery, 192–195
Welcome screen, 17–20
edit and enhance photos, 19
make photo creation, 19
product overview, 17
quickly fix photos, 18
start from scratch, 20
start up in, 20
view and organize photos, 18

Z

Zoom tool, 32–33

Acknowledgements

I would like to thank ED, Lasid, and Simona for modeling for the pictures and also thank all the individuals who contributed photographs for this book.

Picture Copyright © Angelica Lim: page 80
Picture Copyright © Carl Keyes: page 46
Picture Copyright © Ellen Bliss: page 68
Picture Copyright © Ji Yong Kim: page 40, 43, 72, 85, 91, 98, 144, 166, 176
Picture Copyright © Judy Fong: page 158
Picture Copyright © Larry M. Gottschalk: page 59, 126, 138, 147
Picture Copyright © Moon Suk Choi: page 65, 66
Picture Copyright © Pete Gaughan: pages 142, 163